CONTENT AREA LITERACY

An Integrated Approach

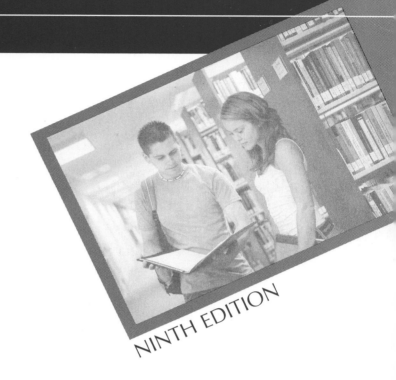

NINTH EDITION

Thomas W. Bean
University of Nevada Las Vegas

John E. Readence
University of Nevada Las Vegas

R. Scott Baldwin
Edinboro University of Pennsylvania

KENDALL/HUNT PUBLISHING COMPANY
4050 Westmark Drive Dubuque, Iowa 52002

Book Team

Chairman and Chief Executive Officer   Mark C. Falb
President and Chief Operating Officer   Chad M. Chandlee
Director of National Book Program   Paul B. Carty
Editorial Developmental Manager   Georgia Botsford
Developmental Editor   Angela Willenbring
Vice President, Operations   Timothy J. Beitzel
Assistant Vice President, Production Services   Christine E. O'Brien
Project Coordinator   Mary Melloy
Permissions Editor   Renae Horstman
Designer   Janell Edwards

Cover images Shutterstock

Library of Congress Catalog Card Number: 2007925448

ISBN 978-0-7575-4026-4

Printed in the United States of America
10   9   8   7   6   5   4   3   2

Brief Contents

Part 1: Learning with Text and Technology

Part 2: Teaching and Learning Strategies

Contents

Preface

Since the publication of the first edition of *Content Area Literacy: An Integrated Approach* in 1981, successive editions have reflected the political, social, and technological evolution of American education. Following the previous edition, the ninth edition focuses on *No Child Left Behind* (NCLB), which was signed into law by President George W. Bush on January 8, 2002. NCLB is a comprehensive and provocative reform of federal education policy, which is redefining national educational priorities, the meaning of proficiency in reading, state assessments of reading, and accountability at every level of education. The ninth edition of *Content Area Literacy: An Integrated Approach* addresses NCLB as it pertains to literacy goals, diversity, technology, and specific teacher strategies for improving student performances on state reading assessments. In addition, this edition presents a national overview of state reading assessments and their implications for NCLB. The ninth edition also includes the following features:

→ Theory and related teaching and learning strategies designed to assist middle and secondary students in reading and learning in the new millennium.

→ A multi-media approach that integrates the book with a CD-ROM and Website.

→ A CD-ROM Digital Supplement which includes instructional video clips presenting selected teaching and learning strategies, numerous articles about reading and writing strategies, authentic chapters from middle school textbooks, and selected, complete literary works such as *The Call of the Wild, The Lady or the Tiger,* and *The Telltale Heart.*

→ The CD-ROM also offers students the ability to search, read, analyze, and synthesize this rich collection of digitized articles, activities, and textbook practice sessions as they navigate the book.

→ An Internet website that includes additional chapter activities as well as hotlinks to other literacy and content area websites.

→ A discussion of current literacy issues.

→ The presentation of new teaching and learning strategies, with SLL strategies woven throughout the text.

This edition consists of two parts. Part 1: Learning with Text and Technology and Part 2: Teaching and Learning Strategies.

Part 1 includes five chapters that introduce content area literacy—

→ Chapter 1 provides a rationale and knowledge base for content area and adolescent literacy as well as a discussion of multiple literacies.

→ Chapter 2 explores the ever-expanding world of technology and its relationship to content area literacy.

→ Chapter 3 follows with an examination of the reading/writing process and a discussion of sociocultural and linguistic variables that influence literacy.

→ Chapter 4 introduces readers to the sociopolitical nature of textbooks and then focuses on quantitative and qualitative procedures for evaluating and introducing textbooks and multimedia materials.

→ Chapter 5 concludes this section of the book with a discussion of naturalistic and standards-based assessment.

Part 2 consists of 7 chapters of strategies for teaching and learning in the content areas—

→ Chapter 6 gives suggestions for unit and lesson planning.

→ Chapter 7 explores young adult and multicultural literacy.

→ Chapter 8 provides principles for effective vocabulary instruction.

→ Chapter 9 addresses principles of comprehension as well as integrated teaching and learning approaches.

→ Chapter 10 looks specifically at strategies for prereading, reading, and postreading.

→ Chapter 11 is about using writing as a vehicle to learn in the content areas.

→ Chapter 12 concludes Part 2 by introducing study strategies and test preparation tactics for state reading assessments.

TWB
JER
RSB

Features of the Ninth Edition

Through the use of several different features, we present a model that reinforces our beliefs and demonstrates that our techniques DO work for teaching in the content areas. Preservice and inservice teachers will refer to this book often when constructing lesson plans and applying strategies in their classrooms.

The page format has been redesigned to provide teachers quick and easy access to the myriad concepts, ideas, and strategies presented in this new ninth edition of *Content Area Literacy*.

In Text Learning Aids

Technology

A long time leader in the content area discipline, this new edition carries on that tradition by providing a complete learning package including a companion Website and a CD-ROM containing video and audio clips that accompanies each book.

Website

This icon indicates that the reader may go to the *Content Area Literacy* Website to access additional information. The *Content Area Literacy* Website

www.kendallhunt.com/contentarealiteracy/

supplements the textbook and the CD-ROM with—

→ Internet activities that expand chapter content by demonstrating how to access current and relevant information for teaching art, literature, science, and other content areas.

→ Hotlinks to Websites such as professional organizations, tradebook locations, and other sources to provide valuable and current information relevant to literacy issues and special interests of subject area specialists.

→ Up-to-date news items about literacy.

CD-ROM

This icon is paired with a reference or citation highlighted in blue. The icon indicates that the highlighted word is the key to finding additional information on the CD-ROM. The CD-ROM that accompanies each textbook contains—

→ Original source material and information on topics such as comprehension strategies, assessments, and multicultural education.

→ *The Call of the Wild* in its entirety.

→ Short stories.

→ Complete chapters from middle and high school textbooks.

→ Video clip presentations demonstrate real-life implementation of instructional strategies.

→ Audio clips provide practice in notetaking and test preparation.

Chapter Openers

Anticipation Guide (Part 1)

Anticipation guides open each chapter in PART 1: LEARNING WITH TEXT AND TECHNOLOGY. These guides present a series of statements that correlate with the content and facilitate discussion of literacy issues presented in each chapter.

Directions: Before reading the chapter, read each statement. Decide whether you agree or disagree with the statement and place a check in the appropriate column. Be prepared to explain your choices.

Vignette (Part 2)

Vignettes open each chapter in PART 2: TEACHING AND LEARNING STRATEGIES. These short vignettes present a classroom scenario that sets the tone of the chapter lesson.

Directions: Before reading the chapter, read and react to the short vignette. Answer the questions that follow and be prepared to justify your responses. Your instructor may ask you to work in pairs or small groups.

Rationale

The rationale section provides background and explains the purpose of the chapter.

Learning Objectives

Learning objectives focus attention on the major literacy issues discussed in each chapter.

Graphic Organizer

The Graphic Organizer provides a preview of new vocabulary and concepts.

Chapter Features

→ Applications—many chapters include practical application exercises to help students gain a concrete understanding of chapter concepts.

→ Consider This—this feature gives examples of material being discussed in the chapter.

→ Glimpse into the Classroom—this feature demonstrates how chapter concepts translate into real-life classroom situations.

End of Chapter Aids

Reaction Guides/Vignettes

These activities reinforce the Anticipation Guides and Vignettes from the beginning of the chapter and confirm the big picture presented in the chapter.

Directions for Reaction Guides (Part 1)—Reconsider your responses to the statements at the beginning of the chapters.

→ If the chapter content supports your original choice, place a check in the Confirmed column. Then write what the text says in your own words under Column A—Why is my choice confirmed?

→ If the chapter content does not support your choice, place a check in the Disconfirmed column. Then write in your own words what the text says in Column B—Why is my choice not confirmed?

Directions for Vignettes (Part 2)—Reread the instructional vignette at the chapter beginning. React to the questions posed.

Mini Projects

Mini projects give you an opportunity to apply information from the chapter.

Website Activity

At the end of each chapter, there is a reference to the *Content Area Literacy* Web Page for the exercises relating to the chapter content.

End of Text Aids

Glossary

The glossary serves as a ready reference for italicized vocabulary terms encountered in each chapter.

Bibliography

Recommended readings are identified by chapter in the bibliography and are given as additional readings to extend and refine the information presented. References are also identified by chapter and listed in the bibliography, thus providing a comprehensive list of references in one section.

Index

Both an author and a subject index are provided for quick page reference for important terms and individuals cited in the text.

About the Authors

THOMAS W. BEAN is a professor of Reading/Literacy and Coordinator of Doctoral Studies in the Department of Curriculum and Instruction at the University of Nevada Las Vegas. His teaching and research interests center on the integration of young adult literature in content area classrooms as well as studies of content teachers' use of multiple texts in print-based and digital classrooms. Tom's hobbies include surfing, kayaking, golfing, and playing blues guitar in the Las Vegas garage band "Out of the Blues."

JOHN E. READENCE is a professor in the College of Education and Dean of the University College at the University of Nevada Las Vegas. His professional interests include research and practice in content area literacy and teacher education. John's personal interests include traveling, collecting art, movies, and his iPod.

R. SCOTT BALDWIN is Dean of Graduate Studies and Research at Edinboro University of Pennsylvania. His professional interests are currently focused on designing web-based degree programs. Scott's hobbies include studying futures markets and trading pork bellies.

PART 1

Learning with Text and Technology

1

CONTENT AREA LITERACY:
Addressing *No Child Left Behind*

Anticipation Guide

		Agree	Disagree
1.	The Federal government should establish the standards for public education.	_____	_____
2.	A content teacher's prime responsibility is to deliver subject matter information.	_____	_____
3.	Reading instruction should be left to reading teachers.	_____	_____
4.	Providing students with a purpose for reading will improve their reading performances.	_____	_____
5.	Upon leaving elementary school, students should have mastered the skills necessary for content literacy.	_____	_____

Rationale

Schools Face Closing If Test Scores Don't Rise
Illiterate Student Sues Local High School
English Only Referendum Looms
High School Dropouts Reach 3,000 Daily

Every year our high schools churn out thousands of students who can't read and understand the fine print on a bag of potato chips. Many more depart with reading skills so inadequate that they can't begin to cope with our print-bound, technological culture. And the public impression appears to be that this problem is chronic and getting worse. Daily newspapers and magazines routinely print articles that blast our public schools and lament how much our students don't know in comparison to Japanese students today or the American students of decades past. There is also a growing realization that the United States is a multicultural society in which disenfranchised ethnic and linguistic minorities are demanding the redefinition of American schools. In addition, we are riding an immigration tsunami which will guarantee that in our public schools 1 child in every 4 will be Hispanic by the year 2020 (Gersten & Woodward, 1994). Diverse and complex issues such as social equity, bilingual education, and formulas for funding public schools combine to make universal literacy in the United States one of the great challenges of the 21st century. For teachers and public schools this challenge is defined by the mandates of *No Child Left Behind*.

This text is based on the conviction that America's literacy dilemmas are ultimately solvable and that each and every teacher can play a role in the resolution. In fact, we believe that programs in which reading is the subject matter are inferior to programs in which each teacher is committed to making students literate with respect to the specific source materials that make up the curriculum.

This chapter will discuss the educational and social meaning of literacy, present a rationale for incorporating literacy strategies into content area classrooms, describe some of the standard misconceptions about content area literacy, and investigate the common reluctance of subject matter specialists to accept responsibility for teaching any reading strategies. Additionally, we will summarize *No Child Left Behind* (NCLB) and its implications for public education and discuss how you, as a classroom teacher, can address the challenges of NCLB in your own classroom.

Learning Objectives

→ Define literacy from historical and social perspectives.

→ Identify the major implications of NCLB.

→ Refute common misconceptions about literacy instruction.

→ State the instructional recommendations that are integrated into the literacy strategies recommended in this text.

Graphic Organizer

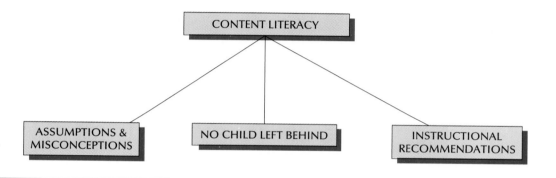

What Is Content Area Literacy?

Literate is derived from the Latin *litterae* (i.e., letters). The standard dictionary definition of literate is to be able to read and write. That seems straightforward except that people aren't simply literate or illiterate: they are literate or illiterate to some degree, which is defined by historical and social contexts. Beginning in 1840 the United States Census Bureau began assessing literacy by asking individuals if they could read and write simple messages in any language. People who answered "Yes" were classified as literate. By this definition 20% of the U.S. population considered themselves illiterate in 1870 as opposed to less than 1% in 1979 (Kaestle, 1991). By the standards of one hundred years ago, virtually all Americans are literate today. But literacy is relative to societal demands, and reading and writing skills that were sufficient in 1670 or 1870 are clearly inadequate in today's world of credit cards, mass advertising, computers, big business, and income tax forms. To illustrate this relativity, Barton (2000) reported that the 25 fastest-growing jobs today have far higher than average literacy demands, while the 25 fastest-declining ones have lower than average literacy demands.

It is widely believed that the ability to read and comprehend the bulk of a daily newspaper is a measure of functional literacy (i.e., how well one needs to read to get by on a day-to-day basis). This might be good enough to meet the job demands of a lumberjack, but probably not the daily reading and writing tasks of a corporate lawyer. Because there are no universal standards for literacy today, we are forced to answer "Literate for what?" in response to the question "Is Frank literate?" In like manner, the issue of literacy in content areas must be contextualized and defined in terms of the reading and writing demands of specific classrooms. For example, students in a 10th-grade biology class are literate to the extent that they can learn with and react appropriately to the written materials (textbooks, lab directions, magazines, etc.) used in the class. Hence, *content area literacy* is defined as the level of reading and writing skill necessary to read, comprehend, and react to appropriate instructional materials in a given subject area. The fundamental purpose of this text is to communicate knowledge and strategies that you can use to help your students become more literate in your subject area.

Finally, we should also mention that questions of what just constitutes content area literacy will continue to evolve as our instructional materials change to accommodate the digital age. As newer forms of text in which students engage (e.g., the Internet, pop culture, teen magazines, music, media sources, young adult novels) mix with traditional forms of text, our strategies for helping students learn will need to evolve also (Bean & Harper, 2006; O'Brien, 2006). However, this does not decrease the importance of students' general competence with traditional forms of print as they still form the basis for students in their dealings with newer literacies (e.g., the Internet) (Wilder & Dressman, 2006) as well as with the standardized tests we use to measure students' abilities.

No Child Left Behind

No Child Left Behind (NCLB) is the latest revision of the Elementary and Secondary Education Act (ESEA) of 1965. The overall purpose of NCLB is to guarantee that each child in the United States is able to meet high standards of learning. The basis of NCLB is a growing dissatisfaction with the costs of public education and the perceived failure of public education to meet the educational needs of all children. The specific goals of the law are as follows:

→ All students will attain proficiency in reading and mathematics by 2013–2014.

→ By 2013–2014 all students will be proficient in reading by the end of third grade.

→ Beginning in 2007 states will assess yearly students' progress in science in each of three grade spans (3–5, 6–9, and 10–12).

→ All students with limited proficiency in English will become proficient in English.

→ All students will be educated in safe and drug-free learning environments.

→ By 2005–2006 all students will be taught by highly qualified teachers.

→ All students will graduate from high school.

The goals of NCLB are not just high-minded notions. The Federal Government has real expectations, and there are a variety of requirements and incentives to ensure that states and schools meet the goals of NCLB. For example, in 2002 all 50 states submitted a comprehensive NCLB plan to the U.S. Department of Education. Each plan defines *proficiency* in reading and mathematics and details how the goals of NCLB will be met by the state. This includes a rigid schedule for schools to demonstrate *annual yearly progress* (AYP) toward each goal. In the case of reading, every state has one or more tests to measure reading achievement in general and state reading standards in particular. The state test(s) must be administered to all children—including those with disabilities or limited proficiency in English—every year in grades 3 through 8. Schools that do not meet the standards for AYP may be subject to corrective action, which in its most severe application would involve firing all of the school's employees and turning the school over to a private company.

In Pennsylvania, for example, the State Board of Education has defined proficiency in reading and mathematics achievement as "above average," which means that in order to meet the conditions of *No Child Left Behind*, 95% of all children are expected to perform at levels that were average in 2001. According to the new law, this goal must be met by school year 2013–2014. Schools that fail to make adequate yearly progress (AYP) in meeting this goal, as defined entirely by test scores in reading and mathematics, will be taken over by the state or privatized. In 2003, for instance, the Pennsylvania Secretary of Education announced that 880 schools in the state were failing to make adequate progress in meeting the objectives of NCLB. Some schools in Philadelphia have already been privatized, and more are likely to follow throughout the United States because the criteria making annual yearly progress increases with every passing year.

The sweeping reforms mandated by NCLB may or may not be in the best long-term interests of our nation. However, we in public education have no choice but to do everything in our power to meet the current AYP goals established by the various states in response to NCLB. School administrators expect teachers to create higher and higher levels of achievement every year, and they expect to see this achievement reflected in state assessments. *We believe that the contents of this book can help you and your students to meet the literacy goals of NCLB.*

No Adolescent Left Behind

The Commission on Adolescent Literacy of the International Reading Association has gone on record to say that adolescents have not been afforded the support that has been given to their beginning reading counterparts at the elementary level. While state and federal funding has increased for programs for younger readers and federal research dollars are focused on beginning readers, monies have decreased and research support is negligible for adolescent readers. The Commission has put forth a position statement (Moore, Bean, Birdyshaw, & Rycik, 1999) which calls for new programmatic efforts to sustain adolescents' literacy growth and revolves around the following principles. Adolescents deserve:

1. Access to a wide variety of reading material that they can and want to read.
2. Instruction that builds both the skill and desire to read increasingly complex materials.
3. Assessment that shows them their strengths as well as their needs and that guides their teachers to design instruction that will best help them grow as readers.
4. Expert teachers who model and provide explicit instruction in reading comprehension and study strategies across the curriculum.

5. Reading specialists who assist individual students having difficulty learning how to read.

6. Teachers who understand the complexities of individual adolescent readers, respect their differences, and respond to their characteristics.

7. Homes, communities, and a nation that will support their efforts to achieve advanced levels of literacy and provide the support necessary for them to succeed.

Assumptions and Misconceptions

Teachers in science, history, and other content areas are frequently reluctant to accept an instructional emphasis that fuses reading with content. In part this is because many content teachers have false assumptions about reading instruction and the reading abilities of students when they arrive in subject matter classrooms (see Table 1.1).

Belief in these assumptions presupposes that students have mastered the processes necessary to enable them to glean essential information from reading, regardless of writing style and content. It also presupposes that students can meaningfully blend new information with prior knowledge and efficiently utilize textbook aids designed to refine and extend important concepts. A close examination of these assumptions reveals how wrong they are.

Reading instruction has been the traditional interest of the elementary school, the assumption being that normal students in normal programs SHOULD enter subject matter classrooms knowing how to read. But consider this:

→ If reading is defined in terms of elementary tasks, e.g., basic decoding skills, the assumption is reasonable.

→ In contrast, the assumption is pure fantasy if reading is defined in terms of subject matter tasks, e.g., expanded homework and independent reading assignments, required note taking in class, and vastly increased dependence upon technology and textbooks with varied and complex organizational patterns.

It does not make sense to assume that students will automatically modify elementary reading skills to suit subject matter reading demands.

Table 1.1

False Assumptions of Content Teachers
1. Students have learned to read in elementary schools.
2. Students have sufficient prior knowledge to cope effectively with the important information in content textbooks.
3. The processes involved in reading and comprehending efficiently in content textbooks are identical to those utilized in reading from basal readers in elementary school.
4. Content reading means teaching phonics and other skills not directly related to their subject areas.
5. Teachers are information dispensers.

APPLICATION 1.1

Read the following paragraph and summarize it in your own words from recall.

We are completely in agreement with him on this point: That symbolization is constitutive of symbolic consciousness will trouble no one who believes in the absolute value of the cartesian cogito. But it must be understood that if symbolization is constitutive of consciousness, it is permissible to perceive that there is an immanent bond of comprehension between the symbolization and the symbol. (Sartre, 1948, p. 65)

Did you have difficulty reading the passage from Sartre? If you were familiar with existential philosophy and Sartre, you might have breezed right through it. However, if this material was foreign to your own personal experiences, adequate comprehension probably proved elusive. In addition, the burden of many new terms and concepts may have caused the passage to seem obscure.

In order to read this passage with full understanding, you would need background knowledge in the subject area and an introduction to the unusual vocabulary and new concepts in the passage. Even then the long, complicated sentences could prove tedious and confusing.

After reading the paragraph from Sartre, you should have some sensitivity for the demands placed on young students in reading their subject matter materials. Students usually lack experiential background and are unfamiliar with the vocabulary and concepts in social studies, science, or any other content areas. It is presumptuous, and possibly damaging, to expect students to perform well automatically with subject-matter texts. In addition, students with Arts and Sciences majors often develop a mind-set to convey a body of information to students, view reading as a simple mechanism for dispensing information, and see no reason to provide instruction in reading and learning with text.

Perhaps a final complication to utilizing content literacy in subject-matter classrooms is the well-intended, but detrimental, slogan that "every teacher is a teacher of reading." Tell social studies teachers, for instance, that they are teachers of reading and you may understand how receptive they are to the concept. If apoplexy does not occur, their certain retort will be that they are teachers of social studies, not reading! The reading model that content teachers usually witness, emphasizing the previously mentioned elementary level skill characteristics, will not encourage them to attend to the reading needs of their classes. Moreover, their resolve that they are subject-matter specialists first is a valid one.

Reexamining the Roles of Teachers and Texts

When subject-matter teachers are surveyed concerning their attitude toward teaching reading in the content areas, they typically give less than an enthusiastic response toward the slogan, "every teacher is a teacher of reading." Ask this same set of teachers their opinion about the statement, "every teacher teaches students to learn with texts," and you will usually hear a favorable response. This latter statement connotes a model of reading instruction that focuses on aiding students in learning with text rather than learning isolated skills.

The authors agree with this reemphasis. Content literacy has too many prior associations with learning to read and skills instruction. Under this reemphasis, content teachers are considered catalysts for learning, whose responsibility it is to aid students in reading and learning with text. The focus of content literacy instruction is on reading to learn, not on learning to read.

Let's examine in depth the roles of the teacher, the reader, and the textbook as each relates to success in learning. First, if texts were meant to be read in isolation, there would be little, if any, need for someone called a teacher. Similarly, if texts are so easy to read that a reader needs little or no help to learn the material, a teacher, again, would be superfluous. Yet, as our Sartre quotation illustrated, this is not normally the case with text materials. Texts are usually challenging and present students with a myriad of problems.

Second, it makes sense to describe content reading as a means of improving communication. There is sort of a long-distance communication that materializes between an author of a text and a reader attempting to comprehend it. The reader is, in effect, trying to communicate with authors of texts by constructing meaning with their words and thoughts. Given, then, the goal of the reader and the difficulty of texts, a facilitator is needed to promote this interaction between reader and text. Indeed, this should be the role of the teacher.

If teachers consider themselves to be information dispensers, then there is no need for textbooks. Teachers who make text reading assignments and then go over in class exactly what is in the text not only make class boring but also encourage students to neglect to read their assignments. This type of teacher is not encouraging the development of independent readers who can take their place as useful citizens and lifelong learners in our society. A teacher who focuses only on content ignores the processes needed by students to comprehend the content in immediate and future reading situations.

The teacher's role is to encourage the thinking processes essential to understanding, i.e., to facilitate learning with text. Teachers, then, can promote this interaction if they conceive of themselves as facilitators of the learning process because they have inherent advantages over textbooks or any other information dispensing device. For instance, teachers have knowledge of at least four skills and processes they can exercise in their teaching that a text cannot—tailoring the message, activating prior knowledge, focusing attention, and monitoring comprehension.

1. **Teachers tailor the message** by adapting their presentations to the needs, abilities, and experiential backgrounds of their students. They already know what students know and do not know and can interact with them during their presentations.
2. **Teachers activate prior knowledge** by reminding students of what they know and how it relates to what they are expected to learn.
3. **Teachers focus attention** by increasing students' interest and motivation to learn new material and by directing them to pay attention to selected pieces of the text.
4. **Teachers monitor comprehension** by checking to see if students understand important parts of a text presentation.

Clearly, texts cannot accomplish any of these tasks.

Nevertheless, while it is true that textbooks cannot do these things, it is also true that textbooks are not designed to do this. They are designed to present information. **Materials don't do the teaching; teachers, by definition, do the teaching,** and this teaching includes helping students acquire the processes necessary for successful learning in content areas.

 STOP! View the CD-ROM video clip on the importance of content area literacy.

What Makes This Textbook Integrated?

We have adopted the following set of instructional recommendations, which are integrated into the strategies you will encounter throughout the book.

Table 1.2

Instructional Recommendations
1. Present content and processes concurrently.
2. Provide guidance in all aspects of the instructional lesson—before, during, and after reading.
3. Use all language processes to help students learn with text.
4. Use small groups to enhance learning.
5. Use technology to promote learning with text.

1. **Present content and processes concurrently.** There are several possible approaches to learning with text—(a) presenting isolated skills; (b) aiming toward content; and, (c) presenting content and processes concurrently.

   a. *Presenting isolated skills* consists of the direct teaching of skills, with no consideration for content. Students use special materials unrelated to the texts students are assigned to learn in their regular classes. This approach, like most skill-centered remedial programs, fails because students also need to be taught how to transfer skills from one material to another. More importantly, they fail to see any purpose in learning skills divorced from content.

   b. *Aiming toward content* focuses on what content to acquire rather than on how to acquire that content. In other words, the teacher sets purposes for reading and during a follow-up discussion checks to see if the purposes were met. This method is unsuccessful because there is no instruction in how to extract the information from the text. Students are told what to do but not how to do it; this is not synonymous with instruction and is not sufficient to improve students' reading abilities.

   c. Students learn best and acquire content most successfully when their attention is focused directly on the material to be learned. *Presenting content and processes concurrently* does this by providing direct instruction in the processes necessary to acquire content in addition to pointing out what content is to be acquired. For example, if the content to be learned is organized into a cause-effect format, the teacher might first present a lesson on organizing content according to that format before giving students the actual content in which they would use their knowledge of that process. Thus, text information is stressed alongside the processes needed to attain it. Specifying what should be attained, without specifying how to do it, is pointless. Taking process into account as well as content acknowledges that: (1) reading is indispensable to the successful learning of all academic subjects, and (2) content as specified in a text is only one part of the dynamic interaction between reader, text, and teacher in classroom learning situations. As a consequence, the learning of content and the teaching of processes to help learn it become **integrated** within a total lesson framework.

2. **Provide guidance in all aspects of the instructional lesson—before, during, and after reading.** Learning content is not simply reading the assigned pages, answering the end-of-chapter questions, and listening to the teacher present what has already been read. Generally, students need to be prepared to read a text, need guidance in reading for selected ideas, and need reinforcement to retain the material learned.

   More specifically, before reading, students need to be aware that using their prior knowledge and having purposes for reading aids the comprehension process. In addition, teachers can explicitly demonstrate to students how to learn with text through *modeling*. In this technique, teachers become role models by explaining how they comprehended something; i.e., a reporting of the mental operations involved in their comprehension of a particular text. Students can then repeat the process in order to comprehend on their own.

   During reading, students are searching for information to satisfy the purposes set by the teacher and/or themselves. The teacher may use some adjunct material to guide the students' search. After reading, teachers check to see if preset purposes have been attained.

   One useful way to give feedback to students is to have a *debriefing* session, which includes self-reports, introspection, and hindsights by students. Debriefing does not cover content alone, but also entails checking out the processes students used to comprehend the text in relation to what was modeled for them. As students become more adept, the demonstration and guidance teachers provide should be faded, or withdrawn, so students can be moved toward independence in their reading and learning. Thus, helping students learn content is **integrated** throughout all phases of the instructional lesson.

3. **Use all language processes to help students learn with text.** The authors believe that all language processes, not just reading, can be utilized as a means to approach learning with text. While reading will undoubtedly remain the major means of dealing with text, other language processes can play key roles in helping students learn content. Indeed, it is suggested that all teachers become language educators and consider using all language processes to enhance students' ability to cope successfully with subject matter materials. Reading and writing are interconnected, and reading should be viewed as a composing process. In effect, writing, listening, and speaking become additional tools to teach more content.

   It is our belief that the receptive language processes of reading and listening should be **integrated** with the expressive processes of writing and speaking to promote thinking and learning with content materials. The integrative aspects of reading and the other language processes are shown in Figure 1.1.

Figure 1.1

Integrative aspects of reading and the other language processes

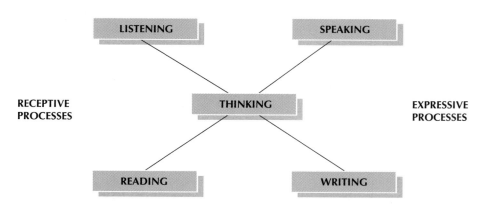

In a system such as this, content reading takes on the larger notions of content communication or content literacy by emphasizing those teaching practices which integrate language processes and thinking as one learns content.

4. **Use small groups to enhance learning.** While the lecture method is the dominant means of instruction in our classrooms, one of the most effective is small group instruction. When students are encouraged to work collaboratively, rather than competitively, with peers, productivity and achievement are enhanced. We realize that the lecture method is prevalent in teaching, yet many of the strategies advocated in this text are best used with, or even require, small group instruction. We recommend such strategies for your consideration because they promote active learning situations and emphasize peer interaction.

   Initial attempts at small group instruction may be chaotic and create management problems; however, this is simply part of learning to interact within a group for both the students and the teacher. Once both are accustomed to such instruction, this method will pave the way for greater output in learning content, both in depth of understanding and in breadth of cognitive and affective experiences. Thus, teachers become cost-efficient when they **integrate** small groups into their teaching (i.e., they enhance the learning environment through good teaching practices which, in turn, create more knowledgeable students).

5. **Use technology to promote learning with text.** Teachers need to be aware of new and emerging technologies as well as how application of these technologies in the classroom will promote students' learning of their subject. In particular, instruction with computers seems most promising as an educational innovation that provides new methods of presenting information, new ways of structuring and organizing instruction, and new ways to motivate students to learn. As schools provide students at all levels with access to technology, it is incumbent upon teachers to **integrate** the use of technology, especially computers, with text and video sources to enhance students' learning in content classrooms.

Strategy Implementation and Reality Checks

The chapters that follow contain dozens of strategies for improving content area literacy, and we trust that you will have an opportunity to experiment with them in real classrooms. Be patient! Don't expect instant results the first time you use a recommended strategy. First attempts at strategy implementation are problematic, and expertise requires time and patience. Try a strategy several times before you render a final judgement on its utility.

We acknowledge that there are limitations to some of the strategies we recommend. For one thing, they tend to be idealized practices that may or may not be realistic in terms of the time and effort required to implement them, given the realities of your teaching environment and the diverse nature of students (O'Brien & Stewart, 2007). There are urban schools, for example, where students are not allowed to take textbooks out of the school because of the high rate at which the books are sold or destroyed by the students. Environmental constraints of this magnitude will vastly alter what makes sense in the way of strategy instruction. In addition, the success of some of the strategies is predicated on the assumption that students want to learn or that they at least are willing to fake wanting to learn in order to get passing grades. In school cultures in which formal learning and grades are viewed as irrelevant, many literacy strategies probably will not work.

On the other hand, it is possible that under teaching conditions that are far from ideal some of these strategies will give you the edge you need to survive and succeed in the profession.

Our advocacy of content literacy instruction is based on the belief that it can better equip preservice and inservice teachers with strategies to facilitate students' learning with text. We do not claim that all strategies we recommend will work for all teachers with all students. Rather, we encourage you to discover for yourself which ones work best for you and your students.

To get a better feel for the philosophy behind this text, examine the list of practices in Application 1.2. These practices will be expanded upon in later chapters. For any immediate clarification of terminology used in the list, consult the glossary.

Reaction Guide

	Confirmed	Disconfirmed
1. The Federal government should establish the standards for public education.	_____	_____
2. A content teacher's prime responsibility is to deliver subject matter information.	_____	_____
3. Reading instruction should be left to reading teachers.	_____	_____
4. Providing students with a purpose for reading will improve their reading performances.	_____	_____
5. Upon leaving elementary school, students should have mastered the skills necessary for content literacy.	_____	_____

A Why my choice is confirmed.	**B** Why my choice is not confirmed.
1. _____ _____	_____ _____
2. _____ _____	_____ _____
3. _____ _____	_____ _____
4. _____ _____	_____ _____
5. _____ _____	_____ _____

APPLICATION 1.2

These practices are recommended for enhancing reading and learning in the content areas. If you are an inservice teacher, check the appropriate number showing how much you do each of these. If you are a preservice teacher, observe a content area teacher to see which practices are used.

1—Almost always
2—Most of the time
3—Sometimes
4—Seldom
5—Never

Recommended Practices for Teaching in Content Areas

	1	2	3	4	5
1. The teacher utilizes all language processes to enhance students' learning with text.					
2. The reading levels of the students are known by the teacher.					
3. Lessons capitalize on students' cultural backgrounds.					
4. The teacher has evaluated the text for the presence or absence of characteristics which make a well-organized text.					
5. Materials for instruction, including the textbook, are chosen to match the reading levels of the students.					
6. Books and other materials are available for students who read below and above the readability level of the text.					
7. Textbook aids, such as illustrations, maps, and graphs, are explained or called to the attention of the students.					
8. Class time is spent discussing how to read the text effectively.					
9. The teacher presents the special vocabulary and concepts introduced in the text materials assigned for reading in the context of a well-planned lesson.					
10. Prior knowledge of the text concepts is activated before reading the text.					
11. Purpose is provided for each reading assignment.					
12. Assignments are stated clearly and concisely.					
13. The teacher adapts instruction to suit the ability and language levels of students.					
14. The teacher asks questions designed to promote thinking at all levels of comprehension.					
15. The teacher provides some form of study guide, listening guide, or outline to aid in comprehension.					
16. The course content requires more than reading a single textbook.					
17. A variety of reference materials and software is made available.					
18. Students are taught to use appropriate reference materials.					
19. Students are encouraged to read widely in materials related to the text.					
20. Small group instruction is used where appropriate.					

Mini Projects

1. Write a sentence or paragraph using the technical vocabulary from your own content field. Exchange this with a class member from a different subject-matter area. Can you understand each other's passage? Why or why not? What might help you increase your understanding?

2. Reflect on your literacy experiences by writing an autobiography of them from your earliest memory of being read to through elementary school, middle school, and high school to the present. Comment on what you read, your feelings associated with reading or being read to, key people who influenced your feelings about reading, and places where you acquired books.

 ## Website Activity

To locate and complete Chapter 1 activities, go to *[www.kendallhunt.com/contentarealiteracy/]*.

2

Technology and Changing Literacies

Anticipation Guide

	Agree	Disagree
1. Technology has had a greater impact on social networking than on school achievement.	_____	_____
2. It is impossible to make the Internet safe for children.	_____	_____
3. Computers and the Internet have replaced textbooks as the dominant instructional tools in public education.	_____	_____
4. The computer is morally neutral.	_____	_____
5. The first electronic computer was built during the U.S. Civil War.	_____	_____

Rationale

In the middle of the last century, automobiles all had manual transmissions and no air conditioning. There were no cellular phones, and there were no convenient ATMs to drive up to for fast cash. Passenger planes were propeller driven only. There were also no televisions, automatic dishwashers, digital clocks, or hundreds of other technological conveniences which are now taken for granted in most American homes.

In spite of the many ways that technology is changing our lives, schools of today are instructionally similar to the schools of hundreds of years ago. Lecture and oral recitation in a teacher-centered environment characterize most secondary classrooms, and the whiteboard is still the prevailing visual aid. The raging revolution in technology should change the fundamentals of classroom instruction, but will it? This chapter examines the impact of technology on content literacy.

Learning Objectives

→ Explain how the meaning of literacy has changed over the last 30 years.
→ State several appropriate uses of computers in the classroom.
→ Define the terms multimedia, wiki, blog, PDA, byte, and WebQuest.
→ Cite several current and potential misuses of the Internet.

Graphic Organizer

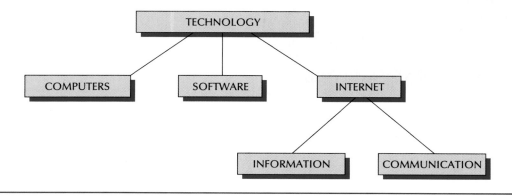

Technology: Reviewing the Past and Imagining Our Future

"The telephone has too many short-comings to be seriously considered as a means of communication. The device is inherently of no value."

Western Union Internal Memo (1876)

"Everything that can be invented has been invented."

U.S. Patent Office Director (1899)

"I think there is a world market for maybe five computers."

Thomas Watson, Chairman of IBM (1943)

"There is not the slightest indication that nuclear energy will ever be obtainable. It would mean that the atom would have to be shattered at will."

Albert Einstein (1932)

"I see no advantage to the graphical user interface."

Bill Gates (1984)

As some of the quotes suggest, even great minds can fail to divine the future or see the potential in technological innovations that in retrospect are obvious. It is easy to chuckle knowingly over the flawed technology predictions of the past. It is much more difficult to predict the future. At the close of the stock market each day there are thousands of analysts and reporters who will tell you with certainty why the market went up or down, but most of them won't even hazard a guess about what the stock market will do the next day. Predicting what technology will do for—or to—the world in the next 50 or 20 or even 5 years is even more difficult. We believe it is safe to say that technology is here to stay and that it is a tsunami of change that will not stop.

Smaller, Faster, and Stronger

The *ENIAC* (Electronic Numerical Integrator and Computer) was the first modern computer and was built in 1946 after scientists realized that information could be represented by the absence or presence of electrical current (pluses and minuses). The ENIAC, which weighed 30 tons, filled a large room, required a staff of engineers to keep it running, and operated with thousands of bulky vacuum tubes.

Today, there are computers thousands of times more powerful than the ENIAC and small enough to fit into the palm of your hand, for example, *PDAs* (Personal Digital Assistants). The portability of PDAs, notebook computers, wireless connectivity, and iPods make it possible for us to communicate and to store and retrieve information almost anywhere (Murphy, 2007). Technological changes are occurring at such a rapid rate that it is almost impossible to predict even the near future. This is particularly true with respect to the storage of information.

A *byte* is the amount of space necessary to store one character, such as a number or letter. A kilobyte is 1,000 bytes, a megabyte is 1,000 kilobytes, a gigabyte is 1,000 megabytes, and a terabyte is 1,000 gigabytes. A terabyte is one trillion bytes (1,000,000,000,000), enough to hold the entire contents of a small college library. Since the last edition of this book, peripheral devices such as floppy disks with 1.2 megabytes of storage and zip disks with 650 megabytes have been replaced by rewritable DVD (digital video disks) and jump drives the size of a stick of gum that can store several gigabytes of information.

Just as computers have become smaller in size and greater in storage capacity, they have also acquired fantastic processing speeds. For example, in June 2005, IBM's eServer Blue Gene Solution computer achieved a computational capacity of 280 teraflops, 280 trillion calculations per second, making it the most powerful supercomputer in the world (Top 500 List, 2005). Processing speeds for personal computers and other devices have soared in a parallel fashion. This smaller-faster-stronger (SFS) phenomenon in computing has resulted in tremendous accomplishments in science and industry, one example of which is the Human Genome Project.

The Human Genome Project, a 16-year project managed by the National Institutes of Health and the U.S Department of Energy, was completed in 2006. The goals of the project were to identify the approximately 25,000 genes in human *DNA* (deoxyribonucleic acid), determine the sequences of the three billion chemical base pairs that make up human DNA, store the information, improve tools for data analyses, transfer information and technology to the private sector, and address ethical, legal, and social issues related to the project. The mapping of human DNA was an incredible scientific accomplishment, and research based on it has the capacity to prevent birth defects, eliminate many diseases, increase the human lifespan, and enhance the intellectual capabilities of humans in the future. On the other hand, there is real potential for misuse of genetic information. Who should have access to personal genetic information, and how should it be used by courts, adoption agencies, insurers, schools, and the medical profession? Technology is a double-edged sword.

The Technology Revolution in American Schools

As of this writing the state of Pennsylvania is planning to spend 200 million dollars over the next three years on a high school reform program called Classrooms for the Future (Pennsylvania Department of Education, 2006). Social studies, English, math, and science classrooms will be equipped with laptops, high speed Internet access, and other advanced technologies; and teachers will receive intensive technology training. The goal of the program is to enable teachers to use technology as an effective teaching tool and to prepare students for a high-tech, global marketplace. Classrooms for the Future is driven by the conviction that technology is the key to higher levels of student achievement. This ambitious project and others like it around the country underscore the importance of technology in the future of education. The question is: Will technology improve achievement in ways that are comparable to the advances in science and industry (e.g., the Human Genome Project)?

 STOP! View the CD-ROM videoclip on the Future of Technology in Education.

Computers have been common in public schools for more than 25 years, and they are on the verge of being ubiquitous. It is readily apparent that high school students know more about digital technologies than the students of a quarter century ago. In addition to exposure in school, 75% of American homes have one or more personal computers with Internet access and 67% of all teenagers carry a cell phone on a regular basis (*CBS News*, 2006). Most students use computers for word processing, conducting Internet searches, and participating in electronic social activities. Far less clear are the contributions of digital technologies to school achievement. Can high school graduates today read and comprehend better than their peers of 25 years ago? Are their mathematical skills superior? Do they know more about biology, economics, history, or any other subject area? One might expect some measurable improvements in achievement after so many years of technology in the classroom. Unfortunately, we are unaware of any systematic research that demonstrates this. Why might it be true that technology has yet to influence academic achievement?

Historically, innovative instructional technology tools such as computers, film, radio, and television have consistently met with resistance from teachers and educators at large. This failure of instructional technologies to be integrated into the classroom has been clearly demonstrated by Larry Cuban (1986) in his book *Teachers and Machines: The Classroom Use of Technology Since 1920*. According to Cuban, instructional technology has consistently failed to bring about the revolutionary changes predicted by its advocates. Beginning with an examination of the introduction of motion pictures in the schools nearly a century ago, and continuing with the introduction of new forms of media such as radio and television, Cuban provides a convincing historical demonstration of how new educational technologies meet with only limited use by teachers in the classroom. For example, during the 1950s and 1960s a variety of mechanical teaching machines were introduced to public schools (Cook, 1962), a decade or more before the invention of microprocessors and digital calculators. At that time there were many educators who believed that teaching machines would change the fundamental character of education—or even replace teachers altogether. But even before microcomputers entered their first classroom, teaching machines had proven to be little more than a curious fad. Will computers in the classroom suffer the same fate?

More recently, Cuban (2003) has argued that after spending billions on technology in schools there are only meager results. Only 2 teachers in 10 are serious users of technology in the classroom, and half of all teachers make no use of technology at all. In addition, computers are used primarily to support low-end applications, such as word processing, that mirror rather than alter and improve existing teaching practices. Placing computers in the classroom will make no difference in achievement unless the technology is accompanied by teachers and students changing their assumptions about teaching and learning. A teacher-centered curriculum with an emphasis on narrowly defined standards and rote memorization combined with an assembly line mentality will render the best of technology impotent.

Other critics of the technology revolution in public schools argue that there is little evidence to support the benefits of computer classroom applications and that technology is a distraction in the classroom and may actually impair intellectual development, writing skills, and problem-solving abilities (Oppenheimer 1997, 2003; Postman, 1999). Given limited school financing and available time for the total curriculum, critics argue that music, art, and other subjects are systematically squeezed out of the curriculum as more instructional time and resources are being devoted to the support of technology. American political and business leaders seem to embrace the notion that technology is good and more of it is better. Only time will reveal the true value of technologically sophisticated classrooms and the unforeseen consequences of technology interventions.

Literacy in the New Millennium

In Chapter 1 we defined content area literacy as the level of reading and writing skill necessary to read, comprehend, and react to appropriate instructional materials in a given subject area. Thirty years ago this definition would have been limited to conventional print mediums such as road signs, newspapers, and textbooks, but now students must also become facile in the use of computers, the Internet, cell phones, software, PDAs, and other technologies directly or indirectly related to reading and writing. Being literate in today's world requires the application of conventional reading and writing skills to software applications and the complicated universe of cyberspace. The term *multiple literacies* is sometimes used to describe the great range of skills required to be literate in today's world (Alvermann, 2001).

Recent research indicates that the ability to take advantage of digital technology is heavily dependent upon conventional print literacy (Wilder & Dressman, 2006). Word recognition, spelling, vocabulary skills, prior knowledge, comprehension strategies, and critical thinking are essential in using the Internet for academic purposes. Students who have difficulty spelling, read slowly, and have a limited understanding of the world outside their immediate community are unlikely to be able to acquire multiple literacies. Clearly, technology cannot replace conventional reading and writing skills. In fact, such skills become even more important in working with technology.

In the last edition of this textbook, we made the statement that ". . . our profession is nowhere near ready to replace teachers and textbooks with technology." However, it appears some schools are already replacing textbooks with laptops and an Internet driven curriculum (Esker, 2006), and many more are exploring the possibilities. To the extent that this becomes a trend in education, a firm grasp of multiple literacies will be essential for every student.

Software, Multimedia, and eBooks

Software refers to applications that run on computers, which include everything from encyclopedias and word processing programs to games and academic programs that support the full range of content areas. *Multimedia* refers to combinations of audio, text, graphics, and animation. Multimedia software refers to computer-based programs that combine two or more multimedia elements.

Software allows students to take part in adventure games or to design their own programs. Programs such as *Carmen Sandiego Great Chase Through Time* allow students to participate in sophisticated simulations in which they manipulate powerful educational databases in order to assemble clues about the whereabouts of a missing detective.

Another example of problem-solving software is *HIP Mathematics* (Center for Image Processing in Education), which uses the image processing software to create lessons related to satellite photography, X-rays, digital elevation models, and other images. Middle-grade students are challenged to solve real-world problems such as calculating the slope of a handicap access ramp, enhancing old photos, and analyzing volcanic plumes using percents, decimals, and ratios. Another example is *Clues in Crime: The Role of Forensic Science in Criminal Investigations* (Duke University). This multimedia introduction to forensic science includes video lessons, lab demonstrations, actual case files, and a true-to-life crime scene investigation that allows students to exercise their problem-solving abilities.

Today there are thousands of multimedia software products available to serve every subject area. For example, Microsoft's *Encarta Africana* is a CD-ROM multimedia encyclopedia that focuses on Africa, Africans, and people of African descent. It includes interactive maps, thousands of articles, photos, video, sound, and 3-D tours of historical sites with commentaries from famous personalities such as Maya Angelou. *Grammar for the Real World* (Knowledge Adventure) is a multimedia program that motivates middle grade students to practice writing, grammar, and language skills in the context of creating their own short films. This software includes advancing levels of difficulty, an on-line grammar reference, and text-to-speech technology that allows students to hear their scripts read back to them.

In addition to using professionally prepared multimedia products, high school students are creating their own sophisticated products using digital video cameras, scanners, DVD burners, and multimedia software such as *iMovie*, *Macromedia*, and *MovieWorks*. These tools are used to create multimedia CD-ROM supplements to high school yearbooks and net-based newspapers. Content area literacy is being redefined by multimedia applications.

Among the thousands of software programs, some are free and some are expensive; some are junk and some offer extraordinary opportunities for enhancing classroom learning. The International Society for Technology in Education (ISTE) *http://iste.org* has established standards for all areas of educational technology and publishes a practical teacher magazine called *Learning & Leading with Technology*. *Children's Technology Review* published by Active Learning Associates reviews software products on a monthly basis and has a searchable database of over 7,000 reviews available to subscribers.

Electronic books, sometimes called eBooks, are a computerized alternative to traditional forms of printed text. They include digital tools that support literacy in ways not possible with traditional books. Electronic books are available as commercially produced CD-ROMs and DVDs, or they can be downloaded from the Internet to stationary computers or to portable eBook readers. For example, eBooks.com (*http://eBooks.com*) sells whole books, chapters, and pages of books of every genre online from publishers all over the world. These electronic books can be downloaded immediately to customers and at lower prices than printed books. The company currently has 69,000 eBooks available. Some eBook readers come with electronic amenities such as touch screen dictionaries. There are two main categories of electronic books: (1) literature, and (2) content area textbooks and other reference materials.

Electronic literature comprises fiction, poetry, drama, and other creative works. Some of the eBooks are simply digitized novels without electronic bells and whistles. Some eBooks are multifaceted programs with note-taking capability, such as *Robert Frost: Poems, Life, Legacy* (Henry Holt), which includes not only searchable text of the complete poems, selected letters, critical essays, and a full-length biography, but also extensive audio of the poet himself reading, archival photographs, and a multimedia documentary.

Electronic content area textbooks and references are, like their paper counterparts, concentrated sources of information. However, the multimedia and rapid search capabilities of the electronic medium clearly enhance the user's experience with video, graphics, and sound. Representative software programs of this type include *American History Explorer* (Learning Co.), *Africa* (Encarta), *Animal Planet* (Discovery Channel Media), *Multimedia Encyclopedia* (Grolier Interactive), and the *Collegiate Dictionary, Deluxe Electronic Edition*, by Merriam-Webster (Baldwin & Murphy, 2002). Finally, some schools have replaced hard paper copies of textbooks with eBooks, and many other schools are experimenting with the concept (Goulsby, 2006).

Internet

The *Internet* is a complex set of interlinking computer networks that began as a project in the U.S. Defense Department's Advanced Research Projects Agency (ARPA) as part of a military strategy in the United States to maintain communications in the event of a nuclear war. The network went operational in 1969 and was initially called the ARPANET. By 1984 there were 1,000 computers connected by the Internet. Today there are hundreds of millions of computers sending tens of billions of emails and doing tens of billions in business transactions on the Internet every day.

Speed, currency, and breadth of information are among the many attributes that make the Internet so dynamic. Email is rapidly replacing regular (snail) mail, and it is now possible to send legal signatures by Internet. Correspondence that formerly took three days now takes three seconds. Another advantage of the Internet is its capacity for constant updating. As a reference source the Internet is far more current than conventional paper documents such as textbooks or even newspapers. The Internet is also possessed of extraordinary subject breadth, and hundreds of online libraries such as EBSCOhost and ProQuest offer media centers and college libraries full-text, searchable databases of thousands of magazines, professional journals, books, and documents whose pages number in the billions. Websites are readily available to address almost every need and interest from buying airplane tickets to finding a local chess club. Some of the applications available on the Internet are nothing short of fantastic. For example, Google Earth (*http://earth.google.com*) combines satellite imagery with maps and the Google search engine to allow the viewer to search the entire surface of the Earth as though one were flying in from space to zero in on the Grand Canyon, the Eiffel Tower in Paris, or even the viewer's own home.

The Dark Side of the Net

Dad: Well, Son, what did you learn in your first year of college?

Son: Well, Dad, I learned that the only substance you can eat or drink in unlimited quantities without dying from it is water.

Dad: That's interesting, what else?

Son: I learned how to make a fertilizer bomb using the Internet.

As enthusiastic as we are about the Internet and the general use of technology to enhance education, we would be remiss if we failed to mention the downside of technology. The Internet is the Wild West of communications. Laws that were designed to protect children, copyrights, and personal privacy are different or entirely inapplicable to the Internet. In addition to good information, the Internet carries enormous amounts of bad information and outright danger. The intellectual scum of society are on-line and prepared to turn the information superhighway into an alleyway for predatory sex, business scams, misinformation, and pathological mayhem (What purpose is served by the creation of computer viruses?). You can buy illegal drugs and child pornography on the Internet just as easily as sporting goods equipment or antiques; and we all seem doomed to receive ridiculous amounts of *spam*, Internet junk mail from the bottom feeders of cyberspace. We are all getting tired of opening up our email accounts only to find dozens of brazen titles such as: MAKE MONEY FAST, CHEAP DRUGS, and NEW ADULT WEBSITE WITH HOT LINKS. For these reasons and many more it is vital that students ask good questions whenever they view a website:

Do the authors of the website identify themselves?

What are the authors' credentials?

Why should I believe the information on this website?

Are the authors informing me for my benefit, or are they biased?

Is the website trying to sell me something or change my beliefs?

Do the authors of the website want information from me, and should I provide it?

Is there any potential danger to me or to others from the website?

According to NetTrekker.Com (2006), one child in four is accidentally exposed to pornography on the Internet, and the average age of a child being exposed to online pornography is 11. It is, therefore, imperative that students be alerted to online dangers and taught to question the values and intentions of the authors of Internet websites and content. While doing research for this edition of *Content Area Literacy*, one of the authors accidentally used the URL *http://www.sin.org* instead of *http://www.sln.org*. The latter is the Science Learning Network, a website that provides links to "Cool Sites" in science. Unfortunately, the author ended up at a sadomasochistic site with content that included "Marquis de Sade: Philosophy in the Bedroom!" In uncontrolled cyberspace, students are never more than a few clicks away from danger.

Additional information on Internet safety is available through iSafe (*http://www.isafe.org*), a non-profit foundation dedicated to protecting the online experiences of youth everywhere. Online protection practices are also available from the American Library Association's *The Librarians' Guide to Great Websites for Kids* (*http://www.ala.org/ala/pio/availablepiomat/librariansguide.htm*).

Thoughtful, critical reading was never more important, and no other technological or intellectual tool will serve the young Internet reader as much as the right question asked at the right time and in the right way (Burke, 2002). Censorship, first amendment rights, and critical reading have never been more relevant to literacy than they are now in relation to the Internet.

Cybraries

Cybrary, a blend of the words cyber and library, is a collection of websites accessible from a single sight and dedicated to a specific subject area. For example, Remember.org is a Cybrary of the Holocaust and shares powerful stories of survival through art, photography, painting, and remembrance (*http://www.remember.org*). Another example is Global Access to Educational Sources: A Cybrary for Middle School and Beyond (*http://www.geocities.com/Athens/Academy/6617?200629*). It is a comprehensive link to collections of websites for academic areas such as art, mathematics, and science. This cybrary also includes links to websites dedicated to Internet resources, new and current events, reference sources, and teacher resources.

Other cybraries are huge compendiums of websites that have been evaluated by educators and deemed safe for student use. For example, *Nettrekker* (*http://www.nettrekker.com*) is a collection of 180,000 educator selected websites, 600 periodicals, 3,000 domestic and international newspapers, and its own search engine. Nettrekker supports specific state standards by providing teachers with online resources, lesson plans, and student activities once the teacher has requested support for a particular standard. The Pennsylvania Department of Education has recently purchased access to Nettrekker for every public school student in the state.

Wikis and Blogs

Wiki is derived from the Hawaiian word for fast and refers to software that supports an open editing environment. This means that anyone can go to a wiki website and edit the text. A wiki is a quick way to collaboratively edit documents and serves as a perpetual collective work of many authors. However, it also means that the validity of the information on the site must always be in question since anyone can alter the content for any reason at any time. The most famous wiki is *Wikipedia* (*http://en.wikipedia.org*), a free online encyclopedia that boasts one and a half million pages of information. An Internet search for a definition will frequently identify Wikipedia as a resource. The information may be interesting but should be digested with skepticism because the content may change at the whim of anyone who visits the site. Another example of a wiki is eBaywiki (*http://ebay.about.com/od/ebaylifestyle/a/el_wiki.htm*), a forum for eBay members to discuss best practices and strategies for buying and selling on eBay.

Blog is short for weblog and is similar in nature to a wiki except that the original material cannot be edited except by the individual who established the blog. Individuals respond to the material published on the blog and to each other. Blogs allow individuals to express their opinions and beliefs on any subject without necessarily identifying themselves. The first blogs began in 2001 and as of this writing there are more than 57 million. There is even a blog search engine called *Technorati* (*http://www.technorati.com*), which finds blogs on almost every subject. Adult bloggers are typically interested in information networking rather than self expression. In contrast, teenage bloggers are primarily concerned with self-expression and social interactions. For instance, a typical profile in LiveJournal (*http://www.livejournal.com*), a teen blog, usually focuses on personal interests, lists of friends, and group memberships. Blogs can also be used for instructional purposes. For example, Darren Kuropatwa, a Canadian math teacher requires students to post summaries of relevant class experiences and reflections (*http://pc20s.blogspot.com/*) (Harris, 2006).

Instructional Practices Using the Internet

A comprehensive discussion of how to integrate technology into the content area classroom is beyond the scope of this book. However, two well documented approaches are the WebQuest (Dodge, 2006) and online literature circles (McNabb, 2006).

WebQuests and Internet Workshops

WebQuest is an inquiry-oriented activity in which some or all of the information acquired from the activity comes directly from the student's interaction with the Internet. It is also an instructional paradigm for integrating the Internet into content area classrooms. The term *Internet Workshop* (Leu & Leu, 2000) is sometimes used when the purpose of the lesson is to teach students how to use the Internet (e.g., navigate, search, document information, avoid dangerous sites, and ask good questions). WebQuests are usually tied directly to the science, social studies, or language arts curriculum. There is no one correct way to conduct WebQuests and Internet Workshops, but they usually have the following steps:

1. Provide students with direct instruction in the use of Internet search strategies and safety precautions.
2. Locate an appropriate Internet site and provide students with the URL (Web address) or bookmark for location.
3. Create an activity that will require students to use the site.
4. Assign the activity allowing enough time for all students to access the site.
5. Encourage students to share their explorations, frustrations, and accomplishments during the workshop session.

An appropriate site is one that is well organized, well documented, and suitable to the age group. Activities may be simple, controlled tasks such as finding a single piece of information, or they may be complex and open-ended, depending upon the age and technological sophistication of the students. Good websites for teachers interested in WebQuests are:

Kathy Schrock's Guide for Educators:
http://school.discovery.com/schrockguide/webquest/webquest.html

The WebQuest Page at San Diego State University:
http://webquest.sdsu.edu/

WebQuest News:
www.webquest.com

Sample WebQuest for Grade 8 General Science

Froguts (*http://www.froguts.com/flash_content/index.html*) is a commercial website that offers schools virtual laboratory experiences. Visit the site and select "Demo."

A. Go to the link called "Froguts." This site will allow you to dissect animals using the computer. Select an animal; dissect it; and answer these questions:

What animal did you dissect? _____

Circle the word that best describes how you felt about this activity:

interested   disgusted   bored   excited

Name one advantage of digital dissections. _____

If you were given a real (dead) animal, do you think you could dissect it based on what you learned from Froguts? Why or why not?

_____

B. Other "cool" science sites are available from the Science Learning Network (*http://www.sln.org*). Go to the Science Learning Network and select a cool site. Name the site and be prepared to share three things about the site that makes it cool.

Site Name: _____

Fact #1: _____

Fact #2: _____

Fact #3: _____

Online Literature Circles

Literature circles are a collaborative approach to instruction that integrates the reading of a book with discussions of themes and background information related to it. Small groups of students at any grade level work together, and each individual selects an aspect of the book for which he or she will provide leadership in research and discussion. For example, if a class were reading *The Diary of Anne Frank*, members of a literature circle might select topics such as World War II, the Holocaust, the history of Warsaw, or ethnic prejudice. These topics would be researched on the Internet with appropriate guidance from the teacher. The CD-ROM that accompanies *Content Area Literacy* includes the complete novel *Call of the Wild*. The activity on the *Content Area Literacy* companion website at *http://www.kendallhunt.com* will guide you in designing a literature circle for *Call of the Wild* using the Internet as a resource.

Conclusions

If the presentation in this chapter seems a bit contradictory, that's because it is. On one hand, we have applauded the tremendous accomplishments in technology and have encouraged its use in content area classrooms. On the other hand, we have been less than enthusiastic about the impact of technology on achievement in American public schools. If technology doesn't improve achievement, why support its expanded use?

We believe that the promise of technology is real but also that it will not be realized until there is a universal commitment to integrate technology into the curriculum. In addition, the curriculum in most schools is driven by textbooks, which are frequently misused to ensure that all students are exposed to the same content and progress through the curriculum at the same pace. Contrast this with the individualistic nature of cyber exploration and blogging. Perhaps the time has come for our profession to question the necessity of all students acquiring the same knowledge base. This might require tossing out the textbooks—or at least making them supplemental—and elevating the Internet, interactive multimedia programs, and original source documents as the primary tools for learning in schools of the future.

Teachers in the content areas need to understand the value of integrating the Internet, multimedia software, and electronic databases into their respective subject areas. Problem solving and the multidimensional exploration of art, history, literature, mathematics, music, and the physical sciences are all possible through multimedia software. What are the advantages of such systems? How will they change the process of learning? Will they significantly affect the traditional role of the teacher? These are just a few of the important questions you and teachers like you will need to address in the near future.

Computer instruction, when combined with video and text sources, promises to be an exciting technological and educational innovation. New methods of presenting traditional information, new methods of problem solving, new ways of organizing and structuring large databases, and new ways of providing personalized instruction are just a few of the opportunities available. Schools must provide students at all levels with access to the new technology and make sure they have equal access to resources whatever their socioeconomic background, race, or gender. At the same time, we must make sure that the new technologies do not limit or impede our capacity to be humane and critical interpreters of the world in which we live and work.

Reaction Guide

	Confirmed	Disconfirmed
1. Technology has had a greater impact on social networking than on school achievement.	_____	_____
2. It is impossible to make the Internet safe for children.	_____	_____
3. Computers and the Internet have replaced textbooks as the dominant instructional tools in public education.	_____	_____
4. The computer is morally neutral.	_____	_____
5. The first electronic computer was built during the U.S. Civil War.	_____	_____

A Why my choice is confirmed.	**B** Why my choice is not confirmed.
1. _____	_____
_____	_____
2. _____	_____
_____	_____
3. _____	_____
_____	_____

4. _____   _____
   _____   _____

5. _____   _____
   _____   _____

Mini Projects

1. This chapter contrasts current societal expectations for computers and related technology with the failed expectations of the teaching machines of the 1950s and 1960s. Read the article, *The Automatization of Socrates,* by Desmond Cook. Were the purposes of the old teaching machines the same as today's educational technology? Do you believe that today's computers and software will succeed where the machines of 40 years ago failed? Why or why not?

2. Discuss the advantages and disadvantages of a multimedia encyclopedia over a traditional printed encyclopedia.

3. Compare and contrast the ENIAC with modern computers that have multimedia capabilities.

4. Explain how the computer revolution might contribute to the social evils of gender bias, stereotyping, and physical violence.

5. American educators have in large part embraced the notion that the use of computers in the schools is inevitable and even desirable. In many respects the increasingly widespread use of computers in our culture and in our schools parallels the introduction of the automobile at the beginning of the previous century. Although the automobile made rapid and convenient travel possible, it also engendered highway construction, air pollution, and frequent accidental deaths. Both from a personal and an educational point of view, what might be some of the hidden costs of introducing computers into our schools? Can these problems be avoided, or are they inevitable?

 Website Activity

To locate and complete Chapter 2 activities, go to [*www.kendallhunt.com/contentarealiteracy/*].

3

Language, Diversity, and Cognition

Anticipation Guide

	Agree	Disagree

1. Knowledge of a student's language is not important in teaching subject matter. _____ _____

2. Programs designed for second language learners help them gain subject matter comprehension. _____ _____

3. Comprehending text material is a creative, constructive process. _____ _____

4. Good teaching will result if one knows the subject and how to teach it. _____ _____

5. Whole class discussion discourages wide student participation. _____ _____

Rationale

The uniquely human acts of reading and writing have been cherished by people for centuries because literacy and power are so closely related. In the young adult book, *From Slave to Abolitionist: The Life of William Wells Brown* (Warner, 1993), African American William Wells Brown provides a harsh, realistic account of his flight from 20 years of slavery and the tearing apart of his family. His autobiography, first published in 1847, reveals the powerful role literacy played in his flight to freedom. Through great personal danger and dedication, William Wells Brown learned to read and write, giving him the voice needed to fight slavery and prejudice for 22 years as a lecturer and author. In 1834, on the run to Canada and freedom, he traded candy for lessons in reading at an abolitionist's home in Ohio. He progressed to a stage where he could read complex texts and, ultimately, contribute to the antislavery movement.

> Soon I bought an arithmetic book and a grammar and studied them equally hard. Next I bought other, general books and in leisure moments, I read them to improve my skills—and my knowledge. This reading of books whenever possible became my lifelong practice. Wherever I might be, there will always be with me a volume of grammar, mathematics, history, or literature. (p. 92)

While students often view content area textbooks as overwhelming and at times dull, for William Wells Brown they represented a route to learning and a voice in the political struggle for freedom. In the early 1830s, teaching an enslaved African American to read was a crime that would result in severe punishment (Nieto, 2004). Denied literacy as a slave, William Wells Brown knew reading and writing were keys to fighting a system that was brutal and unjust.

More recently, scholars have argued that in order to participate as informed citizens in an increasingly global society, students need opportunities to wrestle with problem-based political issues (Banks & Banks,

2005). Critical literacy offers a particularly powerful frame of reference to examine geo-political problems in a variety of content areas, and we consider these ideas as they relate to language and diversity (Harper & Bean, 2007; Stevens & Bean, 2007).

Many immigrant populations continue the struggle to adapt to unfamiliar surroundings in the United States after fleeing conditions of war, poverty, and persecution in their native lands. Schools have experienced an increasing number of non-native speakers of English, and this trend is expected to continue. The United States Census Bureau projects that nearly 90 percent of the population that is expected to increase between 2000 and 2050 will be children of immigrants with a concomitant need for English language instruction (Hadaway & Young, 2006).

Culture and language differences can help or hinder students' progress in content literacy, depending on the knowledge and strategies you, as the teacher, have at your disposal. Students can flourish or flounder in content area classrooms based on what is known about diverse cultures and how lessons are conducted that capitalize on this knowledge. Are multicultural features incorporated in lessons, or are teachers merely maintaining the mainstream European American traditions of individual competition and assimilation?

The contemporary shift from printed texts on a page to online texts on a screen has significant implications for content area teaching and learning (Bean & Wimmer, 2007). Often termed, *New Literacies*, reading Internet and other multimedia texts changes the nature of reading in profound ways. For example, Kress (2003) notes that reading Internet texts often relies more on images with print in support of these visual elements. The cognitive process of navigating through Internet texts adds another dimension to reading where you, as a content teacher, may need to offer additional guidance. Therefore, in this chapter we consider traditional print-based text structures along side newer forms of Internet texts and their unique contributions and problems, particularly for struggling readers (Franzak, 2006; Wilder & Dressman, 2006).

In this chapter, we also explore the related dimensions of language, diversity, and cognition with an eye toward some activities and strategies that will help students' problem-based concept learning. Subsequent chapters will expand on specific strategies in the areas of lesson and unit design, young adult literature, vocabulary, comprehension, writing, studying, and other content area literacy approaches.

Learning Objectives

→ State the linguistic and diverse learner factors that influence reading comprehension and subject area learning.

→ State the cognitive and text-based factors that influence reading comprehension and subject area learning.

Graphic Organizer

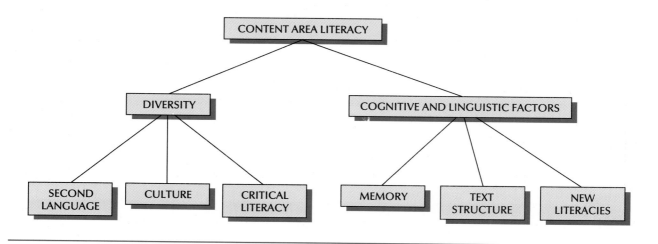

Language

A substantial number of immigrants from Europe and South America who are now middle-aged can recall suppressing their native languages when they arrived in American classrooms. Many have now lost this vital link to their past. For example, Nieto (2004) recalls her degrading experiences as a young Puerto Rican arrival to America. Her native language was Spanish, and teachers quickly transmitted the message that this language was not valued. She struggled simultaneously to learn content area concepts and English as a second language while the potentially powerful boost her native Spanish might have given her was devalued. Nieto argues that teachers can capitalize on a student's native language in content area instruction, especially since most contemporary bilingual education programs provide for the use of the native language as a bridge to using the second language.

Consider This ...

Grace, a Filipino immigrant employed at a rural flower farm in Hawaii, wrote the following query to her employer:

> Claudia,
>
> I have a ? Do you know what is a Bombay. Some one order that but I don't know what is it.
>
> Thanks,
> Grace

Grace formatted her query about the Bombay like a letter but used grammatical structures familiar to her. Nevertheless, she got her message across. As it turned out, Claudia did not know what a "Bombay" was either. At this point in her use of English as a second language, Grace would benefit from a small amount of explicit instruction. She would then have a model to use in future queries.

Programs designed for second language (L2) learning vary according to the emphasis on immersion in the target language (Nieto, 2004). Generally, programs may be characterized as:

a. immersion bilingual education

b. English as a second language

c. transitional bilingual education

d. developmental bilingual education

e. two-way bilingual education.

→ *Immersion bilingual education* is termed submersion by Nieto because it parallels her demoralizing experiences as a native speaker of Spanish expected to abruptly shift into English as the dominant language of instruction.

→ *English as a second language*, or ESL, provides structured lessons in English while the student may choose to maintain facility in the native language. The goal is to learn English through a structured program of lessons.

→ *Transitional bilingual education* consists of content area instruction in the native language while the student engages in ESL instruction with the proviso that the native language will be phased out in three years.

→ *Developmental bilingual education*, in contrast, does not have a time limit for phasing out the native language.

→ *Two-way bilingual education* may be the most attractive because both native English and non-native English speakers learn each other's language while they do the bulk of their content learning in the strong native language.

Two-way bilingual learning, and classrooms where non-native English speakers find their native language is valued and used in content learning, have a number of benefits. Since language and culture are inextricably linked, a teacher who demonstrates respect and enthusiasm for language diversity advances students' self-esteem and identity. A classroom atmosphere where students feel their native language and culture are valued can help reduce the high dropout rates experienced by non-native speakers. Even more importantly, valuing a student's native language helps students from diverse cultures maintain the often close family relationships with parents, siblings, grandparents, and extended family members. In instances where students are immersed in English and denied the use of their native language, the whole network and culture a student knows is treated as if it is less important than mainstream culture. This assimilation model results in real resentment and detachment from one's family. Many successful middle-aged immigrants abandoned their native identities to survive in America and recall these experiences with a good deal of pain.

In essence, once English as a Second Language (ESL) students are engaged in content area learning in history, science, mathematics, and English, they need extra teacher support to cope with academic language (Garcia & Godina, 2004; Hadaway & Young, 2006). Technical vocabulary and the unique expository text structures students encounter in the content areas require additional teacher guidance in the form of visuals, gestures, demonstrations and activity-based, hands-on inquiry learning where students have a chance to practice English language elements (Hadaway & Young, 2006). Hadaway and Young recommend the following specific instructional recommendations for ESL learners:

→ Keeping new vocabulary words in a lesson to a manageable number (7 or fewer).

→ Provide multiple encounters with these words across listening, reading, speaking, and writing.

→ Use words that have high utility and frequency within content areas (e.g., photosynthesis in biology).

→ Support instruction with visuals including graphic organizers, story maps, word banks, and other cognitive mapping approaches (e.g., the herringbone strategy where students list the 5 w's: who, what, when, where, and why in a fishbone format).

In addition, helping students grasp the academic language that underpins classroom instruction is also crucial (Pilgreen, 2006). Academic language includes terms such as "paragraph, bibliography, glossary, graph," and so on. Second language learners are likely to sink or swim depending on the nature of instruction they receive in content area classrooms. Teacher modeling, guided practice in questioning, summarizing text concepts, and using high-level strategies that link students' prior knowledge to text concepts will go a long way toward fostering optimal content learning (Garcia & Godina, 2004). Using literature that connects to ESL students' life experiences and offers opportunities for creative and analytical writing connected to their prior knowledge from diverse contexts will also advance English language development while respecting and supporting students' native language and dialects. The wealth of multicultural literature now available, including novels that feature English and Spanish discourse as well as novels set in international contexts, expand content area learning in social studies and other subject areas.

Today, there is a renaissance of multicultural literature, poetry, and music (Bean, 2006). The following poem, written in Hawaiian Islands Dialect or pidgin, treats a universal topic. Hawaiian poet Leomi L. Bergknut (1997) used unique linguistic structure, intonation, and deep cultural understanding to show how it feels when you are walking across campus and someone gives you "stink eye."

Stink Eye*

You ever give
Sombody one stink eye?
If, you wen do em
Den you know
Wat I stay writen about.

Da udda day wen
I wuz cruizin to class,
I wen feel
Sombody givin me
Da stink eye.

I know,
Cuz I could
Feel em at
Da back
Of my neck.

And da moe I walk,
Da moe I catch
Dat feelin dat make me wonda—
Who stay givin me
Da stink eye?

So, I turn aroun
And I know wuz you!
So, I give
Da stink eye back to you!
Da stink eye!

And den you
Wen stay laugh at me
And den you tell me
"Wat?
Wat you like?"

Stupidhead!
No give me
Da stink eye
Cuz you just might
Not live to regret it!

*Reprinted with permission of
Leomi L. Bergknut (1997) and *Kanilehua*.

 STOP! View the CD-ROM video clip and listen to the author of *Stink Eye* recite her poem in its original dialect.

Au (2000; 2006) has done a substantial amount of curriculum design work focusing on students who speak Hawaiian Islands Dialect in the Kamehameha Early Education Project. She regards reading and writing in any language as a solid foundation for learning. Thus, she recommends having students answer questions using some of their native language as they move toward proficiency in the target language. Hudelson's (2001) extensive work with Spanish speaking students led her to the conclusion that a good foundation in the native language provides a framework for subsequent language learning. Furthermore, she argues that there is no single best way to enhance second language literacy development for second language learners. However, there are a number of approaches and strategies you can use in your content area to value diverse students' existing knowledge and to build on this base.

Second Language Strategies

The most important strategy is to consciously make your classroom an inviting place for all students, but especially for students from diverse cultural and linguistic backgrounds.

BULLETIN BOARD DISPLAYS. Use students' native language in bulletin board displays. This could include signs, news articles, and other items related to your particular content area.

DIALOGUE JOURNALS. Students can make use of dialogue journals, which are discussed in the writing chapter later in this text. Dialogue journals involve the teacher and students writing to each other before the start of a class to ask questions, comment on any confusion over a lesson, and communicate in a free writing fashion where spelling and grammar worries take a back seat to straightforward communication between two people.

LEARNING LOGS. Students write in learning logs their reaction to a specific writing prompt. This helps second language learners focus on the upcoming content topic of a lesson. Students can make predictions, activate prior knowledge, and develop a prereading orientation to an assignment through a well structured learning log prompt.

LABELS. Using labels for items in class that include both English and other languages known to students in the classroom helps expand second language students' technical vocabulary in science, math, social studies, and other content fields.

EXPLANATIONS. Clear, concise explanations of required classroom activities, along with peer support, particularly in editing, help second language students immensely.

APPLICATION 3.1

Take a moment to write a short response to the following prompt. Break into small groups and share your thoughts.

> How do you feel about the notion that a second language learner should be immersed in English and not use his or her native language as a foundation for understanding content lessons?

In addition to these strategies, McCafferty (2002) supported the notion of using the language of literary texts written by authors who were themselves bilingual (e.g., Amy Tan) as a way of helping adolescent second language learners to explore the nuances of the target language. McCafferty (p. 280) alluded to the significant "language shock" experienced by second language learners and a concomitant feeling of alienation when confronted with the subtleties of a new language and culture. In essence, he regarded this difficult dimension of second language acquisition as a threat to the construction of a new identity in the target language and culture. "The opportunity to encounter multiple voices in American English through reading and discussing literary texts can be an important aspect of the acquisition and production of a voice in English for L2 students" (Mc-

Cafferty, p. 281). In Chapter 7 we take up the topic of literature with a particular focus on young adult and multicultural young adult literature. These books offer a powerful vehicle for the exploration of language and teen interaction. For example, Gary Soto's books are often infused with Spanish language phrases intermingling with English narration. This inclusion of second language phrases offers a bridge from the native language to English as a second language.

Language and Culture

Language becomes the surface manifestation of a more subtle and invisible culture. Au (2000) sees culture as a collection of values, beliefs, and standards which influences how students think, feel, and behave in various social settings including classrooms. Nieto (2004) points to a number of potential gaps in mainstream and divergent cultures that manifest themselves in classrooms. For example, she states that textbooks often emphasize a European American perspective while stereotyping, ignoring, or misrepresenting African and Native American contributions. Sociocultural values of various groups may run counter to mainstream classroom values if the teacher fails to be inclusive. For example, Native American students who value respect, harmony, and cooperation may have problems in a competition-oriented classroom. Some cultures disapprove of spotlighting a single student in front of the whole class (Au, 2000). Including more culturally compatible strategies like cooperative learning groups can help you achieve an inclusive, culturally responsive teaching style that is inviting to many students. Given the range of cultural diversity in classrooms, you may find some students view your style as too informal. Some students may regard your classroom as completely disconnected from their community. You can avoid this cultural gap through some labor intensive effort to learn about students' cultures and then design lessons accordingly. Content lessons should, as often as possible, connect the classroom to the problems and diverse values represented by your students. Urban, rural, and suburban communities each have unique contributions to make to instruction.

Instructional Design

The way in which teachers interact with students of diverse cultures may result in students seeing little connection between their native culture and the mainstream classroom value system of individual survival and competition. Unless culturally diverse students see some connection between your teaching and their unique sociocultural experiences, they are likely to just go through the motions in completing text reading assignments, project completion, and other classroom activities. A culturally conscious style of teaching involves creating very direct links between students' community life outside the classroom and the lessons they experience in the classroom (Ladson-Billings, 1995). For example, when students are allowed to bring in their contemporary music as a vehicle for studying conventions of poetry, they are more likely to experience success in reading this genre and they are more likely to tackle more challenging Shakespearean sonnets. In addition, by using music from their respective cultures such as rap, hip hop, reggae, and Hawaiian, students see their respective cultural identities honored and respected. When parents of students visit as scholars in residence to discuss their jobs, their presence clearly demonstrates a direct link between the classroom and community. Without that connection, school is seen as distant and unrelated to day-to-day life for too many adolescents (Bean & Readence, 2002).

Critical Literacy and Culturally Conscious Curriculum

Another important aspect of a culturally conscious pedagogy involves infusing the classroom with a high level of critical literacy. *Critical literacy* is crucial in any content area lesson design, but it is too often absent. Critical literacy, first of all, is not the same as critical thinking (Cervetti, Damico, & Pardeles, 2001; Stevens & Bean, 2007). Critical thinking has been a part of curriculum design in the United States for many years, generally in the form of helping students distinguish facts from opinions, instances of propaganda, and so on. Critical literacy, on the other hand, is aimed at looking behind the text to determine whose agenda is served by the text message, what groups are silenced, and how a text could be rewritten to disrupt these conditions. When we take up the topic of reading comprehension, we will explore in more detail ways to infuse critical literacy in content area classrooms. Critical literacy encourages readers to consider issues of social justice when they encounter a variety of texts that may have obvious or unstated agendas.

By engaging students as critical researchers to investigate and critique popular culture from a social justice stance, disenfranchised and marginalized adolescents are more likely to embrace academic literacy (Morrell, 2004; Pitre, 2007). For example, Ernest Morrell worked with African-American high school students in Los Angeles where they created hip-hop documentaries to protest a racist video game. Students wrote daily journal entries on their laptops and participated in a seminar that treated them as co-researchers. Morrell viewed this curriculum design as culturally conscious and likely to contribute to the development of critical citizens in a collective democracy.

You can increase students' motivation in your content classroom by using activities and participation structures that value a multicultural stance. For example, in English or social studies, students can interview and videotape each other's biographies based on an interview questionnaire they develop (Nieto, 2004). Similarly, in history or English, students can develop oral histories by interviewing family members. These projects show clearly that classrooms value the community they serve, and students are less likely to drop out of a setting that supports their success.

Another multicultural activity we have used in classes involves having students bring in two artifacts that represent their cultures (Maaka, 2001). For example, a student from India brought in a small replica of the Taj Mahal; another student who lost a significant amount of weight and became interested in riding motorcycles explained his various tattoos. Tom, raised in Hawaii, brought in a can of spam and a surf club tee shirt. The point is, the artifacts in our lives offer a window on our unique cultures.

Consider This...

The young adult historical novel *Saturnalia* (Fleischman, 1990), set in Boston during the winter of 1681, provides a poignant account of the main character's search for his lost tribal family. As a printer's indentured servant, his Indian name was changed by his master to the English name William. He sneaks out of the print shop at night after his master's family is in bed to search for his twin Narraganset Indian brother in the cold Boston night. "He had known two worlds, had lived two lives, had even been called by two different names: Weetasket, bestowed by his father at birth, and William, the name he'd worn in his second life, chosen by his second father, the printer, Mr. Currie" (p. 34). The book's rising action culminates in Saturnalia, an ancient Roman holiday when masters and servants trade roles.

Students' Names

Students' names are special and they each have a unique history as well as a wealth of associations. Throughout our history, names have been shaped by the power relationships of the time. You can use the importance and cultural interest of students' names to get to know students' unique contributions to your class. Application 3.2 is a good icebreaker.

APPLICATION 3.2

Your name, especially your last name, has an intricate history that offers a window on your unique culture. Pair up with another student in the content area reading class and ask that student to tell you about his or her name. Do this for both members of the pair and share this information with the whole group.

As a teacher you can devote a section of the bulletin board in your classroom to a name history profile of your students. For example, in one content area class, a student with the last name "Kamalani" in Hawaiian, explained its meaning and significance. "Kama" means child and "lani" means heavenly. Thus, this student's name meant "heavenly child." Another student from Japan had the last name "Ohsuga." Her name denoted a young rice plant with great potential for growth and success. She shared the "kanji" or ideographic symbol for her name, which is: 㐂

This simple activity of pairing, sharing, and discussing class names helps develop a sense of multicultural community in a classroom, and it focuses on an important element of language, one's name. The goal of activities like name sharing is to enable learners from different cultures and perspectives to develop some understanding of another student's world view. This movement toward a multicultural appreciation and related competency is vital for understanding text readings in history, science, music, art, English, economics, and other content areas. This brief name sharing activity can be extended through peer interviewing, video recording of these profiles, and subsequent reading and discussion in a class in social studies or English. Application 3.3 is such an extension.

APPLICATION 3.3

Pair up with another class member and use the survey questions that follow to interview this person about his or her ethnic and cultural biography and values (Kinney, 1993). The interview information can be used to introduce class members, assign small groups, and design lessons that build on students' diversity.

1. Where did your ancestors come from? Country, region, city?

2. Why did they come to _____ (our state, country, etc.)?

3. Where does most of your cultural community live?

4. What are the more popular jobs for your community?

5. What are the popular unique terms and gestures used by the community?

6. Do families stay close geographically as they grow up?

7. Do multiple generations live in the same household?

8. Who are the decision makers in the family?

(continued)

APPLICATION 3.3 *continued*

9. How does the decision-making process happen?

10. How are elders treated in the family and community?

11. How is respect shown?

12. Do family members have certain cultural names? What are the popular names?

13. Who are married children influenced by the most in their decision making? Prioritize.

_____ Children   _____ Grandparents   _____ Cultural leaders

_____ Parents   _____ Nieces/nephews   _____ Spiritual leaders

_____ Siblings   _____ Neighbors   _____ Other

14. What are some special values and beliefs your culture upholds?

15. Is your community focused more on the individual or the group? Please state examples.

16. What are some ways a teacher can act that are culturally appropriate in your community?

Community Projects

In addition to interviewing and developing student profiles of cultural norms, you can institute other projects in your content area that link the school, classroom, and community. In science, students can connect with the community through projects in tree planting and beautification through playground clean-up at a local elementary school. In math or economics, a class can help an elementary school establish an in-school store for supplies or food.

Hobbies, food, and music offer additional areas where unique language and cultural differences can contribute to learning. For example, the African American lyrical patterns found in blues and rap can be used to develop songs to study topics ranging from cell structure in biology to the stages of a revolution in history.

Cooperative learning strategies encompassing small group work with students of diverse cultures and abilities offer yet another means of linking students' sociocultural learning styles and your classroom. For example, Hawaiian students enjoy a participation structure called "talk story" where group performance in a free-flowing discussion of current events, family activities, and community concerns is common. Indeed, the flow of information in "high context" cultures is dominated by oral language networks that rely on talk story exchanges to accomplish the day-to-day business of the community. In contrast, "low context" cultures like many urban, European American communities rely heavily on a paper trail to do business. A profusion of memos, position papers, policy statements, and legal documents characterize the flow of information in a low context culture.

In rural Hawaiian communities talk story as a high context form of "coconut wireless" is still quite common. It saves trees and works remarkably well. Talk story as a cooperative teaching strategy is directly related to the Hawaiian cultural values of "laulima" (cooperation), "ohana" (family), and "lokahi" (unity). Hawaiians and many other Pacific Island and Asian cultures revere their "Kapuna," or elders, for their ability to teach culturally appropriate actions. Indeed, much of the cultural lore that needs to be shared with younger generations is not written down but must be passed along in chants and stories.

Teachers sensitive to the special values of a culture like the Hawaiians or Native Americans design content lessons that place students in small groups to discuss content text readings, react to reading guides, develop projects, and study for exams. Cooperative learning will be discussed in greater detail in subsequent chapters where we demonstrate specific teaching strategies in vocabulary, comprehension, and writing. Cooperative learning has been recommended as a culturally appropriate strategy for students from high context cultures like Native American, African American, and Hawaiian. However, cooperative learning groups mirror the problem-solving approaches used in many low context settings in business and community groups across many cultures. Thus, learning to organize participation structures like cooperative learning will enhance your teaching for most of the students in your content area classes.

In addition to the important sociocultural dimensions that influence content area learning, a number of cognitive and linguistic factors operate as students read and study content area texts and materials.

Cognitive and Linguistic Factors in Text Comprehension

A student's prior knowledge is the vehicle for comprehending new information in a text. This constructivist view of learning argues that knowledge is constructed from experience. A student builds a body of prior knowledge through the accumulation of experiences, and this uniquely personal body of knowledge guides comprehension of subsequent text reading.

Consider This ...

Read the following sentence and see if you can figure out to what it is referring.

The phoscheck dropped left of the cat.

If you lived in a canyon in Southern California where the early fall Santa Ana winds fan wildfires that regularly destroy homes and forests, the term phoscheck would be very familiar from numerous news reports and personal experience. In firefighting operations, phoscheck, a fire retardant, is dropped from helicopters. The term cat refers to a Caterpillar tractor cutting a fire line near where the chemical fire retardant is being dropped.

Prior knowledge, then, is constructed from experience and stored in memory. Understanding how information is organized in memory will help you appreciate individual differences in reading comprehension.

Organization of Prior Knowledge in Memory

Cognitive structure is a term used to describe the way in which an individual stores experiences and concepts. In such structuring, each individual forms a system of categories based largely on common cultural and experiential patterns. For example, Eskimo culture specifies a rich category system for the quality of snow. In Hawaiian culture that category is virtually nonexistent. Such categories serve to aid an individual in organizing and understanding experiences by promoting an efficient memory search of prior experiences during problem-solving tasks. Figure 3.1 depicts a portion of a possible category system for classifying various kinds of mammals.

A category system such as this functions as a representation of knowledge in memory that can be searched to make sense of the surrounding environment. In

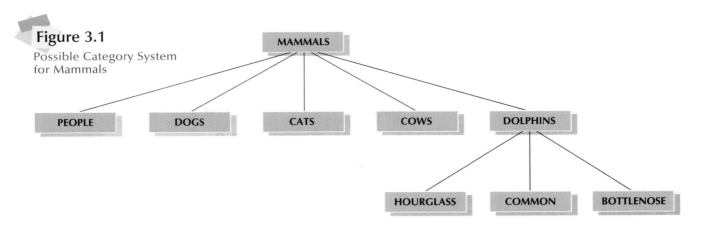

Figure 3.1

Possible Category System for Mammals

general, information located at a high level (e.g., mammals) in our cognitive structure is more easily retrieved than lower level details such as the category of hourglass or bottlenose dolphins. For example, although the category dolphin is readily accessible when we see a dolphin or a picture of one, the more than 50 types of dolphins would be much harder to recall. The accessibility of subsets of a category is highly dependent on individual differences with respect to one's past experience, culture, and interests. A student who was raised near the sea and has a strong interest in marine biology may have a readily accessible and highly detailed cognitive structure for the category dolphins, while the general population of students possess a much less elaborate network for this category.

Most studies of student learning demonstrate the positive effects of prior knowledge as an aid to learning new concepts. Thus, content teachers should help students activate their prior knowledge before they begin a textbook or other reading assignment. Prior knowledge, however, is a double-edged sword and existing knowledge can hinder new learning when students have misconceptions to which they cling. For example, students may believe that all dolphins are the same. Thus, understanding students' prior knowledge for a content topic and how this knowledge is represented and organized is important.

As a student moves into the secondary grades, an ever-expanding wealth of prior knowledge is available to cope with the flood of new information introduced in the content areas. While the concept of cognitive structure explains how this prior knowledge is organized in memory, *schema theory,* patterned after Piaget's formulation, provides a more detailed explanation of comprehension. A person's schema or knowledge structure can be regarded as the central guidance system in the comprehension process. An individual searches existing schemata to make sense of incoming information from the text. The degree to which this incoming information is consistent with the expectations generated from existing schemata determines the presence or absence of comprehension.

While the cognitive structure dimension of schema theory has been a mainstay in comprehension research in reading for many years, others have argued that sociocultural elements need to be included if schema theory is to be useful in classrooms (McVee, Dunsmore, & Gavelek, 2005). Teachers are crucial in guiding students' knowledge acquisition, particularly in complex content area domains. In addition, McVee et al. note that: "Schema and other cognitive processes or structures are embodied—that is, who we are as biological beings determines our sensorial interactions with the world and thus the representations we construct" (p. 555). Thus, in addition to the cognitive demands of any text, other sociocultural elements including race, class, gender, and sex will also influence students' interactions with content area material.

Concept Learning in Content Areas

Consider This ▪ ▪ ▪

Take a moment and consider each of the following statements:

1. All bees sting.
2. If you are bitten by a tarantula in the hills of southern California, you might as well be dead.
3. The earth is flat.

Each of these statements comprise erroneous knowledge structures or misconceptions that students sometimes stubbornly cling to, despite a teacher's best efforts to convince them otherwise. Indeed, the first two misconceptions may be consistent with your schema for bees and tarantulas. Yet a male bee does not have a stinger; you can hold a male bee in your hand without any fear of injury. And, although tarantulas are poisonous and even deadly in South America, the southern California variety are not deadly. Finally, at the secondary and college levels, students generally know that the earth is not flat.

APPLICATION 3.4

In your content area (science, art, math, etc.) you learn a number of concepts (e.g., Newton's second law of motion) that defy common sense or conventional wisdom. Identify two such concepts from your content area and write a statement for each that is the commonly held belief by people who have not studied your field. Share these statements with another class member from a different field. Did they agree or disagree with the two statements. Why? What were their reasons?

Despite potential problems with misconceptions, linking new concepts to some familiar, existing concept remains a powerful strategy we can use to advantage in content teaching. Teachers routinely resort to verbal analogies when they see students looking perplexed. Sometimes these analogies are successful and at times they fail to connect with students' experiences, especially if students are approaching English as a second language. As a content teacher, you need to identify students' existing knowledge and provide experiences in reading, listening, speaking, and writing that help them progress smoothly through tuning and restructuring knowledge. Activities such as the anticipation guide and brainstorming, especially reflective brainstorming written in a dialogue journal, provide us with some sense of students' prior knowledge. We can then anticipate misconceptions that may arise as students read and take measures to help them modify existing information that is naive or in error. In later chapters we introduce specific strategies aimed at exploring students' concept development through reading and writing.

Prior Knowledge of a Topic and Reader Interest

Contemporary models of the reading process present comprehension as a complex interaction of reader knowledge, text variables, reader interest, and the quality of teaching that assists text comprehension. Despite the obvious power of a close match between students' expressed interest and a text that matches those interests, you as the teacher also have a profound impact on interest. As a teacher, you help students establish a purpose and a particular frame of reference or schema for reading text assignments. Because content area assignments often entail reading expository material which may depart from a student's preferred interests, you need to carefully guide students' understanding of text. Building prior knowledge and generating topic interest through purpose setting activities like anticipation-reaction guides can make a difference. In later chapters we introduce systematic procedures for discovering students' reading preferences. More importantly, we introduce techniques a content teacher can employ to insure that students become life-long readers.

Motivation to Learn with Content Texts

When students are confronted with expository textbooks that hold little intrinsic appeal, their motivation for reading and learning may sink to a low ebb. Without adequate teacher guidance and ingenuity, students in content fields such as science and social science may sluggishly go through the motions of learning, dispensing only minimal effort. If you lecture, assign text reading, and ask students only low level factual questions that encourage memorization and forgetting, students are likely to lapse into a reluctant, sluggish mode of participation. If you want to encourage students to actively link new knowledge to their existing background knowledge, to critically evaluate ideas advanced in your class texts and discussions, and to value their growing concept knowledge, the following general principles are important.

You need to provide a supportive, well-structured classroom environment and assignments that are challenging but not frustrating. Your learning objectives should be problem-centered issues worth pursuing rather than busy work that merely encourages memorizing facts and copying text-based definitions. For example, if you are studying a unit on the Constitution with a focus on the Bill of Rights, you might engage students in a discussion of student rights as a prelude to their text reading.

Slicing the complexity of lengthy tasks into manageable increments that students can accomplish in a short period of time helps reduce that feeling of helplessness and inertia associated with tasks students perceive to be beyond their capacity. Similarly, teaching students to set their own realistic learning goals may help reduce frustration. These goals may be in the form of reading a small section of a chapter or answering a specific, reasonable portion of the chapter questions. Along with reducing the scope of a task, providing immediate feedback and rewarding success through pleasurable activities, points, or simply praise will go a long way toward helping students' motivation and interest in your content area.

Finally, opportunities for active student responses to text concepts are crucial to enthusiasm for content learning. Projects, experiments, discussions, debates, role-playing, computer simulations, and student-created multimedia productions all contribute to students' interest in learning content that could otherwise be potentially dull fare. Classroom activities that place students in cooperative learning dyads and triads with their peers, especially if they are engaged in solving problems or grappling with higher order questions, also enhance motivation. In addition, if you provide immediate feedback on how students are succeeding or experiencing difficulty, this too will help them see the value in their efforts. Finally, when students have opportunities to complete finished products, whether they be in the form of essays, reports, multimedia productions, models, a play, artwork, or a gourmet meal, they have a vivid and tangible record of their efforts. We can all remember, possibly in some detail, those learning situations in which we produced something of intrinsic value. You need to strive for lessons that capture these principles. In subsequent chapters we introduce specific strategies designed to involve students actively in content learning. Additionally, we consider those students for whom content learning is especially challenging because of a persistent cycle of failure. We offer strategies for coping with the wide-ranging individual differences typical of our content classrooms.

Guidelines to help students actively link new knowledge to existing knowledge.
Provide a supportive, well-structured classroom environment.
Give assignments that are challenging but not frustrating.
Break up complex, lengthy tasks into manageable increments.
Teach students to set realistic goals.
Provide immediate feedback.
Reward success.
Provide opportunities for active student responses to text.

Memory

This section introduces some important concepts concerning human memory. Since a student's prior knowledge is represented in memory, it is essential that you understand how memory aids or disrupts the efficient use of prior knowledge in the comprehension process.

Cognitive psychologists typically differentiate two aspects of memory—short-term memory and long-term memory. In reality, these terms represent hypothetical constructs about memory rather than particular locations in the brain. Figure 3.2 illustrates the flow of information as it is processed by our memory system.

Figure 3.2   INFORMATION → SHORT-TERM MEMORY → LONG-TERM MEMORY

Short-Term Memory

Short-term memory is often called working memory because it holds information on a temporary basis until the information is either processed into long-term memory or erased to accept more incoming information. Short-term memory contains traces of the most recent information we are attending to at any given moment.

The single most important feature of short-term memory is its limited capacity for storing information. The short-term storage capacity for individual chunks of information is four. Your struggle to retain a new friend's phone number is a concrete example of this principle in operation. Including the area code, a phone number such as 618-296-9149 exceeds the storage capacity of short-term memory. Fortunately, there is a way to circumvent this capcity, limitation. Using a chunking strategy, the phone number 618-296-9149 can be held in short-term memory as three, rather than ten, discrete items (i.e., [618] [296] [9149]). However, short-term memory has a second limitation that even chunking cannot overcome.

The second important feature of short-term memory is its fleeting nature. Information such as a new friend's phone number must be constantly rehearsed if it is to remain available in short-term memory for longer than a few seconds. If attention is diverted for even a moment to something else, the limited storage capacity of short-term memory will be overloaded and the phone number erased to accept the new, incoming information. Both the fleeting duration of short-term memory and its limited storage capacity have important implications for the reading process in general and content teaching in particular.

EFFECTS OF SHORT-TERM MEMORY ON LITERACY. In terms of the reading process in general, if a student plods along in print at a laborious pace attempting to sound-out every unfamiliar word, short-term memory will be overburdened. The result of this word-by-word reading is that students can forget the beginning of a sentence before they get to the end. Students must learn to read text material, including unfamiliar words, in the most efficient way possible to overcome the limits of short-term memory. In Chapter 8 we introduce decoding strategies that encourage fluent reading.

In the content areas, some modes of presenting unfamiliar material may inadvertently impose excessive demands on students' short-term memories. The oral presentation of a large amount of new information in social studies or science may exceed the capacity of students' short-term memories. Problem-solving tasks in mathematics present similar problems. Word problems, which involve temporary storage of one part of the problem while the student simultaneously processes additional information, place excessive demands on the limited storage capacity of short-term memory. Finally, the processing limitations of short-term memory suggest that rote memorization of content material is likely to be an ineffective study strategy. The processing limitations of short-term memory should be kept in mind when a teacher plans or analyzes content teaching and learning tasks.

Long-Term Memory

Long-term memory, or permanent memory, plays an important role in compensating for the limitations of short-term or working memory. In contrast to short-term memory, long-term memory seems to have an infinite capacity for storing information. Long-term memory is the storage system for all our prior knowledge. It comprises our individually complex schema of the world, shaped by cultural experiences and beliefs. As such, long-term memory is a highly organized system. Indeed, the ease with which we can retrieve information from long-term memory is directly related to how well the information was organized at the time of initial processing from short-term memory.

One of the most powerful ways to encode information in long-term memory is through writing. Increasingly, writing is seen as a learning strategy that teachers should integrate across content areas. In Chapter 11 we offer a number of specific writing-to-learn approaches you can weave into your own teaching repertoire to enhance students' comprehension and long-term retention of concepts.

Long-term memory does have one limitation. The rate at which information can be processed into long-term memory is relatively slow. However, the ease with which information is processed into long-term memory depends in large measure on how meaningful the information is in terms of the student's prior knowledge. The more meaningful the information, the more easily it will be processed.

Figure 3.3 summarizes the two major aspects of memory treated in this section. In general, content teachers should acknowledge the importance of prior knowledge and meaningful organization in long-term memory information processing in their teaching. Students will be able to comprehend new information in a content area if you take time to demonstrate how the

Figure 3.3

INFORMATION

SHORT-TERM (WORKING) MEMORY
· CAPACITY: LIMITED
· DURATION: VERY BRIEF
· RETRIEVAL: IMMEDIATE
· INPUT: VERY FAST

DEEP PROCESSING

LONG-TERM (PERMANENT) MEMORY
· CAPACITY: ALMOST UNLIMITED
· DURATION: ALMOST UNLIMITED
· RETRIEVAL: DEPENDS ON ORGANIZATION
· INPUT: RELATIVELY SLOW

new information builds upon and extends what they already know about the topic. And, students will be able to retrieve information from long-term memory if you model and encourage meaningful organization of new information when it is first presented to the class.

Although cognitive factors play a major role in reading comprehension, linguistic factors also influence the reading process. In this section we will describe and demonstrate specific linguistic aspects of written language that interact with cognitive factors to aid or inhibit reading comprehension.

Language of Text

Authors of stories and even challenging scientific text use predictable organization patterns or *text structures*. For example, stories usually begin with a setting and one or more characters. The reader follows the main character's attempts to solve a problem or achieve a goal. This familiar text structure makes it relatively easy for a reader to make predictions about story events. Even more difficult expository text in science has an identifiable pattern of organization. For example, biology texts usually inform the reader about properties and functions of a topic such as carbohydrates or enzymes.

Students who are made aware of the overall structure of a particular text can use this knowledge in comprehending, studying, and discussing key concepts. Moreover, a text that provides a discernible organizational pattern places fewer demands on the limitations of short-term memory than poorly structured text. In Chapter 9 we discuss text structure in detail and introduce comprehension strategies that capitalize on this important linguistic aspect of text.

Contemporary views of what constitutes a text are changing rapidly and we need to consider the multiple texts students typically use. Texts come in many shapes and forms including Internet texts, radio and film media, electronic mail, instant messages, and hosts of other forms. It may be most helpful to think of texts as cultural tools for constructing knowledge rather than encyclopedic collections of information upon which to be tested (Wade & Moje, 2000). Thus, helping students manage a wide array of multiple texts in broad-based thematic units undoubtedly builds on the multi-tasking to which they are accustomed and best prepares them to become independent learners. While the single textbook approach may continue to be found in content area classrooms, students need to be learning how to manage a wider array of text forms, including WebQuests and other multimedia, Internet-based text formats (McNabb, 2006; Moje, Dillon, & O'Brien, 2000).

Language of Students

In addition to features of texts that make them friendly or unfriendly, our earlier discussion of second language learners suggests that students' language facility plays a powerful role in comprehension. If the texts students must read are very distant from their native language, second language students may have difficulty forming the mental pictures necessary for concept learning to occur.

Consider This . . .

The following sentence, adapted from Laird and Jossen (1983, p. 10), illustrates the frustration a second language learner may experience in text material containing vocabulary that is largely unfamiliar.

"Oh! Dakine mea'ai stay so ono," said Wili Wai Kula.

If readers must translate every word of a text with a dictionary or a laborious search through memory, they will have little attention left for comprehension. Moreover, integration of ideas across words and sentences becomes impossible.
Contrast the above example with Laird and Jossen's (1983) original text, *Wili Wai Kula and the Three Mongooses*, a Hawaiian version of the familiar *Goldilocks and the Three Bears*.

"Oh! The mea'ai smells so ono," said a hungry Wili Wai Kula. She tasted the rice and sausage on the biggest plate. It was too hot. Next, she tasted the rice and sausage on the medium-sized plate. It was too cold.

In this instance, some of the vocabulary is unfamiliar. However, your prior knowledge of the original fable, combined with some vocabulary knowledge and context clues should help you comprehend "mea'ai," a Hawaiian word for meal, and "ono," which means good.

Texts for second language learners should strike a delicate balance between familiar and unfamiliar vocabulary. Visual aids and pre-reading guides that help students see how their prior knowledge is related to concepts in the text help students use semantic cues. Otherwise, there is a real tendency for these students to read in a word-by-word fashion or to decode accurately without really comprehending what they have read. Notice that once you see a bridge between the familiar Goldilocks story and the Hawaiian version you can comprehend the selection despite not knowing all the vocabulary. In content areas, students' background knowledge is not likely to be quite this direct. But you can try to select texts that capitalize on familiar topics while adding new information to students' concept learning.

Visual representation of content area concepts helps second language learners connect the new to the known (McNabb, 2006). For example, if students are studying fish in science, the ancient Japanese art of origami will help them develop a hands-on grasp of fish anatomy through paper-cutting, painting, and labeling key parts. Moreover, this form of hands-on activity usually generates many opportunities for language interaction. In addition, the guide material discussed in Part 2 of this text can go a long way toward unlocking text concepts in the target language.

New Literacies and Text Structure

New Literacies refers to newer forms of texts including Internet-based texts, instant messaging (IMing), blogging, e-zines, and a variety of web sites and web page designs (Kist, 2005; O'Brien, 2006). The reason these newer forms of text are important is because they alter how one reads them (McNabb, 2006). For example, to a great extent, the linear and somewhat predictable text structures mentioned earlier (e.g., cell structure and function in biology) shifts when students are reading and navigating Internet-based texts. Indeed, Kress (2003) observed that reading paths in Internet texts vary across multiple sites and call for fairly sophisticated search strategies.

In traditional print-based textbooks, students work with fairly predictable, established text structures (e.g., problem-solution; simple listing of ideas; cause-effect relationships in science). McNabb (2006) notes that online text is characterized by chunks of information organized multisequentially, requiring readers to create their own navigational pathways and structures. In essence, these more unpredictable and varying online text pathways require more teacher guidance, particularly for struggling readers (Wilder & Dressman, 2006). Without careful guidance on your part, students are likely to do cursory searches for information, accepting ideas without critique and producing projects and papers that reflect little thought. Thus, in our view, the increasing use of online texts, while powerful from an information standpoint, is a double-edged sword. Many of the strategies aimed at guiding students understanding of vocabulary and key ideas in content areas become even more crucial as text structures blur and morph into collections of information organized in a wide-ranging panoply of forms on the Internet.

When you engage students in reading multiple texts in your content area, coupled with careful guidance and support to help them make connections across texts, you are preparing them to manage the vast array of information available on the Internet. As we consider vocabulary and comprehension issues in subsequent chapters, we will expand on this changing nature of text and examine strategies that will help students across traditional and newer forms of text.

The Classroom Social Context

In addition to cognitive and linguistic factors, the social context of a classroom has its own linguistic conventions and features. A number of studies, stemming from the anthropological tradition of intensive participant observation, provide us with an emerging picture of teacher-student and student-student interaction that belies a simplistic view of content teaching. The goal of intensive observational study is to uncover the social patterns that influence teacher and student success in constructing meaning.

Social context is as powerful as the following true Glimpse into the Classroom suggests.

Glimpse into the Classroom

In my first year as a ninth-grade English teacher, I had one class of 28 boys and no girls. These young men were the reputed dregs of the school: low achievers, truants, and trouble makers—one was sent to youth detention for robbing the blind man at the post office. I will always remember the day I handed out spelling books with a big number 3 on the front. Most of the boys were reading at a primary school level, and I wanted to have them working with materials at their instructional level. I explained to the class that learning to spell wasn't so difficult and that these spelling books would help them earn better grades in school. They said nothing; but when class was over, 28 copies of Fun With Spelling went into the wastebasket in the back of the room. I never forgot the lesson.

The teacher in this story may have known a lot about English spelling, and he may have had an appropriate instructional strategy in mind, but he failed to consider the social context in which the instruction had to take place. Those ninth-grade boys were not about to walk around a tough, urban school advertising to their peers the fact that they were using third-grade books. Getting kicked out of school or failing English for the year would no doubt have been preferable to them.

Schools are institutions with rules and agendas that tend to reflect the values of adults and the dominant culture and not the social and cultural values of adolescent readers and writers (Gee, 2000; Moje, Dillon, & O'Brien, 2000). Within the school are a variety of subcultures with their own unique beliefs and goals, and they are frequently in conflict with each other. Adults, children, European Americans, Hispanics, African Americans, Haitians, fundamentalist Christians, and many other groups will view the school, its curricula, and your teaching in different ways because these events are filtered through alternative cultural realities (O'Brien & Stewart, 2007). For example, classroom interaction patterns are, at least on the surface, usually orchestrated by the teacher and based on an intuitive or conscious theory of learning. Thus, teachers instruct, question, praise, and monitor students' comprehension in observable patterns that reveal their particular view of reading comprehension. This may range from simply assigning text reading, questioning students orally and giving a test, to the more carefully guided approach we are advocating.

In a classroom that follows our model of content teaching, an observer would expect to see various forms of prereading strategies in use (e.g., Anticipation Guides), small group discussion of text concepts using the guides, and postreading Reaction Guide discussion. Yet even with this guided approach, the classroom remains a social environment with its own hidden curriculum that is shaped by social as well as academic factors. Peer status rankings strongly influence whose voice gets heard and who is silenced, even in small groups (Moje & Dillon, 2006).

Classroom reading and discussion patterns often contain the following dimensions. Students are required only to produce text reproductions that merely reiterate text content. Amidst such low level discussions, they become skilled at procedural display—looking as if they are doing the work and participating while simultaneously carrying on other, more personally interesting and rewarding activities. Thus, a teacher-dominated discussion of text concepts produces an overly passive style of student thinking and participation. In our view, a classroom content lesson coexists with the larger context of the school and the sociolinguistic context of students' lives. A content lesson competes for students' attention amidst other, often more compelling, interests. It is likely to compete successfully if most students have adequate opportunities to participate.

One of the more recent, dominant themes in adolescent literacy now informing our teaching in various content areas is the degree to which classrooms and texts influence students' identity construction (Bean & Readence, 2002). Simplistic, stereotypical views of adolescents have been heavily challenged, arguing for a much more complex portrayal of youth (Lesko, 2001). Older developmental stage theories of adolescence have been deconstructed and replaced with more contemporary views of youth. "Youth are simultaneously young and old, learning and learned, working and in school" (Lesko, p. 197). Thus, adolescents are not at some static plateau where they are waiting to evolve into adults. Rather, they are active individuals with a multitude of interests and identities that shift with varying social contexts. They need to be considered active, critical participants in content learning. We have much to learn from youth as students.

Much of this recent effort to reconceptualize adolescents shows a disconnection between the out-of-school literacy lives of students and the tasks they perform to succeed in school (Alvermann, 2002; Flores-Gonzalez, 2002). For example, a student viewed as only a marginal achiever in school core content areas may write about athletic performance in a running diary when not in school. Although marginalized in terms of literacy performance in school, this same student writes and reflects on running performance eloquently when at home or with peers on the cross country team. The disparity between school and out-of-school identity has been well documented (Moje, 2002). What is truly important in this work is to consciously find ways to incorporate, acknowledge, and build on students' interests as a bridge to content area concepts. For example, running involves the mathematical elements of time, biological elements of cell structure, geography, weather, and attention to attire to maximize performance, among other things. McCarthey and Dressman (2000) recommended developing a curriculum that truly represents students' diversity by focusing on local, situational literacies. "Students would read and critique texts created from multimedia and written from a variety of points of view that reflected the diversity of their racial, social, cultural, and linguistic backgrounds" (p. 548). We agree that capitalizing on students' interests in curriculum design in the content areas is advantageous. For example, students in a biology class interested in running might examine and evaluate the truth claims of various high energy, fluid replacement drinks. In this way, their day-to-day interests from local, situational contexts are connected to issues of health and nutrition, as well as concepts of cellular energy storage.

A number of studies show that transmission of information teaching has changed little over the years. However, if a teacher takes a participatory approach to learning and students have the opportunity to interact with others, more learning takes place (Moje et al., 2000). A traditional transmission approach to teaching concepts from a single textbook disempowers and disenfranchises students, particularly students from diverse cultural and linguistic groups. Moje et al. argue that the text, context, and the learner are interrelated. Since students have multiple identities in and out of school, it behooves the content teacher to help students bridge text concepts with their individual interests and identities whenever possible. For example, a student who wants to be a paramedic is positioned to gain from biology and health sciences, especially if the teachers in these areas are aware of this related interest. Magazines, Internet material, first aid pamphlets, and other forms of text would be naturals to help engage this student in content learning. In addition to knowing something about students' outside-of-school lives, cultural dimensions play a profound role in how students respond to the classroom context (Au, 2000). Moje et al. (2000) urged content teachers to ask themselves: "How will my choices of texts and literacy activities reflect and expand the cultural backgrounds of my learners?" (p. 178). In Chapter 7 we introduce an array of multicultural young adult novels that expand on content area concepts and connect with students' lives.

APPLICATION 3.5

John Ogbu (2007) provides powerful anthropological insights into academic problems commonly experienced by minority children. Obgu also proposes a theory that explains why some ethnic minorities have more success in public schools than others. Read Professor Ogbu's article and write a 1–2 page essay explaining how his research and theories do or do not seem to explain patterns of minority achievement with which you yourself are familiar.

Teacher-student interaction patterns influence students' comprehension and attitude toward the content being studied. Collaborative, small group discussion using pre- and postreading strategies such as Anticipation/Reaction Guides are a good alternative to teacher-centered discussion. We are not suggesting that there is anything wrong with whole group lectures and discussions. But we do believe that small, problem-solving groups can afford greater opportunities for student participation if they are focused on an important topic with clear task guidelines.

In Part 2 of this text we consider comprehension strategies that you may wish to adopt to enhance students' critical reading and discussion. Reflective writing can also form a basis for student-centered sharing and discussion of ideas and issues. These elements of content literacy will be elaborated in subsequent chapters.

Reaction Guide

		Confirmed	Disconfirmed
1.	Knowledge of a student's language is not important in teaching subject matter.	_____	_____
2.	Programs designed for second language learners help them gain subject matter comprehension.	_____	_____
3.	Comprehending text material is a creative, constructive process.	_____	_____
4.	Good teaching will result if one knows the subject and how to teach it.	_____	_____
5.	Whole class discussion discourages wide student participation.	_____	_____

A	B
Why my choice is confirmed.	Why my choice is not confirmed.
1. _____	_____
_____	_____
2. _____	_____
_____	_____
3. _____	_____
_____	_____
4. _____	_____
_____	_____
5. _____	_____
_____	_____

Mini Projects

1. Visit a classroom in your content area and interview the teacher to determine how the issues in the first part of the chapter on language and diversity are handled. Before the interview, develop a few questions to stimulate discussion that focus on sociocultural and linguistic diversity as well as mainstreaming. Share your results with another class member in a discussion.

2. List at least one method you currently use, or plan to use, to assist second language learners' comprehension of concepts in your content area.

3. List at least three methods you currently use, or plan to use, to mobilize students' existing knowledge of topics in your particular content area. Compare your compilation with listings produced by other class members.

4. Visit a classroom in your content area. Based upon your observation notes, analyze the interaction pattern that occurs and determine the level of comprehension emphasized.

Website Activity

To locate and complete Chapter 3 activities, go to [*www.kendallhunt.com/contentarealiteracy/*].

4

Selecting Textbooks and Multimedia Materials

Anticipation Guide

		Agree	Disagree
1.	Censorship is both bad and unnecessary.	_____	_____
2.	Government regulations require that 10th-grade books be written on a 10th-grade reading level.	_____	_____
3.	It is safe to assume that high school students know how to use a textbook index.	_____	_____
4.	The content of subject area textbooks is politically influenced.	_____	_____
5.	The biblical version of creation should be included in biology textbooks that cover evolution.	_____	_____

Rationale

What is a textbook? Broadly speaking, a textbook could be any book which is used in formal study. This might include, for example, novels, reference books, or other works of nonfiction which may or may not have been designed exclusively for schools. More commonly, textbooks refer to books written specifically for school use and designed to summarize a body of knowledge or to present the fundamental principles of a discipline. The American history tomes, literature anthologies, and other textbooks to which you have grown accustomed vary tremendously in their quality. Some offer excellent presentations while others are too difficult for their intended audiences or suffer from poor organization. In addition, as we will demonstrate, the personal values of authors and the agendas of special interest groups cause textbooks which cover the same content to differ in terms of how they represent the truth.

Estimates of the amount of classroom time students spend reading or doing exercises from textbooks range from 55% to 95% (Zahorik, 1991). From the primary grades through college, textbooks are a pervasive element of education in the United States. Assuming that the average student spends five hours per school day using textbooks, the number of hours spent with textbooks exceeds 10,000 by the end of high school $(5 \times 180 \times 12)$. Clearly, how we select those books and what we ask students to do with them will have an enormous impact on how well students learn, what they learn, what they believe, and how well they think.

In this chapter we will examine issues related to the selection and appropriate use of textbooks, first from social and political perspectives and then from an instructional viewpoint. Additionally we will discuss the appropriate selection of multimedia materials. Finally, we will demonstrate a strategy for introducing students to an unfamiliar text.

Learning Objectives

→ Discuss the political and social dilemmas associated with textbook adoption processes.

→ State which quantitative and qualitative factors make a text more or less easy to understand.

→ Employ a checklist of quantitative and qualitative factors to evaluate a textbook and/or multimedia materials for use in your classroom.

→ Conduct a textbook preview to acquaint students with the essential learning aids in a text.

Graphic Organizer

Politics and Textbooks

We customarily associate the word politics with government. However, politics has the broader meaning of any social or cultural arrangement in which people make decisions that have consequences for other people. There are political dimensions to marriage, bridge clubs, and team sports. Public education is no exception.

School systems wrestle with hundreds of political matters every day, and most of them are outside the interest or beyond the control of most classroom teachers. However, there is one political issue which must be of critical concern to every subject area specialist—the selection and interpretation of textbooks. Ultimately, content area teachers are responsible for the accuracy, truth, and representativeness of the textbooks they use. Which stories and essays should be included in literature anthologies, for instance? Because it is impossible to include everything in an anthology, something must be excluded. What stays, what goes, and who makes the decision? Should the biblical version of creation be included in biology texts along with theories that espouse evolution? How explicit should health texts be on subjects of human sexuality, AIDS, and abortion? How these issues are resolved fluctuates over time. Textbooks are not almanac-like tomes of facts. Instead, they are books written and published by human beings whose cultural biases can slant, bend, or bury someone else's version of the truth.

Consider This ...

The following quote is from a World War I vintage geography textbook used by one of the author's grandmothers when she was a high school student (Redway & Hinman, 1916):

> The home of the black or "Negro" race is central and southern Africa and some of the Australian islands. The peoples of this race have coarse woolly or kinky hair, protruding lips, and dark brown or black skin. The black race includes some of the most ignorant people in the world. . . . Most of the yellow race and part of the Malay race have reached some degree of civilization. But some people learn more rapidly than others, and the Caucasian race includes the most enlightened people in the world. (p. 29)

Today we would consider such a racist position unthinkable in a textbook; but such viewpoints were common—even standard—in a country which still did not permit women to vote [The 19th Amendment to the Constitution was ratified in 1920]. Our purpose here is not to condemn the men who wrote your great-grand-parents' school books, but rather to make the following point: What we now observe to be obvious and fatal flaws in a 90-year-old textbook were probably accepted as absolute truths by the children who read the book. Can we afford to place any more faith in the accuracy and moral character of textbooks with a 2007 publication date?

Historical truth is slippery. It is possible, for example, to portray American westward expansion in a variety of ways. One account would describe fanatical, materialistic malcontents who out of greed organized a bloody rebellion against lawfully constituted authority and then murdered or expelled those who remained loyal to the legitimate regime. It would be the tale of a people who institutionalized genocide against American Indians and slavery of African peoples by invoking scriptural revelations of their god. *Bury My Heart at Wounded Knee* by Dee Brown has a graphic description of the treatment of American Indians. If you ever get a chance to read the book, it will not be difficult for you to view European Americans as the bad guys.

In the more traditional account of westward expansion, the nation's past is presented as a triumphant celebration of freedom, social progress, human rights, and individual fulfillment. Starting with the flight of a few enterprising and courageous souls from religious persecution, and continuing with a just and glorious revolution against the oppression of a tyrannical monarch, this would be the tale of virtue, both civic and cultural. This version of American history would portray a happy, freedom-loving people, the product of rugged individualism and hard work. It would be the story of Manifest Destiny with a people resolved to reclaim the wilderness, to civilize the savages, and to spread the principles of democracy across the virgin continent. This view of American history was epitomized in the 1963 movie *How the West Was Won*.

It has been suggested that although both Brown's version and the typical textbook version are extreme, both versions are also true to some degree. Yet one is the approved version that appears in U.S. history textbooks. The latter, familiar version is taught almost universally in American schools as the truth while the former version seldom finds its way into American history books.

Contemporary evaluations of texts of various kinds will benefit from recent work in critical policy analysis. According to Edmondson (2002, p. 114), "critical policy analysts recognize that work in and around schools is unavoidably political, and for this reason, values cannot be separated from facts or choices." Certainly we agree that selecting textbooks and multimedia materials, in part, reflects the belief systems of those who hold power in a school or district as well as a sincere desire to match students with appropriate texts.

Censorship

In early Rome there were magistrates known as censors. Their job was to take an accounting of the people and also to look after public morals. From the magistrates' former duty we have acquired the word census. From their latter commission we have inherited censor and *censorship*. A censor today is someone who indirectly supervises morality by regulating the films, books, music, or other information to which people may have access. The people who assign ratings of G, PG, PG-13, R, and X to movies are censors. Parents are censors when they will not let their children watch South Park because they believe the show is too crude or too violent. A librarian who decides that a book should not be in the school library is a censor. When publishers decide not to put a story into a literature anthology, they are censors—if they exclude the story because they are afraid of reprisals from the National Rifle Association, the American Civil Liberties Union, animal rights activists, or a fundamentalist Christian organization in California.

American schools have been a focal point in censorship battles, especially over the last 20 years. Across the country there have been periodic textbook burnings, book bannings, and school boycotts. In 1982 *The Adventures of Huckleberry Finn* was banned from classrooms in Mark Twain Junior High School in Fairfax County, Virginia, because the book was "racist" and "anti-American" (*The Miami Herald,* April 17, 1982). In some elementary schools the story of Robin Hood is banned because it teaches children to steal.

Censorship issues involving children and schools are not the same as adult censorship issues. With adults the issue usually is constitutional:

> Congress shall make no law respecting an establishment of religion, or prohibiting the free exercise thereof; or abridging the freedom of speech, or of the press; or the right of the people to assemble, and to petition the Government for a redress of grievances.

First Amendment to the Constitution

Presumably, the First Amendment gives adults the right to read whatever they want. However, censorship issues with students are more complex because students, especially young children, are assumed not to have the ability to make sound choices. Someone else makes decisions for them: what movies they may watch, what establishments they may enter, what books they may read, what content they will find in their subject area textbooks. We may feel outraged that books by Judy Blume have been banned from a junior high library—and she has been frequently banned—but few of us would want the same library to carry *Hustler* and *Playgirl* magazines. Either restriction is censorship. When accused of censorship, school officials invariably respond that it is not a matter of censorship but rather a matter of selecting appropriate reading materials for children. They have a point. Censorship in this sense is a fact of life in public education. Books will be chosen for children by someone. The real question revolves around who the someone is that makes the decisions: teachers, administrators, church groups, parents, publishers, or special interest groups in another state.

Textbook Censorship

One of the mightiest—and most hidden—powers in our society rests with those who are in positions to control the meanings of words and the distribution of concepts. Nowhere else in our culture is this power less obvious to the public or more critical to our collective future than in the development of school textbooks.

Textbooks are typically developed as a collaboration between teachers/college professors and an editorial staff within a publishing house. As a rule, the lower the grade level the more the final product is the work of professional editors. In contrast, the content of high school and college texts is more likely to reflect the thinking and writing of teachers/professors.

Publishers are businesses that sell books for money. Their primary responsibility is to shareholders and employees, and not to the abstractions of accuracy and truth. Compared with the profit motive, all other concerns are secondary. In this respect the publishing business is the same as the oil industry, retail furniture stores, and the hotdog stand at the beach. To make a profit the publishers must meet a market demand. If schools will buy more history books if the covers are made more attractive, the publisher will make more attractive covers. If schools will buy more history books if they are made to contain fewer references to Ulysses S. Grant and more references to Robert E. Lee, then you can bet that Grant will wane as Lee rises.

This is not intended to be an indictment of textbook publishers. Most of them are sincere in their efforts to publish quality books for children, but they are under tremendous pressure from schools and special interest groups to censor social science, literature, and physical science textbooks.

Consider This . . .

If you peruse a secondary literature anthology you will probably find that the anthology has been censored so that some or all of the following are absent from every selection:

→   potentially offensive words such as "hell" or "crap"
→   references to any drugs—even aspirin
→   references to any junk foods like potato chips
→   any references—even indirect—to the theory of evolution
→   pejorative comments about any minority groups
→   any sexist language
→   any references to human sexuality
→   any discussions of religion
→   any stories in which children question the values or moral reasoning of their parents.

In reading the list above, you probably feel some of the censored material would not be objectionable to you. Why do all of these aspects of literature have to be removed? The answer is that the most efficient way for publishers to eliminate potential objections from various censors is to self-censor **anything** that **anyone** might find offensive. A fundamental principle of censorship is that censors are sensitive to what is in the text that shouldn't be there. They are seldom worried about what isn't there that should be. Therefore, a special interest group that wants to suppress references to junk foods will not notice that essays about dangerous drugs, information about human sexuality, and pertinent dramas about teenage value systems have bit the dust along with the Twinkies. The result is a carefully homogenized and bland anthology that no longer reflects the adolescent literature it is supposed to represent.

You might imagine that publishers could avoid over-censoring by developing multiple textbooks to suit the needs of individual schools that are more or less progressive, located in different geographic areas, or have different ethnic representations. The problem with this solution is that books are so expensive to develop that the costs of multiple versions is prohibitive. The approximate cost of developing a new literature series, for example, is several million dollars.

Textbook Adoption Policies

Another cause of publisher over-censoring is state textbook adoption policies. When a 10th-grade biology textbook is adopted by a school system, the adoption means that high schools within the school system are permitted to order the book for use in grade 10 biology classes. If the textbook has not been adopted, the book cannot be ordered. There are several reasons for having book adoptions. One reason for adoptions is that publishers give significant discounts when textbooks are purchased in large quantities. It is less expensive to buy 10,000 copies from one publisher than to buy 1,000 copies from 10 different publishers. A second reason for system-wide adoptions is that it provides for quality control. A school system will usually have a textbook adoption committee composed of content area specialists, administrators, and in some cases community leaders or parents. Their task is to evaluate textbooks on the market and choose the one which is most suitable for their school system given the variables of price, text difficulty, methodological approach, and general philosophy. In principle, adoptions can take place at the level of the individual teacher, school, school system, or at the level of the state.

There are now many states that have state textbook adoption programs, and they include three of the most populous states in the country: California, Florida, and Texas. States have adoptions for the same reasons that school systems do: control of costs and curriculum quality. Procedures vary from state to state and subject area to subject area. Typically, a state will cycle through the various subject areas every 5–7 years. Publishers submit textbooks to the appropriate committee, which receives recommendations from individual school systems and special interest groups. The number of books adopted at one time in one subject area varies from 10% to 80% depending upon circumstances. When they buy new textbooks, public schools must then choose from among those on the state adopted list. Once a textbook has been adopted, the tractor trailers roll to book depositories throughout the adoption state. The book depositories are big warehouses that store state adopted books for shipment to nearby schools.

California submits its criteria to publishers years in advance of an adoption decision to let publishers know what the state expects in the way of format and content. If the state of California says it does not want a literature anthology to contain references to junk food, a publisher can tell its editors and authors to censor any and all references to cheeseburgers and fries or risk having its literature series fail the adoption. Failing to make an adoption in California, for instance, means that the publisher cannot sell the textbook or series to public schools in that state until the next cycle of textbook adoptions.

It is not hard to understand why publishers sweat blood over textbook adoptions. The adoption of a textbook in California or Texas may provide enough revenue to pay for the entire cost of developing the book. This is why publishers will cave in to the demands of state adoption committees, many of which are heavily influenced by special interest groups.

For the last 20 years textbook adoption committees, especially in California and Texas, have been strongly influenced by special interest groups such as Educational Research Analysts in Longview, Texas, and Citizens for Excellence in Education. CEE, a California-based, conservative religious organization with 70,000 members, has been successful in forcing five school districts in California to remove textbooks which CEE claims promote satanism and undermine parental authority (Harrington-Lueker, 1991).

Over the years, special interest groups have caused history textbooks, literature anthologies, science books, and even dictionaries to be modified, removed from classrooms, or stricken from the lists of state-approved books. Publishers have become so sensitive to the issues involved that they increasingly censor their own work to avoid the prospect of failing an adoption.

The problem is not the special interest groups themselves. Peaceful political activism is a constitutional right that is guaranteed to all individuals and organizations, including those concerned with the format and content of textbooks and parent empowerment in the education process. The real problem is that the states with the highest levels of coordinated censorship become the common denominator for textbooks across the country. In other words, students in states such as Pennsylvania and Iowa, which do not have state level adoptions, end up using the same textbooks that have been heavily censored to suit the religious, social, or political groups in other states. The truth is that a few people in California exercise considerable control over what students in Pennsylvania are permitted to read.

As you can see, textbooks are not neutral sources of information. They are, in fact, highly politicized. The textbooks you hand to students on the first day of class have been authored by people who have agreed that the publisher is the final authority for what gets written. The textbook has probably been massaged and censored to meet a market demand and to suit the various lobbies that might threaten sales. You cannot afford to assume that a textbook developed for public school consumption is truly representative of any body of knowledge, free of intentional bias, or even factually accurate. Just knowing this makes you a political agent in the instructional process, and the decisions you make about how to use textbooks constitute a political stance of great significance.

Tips for filling the void left by textbooks:

1. Supplement textbooks with trade literature and primary sources of information such as newspapers, professional magazines, unabridged novels, nonfiction single author books, or oral histories. (See Chapter 7 for additional information.)

2. Teach your students how—and then encourage them—to use the library. Do not allow the textbook to become the entire curriculum.

3. Encourage students to read their textbooks critically. The textbook is not always correct, and there must be room for competing points of view.

Readability

Politics aside, there are a number of other instructional issues related to the selection and appropriate use of textbooks. One of the most important of these involves determining the difficulty level of books.

For the last 60 years educators have had an interest in predicting the approximate difficulty of instructional materials. This is commonly referred to as *readability,* a measure of the extent to which a reader finds a given text comprehensible. Ideally, the level of text material can be matched to the appropriate reading level of students. In reality, though, the selection of a core text has been largely based on teacher intuition. Usually, content area teachers choose text materials based primarily on an analysis of the text content. While the content of a core text is certainly important and should reflect a teacher's instructional objectives, there are additional features of the text that merit careful consideration.

The evaluation of printed material can be a highly refined and systematic process given our current understanding of those features that make textbooks understandable and useful as learning tools. Indeed, some striking features of textbooks do increase or diminish the likelihood of student understanding. Therefore, in order to match the difficulty level of the text to the reading level of students, both quantitative and qualitative factors of text material must be evaluated.

Quantitative factors include such language variables as word and sentence length. These factors can be counted and measured with a formula to estimate the grade level designation of text difficulty. *Qualitative factors* are more difficult to determine and include such elements as prior knowledge of the reader, organization of the text, student interest, and a myriad of other important considerations.

Quantitative Factors in Readability Measurement

There are a number of different approaches designed to help the content area teacher estimate the difficulty level of text material. Each approach has inherent advantages and limitations. For example, a teacher can simply guess the grade level of a text. Unfortunately, this approach, while attractive in its speed and simplicity, has not proven to be very reliable.

A second, more reliable approach to an estimate of text difficulty involves the administration of one or two informal tests based on a portion of the text. These procedures will be described in detail in Chapter 5. In this section we will explore a third approach to predicting the difficulty of text material, the use of readability formulas.

Readability formulas are mathematically derived indices of text difficulty based on an analysis of language variables. Over 30 different readability formulas and graphs have been developed, including specialized formulas for appraising foreign language texts. While none of the formulas are absolute measures, they all share some common features that are useful in obtaining a rough estimate of a textbook's readability.

The two most common language variables accounted for in the majority of readability formulas are word and sentence length, and sentence length is thought to be the more reliable of the two. In addition to these two variables of word and sentence length, there are extensive compilations of commonly occurring words which can be used to rate the relative difficulty of a text. Words in the text that are not represented on the master list increase the difficulty rating of the text being considered. Formulas based on extensive word lists lend themselves to computer application. Indeed, they can be quite frustrating to compute using manual methods. We will explore a quick classroom method that retains the reliability of more elaborate computerized formulas—the Raygor Readability Estimate.

Raygor Readability Estimate

The *Raygor Readability Estimate* (Raygor, 1977) is both simple to use and reliable because it eliminates a common source of error found in many readability formulas. While counting sentences in a text sample presents little difficulty, formulas that combine this measure with a syllable count (e.g., the Fry Readability Graph) introduce a moderate potential for error. Two or more evaluators are likely to arrive at divergent answers for the number of syllables in the same text sample. The individual dialects of evaluators and the inherent difficulty in defining exactly what a syllable is, both contribute to unreliable syllable counts among evaluators. A good alternative to a syllable count is determination of the proportion of words with six or more letters in a 100-word text sample.

Following are the directions and the accompanying graph for the Raygor Readability Estimate. Application 4.1 will give you some initial, guided experience with this formula.

Directions for Completing the Raygor Readability Estimate.

1. Count out three 100-word passages at the beginning, middle, and end of a textbook selection. Count proper nouns but not numbers.

2. Count the number of sentences in each 100-word passage, estimating to the nearest tenth for partial sentences.

3. Count the number of words with six or more letters.

4. Average the sentence length and word length measures over the three samples and plot the average on the graph. The grade level nearest the spot marked is the best estimate of the difficulty of the selection.

APPLICATION 4.1

Directions: In order to gain practice using the Raygor Readability Estimate, use one of the following approaches on "Smoking and Smokeless Tobacco" on the CD-ROM. Keep in mind that this text is intended for a high school health class.

Approach A: Follow the directions for the Raygor using only a single 100-word passage you select from "Smoking and Smokeless Tobacco."

Approach B: Get together with two other class members. Each group member should select a different 100-word passage to evaluate from "Smoking and Smokeless Tobacco." Remember to average the three estimates before plotting them on the graph.

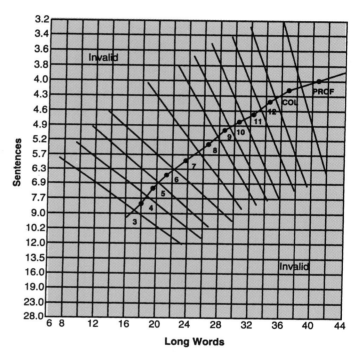

Keep in mind that passage difficulty will fluctuate within the same text. Therefore, the more 100-word samples you evaluate the more likely you are to arrive at a valid grade level designation. Using the Raygor Readability Estimate will provide readability estimates that are accurate within a range of plus or minus one year. In this way you will have a realistic idea of the difficulty level of the text and can begin to judge how effective it may be with your students.

Qualitative Factors in Textbook Evaluation

While readability formulas are useful as one component in the analysis of text material for adoption, they do have some inherent limitations that need to be mentioned. Readability formulas provide an estimate of the linguistic features of print that may influence text difficulty. These surface features typically include the average number of polysyllabic words and the average number of sentences taken from three sample passages in a text. Unfortunately, such measures are not applicable to poetry or the symbolic discourse of such disciplines as mathematics and chemistry. Thus, a number of additional factors need to be considered in a comprehensive evaluation of a text.

First of all, it must be remembered that, generally speaking, attractive, aesthetically pleasing things seem to work better for people, that is, their attractiveness produces more positive emotions, more creative responses, and a greater tolerance for minor difficulties (Norman, 2004). This same phenomenon of human nature applies also to your students and their reaction to the text materials with which they are given to read and learn.

More specifically, the quality of the writing style needs to be given careful consideration. For example, scrambling the word order of a selection would not materially alter the readability rating. Indeed, the scrambled passage would receive the same rating as a passage with acceptable syntax. Therefore, readability formulas are universally insensitive to writing style.

Some readability formulas imply that short sentences are easier to understand than longer sentences. This is certainly not the case, since grammatical structures can aid or disrupt important semantic relations. In the illustration below, example one would be easier to understand than example two, yet readability formulas that use sentence length as an index of difficulty would rate the second example as the less difficult structure.

1. Tim slept late because he was lazy.
2. Tim slept late. He was lazy.

Sentence one is easier to comprehend because the causal relation in the sentence is made explicit by the use of the word because. Conversely, example two disrupts the causal relation, requiring the reader to employ inference in order to establish the implied connection between the two events.

The criticism of short sentences may also be applied to short words. For instance, in the sentence, The dog the cat bit died, not only is the sentence short but also the words are short. Yet, the sentence will provide some difficulty for students because of the unusual grammatical structure. Therefore, the length of words is not necessarily an indicator of easier understanding.

Other text-centered factors deserve careful consideration in the text evaluation process. The abstract concepts and technical vocabulary an author uses are often complex, particularly in content areas such as science. The explanations of complex concepts, such as the process of photosynthesis, may require longer sentences in order to preserve important meaning relationships. Furthermore, since concept load and technical vocabulary are closely related in the content areas, reducing the use of technical terms would dilute important concepts essential to a discipline. One indication of conceptual difficulty in a text is the degree to which technical terms can be translated to more commonly occurring synonyms. For example, the word, compression, is easily substituted using the more familiar term, squeezed. In contrast, a highly specific technical term, like the word photosynthesis, will undoubtedly require a good deal of teacher explanation if students are to cope with this concept in their reading.

Although readability formulas have been used to rewrite text material, the practice of mechanically reducing sentence and word length in a selection is not recommended. While the rewritten version may be easier to read on a surface level than the original, important meaning relationships may be disrupted, making the rewritten version more difficult to comprehend. Readability formulas make no distinction between conceptually important information and trivial ideas. Nor do readability formulas differentiate between coherent writing that flows logically from one idea to the next and incoherent, disorganized prose.

For example, rewritten versions of text often disrupt explicit connections among ideas in the original sentences. At the sentence level, a modest amount of incoherence rarely presents much difficulty. However, if this incoherence extends across sentences, the text may present comprehension problems.

Consider This ...

Reggie wanted to sleep late, but John woke him up early for their trip to the north shore. Just as they were ready to leave, Reggie's girlfriend June arrived. She wanted to go shopping. THEY took the Toyota.

Now answer the following questions:

1. Who went shopping?
2. Who took the Toyota?

Pronouns are notorious for the potential comprehension problems they can cause when antecedents are unclear. However, readability formulas are not intended to measure these more subtle features of a text.

On the other hand, readability formulas do provide an estimate of vocabulary difficulty. Vocabulary difficulty undeniably influences students' comprehension, even when the writing is coherent.

Consider This ...

Nadine perused the grocery shelves, carefully scrutinizing each jar of peanut butter as if they were rare, prehistoric bones. She systematically ignored the organic products in favor of the more familiar brands. Her ARACHIBUTYROPHOBIA had been getting worse lately. She finally chose a jar of creamy style peanut butter, knowing it would never be opened once she got it home.

If the main idea of this passage is at all obscure it is because of the technical, polysyllabic word arachibutyrophobia. This word may look like it should be fear of spiders, but it actually means: fear of getting peanut butter stuck on the roof of the mouth! Notice that a single, precise term like arachibutyrophobia is extremely economical for a writer, in this case encompassing 12 short words.

Readers often rely on an author's organizational structure in their attempts to recall important information. Moreover, some organizational patterns such as comparison-contrast seem more conducive to long-term recall than less cohesive patterns such as simple listing. Readability formulas are not sophisticated enough to account for the influence of these higher level features of text on students' comprehension. For these reasons, readability formulas must be used in combination with other qualitative considerations in order to develop a comprehensive approach to the evaluation of instructional materials.

Readability formulas like the Raygor can only hint at potential problems in text. As you examine texts in your content area, consider how well the author weaves ideas together within and across sentence and paragraph boundaries. Also examine technical vocabulary that may present potential problems.

Contemporary texts supply an abundance of student aids designed to enhance comprehension. These include visual aids such as photographs, line drawings, graphs, tables, and diagrams. Other aids might include pre- and post-questions or questions interspersed within a chapter. Some authors also use *metadiscourse*, or text intrusions in which the author talks directly to the reader about the information in the text, to aid students in comprehending. In addition, a glossary can be valuable in helping students cope with difficult technical vocabulary. Some contemporary texts also include supplemental films and other non-print materials.

All of these devices can be valuable aids to students' understanding; however, none are substitutes for carefully guided instruction. Indeed, the very nature of content learning and content texts implies knowledge to be acquired in conjunction with a course of study. Thus, teacher-centered factors are likely to influence students' comprehension more than all the text-centered factors combined. Content texts are simply not designed to be read and comprehended in isolation, independent of a carefully guided course of instruction. The degree to which a teacher provides a bridge between what the students currently know about a topic and new conceptual information is undoubtedly the essential ingredient in the teaching and learning process. The amount of instructional guidance you provide before, during, and after reading text assignments will significantly affect students' comprehension of even the least challenging text. In the chapters that follow, a number of teaching strategies will be introduced to help you improve students' understanding of text concepts.

Finally, student-centered factors also play a prominent role in content area learning. Two important student-centered factors are the prospective readers' prior knowledge and interest in a course topic. Students generally have a preconceived notion about particular courses and books. Therefore, it is a good practice to have students representing various levels of subject interest and reading achievement directly involved in the text evaluation process. Their opinions and recommendations often provide an alternative perspective which you might find difficult to achieve since your prior knowledge and interest are extensive.

Textbook and Multimedia Evaluation Guidelines and Checklists

In general, students profit from text that adheres to classical principles of good writing. They can best comprehend authors who use frequent examples and graphic aids while avoiding unnecessary jargon. The following procedure for evaluating text material is designed to combine a quantitative measure of readability with additional qualitative factors, including student-centered information.

 A number of different guidelines and related checklists for evaluating text material have been advanced (e.g., Leonard & Penick, 1993; Singer, 2007). While all of these guidelines and checklists are intuitively derived and informal in nature, they comprise the best currently available approach to text evaluation. The 18-item checklist in Figure 4.1 has been adapted from these sources, with some additional factors that are essential to text comprehension.

This text evaluation checklist and decision guide are based on the typical layout of most nonfiction text material. Hence, you may need to adjust the criteria somewhat if you are evaluating fictional material presented in a literary anthology format. The checklist should not be interpreted as a device for categorically accepting or rejecting text material. Rather, the more ways the textbook meets the given criteria, the better and more useful the book will be for your students. Ad-

Figure 4.1

Text Evaluation Checklist

Directions: Enter the intended grade level of the text. Compute an estimate of text readability using the Raygor Readability Estimate. Complete the 18-item checklist to determine the acceptability of the text for your students.

Title of textbook: _____

Author(s): _____

Publisher: _____

Copyright date: _____

Cost: _____

Evaluated by: _____

A. Readability

____ 1. Intended grade level of text: _____. Readability estimate: _____. Is the computed reading level realistic for the students who will be using the text?

B. Format

____ 2. The book is recently copyrighted and the contents genuinely up-to-date.

____ 3. The text is suitable for achieving the stated course objectives.

____ 4. The text contains a table of contents, an index, and a glossary.

____ 5. The table of contents indicates a logical development of the subject matter.

____ 6. When the text refers to a graph, table, or diagram, that aid is situated in close proximity to the textual reference.

____ 7. Captions under graphs, tables, and diagrams are clearly written.

____ 8. Pictures are in color and are contemporary, not dated by dress unless author's intention is to portray a certain period.

____ 9. Various ethnic groups and male and female characters are depicted authentically in the text.

____ 10. The text suggests out-of-class readings and projects to stimulate additional student interest.

C. Organization

____ 11. The main idea(s) or purpose(s) for reading a chapter are stated at the beginning.

____ 12. Difficult new vocabulary words are highlighted, italicized, or underlined.

____ 13. Context clues and synonyms for difficult vocabulary words are used in the text.

____ 14. The writing is coherent in that ideas are clearly developed and related to each other, within and across sentence and paragraph boundaries.

____ 15. New concepts are introduced by relating them to previously learned concepts so that the volume of new information doesn't frustrate students.

____ 16. The text refers to practical, real-life situations and multicultural contexts in which students can relate and have an interest.

____ 17. The text includes references to, and quotations from, other sources and authorities to support its statements.

____ 18. When there are questions and activities at the end of a chapter, they elicit different levels of thinking, ranging from text-explicit to experience-based, problem-solving tasks.

Decision

____ **Appropriate**   ____ **Marginally Appropriate**   ____ **Unacceptable** ditionally, the criteria are broad enough to allow for the exclusion of some items that are simply not present in a particular text. For example, item number 8 would not be included in an evaluation of the text you are reading right now since pictures are not needed to understand the content. Simply code such items as not applicable (N/A) and continue on. Application 4.2 is designed to give you some practice in using the text evaluation checklist on the present text.

In Chapter 2 we introduced multimedia materials as an essential component of content literacy. Therefore, we have also included a checklist for multimedia software (Figure 4.2). Again, the determination of the appropriateness, pedagogical utility, and value of the software relative to other instructional alternatives is ultimately a matter of professional judgment. In the end one must decide if the benefits of the software are worth the price. Note that the number of positive versus negative features of the software by itself means little. If the software requires 128 megabytes of RAM and you only have 64, that one fact alone will probably make your decision.

APPLICATION 4.2

Directions: Using the Text Evaluation Checklist, rate the textbook materials from the chapter, *Matter and Energy in the Web of Life*, on the CD-ROM as to its acceptability for a high school level classroom.

OR

Find a multimedia software program that is designed primarily for education. Evaluate the software using the Multimedia Evaluation Checklist.

Introducing the Textbook to Students

It is unlikely that any single content area text will be the most appropriate for all students in a course. The wide range in students' prior knowledge and subject interests practically insures that your text will be frustrating for some students and too easy for others. Assuming that your particular content area text survives the evaluation checklist and your own informed observations, there is something you can do to help students perceive the text as a familiar learning aid rather than as a threatening obstacle.

You can conduct a preview of the text to acquaint students with the text they will be using. This simple procedure should be introduced early in the term. It will go a long way toward making students feel they can use the text effectively. Undoubtedly, many of us have had the experience of discovering by sheer chance, often halfway through the term, that our text contained a glossary of difficult vocabulary. The preview is designed to guide students to this and other text aids early in the term.

Conducting a Preview of the Text

The following activity should be conducted as a group task. Using Figure 4.3 as a guide, the teacher reads each item on the preview and indicates its location. The guide will help you conduct a preview of the text in your content area.

Figure 4.2

Multimedia Evaluation
Checklist

Title of software: _____

Content area: _____

Instructional objective(s): _____

Prerequisite skills: _____

Publisher: _____

Copyright date: _____

Cost: _____

Evaluated by: _____

A. Configuration Requirements

_____ PC

_____ Macintosh

_____ Other _____

_____ CD-ROM

_____ DVD

_____ Internet access

RAM requirement: _____

Hard drive requirements: _____

Printer requirements: _____

B. Software Friendliness

_____ 1. Readability of directions and other text are appropriate.

_____ 2. Directions are easy to follow.

_____ 3. Feedback to students is clear.

_____ 4. Video, audio, text, and graphics are well integrated.

_____ 5. Students can exit the program at any time.

_____ 6. Students can reenter the program at the point of previous exit.

_____ 7. The program is resistant to disruption from random key strokes.

_____ 8. The program maintains student interest.

C. Teacher Features

_____ 9. The software manual is readable, logical, and comprehensive.

_____ 10. The program includes an assessment component.

_____ 11. The program is applicable to a variety of skill/grade/age levels.

_____ 12. The user level advances automatically.

_____ 13. Graphics are clearly related to the purpose of the software.

_____ 14. The software comes with toll-free technical support.

D. Recommendation

_____ **Highly Appropriate—Purchase immediately**

_____ **Appropriate—Purchase if budget permits**

_____ **Inappropriate—Do not purchase**

Figure 4.3

Previewing Your Text

Name of subject: _____

Title of textbook: _____

Author(s): _____

Author(s) qualifications (e.g., job experience, university degrees): _____
_____

Copyright date: _____

Has the book been revised (brought up to date)?: _____
_____

1. *Prefaces, Forewords,* and *Introductions* contain essentially the same information. These lead-in comments give the author(s) a chance to talk about why the book was written and how it is organized. Often, a suggestion about how to read the book is provided.

   Read the *Preface (Foreword* or *Introduction).* In the space below, use your own words to explain what the *Preface* told you about your text.

   _____
   _____
   _____
   _____

2. The *Table of Contents* provides an early road map of the whole text. It gives a good indication of the learning aids which are provided in the text. Answer the following questions in your own words by referring to the *Table of Contents.*

   (1) Does the organization of topics in the book appear to be logical and easy to follow?

   _____
   _____

   (2) How many total pages are there in your text?

   _____

   (3) How complete do you think the treatment of the subject is in your book (i.e., very complete or only deals with a few aspects of the subject)?

   _____
   _____

   (4) Using the *Table of Contents,* see if your text contains each of the following learning aids. Answer *yes* if you find it, *no* if you don't.

   Glossary _____ Appendix _____ Bibliography _____ Index _____

3. The *Glossary* gives definitions of difficult technical terms used in the text. It is a valuable aid to understanding the vocabulary of a difficult subject. If your text has a *Glossary,* locate at least one difficult word supplied by your teacher and write the definition here.

   _____
   _____
   _____
   _____

Figure 4.3

Previewing Your Text *(continued)*

4. The *Appendix* provides additional information about a topic. An *Appendix* is located in the back of the book and contains information that supports and expands a chapter topic. If your text has an *Appendix* (or *Appendices*), write a list of some of the items you find there.

_____

_____

_____

_____

_____

_____

5. A *Bibliography* gives specific information about authors and books that were consulted during the writing of the text. Some of these books may be recommended as additional reading. The *Bibliography* is usually located at the end of the book (see the *Table of Contents* for its exact location), but it may follow each chapter. Locate the *Bibliography* in your text and write down three books you might want to read in addition to your text.

_____

_____

_____

_____

_____

_____

_____

_____

6. The *Index* provides the fastest means for locating topic information referred to in the text. Locate the *Index* in your book. Study the *Index* and list two or three kinds of information you see there.

_____

_____

_____

_____

7. Many other textual aids, in addition to the *Preface, Table of Contents, Glossary, Appendix, Bibliography,* and *Index,* are included in most texts. See if you can locate each of the following text aids (write *yes* if it's there; *no* if it's not) and indicate in writing how each of these aids might help you understand the subject.

    (1) Questions at the beginning of the chapters

    _____

    _____

    (2) Objectives at the beginning of the chapters

    _____

    _____

Figure 4.3
Previewing Your Text
(continued)

(3) Pictures

_____

_____

(4) Illustrations or diagrams

_____

_____

(5) Graphs

_____

_____

(6) Maps

_____

_____

(7) Words in italics, bold-faced words, large guide words

_____

(8) Pronunciation guide [e.g., paradigm (para dime)]

_____

(9) Footnotes

_____

(10) Headings

_____

(11) Marginal notes

_____

(12) Questions at the ends of chapters

_____

(13) Practice exercises

_____

(14) Other

_____

APPLICATION 4.3

Directions: Using this text as an example, conduct a preview. Did you discover anything of which you weren't aware previously?

In some cases, a teacher may feel it necessary to determine the extent of the students' knowledge about basic textbook elements before conducting a preview. The exercise in Figure 4.4 can also reinforce students' understanding of textbook learning aids. It can be used as a model to develop a similar activity in your own content area.

Figure 4.4

Directions: In column B you will find a brief description of the information contained in a particular textbook learning aid (listed in column A). See if you can match each textbook aid (column A) with its description (column B). Place the letter of the description on the line in front of the textbook aid to which it refers.

A.

____ 1. Index

____ 2. Table of Contents

____ 3. Bibliography

____ 4. Appendix

____ 5. Preface

____ 6. Copyright Date

____ 7. Glossary

B.

A. Author discusses why the book was written and how to read it.

B. The easiest place to locate topic information quickly.

C. Provides additional information about a topic.

D. A road map of how the text is organized.

E. Provides definitions of difficult technical terms.

F. Indicates when the book was published.

G. A listing of what books were consulted in writing the text.

If your text should prove to be unacceptable for some of the students in your content class, there are a number of alternative approaches you can employ. For example, you might consider adopting multiple texts at varying levels of difficulty. Or you can use newspapers, resource speakers, demonstrations, simulations, and discussion groups. Finally, increasing the amount of guidance you provide students before, during, and after reading assignments should go a long way toward making the core text more understandable. Future chapters advance a variety of methods for helping students cope with difficult text material. Such methods range from providing additional guidance in vocabulary development and comprehension to individualizing assignments for some students.

Reaction Guide

	Confirmed	Disconfirmed
1. Censorship is both bad and unnecessary.	_____	_____
2. Government regulations require that 10th-grade books be written on a 10th-grade reading level.	_____	_____
3. It is safe to assume that high school students know how to use a textbook index.	_____	_____
4. The content of subject area textbooks is politically influenced.	_____	_____
5. The biblical version of creation should be included in biology textbooks that cover evolution.	_____	_____

A
Why my choice is confirmed.

B
Why my choice is not confirmed.

1. _____   _____

_____   _____

2. _____   _____
   _____   _____

3. _____   _____
   _____   _____

4. _____   _____
   _____   _____

5. _____   _____
   _____   _____

Mini Projects

1. Apply the Raygor Readability Estimate to a commonly used text in your content area.

2. Complete the text evaluation checklist for the same text you used in mini-project number one. Is the text appropriate for its intended grade level?

3. Go to the *Content Area Literacy* web page. Follow the directions under Chapter 4 "Previewing multimedia software."

Website Activity

To locate and complete Chapter 4 activities, go to [*www.kendallhunt.com/contentarealiteracy/*].

5
Assessment

Anticipation Guide

	Agree	Disagree
1. Assessment should occur naturally as part of teaching and learning.	_____	_____
2. Most state reading assessments are valid measures of reading.	_____	_____
3. Standardized tests provide teachers enough information concerning students' abilities to begin instruction.	_____	_____
4. The best reading tests to administer to students are those which compare them with other students across the nation.	_____	_____
5. Diagnosis is necessary for effective instruction.	_____	_____

Rationale

Instruction is the means by which teachers bridge the gap between what students already know and what they need to know. For instruction to be as effective as possible, teachers must be familiar with a variety of assessment techniques because information about students' abilities and levels of achievement provides a foundation for selecting appropriate teaching strategies. Without assessment information, teachers are forced to make hazardous assumptions about what students do and do not know. In this chapter various types of assessment strategies will be described and recommended for use by content teachers.

Learning Objectives

→ Understand the need for assessment in the content classroom.
→ Describe the differences between formal and informal testing.
→ Utilize various types of assessment strategies.
→ Describe the political and instructional consequences of NCLB.

Graphic Organizer

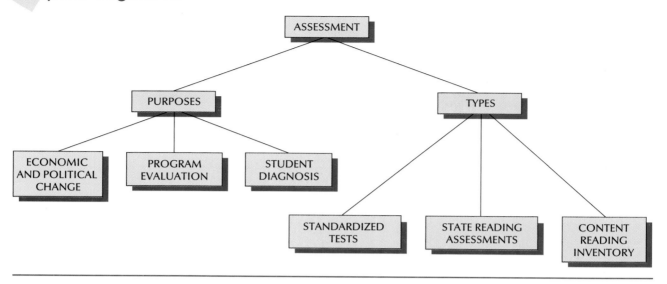

APPLICATION 5.1

Before you begin this chapter, your instructor may want to determine your familiarity with assessment terminology. Use the Knowledge Rating strategy (p. 90) and enter a 3, 2, or 1 rating for each technical term.

Knowledge Rating: Assessment Terminology

Directions: Rate your knowledge of each of the terms below.

Word	3 Can Define/Use It	2 Heard It	1 Don't Know
Norms			
Standard error of measurement			
Passage independence			
Raw score			
Percentile			
Stanine			
Norm-referenced test			
Criterion-referenced test			
Diagnostic test			
Multiple-choice test items			
Performance test items			
Mean			
Standardized test			
Reliability			
Validity			

Purposes for Assessment

In previous editions of this book, the purposes of assessment were limited to program evaluation and student diagnosis. To these we must now add economic and political purposes because high stakes testing is rapidly changing the meaning of education and the curricula in public schools across the country. This chapter will discuss the implications of high stakes reading assessments and how the results are being used to hold public schools accountable for meeting the mandates of *No Child Left Behind*.

The end product of assessment in the content classroom, or any classroom for that matter, is instructional decision-making. Assessment is at best pointless and at worst destructive if it does not lead to intelligent instructional decisions (Afflerbach, 2005). Content area teachers should keep this goal clearly in mind as they conduct assessment procedures.

In the past, various assessments of reading skills and levels of achievement were routinely administered for purposes of program evaluation and student diagnosis. If teachers and schools were free to conduct the business of education with the sole purpose of creating effective curricula for students, the presentations in this chapter could be limited to discussions of program evaluation and student diagnosis. Unfortunately, in recent years reading assessments have become increasingly tied to accountability in public education, and we must add economic/political to the list of purposes of assessment. It is essential that we discuss some of the politics of reading because it will almost certainly influence what and how you teach.

Economic and Political Change

The constant bashing of K–12 public education in the mass media and by politicians at every level of American government appears to be part of a carefully crafted political agenda for public education. A market-based reform movement aimed at corporate takeovers of public schools, the erosion or elimination of teacher certification, reductions in the cost of labor (teachers' salaries), and the shifting of state resources from secular schools to private, faith-based schools drives this agenda. The primary mechanism of this reform movement is the imposition of unattainable standards so that K–12 public education can be conveniently labeled a failure. In Pennsylvania, for example, the State Board of Education has defined proficiency in reading and mathematics achievement as "above average," which means that in order to meet the conditions of *No Child Left Behind*, 95% of all children are expected to perform at levels that are now considered above average. This is not a realistic goal. However, schools that fail to make adequate yearly progress (AYP) in meeting this goal, as defined entirely by test scores in reading and mathematics, will be taken over by the state or privatized. In 2003 the Pennsylvania Secretary of Education announced that 880 schools in the state were failing to make adequate progress in meeting the objectives of NCLB.

The intensity of this anti-public school reform movement varies from state to state, but the phenomenon is national in scope. We believe that the destructive nature of this campaign against public education will eventually become evident to the public and that state boards of education will establish realistic goals and a more honest agenda for public education. In the meantime, we in public education have no choice but to do everything in our power to meet the current AYP goals established by the various states.

Program Evaluation

Program evaluation is usually conducted for accountability purposes and formal tests are usually the devices used. Formal testing instruments, i.e., standardized reading tests, are administered at regular yearly intervals, usually in the fall or spring of the school year. Their function is to monitor student progress in reading. With the help of this assessment, school administrators are able to compare the reading levels of their students with those of other students across the nation at the same grade levels. Although such comparisons may help a particular school district justify its need for federal support for its instructional programs, they are virtually useless for instructional decision-making by teachers with regard to the individual needs of students.

Formal testing may also be used to identify weaknesses in the instructional program. If students in school district A as a whole score low relative to the national average on a particular type of test such as vocabulary or comprehension, that district may decide to examine the emphasis placed on that portion of the reading program. Finally, formal testing may serve as a screening device for those students not performing up to reading program expectations. This should indicate to the school district the need for more intensive diagnostic testing to pinpoint areas of skill weakness in individual students. Unfortunately, the results of these tests may be inappropriately used to refer students to special programs without the benefit of further testing.

Student Diagnosis

The third major purpose for reading assessment is student diagnosis. Student diagnosis can provide teachers with information necessary to make instructional decisions. Informal assessment tools are usually utilized to gather such information (Rakes & Smith, 2007). Specifically, informal tests can be used to diagnose possible reading and learning problems of students. Additionally, such tests can be used to determine the reading levels of students. Knowledge of students' reading and learning problems and reading levels provides a starting point for good teaching. This knowledge eliminates the need to presuppose any learning on the part of the students and provides the essential foundation for instructional decision-making.

One of the more recent educational developments is the use of *standards* to realize these overall purposes for assessment. In Chapter 1 we introduced the notion of standards as a means of delineating what students should know and should be able to do as a result of what they learn in school, with their aim being to make sure all students develop the skills necessary for success in school and in their future careers in the workplace. Standards-based assessment has come into being as individual states (e.g., Michigan, New York) have identified standards at various grade levels (e.g., grades 4, 8, 10) that students must master in a variety of subject-matter areas such as reading, math, and science. Tests are adopted or developed to measure whether or not students have met these grade-level and subject-matter standards. In this way states purport to evaluate schools' instructional programs and, by extension, students' abilities. In some cases states have used this type of assessment to differentiate between adequately and inadequately achieving schools and whether students receive a diploma or only a certificate of completion upon graduation. Though there are problems with the implementation of standards-based assessment [e.g., skepticism that they deal adequately with students of diverse backgrounds (Au, 2000)], standards are a reality in most states, and content area teachers will be expected to teach to the standards prescribed in their subject area.

STOP! View the CD-ROM video clip on the consequences of high-stakes standardized testing.

Descriptive Terminology of Assessment

Before launching into a discussion of the advantages and disadvantages of particular types of tests, we need to introduce several statistical concepts. These concepts are very challenging, and you may need assistance from your instructor.

Formal Tests

Formal tests are often referred to as standardized tests. A *standardized test* is one that is designed to be administered under the same conditions with each administration. For instance, all test-takers should receive identical directions; and if the test is timed, all the test-takers should have exactly the same amount of time to complete the test. Most standardized tests are copyrighted and commercially published. Most standardized tests are also *norm-referenced*, which means that one can only interpret the meaning of a test score by comparing that score with the scores of others who have taken the same test. The scores of those others are called *norms*, and they represent the standard against which the performances of others may be compared.

For example, imagine that the norms established for sixth- and seventh-grade students, respectively, are 40 and 50 items correct on a particular standardized, norm-referenced reading achievement test. Tyrannosaurus Middle School administers this test to its seventh-grade students, and the result is an average of 40 items correct. One could conclude that the students in Tyrannosaurus Middle School achieved on a par with sixth-grade students in the norm group but that their performance was below the average for seventh graders.

To examine the notion of standardized scores more closely, look at Figure 5.1. This is the normal curve, and all standardized scores are based on it. The *normal curve* is a bell-shaped distribution with scores distributed symmetrically around an average score called the *mean*. The number of scores above and below the mean is identical, and the number of individuals who earn the same score decreases with distance from the mean, which makes sense because most people are about average in any kind of assessment. The greatest number of scores (about

Figure 5.1
Normal Curve

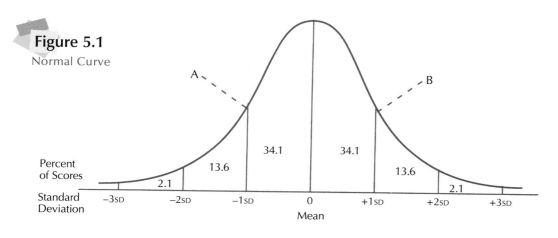

68%) occurs within one standard deviation of the mean—between points A and B in Figure 5.1. A *standard deviation* (SD) is a statistic that tells how much variation there is in a group of scores. For instance, if the scores are close together, the SD will be small. If the scores are widely scattered from low to high, the SD will be large. While it is possible, most teachers do not create standardized, norm-referenced tests because the procedures involved are complex and expensive.

Think of the bell-shaped curve as a narrow, three dimensional glass container into which you could throw marbles. If you filled the container with marbles, most of them would be stacked up in the middle and only a few would be in the tails (sides). The numbers inside the curve above show the percentages of marbles that could fit into the area defined by the lines on either side of the number. Only 2.1% would fit in the area between +2 and +3 SD. A bit more than 68% of the marbles (test scores) would be stacked up in the area between –1 and +1 SD.

The most commonly used scores in standardized testing are the raw score, the stanine, and the percentile rank. A *raw score* is simply the total number of correct items on a test. A *stanine* is the score converted to a standard 9-point scale with a mean of 5 and a standard deviation of 2. A stanine score of 5 is average. Stanine 1 would be a very low score, and a stanine 9 score would be very high. Finally, the *percentile rank* represents the percent of scores equal to and lower than a certain score. It is the position of a score within the entire group of scores. A percentile rank of 60 means the individual has scored as well as or better than 60% of the people who took the test. The percentile rank does not represent the percentage of correct answers.

Informal Tests

Informal assessment tools differ from standardized tests. *Informal tests*, or *criterion-referenced tests*, do not employ the use of norms as standards for comparison. Rather they employ a relative standard, or *criterion*, which implies adequate achievement for a given task or assignment. The score itself has meaning, even without reference to the performances of others. For instance, if the criterion has been set at 60% correct, a student must meet that figure to progress to another level of instruction; otherwise the student might need to work through the unit again and may require some special help to do so. Finally, informal tests are often teacher-made, though some are published. Thus, they can be designed to obtain information specifically related to an individual school's reading program. A second distinction used in describing tests involves survey and diagnostic tests.

Survey Tests

A survey test does what its name implies; it surveys global areas of achievement such as vocabulary and comprehension. *Survey tests* are usually standardized tests and therefore are useful for purposes of group comparisons but not for individual instructional guidelines. No specifics with regard to the global areas of the survey are provided. That is, we are unable to determine what the specific areas of weaknesses in vocabulary and comprehension may be. That is what a diagnostic test endeavors to measure.

Diagnostic Tests

Scores from a *diagnostic test* can indicate strengths and weaknesses in specific skill areas. For example, diagnostic tests provide scores for recognizing main ideas, details, inferences, etc.—the specifics of comprehension. Therefore, it might readily be seen that a standardized, survey-type instrument can be used as a screening device to tell a teacher, for instance, in which global areas a student might be experiencing difficulty. The teacher can then employ diagnostic tests to ascertain which specific areas are causing the difficulty.

Group and Individual Tests

Two other distinctions can be made in discussing testing instruments, neither of which requires a lengthy explanation. There are *group* and *individual* tests. As the names imply, tests may be group-administered or individually administered.

Silent and Oral Tests

The other distinction is between silent and oral tests. Again, as the names imply, tests may be silently or orally administered or employ some combination of the two. Usually, standardized tests utilize a format which requires a group, silent administration. At the other end of the continuum are informal tests which are diagnostic in scope and are administered in an individual, oral format.

Cautions Concerning Standardized Testing

Standardized tests offer some advantages in a total reading assessment program. Because they are administered in a group setting, they do not take the great amount of time that individual testing requires. Since formal tests are administered silently instead of orally, confusion is also kept to a minimum. Additionally, the scores achieved by students allow school districts to compare the performance levels of their students with other students across the nation.

The ease of administration of standardized tests and their use of norms also present some disadvantages. It is essential that content teachers be cognizant of these disadvantages. It is all too easy to obtain students' standardized test scores from their permanent files and make decisions about their abilities based on those scores.

1. What exactly does a score such as 7.0 on reading mean?
2. What exactly are standardized tests measuring?
3. How accurate a picture do I obtain about the reading ability of students from examining their test scores?

The following discussion of cautions concerning standardized tests will answer those questions and others you have in mind.

1. *Inappropriate Norms.* Even though great care is taken by test makers in standardizing a test, the norms established for comparison may be inappropriate for a particular class. The norms may be based on students with whom your students should not be compared.
2. *Extraneous Factors.* It must be emphasized that the scores achieved by a student on a formal test are only a measure of that student's performance at that particular point in time. They may not necessarily be indicative of a student's true ability. An individual's performance may vary radically from day to day depending on extraneous factors which can complicate matters. Factors as

simple as the amount of sleep students had the night before, to factors as complex as the emotional stability of their homes may interfere with students' daily performance in school as well as their performance in testing situations.

3. *Timed Testing.* Most standardized tests employ a time limitation in their administration procedures. Thus, a premium is placed on speed in completing the test. We are all probably reminded of personal experiences with friends or students who may be categorized as slow, but accurate; i.e., students who lack speed in completing tasks but thoroughly weigh alternatives before responding accurately. The slow but thorough reader may fail to complete the comprehension section of a test and thus get a low score when compared to the established norm. In reality, the student's comprehension could be excellent.

4. *Prior Knowledge.* Since comprehension occurs when students are able to associate the unknown with the known, prior knowledge may be a factor in test performance. In fact, there is a question as to whether standardized instruments actually measure reading comprehension or prior knowledge. Test items which may be answered from prior knowledge without the aid of a reading selection are said to be *passage independent.* Items which require students to read a selection in order to answer them correctly are termed *passage dependent.* It may be virtually impossible to eliminate the effect of prior knowledge on test performance. However, depending on the degree to which prior knowledge is a factor in particular test questions, the resulting scores can yield an unfair comparison between individuals.

5. *Comprehension Skills.* Standardized tests of reading comprehension, in many cases, emphasize factual recall of relatively insignificant facts. Is this the type of comprehension utilized in most reading situations? Such tests are at great variance in their demands versus the demands of reading in most school tasks and in everyday life. Certainly factual recall is important, but it is only one dimension of comprehension.

6. *Interest.* Everyone is aware of the effect of interest in reading. In fact, reading comprehension is better when the topic of a passage interests the reader. On the other hand, lack of interest may militate against the completion of a reading task. If the passages to be read on a standardized test are of little or no interest to students, it is bound to affect their ability to answer comprehension questions based on the passage.

7. *Guessing.* Most standardized tests employ a multiple choice format for their questions. They are designed in this manner to facilitate scoring by machines and for convenience. With such a limited format, guessing can unduly raise test scores. If four choices are offered, chances are one in four that a correct guess can be made. In any given test situation, two people with identical reading skills could get different test scores simply because one person happened to guess better that day. In fact, on most standardized tests, it is possible to receive grade-level equivalents, e.g., fourth-grade level, by guessing, that is, by pure chance.

8. *Test Floors and Ceilings.* When formal tests are standardized through averaging scores of students at a particular grade level, limits are placed on the range of performance at that grade level. Students are not supposed to score below a certain grade-level norm or, for that matter, above a certain level in their performance. In effect, the use of *test floors* and *ceilings* may affect the validity of test scores. Specifically, the ceiling of the test may underestimate a more competent student's performance, while the floor may overestimate a less competent student's ability. In effect, the ceiling may penalize better readers

because tests cannot truly measure their ability, while the floor may place a poorer reader at a level where success cannot be achieved. Standardization is designed to predict average performance, not performance at the extremes.

9. *Standard Error of Measurement.* This term indicates the variation in test scores that one might expect if that test were administered repeatedly to an individual student. By adding or subtracting this built-in error to a student's obtained test score, one obtains a range of scores within which the student might actually score. For example, if the standard error of measurement is five months and a student's resulting score is 7.0, the range of scores within which the student might actually have scored is 6.5 to 7.5. Awareness of this factor of built-in error is essential when examining scores on standardized tests.

10. *Fallacy of Grade-Level Reporting.* So what does a score of 7.0 mean? First of all, it is an estimation of performance. Second, it really says little with regard to students' performance; yet it is commonplace to use such scores when discussing reading ability of students. Just because two students both score 7.0 does not mean they are equivalent in reading ability. There are countless ways in which individuals may perform to attain a score of 7.0, yet each performance may be unique. Grade-level scores obscure differential performances of individuals with like scores in the same grade, or in different grades. Further analysis of each student's performance is necessary.

Content teachers must keep these cautions in mind when examining standardized test scores or when provided information concerning them by other school personnel. Such scores provide the basis for comparing group performances and for program evaluation. Many of the factors which cause standardized tests to provide inaccurate scores for individuals (e.g., guessing and personal interests) balance out in group situations, thus making results far more accurate for groups than for individuals. However, they do not provide the kind of information necessary for making instructional decisions (Afflerbach, 2004).

National Overview of State Reading Assessments

NCLB mandates yearly state assessments of reading in grades 3–8. Many states also require reading or language arts tests for high school students. In 2003 we systematically reviewed middle and secondary reading test items for each of the 48 states that published test descriptions and/or had test items released for public review. A state-by-state summary of the results is available in Figure 5.6 located at the end of the chapter. In general, the tests are remarkably similar in form and content. As a group, state reading/language arts assessments for grades 4–12 can be described as timed assessments in which students read both fiction and non-fiction passages and then answer multiple-choice questions. Most of the states also have performance test items, which require the students to respond in writing to the content of one or more passages. Most of the test items focus on passage comprehension or recall of information and include vocabulary questions based on words found in the passages. A majority of the state reading assessments have visual literacy test items requiring interpretation of information from maps, charts, tables, and pictures. About a third of the assessments have test items devoted to locating information or using reference materials. Table 5.1 is a summary showing the number and percentage of the 48 states with various test characteristics. For example, 36 (75%) of the states have some vocabulary test items on their state reading assessments.

Table 5.1

TEST CHARACTERISTIC	NUMBER AND PERCENTAGE OF STATES	
Multiple Choice Items	48	(100%)
Fiction Passages	45	(94%)
Nonfiction Passages	45	(94%)
Passage Independent Items	39	(81%)
Performance Items	39	(81%)
Vocabulary Test Items	36	(75%)
Visual Literacy Questions	30	(62%)
Location of Information Items	18	(38%)
Separate Vocabulary Section	7	(15%)
Matching or True False Items	0	(0%)

Most of the tests have been developed for individual states so that they are coordinated with each state's standards for reading. West Virginia is an exception because it uses the Stanford Achievement Test, a generic standardized reading achievement test. The state assessments of reading are different from most nationally recognized, standardized tests in ways that raise interesting questions about the validity of the state assessments and at the same time make them vulnerable to test preparation techniques.

Test Validity

An evaluation of test validity answers the question: "Does the test measure what it claims to measure?" In the case of reading tests, the assessments should measure reading ability and, to the extent possible, nothing else. There are, of course, no pure reading tests that can assess reading comprehension without also indirectly measuring prior knowledge and general intelligence. However, for the last 30 years, the authors of standardized reading tests have been scrupulous in their attempts to render standardized reading tests as pure as possible; but most of the current state assessments of reading include test items that make it unclear as to just exactly what is being measured by the "reading" tests. These items fall into two categories: performance items and passage independent items.

PERFORMANCE ITEMS. *Performance items* are short essays that ask students to write, for example, a brief summary, an evaluation of the author's purpose, or a prediction of events that goes beyond the passage itself. Usually, the state has a rubric for scoring performance items. There is nothing at all wrong with assessing writing skills and encouraging writing across the curriculum. However, when an assessment that claims to test reading achievement includes performance items and doesn't provide separate scores for reading and writing, these two aspects of literacy are confounded, reducing the validity of the assessment. It is possible to be a good reader and not a good writer.

PASSAGE DEPENDENCE. As previously stated, a test item is passage independent if you can answer it without even reading the passage. If you have to read the passage in order to acquire the information to answer the question correctly, the test item is passage dependent. Reading tests become invalid when test items are passage independent because the questions can be answered based on prior knowledge and logic rather than on reading ability. To the extent that state assessments of reading contain passage independent items, they are measures of general knowledge or achievement instead of reading. Assume, for example, that the question below follows a passage on one of the state reading assessments:

Which of the following countries was a U.S. ally in World War II?

A. England

B. Japan

C. Italy

D. Germany

In this hypothetical case, you would certainly be able to answer the question without having to read the passage. The question would, therefore, be passage independent for you and irrelevant or misleading in any assessment of your reading ability. Instead, the item would assess knowledge of American history. Obviously, a question can be passage independent for one person and passage dependent for another. When a reading test contains too many questions that are passage independent, the test is measuring something besides reading ability.

State reading assessments are riddled with passage independent questions. Some questions are answerable based on general knowledge. Others are designed to test state standards but have formats that make the answer passage independent. For example, one of the standards common to most states, distinguishing fact from opinion, is assessed in the following test item, but the question can be answered without reading the passage. Word clues such as *might* in option C occur frequently in state reading assessments, which means that the answer is found in the question itself rather than the passage.

Which of the following statements expresses an opinion by the author?

A. The Civil War ended in 1865.

B. John Brown died leading a slave revolt.

C. The South might have won the war if Lee had prevailed at Gettysburg.

D. The North had more trains and factories than the South.

Questions about vocabulary are another common form of passage independence in almost all state reading assessments (Figure 5.6). Multiple-choice items regularly include general vocabulary and technical terms taken from a passage. Typically, the words in the multiple-choice questions are not introduced in the passage as new vocabulary but are instead merely words that occur in the passage. The example below is an eighth-grade level item typical of a state assessment:

By using context clues, the reader can determine that the word *cower*, as in "cower behind me," means:

E. jump repeatedly

F. hide fearfully

G. crawl slowly

H. rise quickly

Given the restrictions of time, it is unlikely that a student who did not already know the meaning of *cower* would be able to return to the passage, find the word, and then use context clues to decipher its meaning. This test item is, therefore, passage independent.

Based on our survey of released test items, state reading assessments for middle and secondary students are in reality assessments of reading ability, writing ability, and prior knowledge. This means that many of the tests are of questionable validity as reading assessments and are in many ways more like general achievement tests. However, it also means that a subject-oriented approach to reading to learn makes sense because art, English, foreign language, health, mathematics, music, science, and social studies teachers are the people who build the vocabulary and prior knowledge essential to improved scores on state reading assessments. The nature of the tests also makes it realistic for subject area teachers to prepare students systematically for state assessments without sacrificing curriculum objectives. Test preparation will be discussed in Chapter 12.

NCLB and the High Stakes Assessment of Public Schools

According to NCLB, by the end of the 2013–2014 school year, 95% of *all* children in the United States of America will be proficient in reading and mathematics, and this includes all children from racial and ethnic minorities, children with physical and mental disabilities, children who are economically disadvantaged, and children who have limited English proficiency. It is the responsibility of the schools to ensure that this happens and to make annual yearly progress (AYP) toward this goal. Schools that fail to meet this achievement goal will be taken over by the state or privatized, an action already familiar to many of the schools in Philadelphia, Pennsylvania.

NCLB requires all states to test students in grades 3–8 in reading and mathematics every year using tests such as those described in the previous section of this chapter. The states define proficiency in reading as a cutoff score at each grade level. The percentage of students in each school who must reach proficiency in order for the school to demonstrate AYP will increase each year until by 2014 all children will have become proficient. Tests are administered under secure testing conditions, and the percentage of students reaching proficiency is calculated. If the percentages are too low, the school receives a warning or improvement notice or is scheduled for corrective action. In 2003 there were 1,346 Pennsylvania schools that demonstrated AYP for the previous year and 1,418 (51%) that did not.

The report card in Figure 5.2, adapted from a newspaper article, shows the schools in northwest Pennsylvania that failed to meet AYP for 2002–2003. Checkmarks in the columns adjacent to the name of the school indicate the reasons for the failure. *Please note that if the school fails in any category for any reason, the school is placed on the warning, improvement, or corrective action list.*

→ If fewer than 95% of the students show up for the test, the school failed.

→ If school attendance dropped for the year, even if attendance was very high and the decline was a fraction of 1%, the school failed.

→ If the graduation rate for a high school dropped, even if the graduation rate was very high and the decline was a fraction of 1%, the school failed.

→ If fewer than 45% of the students in the school reached proficiency on the state's standardized reading test, the school failed. Remember that proficiency is defined as above the average performance of students in 2001.

Figure 5.2
Report Card for Northwest Pennsylvania Schools

Local Schools Failing

Schools that fell short of state standards

The state Department of Education released a report detailing results in meeting state testing standards.

Schools that received an improvement notice
Must establish a school improvement team and offer school choice to parents.

	Low PSSA scores					
	Reading	Math	Groups*	Less than 95% participation rate	Falling attendance rates	Falling graduation rates
Jefferson Area School District						
Jefferson Area M.S./H.S.			✓	✓	✓	
Lincoln School District						
Barton Elementary	✓	✓	✓		✓	
Connell Elementary					✓	n/a
Smith Elementary				✓		n/a
Welling Elementary				✓		n/a
Hummer M.S.	✓	✓	✓			n/a
Walker H.S.		✓	✓		✓	n/a
Madison M.S.	✓	✓	✓		✓	
Wilson M.S.	✓	✓	✓			n/a
Washington Community CS						
Washington Community CS	✓		✓			n/a
Jackson S.D.						
Jackson M.S.	✓	✓	✓		✓	n/a
			✓			n/a

Schools that received a warning
No immediate consequences, but they must show improvements to avoid sanctions.

Lincoln County

	Reading	Math	Groups*	Less than 95% participation rate	Falling attendance rates	Falling graduation rates
Jefferson Area S.D.						
Wilson Elementary	✓	✓	✓			n/a
Lincoln S.D.						
Howard H.S.	✓	✓	✓	✓	✓	✓
Peabody H.S.		✓	✓		✓	
Irving Elementary			✓			n/a
West Elementary					✓	n/a
South Elementary	✓		✓			n/a
Smith Elementary			✓			n/a
Jones Elementary	✓		✓		✓	n/a
James S.D.						
James H.S.					✓	✓
Right Avenue M.S.			✓			n/a
Coldstream S.D.						
Coldstream J.S.H.S.					✓	✓
Miller S.D.						
Martin Elementary					✓	n/a
English Township S.D.						
Highland Elementary					✓	
Topper Elementary					✓	n/a
Hillcrest H.S.			✓		✓	n/a
Rosemont High School	✓				✓	
West Lake M.S.					✓	n/a
South East S.D.						
South East Intermediate Elementary					✓	
South East M.S.					✓	✓

Medwick County

	Reading	Math	Groups*	Less than 95% participation rate	Falling attendance rates	Falling graduation rates
Cedar S.D.						
Cedar Lake H.S.			✓		✓	✓
Cedar Valley H.S.			✓		✓	
Frost S.D.						
King Area J.S.H.S.					✓	✓
First District Elementary					✓	n/a
Fillmore Area H.S.			✓		✓	
Fillmore Area M.S.			✓		✓	n/a
Harrison S.D.						
Maplewood Elementary			✓			n/a

*Groups of 40 or more students who are separated from the rest of the student body. These students are either economically disadvantaged, members of racial or ethnic minority groups and have disabilities or limited English fluency.

- → If fewer than 35% of the students in the school reached proficiency in the state's standardized math test, the school failed.
- → If the school had 40 or more students who were in "groups"—special education, ethnic minorities, or limited English proficiency, and any one of those groups failed to meet AYP for any reason, the school failed.

With these criteria for AYP—which become more rigorous with every passing year—it is hard to imagine a public school in Pennsylvania that will not fall to corrective action eventually. Public schools in other states are finding themselves in similar circumstances. It is little wonder that public school personnel are becoming frantic about NCLB and its related assessment programs. There are many potentially negative consequences of NCLB's high stakes testing. Here are just a few of them:

- → Achievement and the value of education are being defined by performances on a few standardized tests in selected areas of the curriculum.
- → Because proficiency in reading and mathematics is being defined by state assessments, schools are teaching to the test. Scores in reading and math may go up, but students may not read, calculate, or think any better than they did in the past.
- → The consequences of failing the tests are so traumatic that schools have no choice but to convert instructional time to test preparation.
- → Schools are curtailing art, music, physical education, and other content areas to increase instruction and test preparation in reading and math.

On the surface, the goals of NCLB are noble indeed. Every child will succeed. Every child will be proficient in reading and math regardless of economic class, race, linguistic ability, or mental disability. These lofty notions are based on the assumption that high stakes testing policies will lead to increased student motivation and academic achievement. Unfortunately, research demonstrates that high stakes tests actually lead to decreases in student motivation and increases in school dropout rates without any positive effect on achievement (Amrein & Berliner, 2003). Are the goals of NCLB realistic? We do not believe so, and our great fear is that in its mad dash to leave no child behind, the federal government will leave all of our children with a public school system in shambles.

Content Reading Inventory

The *content reading inventory* is designed to obtain information about the ability of students to learn successfully with specific text material. Since the content reading inventory is an informal-group-silent-diagnostic assessment, its numerous advantages far outweigh the disadvantage of the time it takes to prepare the instrument:

- → The content reading inventory is quick and easy to administer in a group setting.
- → The content reading inventory is textbook-based. This makes the diagnostic information relevant since it is taken directly from the major source of instruction in the subject matter area.

→ Since it is teacher-made and textbook-based, it provides for ease in scoring. Criteria for judging test answers are objective, eliminating subjectivity as a deterrent in effective scoring.

→ This instrument later may become the basis for teaching. Once the teacher has obtained essential diagnostic information, the test may become an instructional instrument with which the teacher can begin to acquaint students with the author's style and the organization of the textbook.

The content reading inventory consists of three major sections. The first section of the inventory concerns knowledge of, and ability to utilize, the various aids within the textbook or supplemental to it. Specifically, the test covers book parts common to most textbooks such as the table of contents, index, and pictorial aids. The students' ability to use resource aids which supplement the textbook, such as the encyclopedia, are also examined. The premise behind this section of the content reading inventory is that the ability to effectively utilize the internal and external aids of the text is critical to learning with it.

In the last two sections of this inventory, students are asked to read a short three- to four-page selection from the text. Section two then determines the ability to deal with the technical and specialized vocabulary encountered in the reading. Section three examines the ability to comprehend text explicit and implicit information as well as to grasp an author's text structure. A representative content reading inventory, therefore, should contain the following sections:

SECTION I: TEXTUAL READING/STUDY AIDS

A. Internal Aids
   1. Table of Contents
   2. Index
   3. Glossary
   4. Chapter Introduction/Summaries
   5. Pictorial Information
   6. Other Pertinent Aids

B. External Aids
   1. Electronic Databases
   2. Reader's Guide
   3. Encyclopedias
   4. Other Pertinent Aids

SECTION II: VOCABULARY KNOWLEDGE

A. Recall
B. Contextual Meanings

SECTION III: COMPREHENSION

A. Literal Information
B. Nonliteral Information
C. Text Structure

APPLICATION 5.2

Complete the following example of a content reading inventory. It is designed just as you, as the content teacher, would construct and present a content reading inventory to your students. Your task, just as that of your students would be, is to answer the questions. Section I is based on the total text; sections II and III are based upon Chapter 8.

Content Reading Inventory

Section I: Textual Reading/Study Aids

Directions: Using your textbook or your previous knowledge, answer each of the following questions.

A. Internal Aids

1. On what page does Chapter 4 begin? What is the title of the section of which it is a part?

    _____

2. On what page(s) would you find information regarding Critical Media Literacy?

    _____

3. Where would you look in the text to find the definition of "text explicit"?

    _____

4. Of what use is the section entitled Rationale at the beginning of Chapter 8?

    _____

    _____

5. Using the GWP checklist in Chapter 11, what recommendations would you make concerning the student's writing?

    _____

    _____

6. Where would you look to find out how this text is organized?

    _____

B. External Aids

7. What library guide would aid you in locating a book on attitudes and attitude development?

    _____

8. If you were to give an oral report in class about content area literacy and you knew that much of the information you needed would be in current periodicals, what guide would you use to help you find the information?

_____

9. Name one set of encyclopedias. How are the topics in it arranged?

_____

Directions: Read the sections in your text entitled Words and Vocabularies in Chapter 8. Based upon what you have read, answer the questions in sections II and III.

Section II. Vocabulary Knowledge

10. Define the concept of word as used in this text.

_____

11. Compare and contrast denotations and connotations. Provide an example.

_____

_____

12. Define the italicized word as it is used in this sentence: A vocabulary is a *corpus* of many thousands of words and their associated meanings.

_____

_____

13. What term refers to the process by which new information is incorporated into existing schemata?

_____

14. Define the italicized word as used in this sentence: Technical vocabulary words present labels for unfamiliar concepts that must be accommodated by modifying *extant* schemata.

_____

Section III: Comprehension

15. Why do adult language users have little difficulty agreeing whether or not a particular sequence of sounds or symbols is a word?

_____

16. Learning new words (concepts) requires more than a simple explanation by the teacher. Why?

_____

17. What are the largest vocabularies for literate adults?

_____

18. Describe the differences between the words (concepts) "Cold War" and "crass."

_____

_____

19. Describe the process involved with regard to the schemata of students when the word "secant" is presented them.

_____

20. Explain the role of the school with regard to the development of the expressive and receptive vocabularies of students.

_____

21. How is the section entitled Vocabularies organized?

_____

Now that you have completed the content inventory, turn to the end of this chapter (Figure 5.7) for the answers. Classify your performance according to the criteria specified previously for the content reading inventory. The majority of individuals taking this test will find this text adequate for instruction. A few of you may score above or below that level. As can be seen, the content reading inventory can provide the teacher with information concerning the difficulty level of the text as well as specific information concerning students' ability to effectively utilize the textbook. The checklist in Figure 5.3 is provided as a format for teachers to record the information gathered from the content reading inventory.

Figure 5.3
Content Reading Inventory Checklist

Classroom Summary

Subject _____   Title of Text _____

Grade and Section _____   Teacher _____

Student Name	Table of Contents	Index	Glossary	Chapter Introduction/Summary	Pictorial Information	Other Internal Aids	Electronic Databases	Reader's Guide	Encyclopedia	Other External Aids	Vocabulary-Recall	Vocabulary-Context	Literal	Nonliteral	Text Structure
1. John Bead	✓		✓	✓	✓		✓		✓		✓	✓			
2. Tom Rean	✓	✓		✓			✓		✓		✓	✓	✓		✓
3. Scott Bee		✓	✓	✓			✓	✓	✓		✓		✓		✓
4.															
5.															
6.															
7.															

If the results of the content reading inventory indicate student deficiencies in certain areas, teachers may want to use the inventory as an instructional tool. Since the questions asked on the inventory are probably similar to those teachers ask in the classroom, they can expect the students' responses to be similar to those they would make in class discussions. Therefore, the content reading inventory provides the framework for teachers to initiate a preview of the text, as described in Chapter 4. The premise behind this strategy is that the teacher will model the use of the various text parts and efficient use of the author's organizational structure. In this way all students can be effectively introduced to their textbook in a systematic manner. The preview offers students an introduction to proper utilization of the various reading/study aids authors incorporate into textbooks.

Students break into small, cooperative groups and are asked to reach consensus on the correct responses on the content reading inventory. Students who are struggling with the various aspects of the textbook will have the opportunity to experience how other students arrived at their conclusions. Again teachers should follow these small group discussions with a whole-group discussion, insuring an effective introduction to the textbook.

Cooperative groups may be utilized to provide additional practice in areas of need as indicated by an analysis of the summary information sheet with the results of the inventory. For instance, if the class as a whole seems to have difficulty processing text implicit information, the teacher can construct a series of questions emphasizing the use of this skill and assign them to the task groups. Through peer interaction and a whole-group discussion follow-up, the teacher can give students experience with some of the processes necessary to enhance learning with text.

Knowledge of the students' ability to successfully cope with their text material is essential, and the diagnostic use of the textbook enables content teachers to initiate instruction in their classrooms on an informed basis. No assumptions are made about what is already known, and instruction is based upon establishing the background necessary for effective comprehension of new material.

Since only a few items are assessed in each area, the content reading inventory is only a beginning—a point of departure—for assessing students' abilities. In essence, the results of this inventory allow teachers to begin the development of student *portfolios,* or systematic collections of students' work in the classroom (Gillespie, Ford, Gillespie, & Leavell, 1996). As teachers observe students interacting with text in their daily reading and writing assignments, they will acquire additional information that will corroborate or refute the initial findings and add to the portfolios.

Assessing Prior Knowledge

Throughout this book we have stressed the importance of prior knowledge in reading and learning with text. In essence, the more knowledge students bring to the printed page, the more likely they will successfully comprehend the text, particularly if they or the teacher activate the appropriate prior knowledge. Conversely, if students lack, or fail to select, the appropriate prior knowledge, their comprehension may suffer. Therefore, teachers may wish to assess students' knowledge about a topic, making decisions about the quality and quantity of prereading instruction they provide students. If teachers know that students possess a vast store of prior knowledge about a topic under study, it is less necessary to spend great amounts of time in prereading. On the other hand, if students know little about a topic, it benefits teachers to spend time activating and building background knowledge.

In later chapters we will suggest a number of prereading vocabulary and comprehension strategies as well as some prewriting strategies that teachers can use to initiate instruction in the content areas. Though instructional in scope, each of those strategies can provide teachers with relevant knowledge about what students know and do not know about a topic. However, we would like to suggest some techniques for assessing prior knowledge that are easy to implement and can provide teachers with the information necessary for effective instructional planning and teaching.

Knowledge Rating

Knowledge rating (Blachowicz, 1991) is a simple strategy for establishing what students already know about a topic by having them rate how well they know the vocabulary. In planning for the lesson teachers select the vocabulary words they think are needed to understand the concepts to be learned. In doing so teachers develop a sheet that lists that vocabulary and then ask students to rate themselves concerning how well they know the words. To use the example of the topic, Warts and Their Cures, the knowledge rating sheet might resemble the example in Figure 5.4.

Figure 5.4

Knowledge Rating: Warts and Their Cures

Directions: Decide how well you know each of the words below by checking your knowledge for each.

	3	2	1
Word	**Can Define/Use It**	**Heard It**	**Don't Know**
spunk water			
Pliny the Elder			
caustic painting			
electrocautery			
folk treatments			
polyoma virus			
autosuggestion			
nostrums			

Introduce this technique by telling students that in order to get them thinking about the text material they would start by assessing what they already know about the topic. After handing out the sheet, pronounce the words so decoding is not a problem for students. Then ask them to rate their knowledge of each word by checking the appropriate column. The first time this strategy is used teachers may need to model for students exactly what is expected. For instance, students might have some idea of folk treatments and rate it a 2; others may even rate it a 3. On the other hand, students probably would not know nostrums and would give it a 1. After students complete the sheet, teachers tally how many students knew each word. Students' prior knowledge can be ascertained collectively as well as individually. In this way teachers have some information about students' knowledge before making a judgment about the amount of prereading instruction to provide.

Prediction Guide

The *prediction guide* is a series of fact-based statements given to students before they encounter a text assignment. The students indicate whether each statement is true or false. For instance, a teacher about to cover the Cold War in American history might provide students with a series of prediction guide statements. By examining students' responses to each of the guide statements, the teacher can discover not only how much students know about the Cold War, but also what particular aspects about the topic are known or not known. In this way the teacher will gain valuable information for instructional planning. Figure 5.5 is an example

Figure 5.5

Prediction Guide: Bats

Directions: Before you read a text passage on bats, predict which of the statements that follow are true based on what you already know about them. Place a check (✓) on the line next to every true statement.

_____ 1. Bats are the second largest group of mammals.

_____ 2. Some bats are the size of a bumblebee.

_____ 3. Bats transmit disease.

_____ 4. Bats are about as intelligent as dogs.

Bats

Next to the 3,000-odd kinds of rodents, some 900 species of bats make up the second largest order of mammals in the animal kingdom, both in number of species and, by estimation, of individuals alive at any one time. Bats belong to the order Chiroptera, meaning winged hand, and make up nearly one-fourth of all mammalian species.

They range in size from Kitti's hognosed bat, which is the size of a bumblebee and weighs about as much as a penny, to the large fruit-eating bats called flying foxes because of their foxlike faces and their size—they are almost as big as a small fox cub, weighing two pounds and having a wingspan of up to six feet.

Most bats' gargoylelike noses, used for transmitting high-frequency bursts of sound, and their huge ears, used to pick up the echoes from the waves of sound, have contributed to the human perception of bats as eerie, even supernatural, creatures that are probably vicious, filthy, and likely to attack humans and transmit disease.

Recent studies, however, show that bats are gentle; keep themselves meticulously clean; rarely transmit rabies; have a measure of intelligence that scientists equate with that of dogs; can be easily trained; and, in rare cases with a knowledgeable owner, can even become pets.

prediction guide for the topic of bats and the text from which the statements are drawn (adapted from Webster, 1984).

Whether each statement is actually true and how many statements should be used in the guide are not at issue here. What matters is that the statements reflect information the teacher thinks is important for students to know after completing the assignment. In this way teachers will know in what areas to provide prereading instruction.

Before we leave this topic, we would like to caution teachers that prediction guides are characterized as a series of fact-based statements that aid you in assessing students' prior knowledge. Please remember that prediction guides are separate and distinct from anticipation guides, which have opened each chapter of this text thus far and are experience-based statements used to activate students' prior knowledge before they read. You may wish to read the section on anticipation guides in Chapter 10 if this distinction is unclear.

Reaction Guide

	Confirmed	Disconfirmed
1. Assessment should occur naturally as part of teaching and learning.	_____	_____
2. Most state reading assessments are valid measures of reading.	_____	_____
3. Standardized tests provide teachers enough information concerning students' abilities to begin instruction.	_____	_____

4. The best reading tests to administer to students are those which compare them with other students across the nation.   _____   _____

5. Diagnosis is necessary for effective instruction.   _____   _____

<table>
<tr><td align="center">A
Why my choice is confirmed.</td><td align="center">B
Why my choice is not confirmed.</td></tr>
</table>

1. _____   _____

   _____   _____

2. _____   _____

   _____   _____

3. _____   _____

   _____   _____

4. _____   _____

   _____   _____

5. _____   _____

   _____   _____

Mini Projects

1. Interview a school principal, superintendent, or school board member to find out what they think of NCLB.

2. Select one of the techniques for assessing prior knowledge and try it on a small group of students or your peers. Evaluate its effectiveness.

3. Examine a standardized reading test provided by your instructor. Evaluate each subtest of the instrument for the criteria listed below. Use the following classification system: 1 = Satisfactory; 2 = Unsatisfactory; 3 = Not Clear. Add any other evaluative criteria you deem necessary.

   A. Is the stated purpose of each subtest reflected in the test items?

   B. Are the directions clearly written?

   C. Are the test items always passage dependent?

   D. Does the test measure what it purports to measure?

   E. Does the test include performance items?

   F. Is adequate time allowed for the completion of each subtest?

4. Using a content text of your choice, design a content reading inventory. Utilize the procedures described earlier in the chapter. Administer the inventory, if possible, to three students to ascertain their ability to cope with the text. Evaluate the effectiveness of the content inventory as a device for gathering diagnostic information about students.

Website Activity

To locate and complete Chapter 5 activities, go to [www.kendallhunt.com/contentarealiteracy/].

Figure 5.6

Overview of State Reading Assessments

STATES	Are test questions sometimes passage independent?	Are there some fictional passages?	Are there some nonfiction passages?	Is there a separate vocabulary section?	Do questions that follow passages usually include a vocabulary item?	Are there visual literacy questions?	Are there questions related to research and/or location of information?	Multiple Choice	True/False	Performance (Written responses)
AL	Y	Y	Y	N	Y	Y	Y	Y	N	N
AK	Y	Y	Y	N	N	Y	N	Y	N	Y
AZ	Y	Y	Y	N	Y	Y	N	Y	N	N
AR										
CA	Y	Y	Y	Y	Y	Y	N	Y	N	Y
CO	Y	Y	Y	N	Y	N	N	Y	N	Y
CT	Y	Y	Y	N	Y	N	N	Y	N	Y
DE	Y	Y	Y	N	Y	Y	N	Y	N	Y
FL	Y	Y	Y	N	Y	N	N	Y	N	Y
GA	Y	Y	Y	N	Y	Y	Y	Y	N	N
HI		Y	Y					Y	N	Y
ID		Y	Y					Y	N	Y
IL	Y	Y	Y	N	Y	N	N	Y	N	Y
IN	Y	Y	Y	N	Y	Y	N	Y	N	Y
IA								Y		
KS	Y	Y	Y	N	Y	N	N	Y	N	Y
KY								Y	N	Y
LA	Y	Y	Y	N	Y	N	N	Y	N	Y
ME	Y	Y	Y	N	Y	Y	N	Y	N	Y
MD	Y	Y	Y	N	Y	Y	Y	Y	N	Y
MA	Y	Y	Y	N	Y	N	Y	Y	N	Y
MI	Y	Y	Y	N	N	Y	N	Y	N	Y
MN	Y	Y	Y	N	Y	N	N	Y	N	Y
MS	Y	Y	Y	Y	Y	Y		Y	N	Y
MO		Y	Y					Y		Y
MT	Y	Y	Y	Y	Y	Y	N	Y	N	Y
NE								Y		
NV	Y	Y	Y	N	Y	Y	N	Y	N	
NH	Y	Y	Y	N	Y	N	N	Y	N	Y
NJ	Y	Y	Y	N	Y	Y	N	Y	N	Y
NM		Y	Y			Y	Y	Y		Y
NY	Y	Y	Y	N	Y	Y	Y	Y	N	Y
NC	Y	Y	Y	Y	Y	Y	Y	Y	N	Y
ND	Y	Y	Y	N	Y	N	N	Y	N	Y
OH	Y	Y	Y	N	Y	N	Y	Y	N	Y
OK	Y	Y	Y	N	Y	Y	Y	Y	N	Y
OR	Y	Y	Y	N	Y	Y	Y	Y	N	Y
PA	Y	Y	Y	N	Y	Y	Y	Y	N	Y
RI	Y	Y	Y	N	Y	Y	Y	Y	N	Y
SC	Y	Y	Y	N	Y	Y	Y	Y	N	Y
SD	Y	Y	Y	Y	N	Y	Y	Y	N	N
TN		Y	Y	Y				Y		
TX	Y	Y	Y	N	Y	Y	N	Y	N	Y
UT	Y	Y	Y	N	Y	Y	Y	Y	N	Y
VT										
VA	Y	Y	Y	N	Y	Y	Y	Y	N	Y
WA		Y	Y			Y	Y	Y		Y
WV	N	Y	Y	Y	N	Y	Y	Y	N	N
WI	Y	Y	Y	N	Y	N	Y	Y	N	Y
WY	Y	Y	Y	N	Y	N	N	Y	N	Y

Blank = information unavailable

Y = item observed; N = item not observed in available test items

Figure 5.7

Answers for Content Reading Inventory

Section I: Textual Reading/Study Aids

A. Internal Aids

1. Page 51, Learning with Text and Technology. (Table of Contents)
2. Page 187–188. (Index)
3. The glossary.
4. It provides an overview of the chapter. (Chapter Introduction)
5. The student needs help with supporting details, sentence length, and spelling. (Pictorial Information)
6. The preface.

B. External Aids

7. Electronic databases.
8. The reader's guide.
9. Answer open; alphabetically. (Encyclopedias)

Section II: Vocabulary Knowledge

10. A word is a pattern of auditory or visual symbols which represent schemata. (Recall)
11. A denotation of a word is its broad meaning, while a connotation of a word is defined by its subtle shades of meaning and its limiting grammatical and semantic conditions. Examples open. (Recall)
12. A corpus is a body, or collection, of recorded utterances used as a basis for the descriptive analysis of a language. (Context)
13. Assimilation is the process by which new information is incorporated into existing schemata. (Recall)
14. Extant means existing. (Context)

Section III: Comprehension

15. Adult language users have a common sensitivity to the concept of a word because they know speakers do not interrupt words with fillers such as "um" or "uh" during speech. (Literal)
16. Learning new words requires more than a simple explanation because they are not just isolated bits of information. Rather, words are defined by the ways and the extent to which they are related to all other words. (Literal)
17. The largest vocabularies for literate adults are the listening and reading vocabularies because the schemata required for recognizing word meanings in context are more fully developed. (Literal)
18. Crass is a general vocabulary term which is not specifically associated with a teaching area. Cold War is a technical vocabulary term uniquely related to social studies. (Nonliteral)
19. Secant is a technical vocabulary term which requires students to accommodate their schemata by modifying them or creating new ones to learn a novel word. (Nonliteral)
20. Children enter school with developed listening and speaking vocabularies. Instruction in the school enables these children to be exposed to more and more new concepts. Eventually, this exposure enables the listening vocabulary to further expand and the reading vocabulary to overtake the expressive vocabularies. (Nonliteral)
21. The Vocabularies section is organized around a pattern of comparison-contrast as the types of vocabularies are enumerated and discussed. (Author Organization)

PART 2

Teaching and Learning Strategies

6

Unit and Lesson Planning

Vignette

Setting

We are observing Shane Bintliff's ninth-grade United States history class. In a unit on the industrial revolution, Mr. Bintliff, a first-year teacher with an interest in technology as a way of engaging adolescents in learning history, took his students to his high school's computer lab. Although Mr. Bintliff is not well versed in creating WebQuests for his students, he believes that using the Internet to search for information on the industrial revolution will at least interest students in the topic. And, many of his students are reading at the 4th-grade level so he assumes that computer-based texts will be easier to read than the assigned textbook. He wants his students to understand how various machine inventions were influential in improving productivity and transportation. Mr. Bintliff's high school of 3000 students is located in a high-density urban area of the Southwest where language and ethnic differences abound. Significant numbers of students are struggling readers, reading two or more grades below the 9th-grade level.

The Lesson

We observe Mr. Bintliff and his students as they sit down in the computer lab to explore the topic of machine inventions and their influence on productivity and industrialization. Mr. Bintliff tells his students to browse the Internet using the Google search engine, figuring they are well versed in this process. He provides a search prompt to guide their exploration of the Internet. The prompt students are advised to use to begin their search reads:

→ Machine inventions during the industrial revolution

Students type this in and get a number of sites, sequentially listed by this topic. We watch as Shane, a struggling reader, selects the first site that pops up following his key word search. The site provides very traditional looking single-spaced text on the industrial revolution, organized by subheadings such as "The Newcomen and Watt Steam Engines." The vocabulary load in this text includes general terms like "ramifications" and "inefficient," as well as a wide array of technical vocabulary including "micrometer" and "atmospheric." It's Raygor Readability would yield a rating of 12th-grade level, making it well out of the range of Shane's reading level. As a struggling reader, Shane reads around the 4th-grade level, or 5 grade-levels below this text. As a result, Shane briefly scans the text and exits this site. He then selects the next site in the list, but its homepage features a brain tickler puzzle that has nothing to do with the industrial revolution and a sidebar list of "signs of depression." Finally, Shane locates a Wikipedia site that seems a bit more friendly but, by then, he is simply worn out and depressed about his reading. The period ends and Shane has zero information to take back to class to share with his cooperative learning group. Meanwhile, Mr. Bintliff is busy checking the latest travel deals on Expedia.com.

Now that you have had a chance to consider this lesson, write down your thoughts on the following questions:

1. What are the good points about the lesson?
2. What are the weak points about the lesson?
3. What, if anything, would you change about the lesson?

Rationale

In Chapter 3 we discussed the importance of social context in content area literacy. When you plan a *unit of instruction* that may span 3–6 weeks of individual lessons, the success of the unit is dependent upon how well you develop connections between the content and your students' prior knowledge and experiences. Thus, having a clear sense of students' language, culture, and interests is crucial in designing and delivering successful lessons. Planning time is needed to consider instructional purposes and goals. In addition, students' prior knowledge, ability, and motivation should be considered at the planning stage. For example, in the vignette of Mr. Bintliff's introduction to his unit on the industrial revolution, students were let loose in the computer lab to conduct a topic search without much guidance, other than a prompt statement. In Chapter 2 we talked about WebQuests content teachers can develop that structure and guide students' search process. Given that Mr. Bintliff's class had a significant number of struggling readers, careful planning and guidance would have overcome some of the frustration experienced by students like Shane in the vignette. An increasing array of online resources is available to help you create well-designed WebQuests and Internet-based assignments (McNabb, 2006), as well as more traditional print-based aids to lesson and unit planning. We include a short selection of these resources in the Recommended Readings at the close of the chapter. Task analysis of text characteristics such as vocabulary and important concepts should guide lesson planning. Finally, how much time will be available for delivering lessons and what grouping structures might be possible? Even if you do an outstanding job of planning a lesson, it will probably not be flawless the first time through. But planning can alleviate a number of problems related to student boredom, pacing, and evaluation.

As you plan lessons and units following the formats outlined in this chapter, you should keep a journal where you reflect on your teaching. Your professional development as a teacher hinges on constant reflection and efforts to improve lesson design and delivery. In essence, teaching is a process of constant transformation for both students and teachers (Britzman, 2003).

In this chapter, we introduce a format for unit and lesson planning with an emphasis on formulating clear goals and objectives, using exciting hooks or anticipatory set activities, and ensuring that a lesson takes advantage of students' experiences and interests. This framework should be helpful as you explore teaching and learning strategies in vocabulary, comprehension, writing, and studying approaches. In essence, this chapter provides the umbrella for all the individual teaching strategies that follow.

Learning Objectives

→ Use a unit blueprint to develop a 3–6 week unit of instruction in your content area.

→ Use a lesson planning framework to write a lesson plan in your content area.

→ Write lesson objectives that encompass the four elements of expected performance, product, condition, and criteria, applicable to your state curriculum standards.

→ Deliver a 5-minute lesson to your peers based on a hobby or interest area.

→ Deliver a 20-minute microteaching lesson to peers and field experience students in your content area.

→ Deliver a WebQuest as an introduction to a unit in your content area.

Graphic Organizer

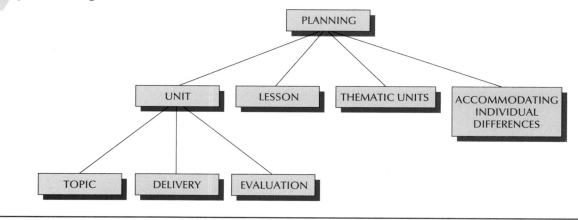

Planning

In the early stages of planning, when you begin to collect materials, draft lessons, and think about what teaching strategies you will use, keep the following points in mind:

Tips for Lesson Planning

1. *Present content and processes concurrently.* The particular teaching strategies you select for an assignment should grow out of a careful content analysis of the material. What is the purpose of the assignment? What text structure does the author use to portray ideas? This analysis should suggest which vocabulary, comprehension, writing, and studying strategies are likely to be most helpful.

2. *Provide guidance in all aspects of the instructional lesson—before, during, and after reading.* Be aware that many students need you to explicitly *model* the content reading process at various stages. They need *feedback* on their attempts to comprehend and they need to have instructional guidance removed once they have a grasp of the material.

3. *Use all language processes to help students learn the material.* Efforts to guide students' understanding of unit and lesson concepts should help them to be effective communicators in speaking, listening, reading, and writing.

4. *Use small groups to enhance learning.* In order for students to become effective at communicating in a content area, they need ample opportunities to risk expressing their ideas. Small group activities encourage risk-taking and expression.

5. *Be patient in new unit and lesson implementation.* It takes teachers and students time to become comfortable with new material. Give your new units and lessons enough trial runs with modifications so you can fully judge their effectiveness.

An additional point to keep in mind is the structure of an instructional unit and its related lessons. We conceive of a typical lesson structure as having three phases: prereading, reading, and postreading.

In **prereading** students apply what they know to what they are learning. Teachers can facilitate this process by appraising and, if need be, increasing students' knowledge of the topic under scrutiny before they begin reading text and course assignments.

In the **reading** phase students are encouraged to think deeply about what they are learning. Teachers can guide this process by insuring that students adopt an active, questioning approach to text through reasoning across a full range of levels of understanding. This involves students not only comprehending what the text explicitly states, but also understanding the text in relation to their own prior knowledge and experiences.

In **postreading**, students refine and extend ideas; teachers can involve students in activities that encourage them to synthesize and organize information for long-term retention.

Bear in mind that these phases are just useful constructs for talking about teaching, learning, and instructional planning. They are not to be blindly adhered to regardless of the instructional situation. Now that we provided some background, it would be interesting to read how some teachers use the textbook in their instructional lessons. Hinchman (2007) provides such a discussion. Finally before we introduce some of the details common to unit and lesson planning, be aware that the following website offers a wealth of guidance for developing sound lesson and unit plans that are likely to maximize students' comprehension [*http://www.internetclassrooms.com/lesson.htm*]. We strongly recommend spending some time browsing this site to gain an understanding of the support being offered in lesson and unit planning across the key dimensions of vocabulary development, comprehension, and study strategies highlighted in Part 2 of our book.

Developing Units and Lessons

A unit may be as short as a single week of instruction or span three to six weeks. In most cases, developing a unit on a topic in your content area will entail using a unit blueprint that contains the following elements:

Unit Blueprint Categories
1. Topic
2. Goals and Objectives
3. Content Outline
4. Learning Activities
5. Resources and Materials
6. Evaluation Plan

In order to understand the role each of these elements plays in planning, we will follow a secondary natural science teacher at a Kauai, Hawaii, high school as she designs a unit entitled Ocean Predators: The Shark. The teacher's name is Toni Avila.

Ms. Avila's unit on the topic, Ocean Predators: The Shark, spans three weeks with a focus on basic shark biology, shark species, and habits of sharks related to attacks reported in the islands. Many of Ms. Avila's students and Ms. Avila are avid watersports enthusiasts. She regularly windsurfs the outer reefs off Poipu Beach and many of her students surf, kayak, scuba dive, fish, and swim in the waters on the south and north sides of the island. Thus, in planning her unit, Ms.

Avila thinks about her students' varied experiences in the nearby Hawaiian waters. She also consults district and state curriculum guideline materials and objectives to include this material in her planning process. And, she goes over all her resource material ranging from texts, tradebooks, videos, Internet web pages, and a set of very large borrowed tiger shark jaws from a marine fisheries friend. In the early planning stages of the unit she has all this material laid out on the living room floor of her apartment. In addition, she is aware of an upcoming exhibit on sharks at a local museum. Finally, the Internet features a number of useful sites about sharks.

Ms. Avila also thinks carefully about the range of students in her class. Her students are heterogeneously grouped, spanning a range of achievement levels and needs. As she reviews all this material, the following unit blueprint emerges over the span of a week.

Blueprint

Topic
Ocean Predators: The Shark

Goal and Objectives
Be able to identify biological features of sharks, species, and know what shark habits influence attacks in Hawaiian waters and how to prevent their occurrence.

1. *The students will be able to identify the biological features of a tiger shark by labeling a shark drawing with its missing features with 100 percent accuracy.*

2. *The students will be able to distinguish dangerous sharks from harmless species by watching slides of various sharks and checking "dangerous" or "harmless" on a paper listing each slide number. They will also be asked to label the species next to each slide number, and the criteria for success at both tasks is 80 percent accuracy overall.*

3. *The students will develop shark education materials (posters, videos, pamphlets) to assist the state's effort to reduce shark attacks. These materials will be judged by a panel of science teachers, community members, and State Fisheries biologists using a scale that includes a) accuracy of information on sharks, b) artistic merit, and c) potential impact on beach safety.*

Content Outline
Ms. Avila goes to the library and checks out a number of resource books on sharks in addition to the class textbook in order to develop a unit content outline that addresses the planned objectives. She also visits key Internet websites on sharks.

Because of the unusually large number of fatal shark attacks attributed to tiger sharks, Ms. Avila decides to focus on this shark as a basis for comparing and contrasting information about other sharks. Based on selectively reading and taking notes on these books, Ms. Avila created the following content outline:

I. Biological Features of a Tiger Shark
   A. A kind of fish which has:
      1. a vertebral column
      2. median fins
      3. breathes using gills
   B. Two groups of jawed fishes
      1. bony fishes
      2. cartilaginous fishes (sharks)

II. Misconceptions about Sharks
   A. Misconceptions:
      1. All sharks are the same
      2. Sharks are color blind
      3. Sharks must turn on their backs to bite
      4. They have simple brains
   B. Facts and Characteristics
      1. 350 species and much diversity
      2. Characteristics:
         a) good vision
         b) sensitivity to vibrations
            1. lateral line organs
            2. ampullae of Lorenzini (jelly filled pores of nerve endings on snout and head to sense electrical impulses in hunting)
         c) no gas bladder like fish to control buoyancy-they must swim to avoid sinking
         d) 5 to 7 gill openings
         e) eyelid protection-nictitating membrane
         f) denticles (toothlike) rather than scales like a fish
         g) inflexible fins-tail fin is the driving force
         h) teeth grow continuously
         i) reproduction is internal

III. Dangerous versus Harmless Sharks
   A. Dangerous sharks (piscivorous feeders)
      1. Tiger
      2. Great White
      3. Hammerhead
   B. Harmless sharks (plankton feeders)
      1. Basking
      2. Megamouth
      3. Whale shark

IV. Preventing Shark Attacks

    A. Sharks hunt using recognized signals of prey:
- *1. thrashing of a wounded fish*
- *2. smell of blood or other body fluids*
- *3. flailing of appendages of weakened prey*

    B. Swimmers should:
- *1. avoid swimming alone*
- *2. wear low contrast clothing*
- *3. avoid wearing shiny jewelry*
- *4. avoid wild splashing and erratic swimming*
- *5. stay close to shore*
- *6. avoid murky rivermouth areas*
- *7. avoid deep channels*
- *8. avoid swimming at night*
- *9. surfers should be alert to sharks-paddle calmly toward shore if one is spotted*
- *10. divers spearing fish should tow their kill on a long line away from their bodies*

Learning Activities

Ms. Avila has taken a class in content area literacy, and she is able to capitalize on a number of teaching strategies. For the opening lesson of this unit she decided to use a comprehension strategy called *Talking Drawings* (McConnell, 1993) to introduce the unit. *Talking Drawings* asks students to draw stick figure drawings that represent what they know about a topic to be studied. These rough sketches become visual prompts for a prereading discussion of the topic in pairs or small groups. Following the text reading, students can revise their talking drawings to include the information they learned, and erroneous information can be removed.

The focus of this opening lesson will be on how sharks hunt for food. Ms. Avila's lesson plan follows. It contains all the elements of a good *lesson plan*: (a) objective(s); (b) set induction; (c) content outline; (d) activities; (e) closure; (f) resources and materials; (g) evaluation; and (h) assignment.

Her objective for this lesson contains the four key elements of any good *objective*: (a) a clear statement of the performance expected of students; (b) the product that should result from this performance; (c) the conditions for demonstrating the expected performance and product; and (d) the criteria for successful demonstration of the expected performance and product. Thus, for the lesson on how sharks hunt for food, Ms. Avila wrote the following lesson plan and related objective:

— —

Ms. Avila's Lesson

Topic: How Sharks Hunt for Food

Objective: Students will verbally discuss their revised shark drawings in groups of four. Students' revised drawings should have two anatomical features that assist hunting for food.

In this objective, the expected performance is a shark drawing. The expected product is a revised version of the original shark drawing. The condition for demonstrating success at this task is a small group discussion of students' revised shark drawings. The criteria for success is the inclusion of two anatomical features that assist sharks in hunting for food.

Set Induction

1. Using the talking drawings format, Ms. Avila has students draw their impressions of a tiger shark's features. The following drawing was produced by one of her students prior to any reading and study about tiger sharks:

Lesson Content Steps, Outline, and Activities

2. Students then shared and discussed their initial drawings in groups of four. A recorder kept track of the information they provided about the shark's features. For example, the group that labeled the previous drawing here understood a few anatomical features of tiger sharks that might be important for hunting. They included the nose and sense of smell, the gills for breathing, and the dorsal fin for swimming. However, they also felt that sharks might navigate to their prey using sonar.

3. A whole group teacher-guided discussion lead to the development of a shark features drawing on the board with labels for those features mentioned by students at this initial stage of the lesson. The second drawing, which resembled a tiger shark more closely than the drawing produced by the group in step 1, had a few additional features useful in hunting, including the pectoral fin.

4. Students were then assigned a text passage to read and Internet material to search.

5. Following text reading, they revised their initial shark drawings:

The final phases of a lesson plan structure consist of: (a) lesson closure; (b) evaluation; and (c) assignment. In the case of the shark lesson, students completed the following steps:

6. Small group sharing of the revised drawings with a recorder keeping track of changes and additions to the original drawings. This small group discussion provided the material for the final lesson activity.

Lesson Closure, Evaluation, and Assignment

7. A whole class discussion resulted in a final composite drawing on the board of the tiger shark and its various anatomical parts that assist hunting. These included the tiger shark's sense of smell and its ability to use its lateral line system or pores along the body to detect vibrations in the water. In addition, highly sensitive pores beneath the shark's snout, termed "ampullae of Lorenzini," assist the shark in the final phases of attack by detecting very weak electrical fields emitted by its prey. In short, the tiger shark is a well equipped hunter, even without sonar.

   To close the lesson, Ms. Avila advised students to read the section in their book on great white sharks, as that topic would be taken up in the next class.

Lesson Resources and Materials

Ms. Avila listed drawing paper, felt tip pens, overhead transparencies, overhead pens, a book on sharks in Hawaii, and Internet search tasks on sharks of Hawaii. Additional learning activities in the overall unit on sharks included shark videos from the local library, a fisheries biologist well known as a shark researcher as a guest speaker, and a field trip back to the local museum where a shark exhibit further countered students' misconceptions about sharks' vision, teeth regeneration, and reproduction. Students also read and critiqued popular novels that involved sharks. They critiqued these based on the accuracy of the scientific information used by the author in describing shark's behavior. In addition, this field trip exposed students to some of the large yet harmless species of sharks, including the whale shark and megamouth. Finally, students were asked to develop shark attack prevention brochures for use by the Department of Fisheries in its community education program.

Unit Resources and Materials

Ms. Avila selected videos, a list of potential guest speakers, felt tip pens, overhead transparencies, media supplies for brochure drafts, and trade books.

Evaluation

This included text-based quizzes and tests, as well as a panel review of students' brochures using specific criteria in a checklist of features. Thus, both ongoing and final project evaluation can be used to judge students' performance within individual lessons and across the overall unit.

Table 6.1 presents the components needed in designing lesson plans for a conventional unit as well as designing lessons within the unit structure.

Table 6.1

Designing Lesson Plans	
CONVENTIONAL UNIT	**LESSON WITHIN THE UNIT STRUCTURE**
1. Topic	1. Topic
2. Goals and Objectives	2. Objectives
3. Content Outline	3. Set Induction
4. Learning Activities	4. Content Outline
5. Resources and Materials	5. Activities
6. Evaluation Plan	6. Closure
	7. Resources and Materials
	8. Evaluation
	9. Assignment

The vocabulary, comprehension, writing, and studying strategies introduced later in the book fit within unit section number 4, Learning Activities. Ms. Avila's use of talking drawings demonstrates how content area literacy strategies fit within the larger framework of a lesson and unit.

All of these planning elements are important, but your delivery of a lesson needs to be flexible enough to allow for students' varying prior knowledge, interest, and achievement. In order to experiment with the process of developing and delivering a lesson, try the activity in Application 6.1.

Five-minute lessons can cover topics like how to polish shoes correctly, how to slice an onion properly, using a kitchen fire extinguisher, making a child's paper helicopter, tuning a guitar, and any number of other possible topics that lend themselves to a single objective. The process of developing and delivering a five-minute lesson will strengthen your skills in lesson planning and delivery that adheres to clear objectives. Remember, a good objective includes four important elements:

a. a clear statement of the performance expected of students;
b. the product that should result from this performance;
c. the conditions for demonstrating the expected performance and product; and
d. the criteria for successful demonstration of the expected performance and product.

APPLICATION 6.1

The Five-Minute Lesson

One of the best ways to get accustomed to lesson planning and delivery is to microteach a brief, five-minute lesson focusing on a single, attainable objective. Using the following example as a model, develop and deliver a five-minute lesson based on your favorite hobby. For instance, a teacher interested in horses devised the following five-minute lesson.

Topic: How to Tie a Quick Release Knot

Objective: Students will be able to verbally state the purpose of the quick release knot in horsemanship with 100 percent accuracy.

Set Induction: "You finish a trail ride with your horse, and it's time to remove the saddle to give your horse a bath. You need to tie your horse while you remove the saddle. How would you do this so you can easily untie your horse if he gets spooked?"

Content Outline and Activity: Demonstrate how to tie the quick release knot using a short piece of halter rope and an overhead transparency showing the steps necessary to tie the knot correctly.

Closure and Assessment: Students in small groups of four will have the group leader verbally state the purpose of the quick release knot with 100 percent accuracy.

Resources and Materials: Transparencies of the quick release knot steps, short halter rope to demonstrate tying the knot around a chair leg, and book on working with horses.

(continued)

The first transparency shows a horse tied correctly with the quick release knot. In an emergency, a sharp tug on the free end will release the horse.

The second transparency in the five-minute lesson shows the four steps needed to tie a quick release knot: (1) Loop the rope through the break away string on the tie down; (2) with the end of the loop, make a bow; (3) tighten the bow to secure the horse; (4) lock the knot by running the loose end through the bow so it will stay secure.

Assignment: Based on this lesson, students would be given short lengths of halter rope to go home and practice the quick release knot for a short performance test at the next class meeting.

The unit and lesson planning framework we have explored so far provides a good beginning point in your planning and use of content area literacy strategies. However, other planning models have been emerging in the last few years that capitalize on core area teacher teams from English, math, science, and social studies engaged in regular lesson and unit planning meetings to develop thematic units that integrate content from diverse subject areas. Another area of increasing importance mentioned in Chapter 3 is total inclusion. How do you plan for a truly diverse, heterogeneous population of students in your classes? We will take up these issues in the next section.

Planning Thematic Units and Lessons

The development and delivery of a *thematic unit* requires a school structure that provides regular planning time for teams of teachers to meet and create curriculum. In addition, a team of core subject area teachers from English, mathematics, science, and social studies typically share the same students. In a secondary school, about 130 students are usually served by a core team of teachers. Additionally, teachers from the elective areas of art, music, industrial arts, and physical education may also be involved in planning *integrated, thematic units*. It is only at the point of actually carrying out the unit for the first time that all the bugs can be worked out. This is equally true for lessons and conventional, single subject units. A well-designed thematic unit contains the following steps.

Steps for creating a powerful Thematic Unit

1. **Create a binding theme.**
   For example, one middle school decided to concentrate on eradicating litter on the campus. The core team teachers and elective teachers developed a quarter term thematic unit on environmental beautification using their campus as a test case. All 130 seventh- and eighth-grade students would be involved in the unit across their various core and elective classes.

2. **Use concept mapping or outlining to brainstorm and design a preliminary plan for the unit. (See Figure 6.1)**

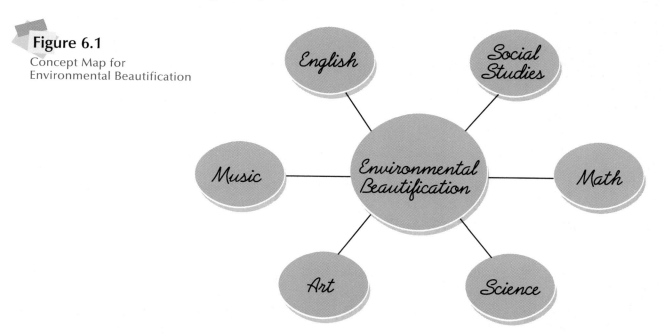

Figure 6.1
Concept Map for
Environmental Beautification

3. **Decide what concepts will be developed within each content area.**

For example, the mathematics, science, and social studies teachers decided to have their students use a campus map and tour the campus to collect specific data on amounts of litter at various key areas of the school. This information was then entered in a computer database, and descriptive bar graphs showing areas of substantial litter were plotted. The English teachers assisted students in writing research reports chronicling the location of litter and potential solutions to the problem. Elective teachers in art had students videotape the data collection process, and ultimately students developed anti-litter posters. In music, they created songs related to litter eradication, and the English classes developed dramatic skits for a whole school assembly to recognize the custodial staff and introduce a campus beautification incentive program. New trash cans were placed at key litter sites mapped by students and a weekly drawing awarded prizes for litter control.

This third step of listing key concepts parallels the lesson and unit planning steps you explored earlier in the chapter, but it relies on all team members coordinating their content around the central theme. Many middle and secondary schools are moving toward this model because it results in students seeing connections across diverse content areas and it allows teachers to track student progress and engage in cooperative problem solving when they notice a student falling behind. Elementary teachers can create thematic, integrated units of instruction within their own classrooms.

4. **Decide how the concepts in step three are connected across content areas.**

Each content area contributes the special skills it has to offer. Thus, the art department capitalized on poster-making talents, the math area on data analysis, the social studies area on mapping skills, science on data collection, and English on report writing. The music teacher gave students a chance to put their ideas to song and rap.

5. **Develop cooperative activities.**

The central, cooperative activity that started this unit was the campus mapping and data collection about litter. This activity necessitated reading materials on environmental beautification and learning a great deal about working in groups with specific assignments for each group member. Some students had to count litter in various locations, others recorded the data, and each team had to share its findings with the other teams mapping campus litter.

6. **Resources.**

A number of websites provide resource materials for lesson planning. These sites change frequently, but they can be found with most popular search engines.

Apart from the library, computer, video, presentation software and hardware, Internet, and other resources needed for this thematic unit, students and teachers were able to receive a small grant from the local Rotary Club to assist in purchasing trash cans and developing posters, brochures, and incentive awards.

When you are designing integrated, thematic units, try to pick topics that are likely to generate excitement and interest. Students should be involved in the planning stages as well as helping to design projects and grouping structures. If possible, seeking whole school involvement is important because it makes clear to students just how crucial this activity is to the whole school. In the case of the litter eradication example, litter was a problem that had gotten steadily worse with everyone assuming someone else—the custodians, teachers, and others—responsible. This was a unit that had an obvious impact on the whole school. Unfortunately, it is rare that our day-to-day curriculum has this kind of obvious impact on students' lives. Carefully planned thematic units can have a tremendous impact, but they do take time to create and implement.

One potential problem in unit planning that we have not yet addressed is the wide range of individual differences that students bring to your classes. You may need to vary lesson assignments in your classes based on students' prior knowledge, interest, reading achievement, language variation, and learning difficulties. In Chapter 3 we reviewed some of the current legislation in the area of inclusion, and we discussed second language learners and various approaches. In the section that follows, we explore the nature of individual differences and consequences for planning instruction.

Accommodating Individual Differences in Planning

Teaching requires helping individuals to change. Learning occurs by making whatever adjustments are necessary in the learning situation, accommodating instructional methods to match student abilities, and guiding students as they try to cope with new learning situations. In Chapter 3 you learned about two factors, among many, that affect students' ability to learn from text—prior knowledge and language knowledge. The quantity and quality of the prior experiences of individuals and their language sophistication vary greatly. Other individual factors that may affect reading achievement as they interact with each other are:

1. physical development
2. emotional development
3. rate of learning
4. mode of learning
5. motivation
6. practice needed.

Because of their interactive nature, it might be difficult to speak of each factor singularly. For instance, physical development may influence one's emotional well-being. The same might be said for rate and mode of learning.

The notion of *passive failure,* or learned helplessness, is another learning difference to be recognized. Students who exhibit passive failure may be defined as those students who are resigned to fail and believe they do not have the ability to succeed in their learning. When faced with failure, they do not persist; they give up. On the other hand, when these students do succeed, they usually attribute it to factors other than themselves, such as luck, good teaching, or the ease of the task. The important point to be made about these students is that they don't fail because of lack of ability; rather, they do not, and will not, employ the appropriate strategies necessary for effective learning.

One last principle regarding individual differences is that sometimes a factor may vary almost as greatly within an individual as it does among individuals. For instance, a student's interest in school may fluctuate dramatically according to subject area. Changing interests, motivations, and life goals are differences that may differ greatly within an individual, especially over time.

A Definition

Accommodating individual differences means many different things to many different people. It does not mean largely undifferentiated, whole-group instruction in which the subject, rather than the student, is the focus of instruction. The problems inherent in such instruction have been recognized for some time. For instance, as far back as 1950, Hunt and Sheldon offered that: "High school teachers must also realize that much of their frustration is derived from attempting to teach forty pupils as if all the children were able to perform on the same level" (pp. 352–353). Nonetheless, the lecture method is still predominant in content area teaching.

At the other extreme is complete individualization in which instruction takes place totally on a one-to-one basis. This may be an ideal to which some educators aspire; however, in the face of the rigors of day-to-day classroom experiences with large numbers of students, complete individualization is an unrealistic and counterproductive goal.

The authors recommend a compromise between the two extremes cited above. It does not embrace complete individualization, which requires individual preparation or text material for each student, nor does it call for the abandonment of grouping strategies. Rather, it incorporates the gamut of grouping procedures—whole group, small-group, and individual—and utilizes these grouping procedures within the structure of unit and lesson planning (Readence & Dishner, 2007).

Grouping, and discussion within grouping procedures, are recommended because the authors feel that active student involvement in a group situation provides for productivity in learning, for example, through plays, science experiments, or unit reviews (Bean, 2002). Students can learn from one another and provide new insight into learning by modeling their thinking for others. Feelings of belonging cannot be disregarded in grouping situations either. Additionally, teachers can move into their most appropriate role, as facilitators of learning, through the use of different group structures.

For example, numerous different types of small groups exist that teachers might employ. Among them are the following:

1. instruction groups—which allow teachers to teach a specific process or issue with more individual contact than is possible in a large group
2. research groups—which gather information on a problem and report the results to the large group
3. debate groups—which present a contest of ideas to the large group
4. digressive groups—which use brainstorming to generate creative solutions to a problem

Types of Small Groups

➲ Instruction
➲ Research
➲ Debate
➲ Digressive

Teachers need to be aware that the idea of making an overnight transformation from total whole-group instruction to the practices for accommodating individual differences is unrealistic. Slow, careful adaptation is crucial to the eventual successful implementation of these practices.

Some Suggestions

In order to realistically consider accommodating students' individual differences, teachers must make modifications in the way they present the textbook within the context of the instructional paradigm. Consequently, you must be willing to make these necessary alterations in order to insure that each student has optimal opportunity to find success in your classroom.

The following are suggested modifications for teachers to consider as they employ the instructional paradigm of prereading, reading, and postreading phases. These include:

1. modifying students' prior knowledge
2. modifying the way in which the material is presented
3. considering alternatives to the text material
4. modifying the assignment made.

These suggestions are the authors' attempts to offer you practical instructional techniques to help you answer the commonly asked question, "What do I do on Monday?"

MODIFICATIONS IN THE PREREADING PHASE. The degree to which readers utilize their prior experiences in reading and learning with text will greatly influence their understanding of that material. Students' failure to associate new information with previously known information as they attempt to assimilate text material increases the difficulty of their comprehension task. Additionally, some students simply do not have the necessary prior knowledge about all the topics they will encounter in text material.

Fortunately, as students prepare to read their texts you can intervene to modify their knowledge of a topic as well as their interest in it. You can provide guided instruction to activate, or modify, students' schemata through the use of prereading strategies. Prereading strategies serve to activate appropriate schemata and then modify them as new information is entered, thus allowing comprehension to occur.

Another way to activate prior knowledge at the prereading stage of an integrated unit is to create a central question that puts students in the role of the problem solvers (Wiggins & McTighe, 2005). Central questions should:

1. tap meaningful issues
2. be provocative and emotionally engaging
3. connect with students' worlds
4. give students active, investigative roles versus passive processing of content
5. allow for multiple responses

For example, in the shark unit, a central question might be, "Why do tiger sharks attack people?" Central questions lend themselves to culminating activities that are based on performance standards. Thus, students may do a performance such as a one-act play, a presentation, a video, or guide a field trip. The possibilities are endless. A well crafted central question will frame a unit and provide an overarching focus for inquiry.

MODIFICATIONS IN THE READING PHASE. Certainly there is cause to wonder about instruction that presents the same material in the same way to all students. Obviously, in this type of instruction no heed is being paid to the differences in the way students learn or how well individual students deal with the difficulty of the concepts and vocabulary inherent in text. Because of these differences, methods for reducing the difficulty level of the learning material need to be considered. With some students it may be necessary to modify the way the material is presented or even the material itself.

Some students may find the text too difficult to read; others may prefer an alternate means of text presentation. In these situations it is advantageous to capitalize on students' ability to listen and comprehend the material. Listening can be an effective means for student readers to communicate with text authors. It is the opinion of the authors that active listening strategies are utilized too infrequently and that students could benefit extensively from such strategies.

The teacher may read aloud the selected passage from the text after instructing students to listen for particular concepts or other purposes. Students who are able to read the text with ease may be asked to read it to other students who are having difficulty with the reading. Another alternative is use of a tape recorder. Either the teacher or selected students may tape a portion of the text for those experiencing difficulty. These students may follow along as the text is being read, again with specific instructions about what they should be listening for. If a more structured approach is desired as students are listening to a selected passage, *listening guides* are suggested. The listening guide is a skeletal outline of the important concepts in the passage presented in the order and relationship in which they are set out in the passage. Students are asked to write in the desired information as they listen to the selection. The task of filling in the listening guides gives students additional guidance through the outline structure provided. Activities for reinforcement and extension may follow as planned.

Figure 6.2 is an example of a listening guide. If a listening guide was employed with the section of Chapter 8 entitled "Principles of Effective Vocabulary Instruction," it might look like this guide.

Figure 6.2
Sample Listening Guide

Principle	Notes
1. _____	_____
	_____
2. _____	_____
	_____
3. _____	_____
	_____
4. _____	_____
	_____

MODIFICATIONS IN THE POSTREADING PHASE. In addition to modifying students' prior knowledge, the method, or the presentation of the material, and assignments required of students may also be modified. Usually the students' comprehension of text material is checked by having them answer a series of questions either found in the chapter's end or in a study guide constructed by the teacher. However, having the whole group of students deal with exactly the same questions is the antithesis of accommodating divergent student abilities.

The use of a technique called *slicing* in assigning tasks to students is suggested as a means to modify assignments. Specifically, slicing refers to simplifying the complexity of these tasks by reexamining those that are required and recasting them to ease the demands placed on students.

Text assignments may be sliced in a variety of ways. Slicing enables teachers to accommodate individual differences by graduating the learning steps involved in completing assignments and by providing structured guidance in doing so. Slicing may be utilized in the following aspects of text assignments: (1) length of passage, (2) scope of information search, and (3) information index.

1. *Length of passage.* Though obviously more of a reading task than a post-reading task, length of passage will be discussed here under the umbrella strategy of slicing. Sometimes assigning a chapter at a time for reading represents too sizeable a chunk of text for some students, yet this size assignment is very prevalent. In some cases, poor readers might be overwhelmed by as little as five pages; therefore, it seems appropriate to consider slicing the length of reading task for certain students to accommodate their divergent abilities. Reading assignments should be varied according to the number of concepts assigned to each student. Slicing the length of the passage to even a section or paragraph might be appropriate for certain students to insure their comprehension. Caution is given regarding pictorial aids in text. Authors sometimes use such aids to express what could take large numbers of words. Such aids might be considered a unit of instruction for some students, while other students may focus on the running text elaborating upon a particular aid.

2. *Scope of information search.* Content textbooks, by their very nature, are bursting with information. It is unrealistic to consider teaching all concepts presented; therefore, the teacher must conduct some form of content analysis in order to make decisions regarding the relative importance of the concepts. The *scope of information search* is determined by the number of concepts for which students are then held responsible. As concepts increase in number, the more exhaustive the scope of the search becomes. On the other hand, the fewer the concepts to be mastered, the more limited the search. The less proficient the student's reading ability, the more difficult an exhaustive search will be, and the greater the chance of negative effects on motivation and retention of new learning. Therefore, slicing the scope of information search according to students' individual differences is appropriate.

The number of concepts for which students are responsible should be dependent upon their differential abilities and the importance of the concepts in the chapter. The number of concepts can be varied by adding or subtracting from the number of assigned tasks on students' end-of-chapter or study guide questions. For example, more proficient readers may be responsible for 12 concepts while others need only deal with three or four. It is cautioned that no matter how many concepts are assigned to individual students in the class, whole-group discussion should follow the completion of their work so that all students are exposed to the selected information.

Two points should be made concerning the scope of information search. First, limiting the search does not necessitate that only literal thinking be involved. It is not the level of thinking that is limited, only the number of concepts. Since all students can think and all students should be involved in higher-level comprehension processes, it is misguided to limit such thinking in an endeavor to reduce the scope of the information search. Second, there is a difference between varying the scope of the search and varying the length of the passage to be read. The number of concepts assigned may be varied while the length of the passage is held constant. For example, in a 3-page selection certain students may be responsible for one concept per page while others may be held responsible for numerous concepts.

3. *Information index.* Keying students into the location of important concepts or in some way structuring their search for that information is the intent of using an *information index*. The extent to which the index is used depends on students' differential abilities, the importance of the information, and the depth of understanding required.

Two ways are suggested for teachers to slice the demands of the learning task using the information index. The first method is to intersperse questions throughout the text. Students can be directed to lightly mark question numbers at the appropriate places in the text chapter. In this way questions can be dealt with at the time they are encountered during the reading, thus slicing the search for the information. For some teachers this marking of questions may also serve as a preliminary step to their eventual development and use of study guides (Chapter 10).

A second method of providing the information index is to provide an actual informational key to the questions. Questions may be keyed to the page, section, paragraph, and/or sentence where students may find the appropriate answer or the information on which the answer is based. This type of information is frequently provided by content teachers when they use study guides with their students. An example of this type of information index is provided below. In this case the students are keyed to the page and paragraph numbers.

What were the causes of the Revolutionary War? (122:2)

Mini Projects

1. Use the "Matter and Energy in the Web of Life" text passage on the CD-ROM and the lesson planning guidelines in this chapter to design a lesson.

   A. Write two learning objectives for a group of secondary students in a wellness class.
   B. Create a possible set induction activity.
   C. Design a learning activity for the lesson.
   D. Brainstorm additional resources and materials for the lesson.
   E. Brainstorm how you would evaluate students' learning with respect to this material.

2. Meet with colleagues from core and elective content areas to design an integrated, thematic unit.

3. Use planning modifications, such as slicing the task, to accommodate student differences for a lesson in your content area.

4. Develop a list of supplementary materials (including Internet material) that you might be able to use to augment or to replace a chapter from a textbook in your content area.

5. Use the Internet to explore state performance and curriculum standards in your content area.

Website Activity

To locate and complete Chapter 6 activities, go to [*www.kendallhunt.com/contentarealiteracy/*].

7

Literature

Vignette

Setting

Two eighth-grade students, Dale Fallon and Sanae Tokunaga, are leaning over the railing on the second story deck of their suburban South Carolina middle school after a lesson in life science. Their teacher, Mr. Cousteau, introduced a lesson on endangered species by bringing in a large, inflatable child's pool toy in the shape and color of a sea turtle. Its vinyl skin made squeaking sounds as he placed the turtle on the table at the front of the room and said, "Today we're going to learn about the green sea turtle." He then launched into a lecture about types of turtles and their habits. The lecture went on for over 20 minutes. Both Dale and Sanae are conscientious students, and they took notes. Many other students slumped in their seats, where they daydreamed and doodled, looking bored. Mr. Cousteau then assigned some text reading and questions to be answered about endangered species in their textbook.

The Lesson

Right before the bell rang, Mr. Cousteau told students they were required to find a fiction book to read about turtles for a book report due to him in one week.

We overhear Dale and Sanae's conversation about the turtle lesson as they talk outside Mr. Cousteau's room during recess.

Dale: "How are we supposed to know what books to read about turtles? That guy is so boring!"

Sanae: "Yeah, my brother had Mrs. Read last year for life science at the other middle school, and they had a classroom library with a whole bunch of really good novels about endangered species. Maybe I can visit his school and see if I can borrow a book there. The only problem is, my brother Roger is now in high school and Mrs. Read moved to Florida."

Dale: "We can ask Mr. Cousteau for more help, but then he'll just get upset and we'll get lousy grades. Let's just go to the library and find a book we can both use for our dumb book report. It's no big deal. I write book reports on books I hate and don't read. Hey, Sanae, I'm sure you've never done that, huh?"

Sanae: "Yeah, right. Sure. All last year in English we had to do these stupid book reports. I just looked for the skinniest books, read the back cover or skimmed the pages, and faked my report."

Dale: "Too bad we can't read about horses instead of turtles."

Sanae: "I guess we won't have time now. We need to get to the library. You want to meet after school? That way we can pick the same stupid book and get this assignment done. I wonder if Mr. Cousteau has ever read any turtle novels himself? I bet he doesn't have a clue about it. He's just giving us work to do without even thinking about how we feel. You know Nathan in class?"

Dale: "You mean the guy who looks like a computer nerd?"

Sanae: "Yeah, that one. Well, his Dad is a marine scientist who specializes in turtle tagging research. Cousteau didn't even ask him about his Dad's work. I read about it in the newspaper."

Dale: "I bet he gets an A on this assignment."

Sanae: "He gets As on everything. Hey, I gotta go to my social studies class in building Q. See you this afternoon."

→ Now that you have had a chance to consider this lesson, write down your thoughts on the following questions:

1. What are the good points about the lesson?
2. What are the weak points about the lesson?
3. What, if anything, would you change about the lesson?

Rationale

Author Jamaica Kincaid grew up on the tiny island of Antigua, governed by British rule. Her memories of the library where she spent so much time recalled the quiet, reflective power of reading a good book.

> If you saw the old library, situated as it was, in a big, old wooden building painted a shade of yellow that is beautiful to people like me, with its wide veranda, its big, always open windows, its rows and rows of shelves filled with books, its beautiful wooden tables and chairs for sitting and reading, if you could hear the sound of its quietness (for the quiet in this library was a sound in itself), the smell of the sea (which was a stone's throw away), the heat of the sun (no building could protect us from that), the beauty of us sitting there like communicants at an altar, taking in, again and again, the fairy tale of how we met you, your right to do the things you did, how beautiful you were, are, and always will be; if you could see all of that in just one glimpse, you would see why my heart would break at the dung heap that now passes for a library in Antigua. (Kincaid, 1988, pp. 42–43)

By 1974, the library was damaged in an earthquake and left unrepaired for over a decade with the mocking sign "repairs are pending" (Kincaid, 1988, p. 42). In her book *A Small Place,* Jamaica Kincaid vividly charts the tensions between native Antiguans, the colonial British, and the more recent Antiguan independence. In truth, Kincaid's book is a multicultural treatise on the complexities of the aftermath of imperial rule, racism, and pride. But the library provided the chance to explore a vast array of books, although they recounted the lives of whites rather than Antigua natives. Nevertheless, as a little girl, Kincaid gravitated toward the lyrical, captivating world of a good book. She said, "I stole many books from this library. I didn't mean to steal the books, really; it's just that once I had read a book I couldn't bear to part with it" (Kincaid, 1988, p. 45).

Unfortunately, many content area teachers assume that librarians, media specialists and English teachers should be the ones to acquaint students with powerful fiction books beyond the required texts in social studies, science, mathematics, and elective areas. Yet the field of young adult literature is a rich treasure trove of books that can illuminate concepts about endangered species like Mr. Cousteau's turtles or the flight of a Nigerian family under a military coup (Naidoo, 2000).

In any content area it is possible to find young adult literature that enriches textbook readings and course concepts. Your task as a content teacher is to become familiar with this rich treasure trove of literature, understand how to survey students' attitudes and interests, and learn about various strategies you can use to link literature and textbook reading. This may sound like a daunting task, but it is really a matter of starting modestly by reading at least one young adult novel keyed to your particular field. Since most of these novels are relatively short, in the range of 125 pages, you may find this process to be every bit as enjoyable as reading the latest adult fiction bestseller.

In addition to reading young adult literature keyed to your field of study, you need to become familiar with the increasingly rich array of multicultural literature. The literary canon of assigned readings in English has been very resistant to change. In this chapter we will introduce some of the growing collection of multicultural young adult literature that can be used in content area teaching.

Learning Objectives

→ Use attitude and interest inventories to survey students' reading attitudes and interests in your content area.

→ Select and use tradebooks linked to units of instruction in your content area.

→ Implement a sustained silent reading program.

→ Use sources of the tradebooks to locate and review books you plan to use in your content area.

→ Create a plan for further development of your knowledge about tradebooks you can use in your discipline.

Graphic Organizer

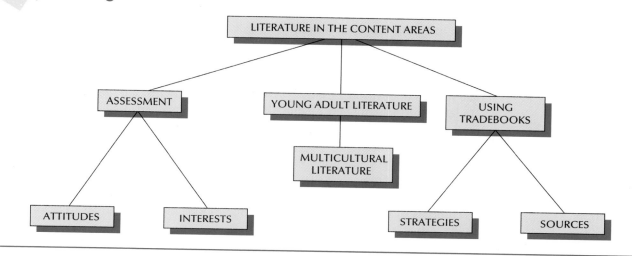

Assessment of Reading Attitudes and Interests

Attitudes

Attitudes may be defined as those feelings that cause a reader to approach or avoid a reading situation. Attitudes toward reading are shaped by a variety of factors. For example, reading attitudes are undoubtedly the result of beliefs finely tuned by culture. The motivation to read is multi-faceted and highly individualistic (Cole, 2003).

In a large-scale survey of 18,185 grade 1 through 6 students' attitudes toward academic and recreational reading, McKenna, Kear, and Ellsworth (1995) noted that reading attitudes declined steadily. By the time students were in 6th grade, they cared little for academic or recreational reading. Unfortunately, declines in voluntary pleasure reading parallel declines in national assessment performance on a variety of reading tasks (Guthrie & Wigfield, 2000). Thus, fostering students engagement in both academic and recreational reading is extremely important for their future success.

Guthrie and Wigfield (2000) pointed to research indicating that students learn more content from interesting texts. Providing interesting texts in a lesson or unit helps bridge the gap between students' pre-existing interests and new content. In addition to being aware of students' attitudes toward interesting texts, it is important to include in the classroom books that relate to their various cultures. Contemporary multicultural young adult literature by authors such as Gary Soto, Walter Dean Myers, and Virginia Hamilton has the power to change students' attitudes toward reading for pleasure, but the visibility of this literature in classrooms is all too rare (Bean, 2000).

A number of studies show the disparity between students' reading interests and the reading they do in school (e.g., Ivey & Broaddus, 2001). This disparity is especially acute for struggling readers and boys (Smith & Wilhelm, 2002; Worthy, Patterson, Salas, Prater, & Turner, 2002). In addition to the value of captivating young adult novels, teen magazines, comics, scary series books, and a host of other recreational reading materials are often absent in classrooms but a regular part of students out-of-school reading lives (Xu, Perkins, & Zunich, 2005). Through careful assessment of students' reading attitudes, as well as their interests, it is possible to create a more enticing collection of reading materials. Indeed, these materials can be keyed to critical learning events in various content areas, and even used to expand students' understanding of classical literature.

ASSESSMENT. Since attitudes are a critical factor in using tradebooks in content classrooms to develop a lifelong love of reading, you need to know how to assess students' attitudes toward reading. There are a number of methods for assessing reading attitudes, including personal interviews, autobiographies, and behavior checklists. The most common method is the self-report questionnaire. The reading attitude survey in Figure 7.1 was developed for use with middle and secondary school students.

This attitude survey may be used as a pre/posttest for determining the affective impact of programs. It is also possible to look at specific areas of reading attitude. For example, in the BJP Survey:

Items 1, 7, 12 = Attitude toward libraries
Items 4, 6, 16, 19 = Reading self-concept
Other items = General attitude toward reading

It is standard procedure for individual scores to be recorded for purposes of counseling students with bad attitudes. We recommend that this not be done. Students with negative attitudes toward reading are not necessarily unintelligent. As a consequence, if they have any reason to think that they will be singled out and/or questioned because of their negative attitudes, they will take the only intelligent option and lie on the survey. The technical name for this is *response bias,* writing down what one believes the examiner wants rather than what the test taker really believes. A second reason for not generating individual scores is that students whose attitudes toward books and reading are so bad that they need counseling are painfully conspicuous most of the time, and no test is needed to identify them. On the other hand, trying to determine whether or not a program has created a positive change in group attitudes requires some objective measure. Therefore, we recommend that attitude surveys be anonymous and that class, grade, and school averages be used to assess groups rather than individuals. Additionally, once data have been gathered concerning the attitudes of students, attention should be given to promoting reading related to content areas.

Figure 7.1

BJP Middle/Secondary Reading Attitude Survey*	Strongly Agree	Agree	Disagree	Strongly Disagree
Directions: This survey tells how you feel about reading and books. The survey is not a test, and it is anonymous. It will not affect your grades or progress in school, but it will help your school to create better programs. Answer as honestly as you can by checking the term or terms which tell how you feel about each statement.				
1. Library books are dull.				
2. Reading is a waste of time.				
3. Reading is one of my hobbies.				
4. I believe I am a better reader than most other students in my grade.				
5. Reading is almost always boring.				
6. Sometimes I think kids younger than I am read better than I do.				
7. I enjoy going to the library for books.				
8. I can read as well as most students who are a year older than I am.				
9. I don't have enough time to read books.				
10. I believe that I am a poor reader.				
11. I would like to belong to a book club.				
12. I like to take library books home.				
13. Teachers want me to read too much.				
14. You can't learn much from reading.				
15. Books can help us to understand other people.				
16. I almost always get A's and B's in reading and English.				
17. I like to have time to read in class.				
18. Reading gets boring after about ten minutes.				
19. Sometimes I get bad grades in reading and English.				
20. I like to read before I go to bed.				

Scoring: The positive items are 3, 4, 7, 8, 11, 12, 15, 16, 17, 20. Give four points for a *SA*, three points for an *A*, two points for a *D*, and one point for a *SD*. For the negative items, 1, 2, 5, 6, 9, 10, 13, 14, 18, 19, score four points for a *SD*, three for a *D*, two for *A*, and one for *SA*. Scores can range from 20 to 80.

60–80 = Good
40–59 = Fair
20–39 = Poor

APPLICATION 7.1

Take the BJP attitude survey. How good is your reading attitude? Be honest!

Interests

Reading *interests* are generally defined as the material students actually select to read while *reading preferences* indicate what they might like to read (Galda, Ash, & Cullinan, 2000). Reading interests are complicated as they are both individualistic and strongly influenced by sociocultural norms and expectations. Knowing something about your students' interests can help you select reading material that will build on this important aspect of their developing identities.

Students naturally prefer to engage in activities that are likely to boost feelings of competence, autonomy, and relatedness to others (Cole, 2003). In addition, reading interests that develop and endure come from feelings of enjoyment and involvement. Recent studies of adolescent males and females reveal their awareness of the complexity of their lives and the degree to which media and some novels oversimplify teen identity (Bean & Harper, 2007; Brozo, Walter, & Placker, 2002; Harper, 2000; Moje 2000). These studies show a level of self-awareness that allows for diverse in- and out-of-school interests, as well as the need to critique simplistic portrayals of gender and teen life. Thus, rather than expecting a homogenization of teen interests, we can expect a good deal of individual diversity within any content area classroom.

APPLICATION 7.2

In a college class with about equal numbers of men and women, have students identify their favorite type of pleasure reading. How are the reading interests of men and women different?

ASSESSMENT. The most useful type of interest assessment is one that permits the teacher to match specific interests with specific materials. However, the general interest inventory is the most common type of interest assessment (see Figure 7.2).

It is possible to create interest inventories with varying degrees of specificity; for instance, sports can be subclassified into baseball, basketball, football, tennis, curling, etc. Baseball could be subdivided into fiction stories, nonfiction books about pitching or hitting, and so on. In much the same manner it is possible to

Figure 7.2

General Interest Inventory

Directions: The purpose of this inventory is to find out what kinds of things you and your classmates are interested in reading. After every topic there is a blank space. On each space give a grade of A, B, C, D, or F based on how much you would like to read about the topic.

An A means: It's wonderful; I love it! An F means: It's terrible; take the topic away and bury it, quick!

Sports _____	Animals _____	History _____
Science Fiction _____	Fantasy _____	Poetry _____
Folklore _____	Romance _____	Family Life _____
Cars _____	Adventure _____	Plays _____
Humor _____	Mystery _____	Human Drama _____
War _____	The Arts _____	Mathematics _____
Supernatural _____	Foreign Lands _____	Health Sciences _____
Science _____		

create an interest inventory for a specific content area. This type of inventory can provide information about group interests as well as guide outside reading for individuals. The U.S. history interest inventory shown in Figure 7.3 is merely one example in an endless chain of possibilities.

Figure 7.3

U.S. History Interest Inventory

Directions: Everyone in your class is going to be doing some outside reading related to American history. The purpose of this inventory is to help you find books that are actually interesting to *you*. After every topic there is a blank space. On the space next to the topic you would *most* like to read about, put a 1. Place a 2 on the space for your next choice. Place a 3 on the third best choice, and so on until you have evaluated every topic. Do *NOT* use any number more than once.

The Colonial Period (1600–1760)

    Biography _____

    Human Drama _____

    Family Life _____

    Freedom and Justice _____

The Revolutionary War Era (1760–1785)

    Biography _____

    Politics _____

    War _____

The Civil War Era (1850–1876)

    Slavery _____

    Famous Battles _____

    Politics _____

    Biography _____

    Human Drama _____

Western and Frontier Life

    Pioneers _____

    Native Americans _____

    Tales of the Wild West _____

World War II (1939–1945)

    Battles in the Pacific _____

    Military Planes _____

    The War in Europe _____

    Atomic Weapons _____

    Freedom and Justice _____

Post World War II America

    Civil Rights _____

    Women's Liberation _____

    Vietnam War _____

    The Presidency _____

    Biographies of African Americans _____

Teachers can modify the interest inventory in Figure 7.3 to fit the needs of their teaching objectives. For instance, students might rank each general topic area (e.g., The Colonial Period) 1, 2, 3, 4 instead of ranking all topics at once. This may enable teachers to find appropriate material for each general topic area as it is encountered.

Young Adult Literature

A cartoon in "The Neighborhood" series by cartoonist Jerry Van Amerongen shows a middle-aged couple, Marian and Guy, sitting in a private booth at an upscale restaurant enjoying what should be a romantic, candlelit dinner. However, both Marian and Guy are fully engaged in reading their respective novels, ignoring each other. The caption below the cartoon reads: Marian and Guy have been together a long time.

Developing a lifelong love of reading is the result of many influences. Family, friends, and teachers all play a role in making reading pleasurable or something to be avoided at all costs. The more you become familiar with contemporary young adult literature the more you can create units that integrate this captivating medium.

Case studies of adolescents' reading habits, especially boys, suggest they spend little of their leisure time reading literature (Smith & Wilhelm, 2002; 2006). As a content area teacher, you can change this apathy or avoidance of young adult literature by becoming personally familiar with at least a small portion of the vast array of books that can be linked to your units and lessons. If you think of adolescents through the lens of your own adolescent experience and the filter of young adult literature from your teen and preteen years, this will limit your horizons. Although we are not saying you should ignore this older literature, we do strongly advocate getting to know the newer young adult authors who portray multicultural characters, actions, and events that more closely mirror those of our students.

The shift toward greater realism in young adult literature began with S. E. Hinton's (1967) *The Outsiders,* written when she was 16. This novel realistically portrayed the passages and transitions adolescents go through as they struggle to find their own identity amidst conflicting peer and family pressures. Young adult literature helps adolescents cope with the dissonance between the ideal and real in daily life by its power to vicariously transport the reader into the lives and times of fictional characters struggling with familiar problems. In more recent times increasingly complex female and multicultural characters emerged. Hispanic authors like Gary Soto offered a positive, insider's view of life in the barrio. Asian American literature explored racial discrimination and oppression. The Vietnam war has been widely chronicled in powerful young adult novels like Walter Dean Myers' (1988) *Fallen Angels.* Myers' novel is a poignant account of two young African American soldiers immersed in the rice paddy skirmishes that robbed their adolescence and forever changed their lives.

Unlike textbooks that present facts to be considered and used in solving problems in science or math, discussing policies in history, or reading the notes of a scale in music, fiction by its nature propels students into high level interpretive thinking. Indeed, critical literacy, by definition, asks readers to carefully examine how characters cope with power relations and, in particular, the way social and cultural forces shape their lives (Lewison & Leland, 2002). Critical literacy moves the reader beyond response (Rosenblatt, 1978) to examine novels as social constructions that position characters in various ways in terms of gender, ethnicity, class, and race (Bean & Moni, 2003; Stevens & Bean, 2007). Students are encouraged to examine gaps and silences wherein some characters have strong voices and power and others are left by the wayside. Later in this chapter we explore some of the questions you may want to have students explore as you link young adult literature and content area teaching.

What exactly is *young adult literature*? We like the definition supplied by Nilsen and Donelson (2005, p. 1). They define *young adult literature* as "anything that readers between the approximate ages of 12 and 18 choose to read." Young adult literature encompasses a wide range of genres including mystery, adventure, science fiction, romance, supernatural, fantasy, sports, humor, and historical fiction. Typical themes revolve around family relationships, rites of passage, alienation, friends and society, death, disabilities, drugs and alcohol, and sexual relationships. A number of powerful novels explore how to define oneself outside the family, coping with the reality that parents are less than perfect, carving out one's own set of moral, ethical, religious, and political principles, developing positive healthy relationships, and projecting possible futures and career choices (Stover & Tway, 1992). For example, Woodson's (2002) powerful novel, *Hush*, explores the life of an African American teenage girl, uprooted from her familiar home when her Dad is placed in a witness protection program.

Unfortunately, very few content teachers seem to use or know much about young adult literature. Rather, they often see all literature as the English teacher's exclusive domain and responsibility. Worse still, many teachers have never read a young adult novel, let alone a contemporary young adult novel.

The purpose of using young adult literature in your content area is to enhance students' content learning. This is a different focus than the English teacher's interest in appreciation and analysis of literature. You can focus on locating those books best keyed to concepts and issues in your course. For example, a history teacher could enrich a unit on slavery with Warner's (1976) diary account, *From Slave to Abolitionist: The Life of William Wells Brown*. This poignant book propels the reader into the day-to-day trials of William Wells Brown, a young slave who eventually escapes his tormentors to become a significant abolitionist writer in the 1850s. His writing far surpasses that of any textbook in its ability to grab the attention of young readers. Similarly, young adult novels like *Code Orange* (Cooney, 2005) and *Chasing Vermeer* (Balliett, 2005), dealing with science and mathematics issues, and a host of other young adult works offer a rich array of choices to expand students' understanding of content area concepts, particularly in the core subject areas of English, history, mathematics, and science. Locating useful booklists by topic and theme is relatively easy with online support, and we offer a selected list of tradebooks by content area at the close of this chapter to help you get started.

Creating a Classroom Library

Tradebooks must survive on the open market. These are the books you find at popular bookstores, where there is usually a section on young adult literature. Since there is no perfect list of tradebooks to be used with every content area, as a teacher you need to explore books keyed to your area and develop a classroom library (Nilsen & Donelson, 2005). Given the labor intensive requirements of creating a classroom library, we suggest you start small by getting to know one or two contemporary young adult novels that relate to one or two topics in your content teaching. We include an annotated bibliography of tradebooks keyed to various content areas at the end of the chapter, but it is important to realize that the list is one we created. You need to develop your own unique collection of novels, magazines, and enjoyable reading material that expands on textbook and class concepts. For example, some authorities on using literature in classrooms recommend creating book clusters (Savage, 1994). A book cluster is a graphic organizer with the title of a unit like sharks and a listing of tradebooks that relate to the unit. Often, the school librarian and/or media specialist can be helpful in suggesting books to use with your proposed unit. In addition, websites like the one offered by the American Library Association as well as international sites can be helpful.

Multicultural Literature

One of the most exciting dimensions of young adult literature is the growing number of multicultural books portraying characters' experiences from a bicultural perspective. Books about African Americans, Asian Americans, Native Americans, Hispanics, Pacific Islanders, and the disabled fit within this category. The best of this body of literature affords an opportunity for students to see themselves in the books they read, provided the multicultural literature selected portrays characters in a culturally authentic fashion.

For example, one of Soto's novels, *Buried Onions* (Soto, 1997) charts the struggles of Eddie at 19, trying to find a way out of his Fresno Barrio. Throughout the novel, Eddie faces ethical dilemmas that form the basis for powerful classroom discussion and writing (Bean & Rigoni, 2000). We have used this novel in high school social studies to engage students in journaling with university graduate students about how they would handle Eddie's problems with his relatives and the police. The novel lends itself to social studies classrooms and issues of citizenship and social justice. In addition, guidance classes might center discussion on the gang issues dealt with in the novel. The writing is lyrical and peppered with Spanish phrases. Consistent with many other Soto novels, this one includes a glossary of Spanish terms.

In a sequel to *Buried Onions* entitled *The Afterlife* (Soto, 2003) Chuy, Eddie's cousin in *Buried Onions,* is murdered early in the novel at a high school dance, leaving him to wander Fresno as a ghost. This novel and others offer sites for exploring the social construction of adolescents, often treated as invisible in larger society (Bean & Harper, 2004). Multicultural literature is typically outside the accepted canon of traditional required reading that includes books such as *The Scarlet Letter* and Shakespeare's writing. Yet, all students "have the right to see themselves in what and how we teach" (Gray, 2003, p. 82). Heriberto Godina (1996) recounted his struggles as a teacher to establish a multicultural literature strand at his middle school. He was able, through the use of his own funds and a desire to move beyond one-shot multicultural food days, to engage students in his English classes in the reading and discussion of Rudolfo Anaya's (1972) *Bless Me Ultima.* "Students began to see reflections of themselves in text, and this provided them with a familiar path for thinking critically and scaffolded their writing" (p. 546). Godina makes a persuasive argument for integrating classical, widely accepted canonical literature, and multicultural literature.

In a very powerful classroom project in Corpus Christi, Texas, aimed at integrating multicultural literature and community talents, Brozo, Valerio, and Salazar (1996) also used *Bless Me Ultima* as a basis for exploring cross-cultural approaches to healing. By using take home learning packets that involved making herbal tea, they were able to bring parents into the novel reading and discussion. This community connection made the novel's setting in south Texas come alive for students and families.

As Godina (1996) and Brozo et al. (1996) found, when students see themselves reflected in their reading, they view the content classroom as a place of direct relevance to their lives. Reading at the secondary level, as it has so often been described in literacy autobiographies, is no longer work or a task to complete. Rather, reading has powerful, personal meaning for adolescents' identity development.

Nieto (2003) argues that, to effectively use multicultural literature in the classroom, teachers must become multicultural themselves. The best of multicultural literature confronts racism, bias, and oppression head on. Thus, social issues are a good starting point for selecting multicultural literature. Students from diverse cultures gain pride in their ethnic origins when they see a character overcome obstacles to succeed. They gain a complex view of American and world societies and issues of social justice.

What constitutes good multicultural literature? A number of writers have wrestled with this issue. You should try to select books that sensitively and accurately depict characters. For example, in Asian-Pacific young adult literature, authors should go beyond stereotypes, avoid historical distortions or omissions, avoid the "super minority" view, and reflect the changing status of women (Aoki, 1993, p. 122). Additionally, young adult literature should shun tokenism where characters from divergent cultures are mere window dressing in a story (Stover & Tway, 1992). These novels should give the reader an honest, accurate portrayal of the human condition experienced by students from various cultures. For example, Linda Crew's (1989) *Children of the River* follows a young girl named Sundara as she escapes her war-torn home in Cambodia in 1975 to journey to Oregon. She encounters the subtle prejudice of the time in the local high school where she falls in love with the school's football star. She grapples with her parents' beliefs and the bicultural upheaval experienced by many students in secondary schools. This type of historical fiction helps personalize history for students, and it helps them see the cause and effect structure of history. In contrast, textbooks present a profusion of objectively documented facts that lose the flavor of the human experience. The best young adult literature is historically accurate, but human drama is at the forefront rather than places and dates.

Once you have browsed sources of young adult and multicultural young adult literature, found some that relates to topics in your discipline, and taken the time to read a few books, how can you make these books an integral part of your classroom teaching? In the section that follows we offer a few ideas for using literature across the various content fields.

Using Tradebooks

Tradebooks offer one of the best ways to delve into other cultures or to see how other people cope with the problems inherent in being a young adult. A good novel can illuminate otherwise dull facts in history, science, mathematics, and the elective fields of art, music, physical education, health, agriculture, industrial arts, and a variety of other curricular areas. You really can't afford not to tap this rich resource in your content teaching (Baldwin & Leavell, 2007). The chance to influence students' lifelong love of reading as well as the potential to improve their concept understanding and critical reading in your subject is too important a task to leave exclusively to the adopted textbook. And, the evidence in support of tradebooks in improving content learning is substantial and growing. For example, students in sixth grade learning about China through a literature-based approach significantly outpaced a group of their peers engaged in textbook study of China on an 88-item concept acquisition test (Guzzetti, Kowalinski, & McGowan, 1992).

Nonfiction tradebooks can be used to explore text-based topics and as a means to engage students in synthesizing ideas from diverse sources. The librarian is key to locating a good collection of nonfiction tradebooks to support any unit you are working on. In addition, local district resources and the Internet offer resources students can learn to explore independently. For example, in a recent literature response project, 9th-grade students in English visited the Las Vegas Indian Center and consulted the Internet to learn more about Navajo burial practices. They then used this information to critique and write about the authenticity of Navajo burial traditions described in a novel they were reading and discussing (Bean, Valerio, Money Senior, & White, 1999). Additionally, contemporary young adult literature like Joseph Bruchac's (2006) *Geronimo* treats the capture and imprisonment of the Apache from an insider's point of view that counters earlier accounts viewing Native Americans as savages. Powerful young adult novels like this one can be integrated with content area classes in social studies to give your students a more in depth understanding of history.

Nonfiction tradebooks and Internet resources are often informative, visually attractive, lively, and up-to-date. Although students may be unaccustomed to reading across multiple sources, taking notes, and synthesizing information, they are unlikely to learn these crucial skills without practice. Indeed, as they move into college and work, these will prove to be essential skills for success. Palmer and Stewart (1997) emphasize the need for teacher guidance in how to read, retrieve, and restructure information in nonfiction tradebooks and other sources.

Reading Aloud to Students

Most contemporary young adult novels lend themselves to reading aloud (Albright, 2002; Serafini & Giorgis, 2003). For example, Marie Lee's (1997) novel, *Necessary Roughness,* follows main character, Chan Kim, from a cohesive, Korean American community in Los Angeles to a new school in rural Minnesota. Chan plays football and endures overt and sometimes violent discrimination from his teammates and others. The novel should be preceded by a cultural history of Korean immigration patterns to the United States because Chan's Dad in the novel represents the old world and its norms. Chan tries hard to assimilate, caught between his father's old ways and his teammates' rancor. Marie Lee's writing flows and the novel's vivid scenes and surprise ending generate vibrant classroom discussion.

Short story collections also offer excellent narratives for reading aloud. For example, Donald Gallo's (2004) *First Crossings: Stories about Teen Immigrants* can be read aloud and serve as a springboard to students' recounting, in writing or multimedia, their own experiences with immigration or a move to a new home and school. In addition, non-fiction accounts of adolescents living in war zones like *Thura's Diary* (Al-Windawi, 2004) provide an adolescent insider's look at life in the Middle East. These shorter collections are ideal for reading aloud, but novels can also be sub-divided into read aloud sections.

We recommend starting modestly by identifying a unit where you can include a young adult tradebook novel of about 125 pages. In selecting a novel to read aloud, look for books that have rich, lyrical language. For example, in a unit on slavery, Mary Lyons' (1992) *Letters from a Slave Girl: The Story of Harriet Jacobs,* takes place in 1861 and vividly recounts Harriet's 7 years of confinement in a relative's storeroom before gaining her freedom. The autobiographical letters that formed the basis for this story accurately portray the dialect of the time. At 158 pages, *Letters from a Slave Girl: The Story of Harriet Jacobs* is an ideal read aloud book.

Read the novel once and then skim through it to identify prediction points and places where you can stop reading at the end of a class period. Allow about 10 minutes at the end of a period to read from the novel and build on concepts introduced in the text and other class activities. With some young adult literature, videos can be located to further illuminate events of the time in compelling human terms. We recommend practicing your read aloud with a cassette recorder to ensure you are likely to capture students' attention. In addition, using prediction questions like "What do you predict will happen to Harriet? Will she gain her freedom?" Or, experience-based questions like "What would you do if you were Harriet?" involve students in the story plot and upcoming events. With some novels you can omit passages that you feel do not move the story forward.

Sustained Silent Reading (SSR)

Bard College literature professor and writer, Chinua Achebe, is a Nigerian Ibo villager and is now one of the most influential African intellectuals of our time

(Winkler, 1994). The headmaster of his secondary school in Nigeria had a rule that after class, three days-per-week, students closed their textbooks and read novels, poetry, or anything for pleasure. Achebe attributed his love for literature to this period of his life. However, he did not see himself or other Africans portrayed in the stories he read, so he set out to become a writer. His first novel, *Things Fall Apart* (1958), has been translated into over 50 languages.

Sustained Silent Reading is a systematic program that establishes regular reading times for students. Its fundamental objective is to provide students with an opportunity to practice their reading skills using pleasurable content-related materials. Sustained Silent Reading has the potential to immerse students in pleasurable reading where they achieve what psychologist Csikszentmihalyi (2002) calls flow. In a state of flow, reading is spontaneous and effortless with the reader unaware of time passing. SSR has a positive impact on students' attitudes toward reading and their long-term interest in reading for pleasure.

There are two separate phases in SSR: (a) instructional readiness, and (b) the reading activity itself. The books can be selected to match a content unit like the slavery example in the read aloud section discussed previously, or books may be self-selected by students if you have a well-stocked classroom library or helpful librarian.

INSTRUCTIONAL READINESS. Discuss SSR with students. Let them know how the activity will be carried out and why they are doing it. Emphasize that SSR is supposed to be a pleasurable activity. Tell them that they will not be graded or asked comprehension questions over what they read. It is important to ensure that students are actually reading during SSR and not simply napping with their eyes open. In an action research study at one urban high school, Fisher (2004) and colleagues observed and charted the fact that fewer than 33 percent of the students participating in the SSR period were actually reading. As a solution to this problem, students in video classes developed a powerful commercial showing how SSR should look in practice. In addition, teachers engaged in professional development sessions to improve the success rate of SSR in their school and a funded grant helped with purchasing contemporary young adult books like *Monster* (Myers, 1999). Following these changes to the program, follow-up data revealed that 88 percent of the students were actually reading during SSR.

Textbooks are seldom selected for pleasure reading, and comics, magazines, and newspapers lend themselves to picture looking rather than reading. If you plan to use SSR to further expand students' understanding of events in history, science, or mathematics units, then you will need a well-stocked collection of young adult novels from which students can select. Your guidance in this area will be crucial as students often have no idea what books match their interests within a content area like science or history. An interest inventory and your own familiarity with literature related to your field will be important preparatory steps before launching into SSR.

Guidelines to help students actively link new knowledge to existing knowledge.

Once you have completed the instructional readiness stage, engage students in the activity of Sustained Silent Reading.

1. Everyone must read, and this includes the teacher. SSR is not a ministudy period for students, and it is not a break or prep period for teachers. Doing homework, getting coffee, grading papers, and other extraneous activities are put aside to allow time for pleasure reading. It is essential that the teacher model SSR by reading right along with students.

2. SSR should be uninterrupted. *Let students know that they are not to sharpen pencils, gossip, or ask questions like "Ms._____, what's this word mean?" In addition, colleagues should know that they are not to disturb a class during SSR. It may be worthwhile to hang a sign on the door: "SSR IN PROGRESS. DO NOT DISTURB!"*

3. The SSR period *should be set at the beginning of the year to ensure the activity is accomplished. SSR has a settling effect on a class. Ideally, SSR should occur on a regularly scheduled basis. We strongly encourage SSR as often as it is realistically possible in your classroom.*

4. The time limits *for SSR will need to vary according to the age and general maturity of the class. We recommend beginning with five minutes and then gradually increasing the time as students adjust to the routine and develop a capacity to attend to reading for more than brief periods of time. Be careful not to increase the time too quickly, perhaps a minute every week or two. Each teacher should judge the amount of time to be allocated to SSR based upon student abilities and curricular demands.*

    The benefits that can be gained from reading pleasurable content-related material will enrich your instruction, particularly if students are reading material related to the topic under discussion. It is suggested that coupling the findings of the interest inventory previously administered with the time to read those materials during SSR in your classroom will be most beneficial and rewarding for future learning of subject matter material.

5. Time SSR with care. *We suggest using a kitchen timer placed on your desk and facing away from the students so they won't stare at it. For the same reason, wall clocks make bad timing devices as some students become clock-watchers. Avoid using your wristwatch since that encourages students to ask you about time remaining. Simply tell them that the kitchen timer will always indicate when SSR is over for the day.*

6. Avoid doing SSR immediately prior to tests *since it will be difficult—maybe even painful—for students to concentrate knowing that a quiz or test is imminent. On test days, shift SSR to some later part of the class period.*

7. Problem students *can be handled in the following manner. You may have some students whose aversion to reading is so profound that they will refuse, initially, to participate in SSR. The very idea of reading for fun will be totally foreign to some students. Do not badger or pressure them. You can force people to do something, but you can't make them like it. Let problem students "sleep," just as long as they don't bother the group. As these students see others enjoying SSR, they should come to find reading preferable to inactivity.*

    Let the class know that intentional disruption will result in termination of SSR for the day. If a student does something that causes half the class to stop reading, simply say: "I'm sorry, but our SSR is over for today. Put your books away and begin _____." Move right along to the next scheduled activity without acknowledging the culprits or their actions. Because SSR is inherently pleasurable, peer pressure should serve to reduce individual disruptions.

Literature Response Journals and Other Response Strategies

Both reading aloud to students and SSR lend themselves to some follow-up dialogue about the book or books being read. Indeed, students generally want to discuss powerful literature, and this is a good opportunity to build on content learning. *Literature response journals* ask students to reflect on their reading and share these reflections with the teacher, peers, or parents for further written dialogue (Bean, 2002). You can give students a few minutes after SSR or reading aloud to write in their journals about how they might handle the situation the main character is in or what they predict will happen next. We recommend collecting journals and responding to them for extra student points. You can collect a few journals each time or collect all of them depending on the schedule you establish with students.

In addition to journal writing about tradebook selections, you can organize a panel discussion or debate that asks students to take a position the main character in a novel might advocate or oppose. For example, in *Saturnalia* (Fleischman, 1990) William, the main character, has a chance to flee Boston with his Narraganset Indian uncle. Students can debate the plusses and minuses of William's ultimate decision in a society that took indentured servitude for granted.

Using overlapping Venn diagrams, you can compare and contrast cultural mores in multicultural literature. For example, in Crew's (1989) *Children of the River,* Sundara, a Cambodian teenager, struggles with the old ways of her relatives and the contrasting brashness of her Oregon classmates. A Venn diagram (Figure 7.4) consisting of two overlapping circles can be used to discuss those cultural norms that are distinct to Cambodian and European American cultures and those norms that seem to overlap.

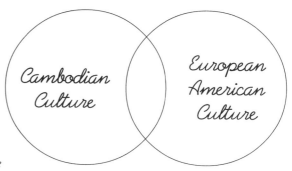

Figure 7.4
Venn Diagram for *Children of the River*

Art, role-playing, music, and drama offer additional ways of responding to literature. For example, Miller (1993) had a group of at-risk adolescent females read four novels that exemplified strong women characters. Based on their reading of Walker's (1983) widely known novel, *The Color Purple,* these students created drawings of the main character, Celie, at the beginning of the book and, again, as a stronger person at the end of the book. Or, a strategy like Talking Drawings, introduced in Chapter 6, can be used to create before and after reading drawings about a novel or its characters.

Students engaged in reading international multicultural literature like Gwynne's (2000) Australian-based aboriginal novel, *Nukkin ya,* can e-mail students in an Australian site to gain an insider's understanding of the sociocultural issues explored in international multicultural novels (Bean & Moni, 2003). Novel e-mail discussions offer a venue for production exploration of key events in a novel (Love, 2002). Or, as a contemporary alternative to writing, they can make a video with one student interviewing another or a panel of students about the book just read.

Finally, students can write authentic book reviews for online sites like Amazon.com or blogs that can be shared with other adolescent readers. These sites offer real audiences for student writing, and they see their work in venues that generate a significant number of hits by a large readership. Someone once said "a book report is the penalty for reading a book." But authentic book reviews serve a real purpose and provide an audience that goes beyond the teacher as sole audience and judge. In addition to the response modes mentioned, a host of other responses to literature can enliven content area classrooms.

Book Clubs

Book Clubs in content classrooms offer another way to engage students in reading and sharing their interpretations of fiction and nonfiction tradebooks. Book clubs involve small groups of 3–5 students gathering to discuss a common reading (Gray, 2003; McMahon & Raphael, 1997). This sharing helps clarify areas of confusion in reading a novel or other selection, and it offers a good forum for collectively creating interpretations, critiques, and ownership of ideas.

Book clubs can be used in content fields like social studies to expand students' learning. For example, studying World War II through novels that view events from a Japanese perspective helps students evaluate textbook accounts critically.

In addition, guided reading across multiple sources helps students learn how to synthesize information.

In a book club discussion in one of our classes, students enrolled in a content area literacy course read David Klass's award winning novel, *California Blue* (Klass, 1994). John, a high school student and the main character, finds a special butterfly while jogging in the woods in a logging area of Northern California. It turns out the butterfly is endangered and the livelihood of the town is about to be threatened because of John's discovery. About halfway through the novel, John longs to tell his Dad about his discovery but realizes there is great risk involved as his family also earns their living through logging. He feels very alone and decides to keep his discovery to himself, ultimately sharing it with his biology teacher and others he decides to trust. In order to prepare for book club discussion of this and other key episodes in the novel, students kept reading logs. Open-ended prompt questions helped students jog their thinking and writing about these episodes. For example, in this episode, students were asked to write and talk about how they would handle the situation where John wants to tell his Dad about his discovery the next day at breakfast. This prompt question generated a wide array of responses and personal stories about family styles. Some students said they would be secretive because of severe consequences in their families, and others indicated they would take the risk of being restricted or worse to stand for their beliefs. This particular novel is ideal for exploring a range of science and social science issues, particularly issues of citizenship and decision making.

A host of new novels emerge each year that you can use to expand students' grasp of content area topics. For example, in a biology class considering the topic of infectious diseases, the young adult novel *Code Orange* (Cooney, 2005) offers a suspenseful look at a potentially fatal virus that could wipe out the entire population of New York City. Roland Smith's (2005) novel, *Cryptid Hunters,* takes the reader on a fast-paced journey to the Congo. The novel is based on cryptozoology involving the search for and study of mysterious and sometimes mythical animals such as Sasquatch and the Loch Ness monster. Similarly, Nancy Werlin's (2004) award winning mystery, *Double Helix,* capitalizes on students' interest in CSI and other crime detection television series. Your media specialist and librarian can help you create a print-rich environment in your particular content area that is likely to increase students' interest and engagement in both fiction and nonfiction selections.

When you decide to implement book clubs in your classroom, take some time to learn more about other teachers' experiences with this exciting addition to a content classroom. In the recommended reading section for this chapter, we offer selections to help you get started.

Novel Journal

The *Novel Journal* (Benedicty, 1995) engages students in writing about their reactions to a novel within a 7- or 10-week unit structure. Students write in their journals on a regular basis in response to events in the novel they are reading as a group. The reading schedules for the unit are included at the front of the journal, followed by a menu of essay questions for the final written in-class essay exam. Thus, students have a preview of the final performance task. Questions usually center on themes (e.g., belonging, loneliness) and ask students to compare how various characters cope with the events in their lives. For example, in many young adult novels, identity development is a recurring theme that lends itself to a series of questions which could guide novel journal entries. In addition, the novel journal can feature drawings, vocabulary development, examples of metaphors and their interpretation (e.g., the significance of "buried onions" in Soto's 1997 novel by the same name), rap lyrics, and a host of other creative responses.

Readers Theater

Readers Theater involves a presentation of material that is read aloud in an expressive and dramatic fashion by two or more readers (Young & Vardell, 1993). Readers theater offers students oral reading and group presentation practice and a chance to review concepts so they can effectively deliver a performance. To engage students in readers theater you need to:

a. select passages from a novel that move the story forward;
b. reproduce these sections;
c. delete non-critical lines;
d. divide the parts for each student to deliver;
e. label reader parts with students' names; and,
f. model the process of reading aloud in a dramatic fashion.

APPLICATION 7.3

The CD-ROM includes the complete text of Jack London's *The Call of the Wild*. Use the novel to select passages and practice readers theater.

Dinner Party

Dinner Party is based on the idea that you could invite characters from a young adult novel (or other forms of text, including nonfiction) to your home for dinner and conversation (Vogt, 2002). The purpose of dinner party is for students to take on the role of specific characters in response to prompt questions you develop. Dinner party is a postreading strategy and assumes students have read the novel or at least the section being discussed. In addition, dinner party, consistent with contemporary theories of critical literacy, offers an opportunity for silenced characters in a novel to have a voice. The following steps will be helpful in guiding a dinner party discussion in your classroom:

a. Decide which characters from the novel will be part of a panel discussion. About 5 to 6 characters, including some whose voices were silenced in the novel, will be about right. You may want to have multiple small groups engaged in dinner party discussion.
b. Assign one of the group members the role of moderator.
c. Provide an initial prompt question to get the discussion rolling.
d. Use an excerpt from the novel or an especially conflict-ridden scene to entice students into the discussion.
e. Debrief at the end of the role-playing to illuminate important issues that were revealed in the discussion and any content concepts that were considered.

In the example that follows, an excerpt from Klass's (1996) young adult novel, *Danger Zone* takes up the issue of racism within a U.S. all-star basketball team slated to play in Italy.

Danger Zone

Plot Summary:

Jimmy Doyle, a high school basketball player from a small town in Minnesota, has been selected to play on an American Dream Team slated to compete in Italy. In this scene, he has just completed his first scrimmage with the team. This illustration of Dinner Party involves three major players. Two students volunteer to play Jimmy and Augustus LeMay, an African American player from South Central Los Angeles. Both players are interviewed by a third volunteer playing the role of the team coach.

The key to the conflict in the novel is the fact that both Jimmy and Augustus carry misconceptions about each other. Jimmy thinks Augustus is lucky to live in Los Angeles with its warm climate and beaches. In actuality, Augustus grew up in a tough neighborhood where his Dad was killed. Moreover, Jimmy replaced Augustus's cousin Devonne after a team infraction, further aggravating the tension between them. Augustus views Jimmy as a rich white kid, but Jimmy is from a poor family, and his Dad died of a heart attack shortly before the team selection, leaving his Mom in difficult financial shape. These layers of truth emerge as the novel unfolds.

Excerpt from the novel (Klass, 1996, p. 67):

Augustus (referring to his cousin, Devonne):

They dropped him to put some whitebread on our team. That's you, Mr. Minnesota.

Jimmy:

I am white and I'm from Minnesota. So what? I still don't get it.

Augustus:

It's just that I don't have much patience with the . . . . jive that says a team representing America has to have some rich, blond-haired stiff who wouldn't last five minutes on any playground in this city.

Jimmy:

I lost all control and swung at him. Then he stepped forward and hit me twice, bam, bam, first on the side of the head and then in the stomach. I found myself lying on my back on the gym floor.

Prompt Question:

In the role of the team coach, what would you want to find out about this fight from Jimmy and Augustus? What advice would you give them once they each tell their respective sides of the story?

Dinner party is a highly engaging discussion strategy that often leads students to surprisingly creative dramatic performances. Most importantly, it allows for vibrant follow-up discussion aimed at considering both main character voices as well as those characters who may have had little voice in the novel. For example, Jimmy's Mom supported his joining the all-star team, but her strength and voice were largely silent in the novel. During dinner party, you can include characters to transform these gaps and silences.

In the area of social studies, a vibrant collection of novels can serve to illuminate and enliven discussions of often abstract or taken-for-granted concepts like freedom and democracy (Bean & Harper, 2006; Harper & Bean, 2006), For example, award-winning novels like *The Breadwinner* by Deborah Ellis (2000), set in Afghanistan, chronicle Afghan women's rights amidst Taliban rule. In a United States urban context, Sharon Flake's (2001) *Money Hungry* takes the reader inside a single parent African-American home where the main character, 13-year-old Raspberry, struggles to make ends meet and avoid becoming homeless. Both these novels have sequels and their authors continue to produce additional titles listed in the recommended reading section of the chapter. In addition to creative response strategies like Dinner Party, you can infuse any literature and text discussion with elements of critical literacy examining an array of social justice issues including racism, gay and lesbian issues (Blackburn & Buckley, 2005), and violence (Franzak & Noll, 2006). Critical literacy questions move the reader into a wide angle lens view of characters, social practices, and the non-neutrality of any text (Stevens & Bean, 2007).

Critical Literacy Discussion

Critical Literacy Discussion takes a close look at power relationships among characters in a discussion of a novel. Students are asked to carefully consider who has a voice in the novel and how various characters are positioned and treated by others. Novels are viewed as social constructions subject to multiple interpretations. Thus, the narrative world of a novel can be deconstructed through critical questions about gender, race, and class stereotyping (Bean & Moni, 2003; Stevens & Bean, 2007). In the illustration that follows, we pose some generic critical questions along with an excerpt from an Australian novel, *Deadly Unna?* (Gwynne, 1998), centered on two adjacent but ethnically divided communities, one Aboriginal, the other white. Set in a remote fishing community, Aboriginal students walk from their neighborhood to the local high school in the white fishing community. They excel at the fast-paced Aussie football but, outside of this arena, little cross-cultural interchange occurs. During the course of the novel, an Aboriginal player, Dumby Red, is killed in a pub robbery in the white community. Racial tensions underpin this novel and its sequel, *Nunkin Ya* (Gwynne, 2000), when Gary Black, one of the white Aussie players, falls in love with Dumby Red's sister, Clarence. Their affection for each other begins in Gwynne's first novel, *Deadly Unna?*, and the scene that follows foreshadows some of the tensions that escalate between the two communities as the novel unfolds. The derogatory term for Aboriginal people in the white fishing community where Gary Black lives is "Boongs," and this term marks the beginning of the conflict that escalates in the story.

Excerpt from the novel (Gwynne, 1998, p. 121):

In this scene, Gary Black has left their winning high school team celebration dinner with Clarence, an Aboriginal girl whose brother is Dumby Red, a star player but destined for a violent death later in the novel. They go down to an old shed by the fishing harbor to smoke cigarettes. They sit on opposite seats in the shed, which smells of fish guts, cigarette smoke, and stale beer.

Gary:

> The smell didn't really bother me, but something else did. Right above where Clarence was sitting was some graffiti. BOONGS PISS OFF it said . . . . BOONGS PISS OFF had been there for ages. I wasn't sure if Clarence had seen it; she didn't say anything. Still, I didn't feel comfortable. I hadn't written it, but I hadn't scratched it out either.

Critical Questions:

1. Who has a voice in this discourse? Who does not have a voice?
2. What are the power relationships involved?
3. What race, class, and gender issues are highlighted?
4. What ideologies are operating to shape this discourse?
5. How could this discourse be shaped differently? For example, if you were to rewrite this passage, how would you change it?

Additional questions can be created to further deconstruct critical elements of key sections of a young adult novel, in this case aimed at illuminating social justice issues. Critical literacy moves beyond reader response and the individual to consider larger, societal problems and issues often raised in contemporary young adult fiction.

Body Biographies

Body Biographies involve creating a multimedia interpretation of a character in a novel, short story, or major figure in any content area (Boyd, 2003; Smagorinsky & O'Donnell-Allen, 1998). They can be displayed around the classroom and discussed in a gallery walk where small groups of students explain their illustrations. Following are the steps:

1. Students in small groups place a 7-foot long sheet of butcher paper on the floor and have one student lie down on it. Another student needs to draw an outline of the student's body on the butcher paper.
2. Students in small groups then fill in the body outline with artistic representations of the character's traits, relationships, motivations, and experiences. These can be drawings, clip art, or other multimedia. The body biography should also include relevant quotations and original text about the character. The following details are important to consider in the development of a well-designed body biography and could be included on a rubric for grading this small group work:

   → Placement of the art is important (e.g., the character's heart could feature important relationships).
   → The body biography should help an audience visualize the character's virtues and vices.
   → The effective use of color should help symbolize elements of the character's personality.
   → The effective use of symbols and objects helps capture the character's various dimensions.
   → Poetry can also be used to portray various dimensions of the character.
   → Try to portray contrasting views of the character (e.g., self-view versus how others perceive the character).
   → If the character changes over the course of the story, use text and artwork to show this transformation.

Body biographies offer yet another, creative means for students to explore the complex and often contradictory elements of characters in contemporary young adult fiction. In our experience, this postreading strategy engenders a high degree of engagement and creativity.

Library Power

Good school libraries contain thousands of fascinating novels, biographies, periodicals, and reference works, all waiting to be discovered. The unfortunate thing is that many students never discover the pleasures and satisfactions of the library. You as a content teacher can introduce students to the wealth of the school library. The following guidelines suggest some of the ways you can do this.

→ *Meet the Librarian, Media Specialist, and the Library.* It makes sense that before you can guide students in the uses of the library, you need to familiarize yourself with its organization and resources. Find out what periodicals, reference works, videos, and other media are available for your subject area. Most librarians are anxious to help faculty members identify, catalogue, and order materials.

→ *Library Orientation.* The school librarian or media specialist is an expert in location skills necessary for finding information. Take advantage of those skills by setting up library orientations for groups of students. Even in senior high school, many students will not know how to use the computerized databases to locate books and materials. Some students will not be able to find a work of fiction. The librarian can provide this basic information as well as answer questions about library hours and special rules.

Glimpse into the Classroom

Imagine that you are a high school American history teacher. You want your students to read beyond the class textbook, and you want them to enjoy their outside reading as much as possible. In order to meet this objective you do the following things:

1. You create a list of broad topics from American history, for example, Freedom and Justice.

2. With the help of the librarian, you catalogue the titles in the school library that fit each topic. (Obviously, the difficulty of the task is determined by the size of the library, the number of topics, and the number of books you require for each topic.)

3. Create an interest inventory which reflects the original topics, in this case the U.S. History Interest Inventory cited previously.

4. Administer the inventory to students and then recommend specific titles to individual students on the basis of expressed interest.

The following 10 selected titles reflect the freedom and justice topic on the U.S. History Interest Inventory.

Bruchac, J. (2005). *Pochahontas.* Orlando, FL: Harcourt.

Bruchac, J. (2006). *Geronimo.* New York: Scholastic.

Carlson, L. M. (Ed.). (2005). *Mocassin thunder: American Indian stories for today.* New York: HarperCollins.

Fleischman, P. (1990). *Saturnalia.* New York: HarperCollins.

Houston, J. W., & Huston, J. D. (1973). *Farewell to Manzanar.* New York: Bantam.

Myers, W. D. (1988). *Fallen angels.* New York: Scholastic.

Ryan, P. M. (2000). *Esperanza rising.* New York: Scholastic.

Salisbury, G. (2005). *Eyes of the emperor.* New York: Wendy Lamb.

Taylor, M. D. (1976). *Roll of thunder, hear my cry.* New York: Trumpet Club.

Warner, L. S. (1976). *From slave to abolitionist: The life of William Wells Brown.* New York: Dial.

As recommended earlier in this chapter, perhaps the best way to begin using tradebook novels in your content area is to read one or two young adult novels a year, starting small and building your collection slowly. That way, you will truly have ownership of the books you read aloud to students and recommend they read. Your book discussions will be more informed, and you will be modeling your own interest in young adult literature. Where can you locate tradebooks to use in your content area? And what are some good books in the divergent content areas of science, mathematics, music, social studies, and other content areas? In the section that follows we provide a listing of useful sources as you search for books in your own unit and lesson planning. We also indicate a few books that we have found to be useful in expanding students' knowledge in science, history, mathematics, social studies, and other areas.

Sources of Tradebooks

As a content area teacher in science, social studies, mathematics, English, music, physical education, agriculture, art, and other areas, you may be interested in locating contemporary young adult literature and other tradebooks. The librarian, the Internet, book reviews in journals, teacher conventions, mall bookstores, specialty children's book stores, and publishers' catalogs are some of the possible sources. Keep in mind that there is no substitute for browsing your local bookstore, reading the first few pages of a young adult novel you think might key into your content area, and spending some time reading it. The process of finding just the right book to read aloud, including it in SSR, and integrating it with a unit in your field is labor intensive. Viewing the development of your own bibliography of tradebooks for your content area over the span of 3–5 years is a reasonable goal. Any of the following sources can help you get started.

Sources of Tradebooks

- ⮂ Librarians
- ⮂ Journals
- ⮂ Book Reviews
- ⮂ Teacher Conventions
- ⮂ Mall Bookstores
- ⮂ Specialty Children's Bookstores
- ⮂ Publishers Catalogs
- ⮂ Local Bookstores

JOURNALS.

Young Adult Choices. Each year, the November issue of the *Journal of Adolescent & Adult Literacy* (International Reading Association) publishes an annotated list of recommended books that a team of young adults selected.

The *English Journal,* published by the National Council Teachers of English, also features young adult literature reviews. It is published eight times per year.

ANNOTATED BIBLIOGRAPHIES AND BOOK REVIEWS. Most annotated bibliographies are organized by content area or theme, making it easy to locate books within the topic area you need. These bibliographies are a good starting point, but ultimately, you need to create your own unique bibliography.

ALAN Review. Assembly on Literature for Adolescents, National Council of Teachers of English. Published three times each year.

The American Library Association lists the annual Top 10 Best Books for Young Adults on their website at: *http://www.ala.org/yalsa/booklists/bbya/.*

Internet sources (e.g., *Amazon.com*) also include reviews of novels.

CONVENTIONS AND CATALOGS. Most professional association annual and regional conventions feature a large exhibit hall filled with publishers' displays of books and materials. This is a great place to browse, collect catalogs, and put your name on publishers' mailing lists so you can stay in touch with new books. For example, the annual California Reading Association convention each November features an extensive array of publishers' exhibits with a focus on California's literature initiative. Specialty bookstores display their books and feature a quarterly newsletter with annotations and book ordering information. Other book suppliers have a special emphasis on multicultural books, particularly Asian novels and nonfiction. Publishers like Scholastic in New York have extensive, annotated catalogs and classroom book club order forms.

LOCAL SOURCES. Your local teacher materials and supplies store and the school and public libraries are good places to browse. Local business and philanthropic clubs are usually interested in raising funds to support literacy activities in classrooms. This is an often overlooked source of support. Purchasing a classroom set of books for a unit on endangered species in science may seem prohibitive. But with the help of a small grant from a local philanthropic organization, you can at least get started.

CREATING YOUR OWN BIBLIOGRAPHY. Book lists, catalogs, and journal recommendations of books are convenient, but no substitute for browsing, locating a book you think might key into a unit you teach, and reading it. Table 7.1 includes some of the content areas in which tradebooks can be used to illuminate textbook concepts. Many books are also appropriate for art, music, mathematics, agriculture, industrial arts, foreign language, drama, health, guidance, and physical education. This bibliography is merely a brief listing to get you started on developing your own collection of books and materials.

As a content teacher, with a well-developed knowledge of students' reading attitudes and interests, as well as a working knowledge of young adult literature you can tie to your units, you will make learning in your classroom a rich experience.

Table 7.1

Annotated List of Tradebooks for Content Areas

ENGLISH

Christenbury, L. (1995). *Books for you: An annotated book list for senior high students.* Urbana, IL: National Council of Teachers of English.

Loughery, J. (1993). *First sightings: Contemporary stories of American youth.* New York: Persea. (ISBN 0-89255-187-9). This anthology contains 20 stories selected from a variety of award winning authors.

Mazer, A. (1993). *American street: A multicultural anthology of stories.* New York: Persea. (ISBN 0-89255-191-7). Includes short stories from Native American author Duane Big Eagle and "The No Guitar Blues" by Gary Soto. A wide range of cultures and times are represented in this anthology.

Tannenbaum, J. (2006). *Solid ground.* San Francisco, CA: WritersCorp. Written by adolescent writers based in San Francisco, this edited collection of poetry by urban youth captures life in a vibrant city, 100 years after the great earthquake of 1906.

HISTORY AND GEOGRAPHY

Choi, S. N. (1991). *Year of impossible goodbyes.* New York: Dell. (ISBN 0-440-40759-1). Chronicles the occupation of Korea in 1945 and its impact on one family.

Ellis, D. (2000). *The breadwinner.* Toronto, Canada: Groundwood Books. This novel explores life in Afghanistan through the eyes of a young girl living under Taliban rule.

Fleischman, P. (1990). *Saturnalia.* New York: HarperCollins. (ISBN 006-447089-X). William is a Narraganset Indian in colonial Boston where he must serve as an indentured servant to a printer. It is 1681 and the servants await Saturnalia, a 24-hour respite when servants and masters trade places.

Myers, W. D. (1988). *Fallen angels.* New York: Scholastic. (ISBN 0-59040943-3). The Vietnam War in 1968 through the eyes of a 17-year-old African American soldier from New York.

Naidoo, B. (2000). *The other side of truth.* New York: HarperCollins. Follows a 12-year-old Sade into a forced exile from Nigeria to London following the murder of her mother, caught in the crossfire of an assassination plot aimed at her journalist father for protesting the military government in Lagos, Nigeria.

Ryan, P. (2000). *Esperanza rising.* New York: Scholastic. A young girl's life in a Mexican farm labor camp during the Great Depression is the setting for this novel.

Slade, A. (2001). *Dust.* Toronto, Ontario, Canada: HarperCollins. Canadian prairie life during the Dustbowl forms the backdrop for this young adult fantasy.

(continued)

HISTORY AND GEOGRAPHY *(continued)*

Taylor, M. D. (1976). *Roll of thunder, hear my cry.* New York: Trumpet Club. (ISBN 0-440-84387-1). The Logan family in Mississippi in the 1930s struggle with discrimination, racism, and oppression.

Uchida, Y. (1983). *The best bad thing.* New York: Macmillan. (ISBN 0689-71069-0). Rinko, a Japanese American living in California in the 1930s, experiences prejudice.

Yep, L. (1993). *Dragons's gate.* New York: HarperCollins. This novel chronicles the Chinese workers' experiences while building the transcontinental railroad in brutal physical and psychological conditions.

ART AND MUSIC

Balliett, B. (2005). *Chasing Vermeer.* New York: Scholastic. This young adult novel revolves around an international art scandal and incorporates elements of problem solving overlapping with geometry and the linear quality of Dutch painter Vermeer's art.

Landis, J. D. (1989). *The band never dances.* New York: HarperCollins. The main character is a female drummer who rides the wave of success into the world of rock arenas while simultaneously struggling with her brother's suicide.

PHYSICAL EDUCATION

Cannon, A. E. (1990). *The shadow brothers.* New York: Bantam. Recounts the problems Marcus and his Navajo foster brother Henry experience in high school track and through Henry's growing interest in his Navajo culture, which propels him away from his foster family.

Klass, D. (2002). *Home of the braves.* New York: Farrar, Straus, and Giroux. Chronicles the experiences of a senior high soccer captain, Joe Brickman, and a Brazilian soccer star who transforms the team, resulting in tensions with Lawndale High's football players.

Klass, D. (1996). *Danger zone.* New York: Scholastic. Racial tensions swirl around a star basketball team getting ready to play in Italy. African American player Augustus LeMay and a new player, Jimmy Doyle, clash on and off the court.

Lipsyte, R. (1993). *The chief.* New York: HarperCollins. In this ongoing series, Lipsyte presents an insider's view of the gritty world of boxing.

Myers, W. D. (1996). *Slam!* New York: Scholastic. "Slam" Harris's superb basketball playing offers a way out of New York's inner city, but his grades haunt his dreams.

Zusak, M. (2000). *Fighting Ruben Wolfe.* New York: Scholastic. A strong novel set in the rough world of illegal boxing and betting.

SCIENCE, MATHEMATICS AND TECHNOLOGY

Anderson, L. H. (2002). *Catalyst.* New York: Penguin. This novel features a main character with a strong interest in math and science and a related desire to organize her world based on logic. Needless to say, life intervenes, disrupting her orderly world.

Cooney, C. B. (2005). *Code orange.* New York: Delacorte. The main character in this thriller finds a virus that has the potential to wipeout New York City. Combining suspense, mystery, and allusions to the powerful pull of technology in adolescents' lives, this novel links nicely to problem solving in biology around the topic of infectious diseases.

George, J. C. (1989). *Shark beneath the reef.* New York: HarperCollins. (ISBN 0-06-440308-4). Fourteen-year-old Tomas Torres wants to become a marine biologist and struggles with staying or dropping out of school.

Hobbs, W. (1988). *Changes in latitudes.* New York: Avon. (ISBN 0-38071-619-4). A family vacation in Mexico leads to Teddy's interest in turtles and efforts to protect their welfare as endangered species.

Johansen, K. V. (2006). *The Cassandra virus.* Victoria, BC, Canada: Orca. This short novel deals with computer viruses from the point of view of a bored student over summer vacation. Orca publishes a number of short titles on topics in science (e.g., tornadoes), generally running about 100 to 150 pages.

Klass, D. (1994). *California blue.* New York: Scholastic. John, the main character, discovers the double-edged sword of trying to protect an endangered butterfly in a small logging community.

SOCIAL STUDIES: CULTURAL AND ETHNIC IDENTITY

Al-Windawi, T. (2004). *Thura's diary.* London, England: Penguin. This account chronicles the war in Baghdad from the point-of-view of an Iraqi teenager. Along with young adult novels and other non-fiction accounts of adolescents in war zones, these selections offer powerful insights into the human impact of global conflicts.

Chock, E., Harstad, J. R., Lum, D. H. Y., & Teter, B. (1998). *Growing up local: An anthology of poetry and prose from Hawai'i.* Honolulu, HI: Bamboo Ridge. This collection of short stories and poetry includes the major authors from Hawai'i (e.g., Lois Ann Yamanaka) as well as new teen voices. The writing is true to Hawai'i's local scene with pidgin dialect an integral part of many of the author's voices.

Ellis, D. (2002). *Parvana's journey.* Toronto, Ontario, Canada: Groundwood.

Ellis, D. (2003). *Mud city.* Toronto, Ontario, Canada: Groundwood. Each of these sequels to Ellis's (2000) award winning book, *The Breadwinner,* trace a young adolescent girl's flight from war-torn Afghanistan to the streets of Peshawar, Pakistan. These books and others in this list, set in the Middle East, offer a strong collection of writing to support a unit in world history or cultural geography.

SOCIAL STUDIES: CULTURAL AND ETHNIC IDENTITY (*continued*)

Ellis, D. (2004). *Three wishes: Palistinian and Israeli children speak.* Toronto, Ontario, Canada: Groundwood. Adolescents in the Middle East candidly describe their lives and advance proposals for peace. Much like *Thura's diary* (annotated earlier), this series of young voices provides a compelling, insider's view of war.

Flake, S. (2001). *Money hungry.* New York: Hyperion Paperbacks. Thirteen-year-old African American character Raspberry Hill has lived in a car and project housing. Her fear of becoming homeless drives her entrepreneurial efforts, but she is constantly in trouble with endless schemes to make and keep cash on hand.

Flake, S. (2004). *Begging for change.* New York: Hyperion. This sequel to Sharon Flake's (2001) earlier novel, *Money Hungry,* continues Raspberry's quest for a permanent home for herself and her mom, as well as Raspberry's pursuit of financial security.

Gallo, D. R. (2004). *First crossings: Stories about teen immigrants.* New York: Candlewick Press. Donald Gallo's short story collections always feature engaging accounts to which adolescents can relate.

Hamilton, V. (1993). *Plain city.* New York: Scholastic. Buhlaire Sims slowly forms a positive sense of the good dimensions of her life imparted by her African American mother and long-departed half-Caucasian dad.

Hernandez, I. B. (1992). *Heartbeat drumbeat.* Houston, TX: Arte Publico Press. This novel chronicles Morgana Cruz's search for her identity based on her mother's Navajo traditions and her father's Mexican culture.

Lee, M. (1992). *Finding my voice.* Boston, MA: Houghton Mifflin. A Korean American high school student, Ellen Sung, struggles with violent racism and its impact on her identity in a small Minnesota town.

Lee, M. (1997). *Necessary roughness.* New York: HarperCollins. Chan Kims' family moves in his senior year from a close-knit Los Angeles Korean American community to a rural Minnesota town. Chan begins to play football there amidst prejudice and his father's old world expectations.

McMillen, G. K. (2005). *School for Hawaiian girls.* Sag Harbor, New York: Permanent Press. Spanning the 1920s to the 1980s, this young adult novel recounts the murder and rape of 16-year-old Lydia Kaluhi. A novel of struggle and cultural survival, much like Salisbury's (2005) *Eyes of the Emperor,* it could fit within a United States history course by offering an insider's postcolonial lens of past events.

Myers, W. D. (2000). *Monster.* New York: Scholastic. Sixteen-year-old Steve Harmon's trial in the murder of a convenience store owner during a robbery forms the backdrop for his simultaneously writing a screenplay about the trial and wrestling with the moral dilemmas in his life. This avante-garde novel, written by Walter Dean Myers and illustrated by his son, Chris Myers, moves the young adult novel into a multi-task framework familiar to contemporary teens.

Myers, W. D. (2003). *The beast.* New York: Scholastic. The main characters in this powerful novel represent the varying opportunities available to urban youth, often beset by street pressures to embrace drug addiction. The double-edged sword of community and family loyalty, and the need to form an independent life play out in this story.

Rifa'I, A., & Ainbinder, O. (2003). *We just want to live here.* New York: St. Martin's Griffen. Two 18-year-old girls, one Palestinian and the other Israeli, attend a student exchange program in Switzerland. Following their return to their respective homes, they continued corresponding. The resulting letters, compiled by Middle East correspondent Sylke Temple, provide a strongly human picture of their lives amidst suicide bombings and constant restrictions on their mobility. Along with Thura's diary and Deborah Ellis's trilogy, this book could support a unit in world history or geography.

Soto, G. (1997). *Buried onions.* New York: Scholastic. Nineteen-year-old Eddie drops out of school to work at menial jobs, avoid gang confrontations, and find a way to cope with constant problems in a Fresno barrio.

Soto, G. (2003). *The afterlife.* Orlando, FL: Harcourt. This sequel to Gary Soto's (1997) *Buried Onions* follows Chuy, Eddie's cousin, who was murdered in that novel and returns as a ghost with powers that allow him to take a wide-angle look at his neighborhood, family, and barrio life in Fresno, CA.

Now go back to the literature vignette at the beginning of the chapter. React again to the lesson as you did before. Compare your answers with those you made before you read the chapter.

Mini Projects

1. Interview two adolescent students, one male and one female, to determine: a) what their reading interests are, and, b) to what extent their interests are represented in the classroom by the content area reading they do in school.

2. Administer the BJP attitude survey presented in this chapter to a group of middle or secondary students. Summarize the results.

3. Create a reading interest inventory for your content area.

4. Read one young adult novel related to your content area and share it with another person in your field. Use the novel in a read aloud or SSR fashion within a unit of instruction in your content area.

5. Develop a bibliography of young adult literature for use in your content area. Use Internet resources to research contemporary young adult books.

Website Activity

To locate and complete Chapter 7 activities, go to [*www.kendallhunt.com/contentarealiteracy/*].

8

Vocabulary

Vignette

Setting

Matha Matix's seventh-grade math class, a diverse group of students in a multicultural setting. In her unit on Geometry, Ms. Matix is teaching a lesson on angles.

The Lesson

Ms. Matix begins class by listing the following words on the board: straight, right, obtuse, acute, vertical, corresponding, adjacent, complementary, and supplementary. She then goes back to each word, pronounces it, provides a definition, and gives a pictorial example. Some students are seen to be writing in their notes. She emphasizes to the class that they will be using the words throughout the lesson on angles. Later, as the bell rings, Ms. Matix gives a homework assignment and tells students they will review the vocabulary words the next day as they go over the assignment.

→ Bearing in mind that much of this lesson concerns vocabulary, jot down your thoughts on the following questions:

1. What are the good points about the lesson?
2. What are the weak points about the lesson?
3. What, if anything, would you change about the lesson?

Rationale

Sometimes a mob might "grift" all day without "turning them over," but this is unlikely except in the case of a "jug mob" which takes a limited number of "pokes." Any pick-pocket who has on his person more than one wallet is something of a hazard both to himself and to the mob, for each wallet can count as a separate offense if he should be caught. Therefore, it is safer to have cash only. "Class mobs" usually count the money each time they "skin the pokes," one stall commonly is responsible for all of it, and an accounting in full is made at the end of the day. (Maurer, 1955, p. 194)

All groups of people, whether they be pickpockets, bridge players, or educators, share special idioms and technical terminology which characterize the group. "Insiders" use this vocabulary freely and through it gain access to the collective knowledge of the group. Likewise, "outsiders" are identified as such and are restricted in their social and intellectual intercourse with the group due, in part, to their ignorance of its specialized vocabulary.

The task of the content teacher is to help students become insiders whose minds move with facility in the fields of science, English, social studies, or mathematics. To a large extent, this is accomplished by teaching them the technical terminology of each discipline. The following example, in which one student is explaining a math problem to another student, suggests the gravity of vocabulary acquisition in content areas.

"I don't remember what you call it, but it's like if you have three numbers—5, 9, and 6—and you want to multiply them. It doesn't matter what order you do it in. You always get the same answer, 270."

This student apparently understands the concept of the commutative principle, the process of combining elements in such a manner that the order of multiplication is unimportant. Unfortunately, not knowing the word for this concept limits the student's capacity to utilize it. For instance, one might expect the student's reading or listening comprehension to be seriously impaired, given the following textbook statement, ". . . The commutative principle applies to the preceding series of algebraic equations."

In all content areas, new concepts are sequentially introduced and defined in terms of concepts presented earlier. As students progress through texts, reading comprehension can diminish to the point of extinction if students have failed to master the words that symbolize important concepts, even when they have mastered the concepts themselves! In addition, teaching vocabulary can have a powerful and positive impact on reading comprehension. For this reason, considerable attention to vocabulary is fundamental to the purposes of every classroom teacher.

Learning Objectives

→ Discuss the pros and cons of various decoding strategies.
→ Understand the general principles of vocabulary instruction.
→ Justify direct vocabulary instruction as an essential component in your own content area.
→ Implement a variety of instructional strategies for introducing and reinforcing new vocabulary.

Graphic Organizer

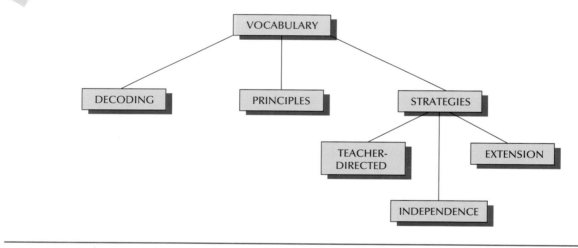

Words

For a variety of technical reasons, the concept of "word" is extremely difficult to define as a unit of language. Curiously, adult language users have little difficulty agreeing whether or not a particular sequence of sounds or symbols is a word. This common sensitivity to the concept of word is a result of defining words as prefabricated units which speakers know are not to be interrupted with linguistic fillers such as "um" or "uh" during speech. For instance, it would be quite natural for a speaker to say "The-workman-um-will-finish-um-Saturday," but not to say, "The-work-um-man-will-fin-um-ish-Saturday."

Words may also be described in terms of semantic relationships; and, since the focus of this chapter is on the meanings of words rather than the sounds of words, the following definition is offered:

A *word* is a pattern of auditory or visual symbols which represent schemata (concepts).

The most important characteristic of this definition is the inclusion of *schemata*, because it suggests that word meanings—for individual persons—are in an endless state of flux. The concepts which words represent are constantly being modified by daily experiences during which: (1) new information is fitted into existing schemata, or (2) radically new or discordant information is accommodated through the modification of schemata.

Consider This ...

For instance, most people have internalized the concept of cat, but do they know all breeds by name? Could they correctly identify the habitats and mating customs of each? Could they name a type of cat which does not have retractable claws? If not, then there is a clear potential for the modification of their cat schema.

The point is that the question of knowing the meaning of a word is not subject to a simple yes or no. There is always a need for qualification because a word is known or unknown, strange or familiar, to some degree which is determined by the richness of its known associations.

Learning a new word (concept) requires more than a simple explanation, because individual words are not simple isolated bits of information. Words are defined by the ways and the extent to which they are related to all other words. For instance, it would be possible to define the concept "anchor" as a device used on a boat or ship to keep the vessel stationary. However, such a definition does little to build an anchor schema that will allow a student to comprehend and use the word at will. A more effective strategy, one that builds a richer schema, might entail the following:

1. demonstrating the variation in sizes and shapes of anchors;
2. letting students touch or try to lift an anchor;
3. explaining how sailors get an anchor in and out of the water;
4. describing how an anchor keeps a ship from drifting; and
5. explaining why it is a good idea to keep boats from drifting.

On a more abstract level, knowing a word requires understanding its connotations as well as its denotations—sometimes referred to as contextual versus definitional knowledge.

→ The *denotation* of a word is its broad meaning; in this sense, old/aged, end/finale, and surface/superficial are synonymous pairs of words.

→ A word's *connotations* are its subtle shades of meaning and the specific contextual conditions in which it can occur.

Connotations are meanings that differentiate among words which would otherwise be considered synonyms. Connotatively, old and aged are not synonyms because they cannot be used in the same contexts. For example, you can talk about "an old rock" but not "an aged rock" because aged connotes "living" as in "an aged woman." In this sense, there are probably few, if any, exact synonyms in English.

Consider This ...

The following four sentences were written by students in a ninth-grade English class. The sentences were constructed as part of an assignment in which the students wrote sentences and then made word substitutions based on an inspection of the classroom thesaurus. The italicized words are those selected from the thesaurus.

1. The dirty old man went to church to ask God for *immunity*.
2. The car had a *putrefaction*.
3. It was clear from her actions that Susan was a fine *madam*.
4. It pays to be a *chivalrous* driver.

Aside from the amusing pictures which some of these sentences paint, what precisely is wrong with them? Denotatively, the words selected from the thesaurus are quite reasonable since pairs like immunity/forgiveness and breakdown/putrefaction are synonymous, or at least closely related in meaning. However, the members of each pair have different connotations that make them unacceptable substitutes in most contexts. For instance, putrefaction connotes a breakdown of a biological nature, and it is anomalous to use the word in reference to something made of such things as steel and rubber.

What we are suggesting is that the acquisition of new word meanings is sufficiently complex that vocabulary instruction should not be consigned to a mindless list of strange words followed by one-line definitions. If it is, the lack of examples and supporting contexts will doom students' understanding of new words to be both superficial and tentative.

Vocabularies

A *vocabulary* is a corpus of many thousands of words and their associated meanings. An individual's vocabulary may be analyzed in several ways. For instance, every person has a *receptive* vocabulary and an *expressive* vocabulary. Receptive refers to words that can be read and comprehended in print or heard and understood in spoken context. Expressive refers to lexical items which a person can use properly when speaking or writing. In a sense, people have four vocabularies: listening, reading, speaking, and writing, and these categories are not mutually inclusive. Children usually begin school with respectable listening and speaking vocabularies but considerably less reading and writing vocabularies. On the other hand, the listening and reading vocabularies of literate adults—and secondary students—far outstrip their speaking and writing vocabularies. This is true because the schemata necessary to place words in proper contexts must be more fully developed than those required for recognizing word meanings when context has already been provided.

Finally, vocabularies may be classified as *technical* or *general*. Technical vocabulary refers to words such as denouement, secant, Bull Market, secede, etc., which are uniquely or usually related to individual academic disciplines. General vocabulary refers to words that are not specifically associated with any one teaching area, e.g., germane, astute, and ubiquitous.

By the time students are intellectually prepared to learn words such as germane or astute, they already possess the concepts which those words symbolize, i.e., significant/relevant and alert/perceptive. Consequently, germane and astute are new, perhaps more efficient, labels for previously acquired concepts. Learning them does not demand a radical modification of existing concepts. In contrast, technical vocabulary present labels for unfamiliar concepts.

Content area teachers are primarily concerned with transmitting novel information and helping students develop new concepts, e.g., Bull Market or secant. For this reason, the focus of the present chapter will be on the teaching of technical vocabulary and a general strategy for independently decoding unfamiliar words.

Decoding Unfamiliar Vocabulary

Decoding is a process whereby a coded message is converted back into thought. For example, a chef reads a waiter's written message about your order and decodes it, that is, comprehends how you want your steak prepared.

The process is similar in content area textbook communication. Authors put down their thoughts in a written form that their readers then decode. When the decoding process breaks down, comprehension suffers. In our opinion the major stumbling block to efficient decoding of text is students' inability to cope with words and concepts that are unfamiliar to them. There are three basic strategies for unlocking the meanings of unfamiliar words in text: *morphemic analysis, context clues*, and *external references*.

Morphemic Analysis

When students encounter long words in print, it is valuable to break such words into more manageable parts. It is well known that a word part may have a meaning of its own. Such a word part is called a morpheme. A *morpheme* is the smallest unit of language which has an associated meaning; i.e., it possesses a definite meaning and cannot be subdivided into smaller units which have meaning. There are two types of morphemes, free and bound.

→ A *free morpheme* can function alone as a word, e.g., "some" or "thing."

→ *Bound morphemes* are those meaningful language units that occur only as attachments to words or other morphemes, e.g., "tele-," "-er," or "-cide." In essence, they are prefixes, suffixes, or roots.

Just as a word may be a symbol that represents a schema in our knowledge structure, so may a word part or morpheme. Additionally, two or more morphemes may combine to give a combination of ideas, thus modifying a schema. For instance, "blue" and "berry," two separate morphemes, may be combined to form a new or modified schema conveying a combination of meanings. Thus, *morphemic analysis* is a process by which readers can determine the meaning of an unfamiliar word by analyzing its component parts.

Attention to word parts to reveal the meanings of unfamiliar words is a process that goes on all the time. For instance, if a reader encounters a word such as "patricide" in a contextual setting, the reader is likely to focus on the morphemes of the word, "patri-" and "-cide" to determine its meaning, particularly if the context is anomalous, or provides no clear interpretation. Such an anomalous context would be:

Robert has committed patricide.

Of course, the reader cannot perform such an analysis if the reader does not have prior knowledge of the two morphemes in patricide. Yet because morphemic analysis focuses on meaning, it provides a more sensible approach to analyzing unfamiliar words than does phonics. Additionally, approximately 80 percent of the words listed in an English dictionary contain words which are composed of Latin or Greek morphemes. Consequently, a knowledge of these roots and affixes can be valuable in analyzing and remembering the meanings of unfamiliar polysyllabic words.

The authors are certainly not arguing that content teachers should have their students master lists of affixes and roots. This procedure is restrictive in that students memorize without meaningful context. Inserting information into long-term memory is best accomplished by making the information interesting and relevant—descriptors that hardly apply to lengthy lists of strange-looking morphemes.

APPLICATION 8.1

Use your knowledge of morphemes to analyze the following unfamiliar polysyllabic word. Try to derive the meaning of it.

PNEUMONOULTRAMICROSCOPICSILICOVOLCANOCONIOSIS

Were you able to arrive at a definition without consulting a dictionary, or did you panic because the word appears ominous? What you have encountered is one of the longest words in the English language, yet one that readily lends itself to morphemic analysis. Perhaps the following context will help you come up with the definition:

Because of his proximity to Mount St. Helens, he contracted pneumonoultramicroscopicsilicovolcanoconiosis.

Using the context clues present in the sentence, in combination with your knowledge of morphemes, probably gave you the definition. The following morphemes are present in the word:

Pneumono—related to the lungs

Ultra—transcending; super

Micro—small

Scopic—related to a viewing instrument

Silico—the mineral, silicon

Volcano—eruption in the earth from which molten rock, steam, and dust issue

Coni (konis)—dust

Osis—referring to a disease condition

Thus, pneumonoultramicroscopicsilicovolcanoconiosis is a disease of the lungs caused by habitual inhalation of very fine silicon dust particles.

In summary, what we are suggesting is that knowledge of morphemes has the potential for transfer to unfamiliar words that possess the same morphemes. Students should be taught to apply their knowledge of word parts to unfamiliar words they encounter. In this way they are encouraged to discover their own generalizations by intelligent inference or informed guessing. For instance, in the word you were asked to analyze in Application 8.1, you may not have extracted the morpheme, "pneumon" and attached meaning to it directly. Rather, you may have associated the morpheme with the word "pneumonia" to arrive at a meaning for it. It is this type of learning process that the authors advocate.

Context Clues

All human experience is context dependent. Indeed, human behavior can hardly be interpreted without context. As an example, consider the question, "Is it OK for me to take my clothes off?" The answer obviously depends upon the context—at a nudist colony, yes; in church, no! Context is, therefore, a necessary and natural part of human functioning. Such is also the case in reading. For instance, if given the sentence, "Jo Ann loves her new red _____," you would be able to supply a word in the blank even though no graphophonic information is present. Additionally, many investigators in reading education have stressed the importance of readers' use of context in interpreting and verifying the meaning of words and sentences to be comprehended. The appropriate use of context leads to more effective processing and overall accuracy in deriving the meaning of unfamiliar words. It is in combination with readers' experiential background that the analysis of context provides meaning to the semantic subtleties of print.

To assess the value of context clues in decoding new vocabulary, we need to examine how context can supply meaning. There are three main types of *context clues:*

A. Definition: The word is defined, usually in the same sentence. For example:
   1. *Uxoricide,* which means to murder one's wife, is the ultimate form of marital abuse.

B. Description: The word is described by the context in such a way that the reader can take a good guess at its meaning. For example:
   2. Their *vociferous* chatter made me wish I had ear plugs.

C. Contrast: The word is compared with some other word or concept, often an opposite. For example:
   3. Mike was *loquacious* while Susan said very little.

Most textbooks rely on context clues when introducing new concepts. Generally, these new words are *italicized*, <u>underlined</u>, or written in **bold print** to call attention to the fact that a new word is being introduced. Typically, the context clue is some form of definition.

It is fairly obvious that context clues work in the sentences above, and students are capable of using such clues when they are presented. The real issue is whether or not sentences such as those in (B) and (C) above occur with sufficient frequency to make context clues a valid strategy for decoding unfamiliar words. Research based on the naturally occurring prose of novels, magazines, and textbooks strongly suggests that context clues are not nearly as useful for decoding unfamiliar words as has traditionally been assumed (Schatz & Baldwin, 1986). Rather, both definitional and contextual information are crucial for learning new vocabulary, along with multiple encounters with new words.

Moreover, context clues only seem to work well in the decoding process when the word in question is redundant with the passage and, therefore, unimportant to the overall meaning of the passage. Since the major purpose of a decoding strategy is to promote comprehension during reading, context clues are less valuable than external references as an independent decoding strategy.

External References

An *external reference* is a source of information that falls outside the passage in which the unfamiliar word occurs. In this sense phonics, context clues, and morphemic analysis are internal sources of information, while textbook aids, dictionaries, and encyclopedias are external.

Textbook Aids

Textbook aids are elements included in the text to help students with new vocabulary. When students come to an unfamiliar word, context clues and morphemic analysis usually will not be enough to decode its meaning. In most cases, references outside the passage must be used to find the meaning of the unknown words. The three most important references are the glossary, index, and dictionary.

GLOSSARY. A *glossary* is an alphabetized list of the technical words used in a textbook. With each word is the definition of the word as it is used in the book. For instance, the glossary in this text is located toward the end of the book. Not all textbooks have glossaries, but those that do usually place the glossary at the back of the book. Sometimes authors put the glossary at the beginning or end of each chapter in the text.

INDEX. When a textbook does not contain a glossary, the index is another good reference for finding word meanings. An *index* is an alphabetized list of important terms and topics included in the text. It is always located at the back of the text. Locate the index for this textbook. The index lists the page numbers in the text where information can be found on each topic. Frequently, the word for which a student is hunting will be defined in context on one of those pages. This is particularly true of technical vocabulary.

DICTIONARY. When students need to find the meaning of a nontechnical word, they should use a dictionary. The standard word dictionary is undoubtedly the most commonly used of all reference tools. Unfortunately, it is also probably one of the most misunderstood and misused. Because the dictionary is used so widely, teachers have a tendency to assume that students know how to use a dictionary. This is a dangerous assumption.

Consider This ...

For example, one of the authors once asked a ninth grader in his English class to look up the word "embroil." After a few minutes he returned to the student's desk only to find her moving her finger laboriously from entry to entry on page four of the As. The student did not know that words in a dictionary are arranged alphabetically! This remarkable incident led the author to discover that half the class did not know what guide words were, and that over half did not know how to use the pronunciation key or choose from among the multiple definitions of a word.

If you want your students to use the dictionary, particularly for verifying the meanings of unfamiliar words in print, it is worth your time to diagnose their familiarity with this important book. The guide words and entry in Figure 8.1 indicate the most common and important features of dictionaries.

Dictionary skills can be assessed informally by asking students to seek out and explain the various features of specific entries in the dictionary. This can easily

Figure 8.1

Features of the Dictionary

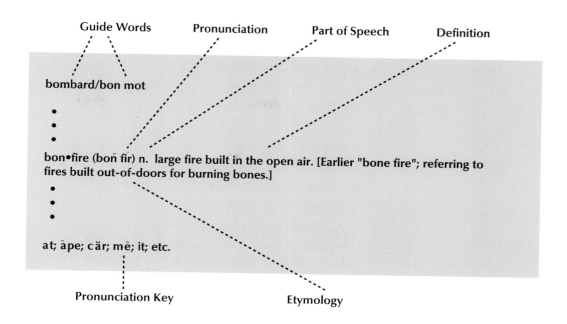

be conducted as a group activity in which students must find an answer and then explain how they arrived at it. For example:

> "Turn to page 253 of your dictionary and figure out how to pronounce the word "___" (e.g., "daguerreotype" is written on the board). Raise your hand when you have the answer, but be prepared to explain to the rest of the class how you got it."

Once you have ascertained which dictionary features students need to practice, discuss them and then provide practice in identifying and interpreting those features. It is, of course, possible to create exercises for students. However, a simpler and more enjoyable activity is for students to compete with each other or with the clock to see how fast they can identify parts of speech, specific guide words, etymologies, and so on.

For those students interested in pursuing the dictionary through the Internet, they are directed to One Look Dictionaries (Available: *www.onelook.com*). This is a website which can search the dictionary world to provide comprehensive definitions of words.

APPLICATION 8.2

Directions: Create an activity for giving middle or secondary students practice in using one or more features of the dictionary.

A General Decoding Strategy for Textbooks

When students encounter an unfamiliar word as they are reading, they should first finish reading the sentence. If they determine the word is crucial for comprehension, we recommend that they rely heavily on external references, following these steps:

1. Decide whether the word is technical or general. When in doubt, assume the word is technical.
2. If the word is technical:
   a. Try the glossary first.
   b. Then try the index.
   c. Then try the dictionary.
3. If the word is general:
   a. Try the dictionary first.
   b. Then try the glossary.
   c. Then try the index.
4. After finding a meaning for the word, check the meaning in the context of the sentence to make sure that the definition fits. This is particularly important when using a dictionary. Context is critical as a verification procedure.

This strategy is recommended as a way for students to deal systematically and independently with unfamiliar words in print. The strategy concentrates on meaning since that is the task of students when they are reading textbook assignments. The strategy also avoids the pitfalls of haphazard or misleading guessing associated with context clues and morphemic analysis. Those who are knowledgeable in a subject area do not need to guess at the meanings of important words; those who are less knowledgeable should not.

Principles for Effective Vocabulary Instruction

If there is one thing which contributes most heavily to the burdens of learning technical vocabulary, it is the simple lack of direct instruction. Teachers frequently assume that students will automatically assimilate new words just because they are introduced in textbook assignments. This is a mistake. While incidental learning of word meanings may occur with narrative, story-type material, even across cultures (Shu, Anderson, & Zhang, 1995), this will, more than likely, not occur with textbook material. Additionally, while textbook publishers may think vocabulary instruction is important, they do little to provide teachers with activities to develop vocabulary beyond word puzzles (Harmon, Hedrick, & Fox, 2000). Consequently, almost any kind of direct instruction you provide is better than none at all. The following principles should be considered in conjunction with the specific teaching strategies presented later in the chapter as well as the information presented about lesson and unit planning in Chapter 6. Additional suggestions and instructional implications for vocabulary development for English Language Learners (ELL) are provided in Butcher and Ramirez (2007).

Be an Enthusiastic Model of Vocabulary Use

Reach out to your students and make them see that you believe vocabulary development is something more than a dead paragraph from your teacher's syllabus. Let them see you using a dictionary once in awhile, and make an effort to use words you expect the students to learn. In addition to exemplifying new terms in appropriate verbal contexts, you will be demonstrating that they have some practical value. Nothing will facilitate the acquisition of vocabulary more than the enthusiasm which you convey to students.

Make Vocabulary Meaningful

Vocabulary instruction should have a long-term impact upon individual powers of communication and concept development. A vocabulary program that encourages students to squeeze the definitions for 20 words into a temporary memory store so that they can pass Friday's quiz is a waste of time. New words and their meanings must be stored in long-term memory if they are to add to the students' powers of perception and articulation. As we pointed out in Chapter 3, placing information in long-term memory is difficult unless the information is meaningful in terms of prior knowledge. Consequently, new words should be:

1. defined in multiple contexts;
2. drawn from reading or other experiences immediately pertinent to the student; and
3. defined in terms and with examples that clearly fall within the boundaries of the students' prior knowledge.

In general, the greater the quantity of meaningful associations that teachers can tie to new words, the greater the likelihood that the students will remember and use them (Cunningham, 2007).

Reinforce Vocabulary

Give students an opportunity to use their new words as they read, write, speak, and listen. There is no substitute for meaningful practice. Drill, practice, and multiple exposures to a new word in various contexts will improve word knowledge and comprehension.

Be Eclectic

There are as many good ways to teach vocabulary as there are creative teachers, and probably no single one is best. However, any method can become boring if it is overused. A successful vocabulary program will employ a variety of methods. Moreover, research indicates that a balanced program emphasizing both contextual and definitional strategies works best (Blachowicz & Fisher, 2000; Graves & Watts-Taffe, 2002).

Teaching new vocabulary prior to reading assignments is a direct application of the *readiness principle*. Readiness refers to the mental state in which an individual is prepared to derive maximum meaning from a learning situation, with a minimum of frustration. Preteaching content area vocabulary is a readiness aid that gives students direction and purpose for reading.

Introducing vocabulary facilitates reading comprehension by reducing the number of unfamiliar words in textbook reading assignments. If new terms are introduced in a meaningful and interesting manner, this will reinforce vocabulary, generate enthusiasm for the reading task, and provide background information that will help students relate what they know to the content of the text. The strategies for introducing vocabulary that follow are adaptable to reading assignments in most content areas.

Troubleshoot reading assignments for the students by identifying important words that are likely to engender confusion as they read. Then introduce those words before they begin their reading assignments. By introducing difficult terminology, the teacher will facilitate the retention of pivotal vocabulary, provide students with critical prior knowledge of the content they are being asked to assimilate, and improve reading comprehension by reducing the number of alien words in the text. In most subject areas, reading assignments introduce so many unfamiliar words that it is impossible to teach all of them.

Tips for selecting words to teach

1. Restrict your selections to words that are critical to comprehending the selection.
2. Choose words that define key concepts.
3. Choose terms that you might include on a test.
4. Choose words that have a new technical meaning in addition to a general, familiar meaning, e.g., "complementary" angles as opposed to "complimentary" actions in social situations.
5. Ignore terms that will be of little or no use once a student has passed the test.
6. Don't spend time reinforcing the meanings of words just because they appear in italics. Words should also meet the criteria in 1–4 above.

Teacher-Directed Strategies

In addition to preteaching strategies, it is also good teaching to reinforce new vocabulary after reading. Reinforcing new vocabulary allows students to review the words that you introduced before reading and words they encountered during reading. In essence, reinforcement makes the words more meaningful to students. The following teacher-directed strategies for introducing and reinforcing vocabulary are adaptable to reading assignments in most content areas and should be modified as necessary to fit the idiosyncratic nature of individual classrooms.

Teacher-Directed Vocabulary Strategies

- ➲ Contextual Redefinition
- ➲ Personal Glossary
- ➲ Graphic Organizers
- ➲ Word Origins
- ➲ Semantic Mapping
- ➲ Clues and Questions

Contextual Redefinition

The authors recommend a strategy described by Tierney and Readence (2005) for its simplicity and ease for content teachers. To illustrate contextual redefinition, define each of the following words using only your own prior knowledge.

1. Carapace _____
2. Nonsectarian _____
3. Insipid _____

Were you able to write a definition without going to a dictionary? If not, read the following sentences and see if they help you with the definition of the words. After you write a definition, check the dictionary for your definition.

1. Without its *carapace,* the turtle would be subject to certain death from its enemies or the elements.
2. Although he was a believer in God, he had a *nonsectarian* attitude toward religion.
3. His teaching lacked spirit. He had presented his lesson in a dull manner, failing to challenge or stimulate the students. The teacher knew he had made an *insipid* presentation.

Did the sentences help you with the meaning of the unknown words? If they did, you were utilizing the surrounding context as clues to the meaning of the words. *Contextual redefinition* is a strategy that introduces new vocabulary in rich contexts that help to define words and facilitate memory by giving the words meaningful associations.

Steps for Contextual Redefinition

1. **Select Unfamiliar Words.** Identify those words that may present trouble to your students and that may be central to understanding the important concepts they will encounter in their reading. Select only a few words to be presented at one time to prevent the lesson from becoming tedious.

2. **Write a Sentence.** An appropriate context for each word should be written with clues to its meaning. The categories of clues discussed earlier should be utilized in the writing of these sentences. In the sample sentences provided, "carapace" could be identified by previous experience, "nonsectarian" by comparison and contrast, and "insipid" by description or mood. If such a context already exists in the text material the students are about to read, it is appropriate to use that in lieu of creating a new context for it.

3. **Present the Words in Isolation.** Using the chalkboard or a transparency, ask students to provide you with a meaning for the unfamiliar word. Some guesses may be off-base or even humorous, but students should be asked to come to a consensus about the best meaning.

4. **Present the Words in a Sentence.** Using the sentence you developed previously, now present the word in context. Again, ask the students to provide a meaning for the unfamiliar word. It is important that students who volunteer definitions defend their guess by providing the rationale for it. In this way poor readers will be able to experience the thinking processes of other students and how they arrive at meaning. In essence, students can act as models for each other.

5. **Dictionary Verification.** A volunteer or volunteers can look up the word in the dictionary to verify the guesses offered by the class. This step also provides students and the teacher an opportunity to examine any morphemes present in the word and how they might help in its verification.

Students gain several benefits from this strategy. First, they realize that trying to identify an unfamiliar word by simply focusing on the word as an isolated element is frustrating, it makes for haphazard guessing, and it probably is not very accurate. They are prompted to develop more reliable methods for determining meaning. Second, students become actively involved in a more profitable process of discovering new words rather than in the rote memorization of them. Finally, the dictionary is cast in its most appropriate role—that of a tool used to verify the meanings of unfamiliar words by selecting the definition that is syntactically and semantically acceptable in a particular context.

Personal Glossary

Having students keep a *Personal Glossary* is a valuable addition to the Context Redefinition strategy (Baldwin, Readence, & Bean, 2004). A personal glossary will aid students' long-term retention of word definitions. The following steps demonstrate how to guide students' development of their own personal glossaries.

Steps for Personal Glossary Development

1. **Introduce the Glossary Format.** While the format for entries in a standard dictionary is comprehensive, it may present more features than are necessary for students' personal glossaries. We recommend the following components for a personal glossary: (a) the word, (b) its definition, and (c) a sentence using the word in context. You may find that the pronunciation of the word, its part of speech, and/or its etymology useful for your students. Introduce the format you want your students to use and show students how their personal glossary should look. For instance, using our previous example, *bonfire*, a personal glossary entry might look like the following:

   bonfire

   Definition: large fire built in the open air.

   Sentence: The football team built a bonfire at its party to celebrate its victory over their main rival.

2. **Direct Students in Its Usage.** Since the personal glossary is used individually by students to help them retain word meanings, tell students to enter those words introduced by you that were difficult for them as well as words they encounter in their own class reading which are problematic. Explain that their glossaries are their responsibility to maintain and that they are important to help them learn and retain key vocabulary words and their meanings, particularly if you use them on a test. Demonstrate that they can use the words to quiz themselves about the definition of the word and how it might be used in a sentence. Emphasize that they can make the words part of their permanent vocabulary through periodic rehearsal of the words' definitions and their use in context.

Graphic Organizers

A *graphic organizer* is a visual aid which defines hierarchical relationships among concepts. It lends itself particularly well to the teaching of technical vocabulary. The graphic organizer may be used in a variety of ways. It may be used as an introductory strategy, as exemplified by the organizers at the beginning of each chapter in this text. Such usage is designed to provide relational guides to the prose that follows them. A graphic organizer may also be used as a postreading technique to reinforce and summarize. Additionally, the graphic organizer is one strategy that can be used in the same lesson to enhance both readiness and recall of material. In all cases, the graphic organizer can be an excellent mechanism for defining related concepts. Certainly, modeling the use of graphic organizers for students will help them see their usefulness.

Steps for Generating Graphic Organizers

1. **Concept Identification.** An analysis of the content is undertaken to identify all new terms and concepts that will be introduced in the reading assignment. Since there will often be a large number of these terms and concepts, it will save time simply to mark them in your own text. The following list was derived from one chapter in a science text dealing with matter and how it is structured.

   Structure of matter   Natural elements
   Elements   Compounds

Metals	Nonmetals
Nucleus	Atoms
Mixtures	Physical combination
Natural elements	Orbits
Particles	Electrons
Protons	Neutrons
Electron shell	Energy levels
Molecule	Electrolysis
Inert gases	
Positive electrical charge	
Negative electrical charge	
Atomic theory of matter	
Law of definite or constant proportions	
Chemical combinations	

2. **Concept Selection.** In order to prevent the organizer from being overly complex, it is critical to prune the initial list until it consists only of superordinate concepts, i.e., those that are most important or most essential to the integrity of the reading selection. The organizer is supposed to supplement the reading assignment, not replace it. Once the list has been reduced, subclassify the remaining terms in an informal outline.

Structure of matter
    Chemical combinations
        Compounds
        Molecules
        Elements

    Natural elements
        Metals
        Nonmetals

    Physical combinations
        Mixtures
            Compounds
            Elements

3. **Diagram Construction.** Arrange the terms in a tree diagram which reflects the structure established in Step 2. (See Figure 8.2.)

4. **Initial Evaluation.** Once you have created the organizer, step back and evaluate it. Does the organizer accurately convey the concepts you wish to teach? If not, massage the diagram until you are satisfied. One of the advantages of the graphic organizer is that it helps teachers to organize and clarify their own purposes. In addition to accuracy, consider the complexity of the diagram. Students can be overwhelmed if the visual display is too complicated. Under such conditions it may be desirable to present the organizer piece-by-piece.

5. **Organizer Presentation.** The physical presentation of the organizer is unimportant. Handouts, a permanent poster, overhead transparency, or chalkboard may be used as the teacher's resources dictate. The time required for the presentation will vary depending upon the complexity of the organizer and the extent to which the concepts in question are unfamiliar to students. Begin the presentation with a general explanation of the purpose of the organizer and an explanation of how a tree diagram works. Talk students through the orga-

Figure 8.2

Graphic Organizer on the Structure of Matter

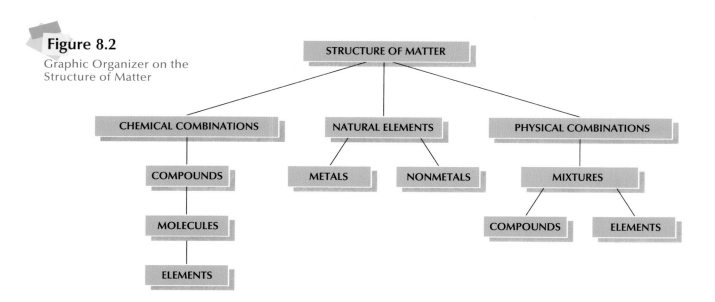

nizer, explaining each term, encouraging student questions and discussion, and indicating the ways in which terms are related to each other. In so doing you will be developing vocabulary, improving reading comprehension, and enriching schemata in ways which will make subject matter more meaningful to students.

APPLICATION 8.3

Directions: Using the following words, create a graphic organizer. Be prepared to justify your arrangement.

Vertebrate	Mammal	Invertebrate
Snake	Grasshopper	Reptile
Cockroach	Crustacean	Aardvark
Animal	Whale	Insect
Lobster	Shrimp	Crocodile

Word Origins (Etymologies)

Introductory strategies for vocabulary will be successful to the extent that they are interesting and build meaningful schemata. Etymologies offer a colorful means of helping students remember word meanings. This is especially true for social studies and English where many relevant words have interesting etymologies.

The *etymology* of a word is its history, where it originated, and how it came to be a part of the language. Language is not a static feature of human behavior; all languages are in a constant state of change. Grammar mutates from one form to another; lexical items become popular and then fall into disuse, e.g., "groovy." The meanings of words change, too. Every word that is now a part of the English language has a past, a present, and a future. Many word histories are quite interesting and can add flavor to an otherwise banal vocabulary lesson.

The etymological portion of a dictionary entry follows the pronunciation guide and part of speech and is enclosed in bold face brackets, although some dictionaries don't include any etymological information at all.

vent	conduit	volcanic bombs
gas	blocks	tsunami
explosions	plug	Krakatoa
pressure	hell	terrifying
plate tectonics	magma	shield volcano

4. Organize the words into a diagram as in Figure 8.3.

Figure 8.3

Semantic Map Using the
Topic Volcano

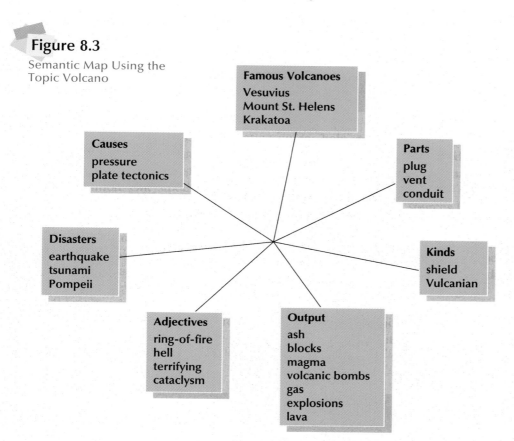

5. Students share words while you write them on the board. As new categories emerge, give the map new arms or add categories of your own. The diagram itself can be as simple or as complex as you desire.

6. Have students give names to the various categories or break categories into subcategories.

Famous Volcanoes
Parts of Volcanoes
Adjectives That Describe Volcanoes
Causes of Volcanoes

Volcanic Output
Related Disasters
Kinds of Volcanoes

7. Perhaps the most important step in this activity is the discussion and questioning activities that accompany the diagram. For example:

a. Why are volcanoes considered disastrous?

b. Which do you think was the all-time most disastrous volcano?

c. Why is "ring-of-fire" a good name?

d. In what ways are Mauna Loa and Vesuvius different? How are they the same?

e. Tell what it would have been like to be on the island of Krakatoa in 1883.

f. "Mark, imagine that you are Krakatoa. Susan, imagine that you are Mount St. Helens. Now, each of you try to convince the other that you are the world's greatest volcano."

APPLICATION 8.5

Directions: Imagine that you have just finished teaching a series of units on human physiology, e.g., parts of the body. Describe how you would conduct an appropriate semantic mapping lesson with your class. Be sure to include the following:

1. 20–30 terms likely to be elicited from students.

2. Probable groups and labels for those terms.

Clues and Questions

This procedure is designed to help students review technical vocabulary. What makes *Clues and Questions* interesting is the fact that students provide the questions as well as the answers.

The teacher begins by collecting content area vocabulary for students to review. Each word is typed on a notecard and placed in a shoebox or card file. Students randomly select several of these cards. Their task is to write questions whose answers are the words on each card.

The teacher encourages the students to use the textbook index to find where their vocabulary words are introduced and used. In addition, the teacher provides examples of different kinds of questions and clues, e.g., definition, analogy, comparison-contrast, context (see the following example on "molecule"). As students finish writing questions, the teacher checks them for clarity and accuracy and then has the student print them on the vocabulary card directly below the word.

When the vocabulary cards have been completed, the class is subdivided into small groups, with each group having a portion of the vocabulary cards. One student shows a card to the others in the group but does not look at the card. Each of the other students asks a question or supplies a clue until the word is identified. The activity proceeds in round robin fashion until the cards have been exhausted, at which point students exchange cards and the clue sessions begin anew.

As a vocabulary builder, the clues and questions procedure has a number of strengths. First, allowing students to create their own questions for a game gives them a novel purpose for using the text. Second, students will benefit from trying to write clear and meaningful questions. And third, participating in the vocabulary review itself will enlarge and reinforce students' technical vocabularies.

Molecule

1. _____ is to compound as atom is to element.

2. What is the smallest unit of a compound which retains all the characteristics of that compound?

3. Two hydrogen atoms and one oxygen atom make one _____ of water.

Strategies for Vocabulary Independence

It is essential that students develop strategies that continue to serve them when they do not have teachers to guide them whenever they encounter a new vocabulary word. In other words, students need to have their own repertoire of strategies to help them learn new words independently. In this section we describe four strategies that are relatively easy for students to learn and use across various content areas. However, as with any learning strategy, students will need to be shown how to apply them when reading and learning with text.

Vocabulary Independence Strategies

- ➲ Verbal and Visual Word Association
- ➲ Vocabulary Self-Collection
- ➲ Word Map
- ➲ TOAST

Verbal and Visual Word Association

Students can use this strategy on their own to learn and retain both general and technical vocabulary. The *verbal and visual word association strategy* we describe here was especially effective for diverse and/or low achieving students (Hopkins & Bean, 1998–1999). In our own work we have found that this strategy can be learned and used effectively, with adaptations, by second language learners in content area classes.

Suppose you are reading along in a novel and you encounter the following passage:

> "Joan had recently taken up jogging. She used to live life in the fast lane—staying out all night dancing and partying till dawn. Now that she was middle-aged, Joan strived for a more *salubrious* lifestyle."

The word "salubrious" is a general vocabulary term not well known by most people. Let's assume you need to learn and remember this word. The following steps of the verbal and visual word association strategy will help you associate the word salubrious with personal experiences.

1. Draw a square with four boxes in it. Write the word salubrious in the top left hand square and its definition in the bottom left hand square (see Figure 8.4). Salubrious, as you may have guessed by now, means healthful. Hence, Joan's jogging suggests she is now leading a salubrious lifestyle.

2. Now in the top right hand square you need to write a personal association for the word salubrious—something you do in your own life that is salubrious. For example, surfing is a healthful activity so you might put that in the upper right hand square.

3. In the bottom right hand square you need to include a word that describes something you do or something you experience that is not salubrious. Thus, smoking, an unhealthful habit, might go here. This verbal association for the word salubrious can then be used to study and retain a personally meaningful conception of the word. In speaking and writing activities, the word salubrious is one you might feel comfortable using.

A student in social studies trying to learn the word "diplomatic" formed the following verbal association in Figure 8.5. His association for someone who is diplomatic was

Figure 8.4

Verbal and Visual Word Association for "Salubrious"

Salubrious	Surfing
Promoting Health	Smoking

Figure 8.5

Verbal and Visual Association for "Diplomatic"

Diplomatic	Franklin D. Roosevelt
Skilled in International Relations	Adolf Hitler

Franklin D. Roosevelt, a successful American diplomat of World War II. This student's non-example, also from World War II—someone who is clearly not a diplomatic person—was Adolf Hitler.

Figure 8.6

Verbal and Visual Association for "Nocturnal"

Nocturnal	
Active at Night	Owl

STRATEGY MODIFICATION. Second language students benefit from a modification of the original verbal association strategy. By including a visual association with the verbal symbol and omitting the non-example, second language students can quickly grasp and learn unfamiliar general and technical vocabulary. For example, the word "nocturnal" can be associated with the drawing of a half moon and stars against a black background (see Figure 8.6). Then, in the lower right hand corner, this student's personal association, "owl," is written to reinforce the idea of a creature that hunts at night. Thus, concept development was enhanced with this strategy modification by providing additional reinforcement rather than the constructive non-example.

The visual and verbal association strategy can be introduced to students easily and, given some guided practice, it should quickly become part of their repertoire of independent strategies for learning new vocabulary. It works best for nouns and descriptive adjectives. Highly technical terms such as "photosynthesis" require the more elaborate conceptual networks that may be formed using a graphic organizer, semantic mapping, or the vocabulary self-collection strategy that follows.

STOP! View the CD-ROM video clip showing the creative products of the verbal and visual word association strategy with middle school students.

Vocabulary Self-Collection

Given the enormous numbers of new words that students encounter in reading assignments, it is not surprising that most students have a difficult time deciding which unfamiliar words to learn. The *vocabulary self-collection* strategy (VSS) (Ruddell & Shearer, 2002) is a vocabulary acquisition technique that is designed to teach students how to select the most important vocabulary from reading assignments. VSS should first be introduced as a postreading group activity.

Guidelines for Vocabulary Self-Collection.
1. *Student teams identify a word or term important for learning content information. The teacher identifies one word or term.*
2. *Teacher writes the words on the chalkboard as teams give definitions from context.*
3. *Class members add any information they can to each definition.*
4. *Teacher and students consult external references, e.g., glossary, index, and dictionary, for definitions that are incomplete or unclear.*
5. *Students and teacher discuss and then narrow the list to a predetermined number of words for a final class list.*
6. *Students record the class list with agreed-upon definitions in notebooks, vocabulary journals, or on notecards.*
7. *Class list words are used in extension activities and class tests.*

Word Map

Once students are proficient at categorizing technical vocabulary through the semantic mapping strategy, they can learn to use word maps to develop ownership of important terminology. Word maps provide students with a procedure for independently studying content area vocabulary (Tierney & Readence, 2005). A *word map* is a visual representation of a definition, displaying three categories of semantic knowledge: (a) the general class or category to which the concept belongs; (b) the primary properties of the concept and how these properties distinguish it from other members of the class; and (c) examples of the concept.

Figure 8.7 demonstrates a student's effort to develop a word map in science class for the word "reptile." Steps to make students independent users of word maps follow:

1. Discuss the word map with students, emphasizing its value as a word study technique.
2. Walk through the incomplete word map, modeling the process with familiar words like "skateboard," "ice cream," "computer," and "sandwich." Have students brainstorm associations for these words as you would in semantic mapping, and then align the associations with category labels.
3. Give students independent guided practice with technical words in a rich sentence context. Then progress to words in less rich contexts that require students to consult another source of information such as a dictionary, glossary, or encyclopedia.

After students have constructed a word map, you may want to add the requirement that they then create a sentence using the word to see if they have, in fact, internalized its meaning and truly own the word in writing and speaking. For example, the student studying reptiles wrote: "Snakes are a reptile most people fear." This sentence demonstrates that the student knows specific examples of reptiles.

Figure 8.7

Word Map for "Reptile"

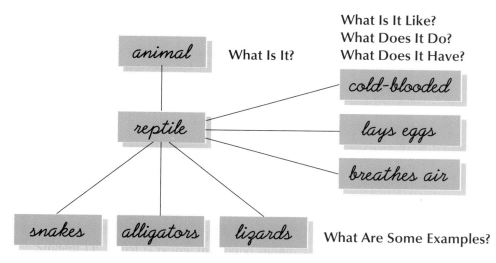

TOAST

A final strategy to help students achieve vocabulary independence is *TOAST*, an acronym which corresponds to the steps in the procedure—*t*est, *o*rganize, *a*nchor, *s*ay, and *t*est. TOAST was developed by Dana and Rodriguez (1992) to provide students with a system for independently studying vocabulary so they can learn at their own rate and focus on the words which seem the most difficult. For many students TOAST represents a viable alternative to the method they themselves use as a means of studying words—which is probably unsystematic at best. Additionally, the strategy is a good rehearsal activity for second language learners. TOAST is comprised of the following steps:

Test
Organize
Anchor
Say
Test

Test   Students first pretest themselves on new vocabulary introduced to them in class; by doing so, they determine which words are already known to them, which ones they are somewhat familiar with, and which require additional study time. Students can make vocabulary cards with the word to be learned on one side and the definition and a sentence with that word on the other side. An alternative is to use a piece of paper folded so a column of words to be learned is on one side and the identifying information is on the larger side of the paper and folded underneath. Students examine each word and attempt to guess the definition and provide a sentence; guesses could be verified by checking the other side of the card or paper. The pretest could be oral, silent, or written. It also may be done with a partner if time and circumstances allow.

Organize   Students organize their words into some framework that will enhance their ability to learn the new vocabulary. They might arrange them into semantically-related groups or place them into categories according to structural similarities. They might also arrange them according to degree of familiarity or unfamiliarity. Some type of organization is important, as it helps students mnemonically and facilitates their learning of the words.

Anchor   Some type of strategy is necessary for students to commit the words to long-term memory. This might entail, but not be limited to: (a) working with a partner to teach and test each other, or even compete with one another; (b) using a tape recorder to tape, listen, and recite definitions and sentences; (c) using timed trials to figure out improvement over a series of trials in writing or reciting the words and their definitions; (d) trying to find another word which would act as a mnemonic link to the target word; or (e) examining the morphemes present in each word.

Say   This step constitutes the review stage of the procedure. To avoid forgetting newly learned words, words must be periodically rehearsed and reviewed. The first review session should occur 5–10 minutes after learning the words; other review sessions can occur later the same day, a week later, and just before the test. Vocabulary that has been forgotten should be relearned using the anchoring strategies from the previous step.

Test   Students need to conduct a posttest after each review to check how well they have learned the words. This test may be conducted in the same way as the pretest.

Extension Activities

Extension activities are pencil and paper exercises designed to reinforce and expand the schemata of newly acquired content area vocabulary. These activities allow students to explore word relationships and, in general, to manipulate and practice new terminology in a variety of ways. Recall and memorization are certainly a part of extension activities; however, these activities should also force students to think about the terms they are learning. The following extension activities are examples of exercises that teachers can use to enhance the acquisition of vocabulary in their own content area classrooms.

Analogies

Word analogies are useful thinking exercises. They require students to draw inferences, and they are an attractive method of exposing subtle word associations. In addition, analogies lend themselves to creative and divergent thinking. A word of caution—analogies can be extremely difficult, especially for students who have never worked with them. Be prepared to provide students with simple analogies which can be used as models for verbalizing relationships. For instance:

> *Night* is to *day* as *big* is to _____
> Large, black, little, simple
> *Verbalization:* Night is the opposite of day, so big must be the opposite of something.
>
> What is the opposite of big? Little.

Analogies are easier to complete if answers are provided; however, that leaves only one correct answer for each analogy. If no answers are provided, the analogies are more difficult, but they allow for divergent answers and interesting discussion. (See Figure 8.8.) The decision should be based on the capabilities of the class.

Pencil and Paper Extension Exercises

- Analogies
- Hidden Word Puzzles
- Matching Definitions to Scrambled Words
- Crossword Puzzles

Figure 8.8
Sample Analogy Activity

Directions: The following analogies are about science vocabulary that we have just studied. Pick the answer you feel makes the most sense.

1. *Gas* is to *liquid* as *liquid* is to _____
2. *Proton* is to *positive* as *electron* is to _____
3. *Atom* is to *element* as _____ is to *compound*
4. *Physical* is to *mixture* as _____ is to *compound*
5. *Hg* is to *mercury* as _____ is to *silver*

Solid	Atomic	Water	Energy	Molecule	Negative
K	S	Chemical	Ag	Salt	

Hidden Word Puzzles

Hidden word puzzles are activities that almost all students will respond to positively. Consequently, they make good motivational devices for vocabulary review. Hidden word puzzles are easy to make, using computer software. A word of caution—always give clues that define the hidden words in some way. If the clues are eliminated, the hidden word puzzle simply becomes an exercise in word recognition rather than an extension activity for vocabulary development.

Matching Definitions to Scrambled Words

This exercise provides straightforward reinforcement for meanings of basic vocabulary. Scrambling the spellings adds an extra challenge and makes the activity more interesting. See Figure 8.9 for an example.

Figure 8.9
Sample Scrambled Words Activity

Directions: Below are two lists. The numbered list on the left is composed of some basic math terms that we have studied. (Notice that the spellings are mixed-up.) The lettered list on the right is composed of definitions for the math terms. Place the letter of each definition on the line next to the appropriate math term.

1. rcleci _____
2. ip _____
3. ets _____
4. toinp _____
5. recpiorclas _____
6. nogatnep _____
7. hcord _____
8. irccumfreence _____
9. daiemtre _____
10. miepr _____

A. A number that has only two whole number factors

B. A line segment with endpoints on a circle

C. A closed curved figure on which every point is an equal distance from a fixed point within the curve

D. 3.14159265

E. Two of these are necessary to determine a line

F. A polygon that has five sides

G. A collection of mathematical elements that have something in common

H. A chord running through the center of a circle

I. Two fractions whose product is 1

J. The perimeter of a circle

Crossword Puzzles

The best way to develop your own puzzles is to use crossword puzzle generator software. Many of these programs offer free demonstration downloads on the web. They allow you to use your own word lists or to tap into their previously set-up dictionaries to develop crossword puzzles. We suggest you consider searching for your own crossword puzzle software on the web. You'll find this can be a lot of fun!

NOW go back to the vocabulary vignette at the beginning of the chapter. React again to the lesson as you did before. Compare your answers with those you made before you read the chapter.

Mini Projects

Using the text chapter on the CD-ROM entitled "The Use and Misuse of Alcohol," do one or all of the following:

1. Choose a teacher-directed vocabulary strategy from Chapter 8 and design an activity appropriate for use in a high school health class.

2. Select a strategy for vocabulary independence and demonstrate how you would use it with students.

3. Develop an extension activity to foster creative and divergent thinking about the key vocabulary related to alcohol.

Website Activity

To locate and complete Chapter 8 activities, go to [*www.kendallhunt.com/contentarealiteracy/*].

Comprehension:
Principles and Integrated Approaches

Vignette

Setting

Jake Spear's ninth-grade literature class. Mr. Spear is in his first teaching job in a diverse urban high school. As the class nears an end, he is about to introduce the next novel the students will read, *Les Miserables* by Victor Hugo.

The Lesson

Mr. Spear: "Today we are about to begin reading our next class novel, *Les Miserables* by Victor Hugo. Does anyone know anything about it?"

Eunsook: "I think it's a play that my parents went to see."

Mr. Spear: "Yes. Anything else?"

Students: Some shuffling of papers and yawning is seen to occur.

Mr. Spear: "Okay. This play is set in France in the 18th century. What do you know about that time?"

Manuel: "Wasn't France involved in a revolution?"

Mr. Spear: "Yes, what else?"

Students: Many heads are bowed and some students seem to be occupied with other things.

Mr. Spear: "Well, I believe we're in for a treat in reading this novel. It is one of my all time favorite works of literature, and I'm sure after reading it you'll think the same!"

Students: Two students are passing notes to one another. Others are seen staring off into space.

Mr. Spear: "I want you to read the first 20 pages of the novel for tomorrow. In reading these pages, I'd like you to think about the answers to some questions I'm going to pass out about your reading. Any questions?" He begins to pass out the questions.

Billy: "When did you say we had to read the pages by?" The bell rings.

→ Keeping in mind what you already know about the comprehension process, jot down your thoughts on the following questions:

1. What are the good points about the lesson?
2. What are the weak points about the lesson?
3. What, if anything, would you change about the lesson?

Rationale

Comprehension of challenging ideas in a content area is rarely easy for students. No collection of textbook aids can substitute for the careful guidance you can provide. Academic literacy ultimately requires the ability to monitor one's comprehension independently. By engaging students in participatory, guided instruction in comprehension, they can move successfully toward independent comprehension strategies. In order to accomplish this in your particular content area, you must have a working knowledge of some basic notions about the comprehension process and an array of strategies at your disposal.

In the next two chapters we will explore the comprehension process. Specifically, in Chapter 10 we will examine various strategies to facilitate the comprehension process before, during, and after reading. The aim of this chapter is to explore some principles of comprehension and how they are linked to the instructional lesson. Then, we describe various strategies and how they are integrated across the lesson.

Learning Objectives

→ Be able to explain the principles of guiding comprehension in a content area.

→ Be able to apply specific integrated strategies in your content area which provide guidance before, during, and after reading.

Graphic Organizer

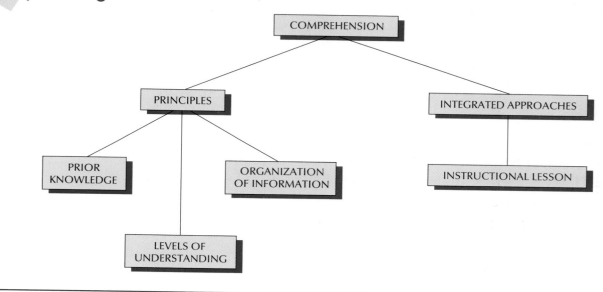

Principles of Comprehension

A comprehensive content area lesson displays an awareness of three psychological principles in the comprehension process. These principles include: (1) the importance of students' prior knowledge in the acquisition of new information; (2) the level of understanding to be achieved in the lesson; and (3) the organization of information to aid long-term retention. Let's examine each of these principles and their respective instructional stages in more detail.

Prior Knowledge

The first principle of comprehending unfamiliar content area material is embodied by students applying what they already know to what they are learning. We have emphasized this point from the very beginning of this text and reinforced it further in our discussion of the reading process in Chapter 3. Through guided in-

Principles of Comprehension

➲ Prior Knowledge
➲ Levels of Understanding
➲ Organization of Information

struction, we can activate, appraise and, if need be, increase students' knowledge of a topic before they begin learning with the text. Teachers can accomplish this task by using a variety of prereading strategies.

Levels of Understanding

The second principle of comprehension emphasizes the fact that content material frequently demands in-depth study beyond the factual, literal level for adequate understanding and application in future lessons. Thus, students must be encouraged to think deeply about what they are learning, as it is a key factor in the retention of information. A content teacher can guide this process during the reading stage by insuring that students adopt an active, self-questioning approach to the text (Taboada & Guthrie, 2006). In order to construct lessons that guide students in the assimilation of factual text concepts with their own experiences, it is helpful to have a procedure for characterizing different levels of understanding. Those levels are *text explicit*, *text implicit*, and *experience-based*. Students should be given every opportunity to reason across this full range of understanding.

These categories, in our opinion, offer the best description of the processes involved in comprehending text at various levels of understanding. This simple framework captures the essence of comprehension—the interaction of prior experience with printed information. In order to gain a more concrete understanding of the three categories, try the following activity.

Levels of Understanding

⊃ Text Explicit
⊃ Text Implicit
⊃ Experience-based

APPLICATION 9.1

Read the paragraph below and answer the questions that follow.

Failing to remember things is a problem that plagues most of us. We forget to perform routine tasks like stopping at a grocery store on the way home or picking up the dry cleaning. Worse still, we may forget important information such as a new student's name. Fortunately, there are some reasonable solutions to our forgetfulness.

Q: 1. What is a problem that plagues most of us?

A:

Q: 2. What specific group or audience is the paragraph addressing?

A:

Q: 3. What are your solutions to the problem posed in the paragraph?

A:

In answering question one from the Application 9.1, What is a problem that plagues most of us?, your response, forgetfulness, was taken directly from the text. In fact, you were able to point to the answer in the paragraph because it was literally stated by the author. Such comprehension is called ***text explicit***.

In question two, What specific group or audience is the paragraph addressing?, you had to engage in a different type of comprehension from question one. Your response did not come explicitly from the text; rather, it had to be inferred from a hint in the passage. The phrase, *new student's name* implies that teachers are the audience being addressed. When you must infer from the text to derive an answer to a question, you are engaging in ***text implicit*** comprehension.

Finally, answering question three, *What are your solutions to the problem posed in the paragraph?*, requires still another form of comprehension. Your response this time was drawn from your previous experience. You had to search your schema for strategies you might use to remember a new student's name. In doing so, you may have responded in a number of different ways, including bizarre associations, where the student sits, and so on. Your inference was not derived from the text, but from your existing schema or knowledge structure. This is called ***experience-based*** comprehension. This type of thinking is at the heart of curiosity, invention, and problem-solving. It is also one of the most neglected forms of questioning in many classrooms.

Explicating Levels of Comprehension

Let's examine each of the three levels of comprehension in depth. We will be examining question and answer relationships, rather than classifying questions in isolation.

TEXT EXPLICIT COMPREHENSION. This involves getting the facts of a passage, as stated by the author. The question asked is based directly on the text, and the answer is explicitly cued by the language of the text. Raphael, Highfield, & Au (2006), in an effort to use language familiar to students, use the phrase, **right there on the page**, to describe text explicit comprehension. Answers are literally found on the page and readers can actually point to the answer. In essence, you are reading the lines. Text explicit comprehension requires you to tell what the author said, and there is usually only one answer. Therefore, answers to such questions have no middle ground—they are either right or wrong.

Text implicit and experience-based comprehension, on the other hand, require you to think about your answers—they are not explicitly stated by the author, and answers may vary depending on each respondent's experiential background. In fact, the less the text is involved and the more experiential background comes into play, the larger the number of possible answers.

TEXT IMPLICIT COMPREHENSION. This involves answering a question derived directly from the language of the text, but also requires the reader to derive an answer when no obvious clues to it are visible in the passage. You are asked to infer what the author meant. Thus, the relationship between the question and the answer is implicit; it necessarily requires some logic to get from the question to the answer. Raphael, Highfield & Au (2006) call this **think and search**. As such, questions that require paraphrases of text information result in text implicit comprehension. In essence, you take the facts presented by the author and add knowledge from your experiential background to derive a reasonable implicit relationship. In other words, you are asked to read between the lines.

EXPERIENCE-BASED COMPREHENSION. This results when a question is asked and the plausible answer is derived almost exclusively from previous knowledge. Thus, the answer cannot be derived directly from the text. In Raphael, Highfield & Au's (2006) words, you are **on your own**. Students draw inferences from previous knowledge; hence, they are involved in reading beyond the lines.

Summarized in Table 9.1 are the distinctions between the three levels of comprehension:

Table 9.1

	INFORMATION SOURCE			# OF POSSIBLE	ALTERNATE
LEVEL	**QUESTION**	**INFERENCE**	**ANSWER**	**ANSWERS**	**DEFINITION**
Text Explicit	Text	No	Text	One	Right on the Page
Text Implicit	Text	Yes	Text	One Plus	Think and Search
Experience-based	Text	Yes	Reader	Many	On Your Own

Table title: **Levels of Comprehension**

Implications Concerning Questions

Questions are one of the most prominent forms of comprehension instruction used. Questions are used to activate students' memory processes of text, focus their attention on significant aspects of text material, and aid them in synthesizing seemingly different parts of text into a coherent whole. Teachers who are good questioners promote the process of comprehension, as well as modeling and scaffolding student self-questioning. However, there are certain considerations you should be aware of when you attempt to use questions effectively.

Use All types of Questions.

1. It takes time and thought to compose good questions. Good questions do not flow like water from a fountain. You need to examine carefully the material you have covered in order to ascertain the best kinds of questions to ask. You possess a wealth of information concerning your subject matter area; students do not. Asking questions that come from your knowledge base, rather than from the text, will do nothing more than confuse and befuddle your students.

2. In asking good questions, be sure not to ask too many text explicit questions. Answers to such questions, though they form the basis for questions at higher levels of comprehension, require little or no thought, do not challenge the student, and do not enhance your role as a facilitator of learning.

3. Asking questions at higher levels of comprehension requires that you give students the freedom to respond. Without this, you may inhibit divergent responses.

4. Be aware that sometimes you may not get the type of comprehension you expect. For example, consider the following sentences:

   > Tom rode through the park at a slow gait, thinking about the day's activities. As Tom daydreamed, she searched the afternoon shadows for a few blades of grass.

   Your intended text implicit question to students might be: What kind of animal is Tom riding? Although most students are likely to respond, horse, a few may say, mare. Thus, at times you may be pleasantly surprised at divergent, high-level responses to a seemingly straightforward question. The student has just processed your question differently to draw the above mentioned inference. The point is that you should be prepared for divergent responses to your expectations.

5. The levels of comprehension model has implications for textbook questions, also. Take care to avoid relying entirely on questions provided by text authors. Such questions are written by experts in their field, and as good as these authors may be, they can't possibly understand your students' special needs. Only you, their teacher, can tailor questions that will involve your particular

students in comprehension at varying levels. Questions so intended by text authors may not accomplish that task.

6. Students can be taught to generate their own questions. If you truly want your students to become active, critical readers of text, you need to become familiar with strategies designed to help them develop a questioning approach to reading (Stevens, 2001; Stevens & Bean, 2007). Helping students adopt this inquisitive stance can boost students' interest in pursuing a topic that may otherwise seem distant from their own personal lives.

7. Though questions are a major means to teach students, the value of statements should not be neglected (Bean, 2000; Tierney & Readence, 2005). It is suggested that using statements at first will help students to recognize information before they are required to produce it through the use of questions. Such statements will simulate comprehension at higher levels of thinking and familiarize students with that process. Once familiarity has been achieved, questions again become an appropriate and valuable way to help students comprehend text material. In the next chapter we will discuss the Anticipation-Reaction Guide, a strategy which exemplifies the value of statements as a means of enhancing students' comprehension.

Organization of Information

The third principle of understanding, organizing for long-term retention of information, is the most often neglected aspect of comprehension instruction. In the postreading phase, ideas are refined and extended. Additionally, this final instructional stage relates directly to how well new information will be understood in a subsequent lesson. The postreading stage of a lesson must involve activities that encourage students to synthesize and organize information.

Specifically, organization of information relates to the ability to perceive an author's *text structure* or organizational pattern. When you alert students to the structure of an author's thoughts, you provide students with a powerful strategy for organizing information in a memorable fashion. Moreover, as you develop strategies to guide students' comprehension, your analysis of a text passage should reveal the author's pattern of organization. With adequate guidance, students can eventually become adept at detecting an author's structure independently.

The following activity (Application 9.2) will give you an idea of your well-developed, largely unconscious use of patterns in your own reading.

APPLICATION 9.2

Read the following sentences. Place them in the proper order of occurrence.

He was well thought of by his peers.

John volunteered for extracurricular activities.

His principal gave him an excellent recommendation for the university doctoral program.

He never missed school unless he was very ill.

John was a conscientious teacher.

Recognizing the structure of prose is a great aid for students in comprehending and recalling text material. Students who can perceive the structure that binds the ideas in text will understand and remember ideas much better than if they are viewed only as separate entities (McGee & Richgels, 2007). In Application 9.2, your recognition of the *cause-effect* pattern should have enabled you to organize the text in its proper sequence. Because John was such a good teacher and did fine things for his school, his principal was only too happy to fulfill his desire. Additionally, with your knowledge of the apparent organizational pattern, you, more than likely, started the sequence with, John was a conscientious teacher, because the other attributes concerning his abilities logically follow that topic sentence. This same knowledge allowed you to place this sentence last: His principal gave him an excellent recommendation for the university doctoral program. In essence, your knowledge about the world and the organization of text allowed you to make logical predictions about the arrangement and sequence of the above sentences. It is this same knowledge that students use, or should be taught to use, with their context textbooks.

Helping your students perceive an author's text structure gives them a valuable independent strategy they can use to comprehend text efficiently. Teaching students to think like authors makes them more aware of text structure patterns which provide a framework for remembering important content. For example, history texts often feature a problem-solution text pattern. Placing this pattern in a visual frame assists students in writing a summary of the major ideas and supporting details highlighted in the passage. Thus, a frame guide in history would include three items: (a) a sentence explaining what the problem is; (b) a second sentence telling what action has been taken to solve the problem; and (c) a third sentence explaining what happened as a result of this action. Students can then develop coherent summaries using information in each section of the frame. Your efforts to help students use text structure in comprehension and recall will reap benefits in their reading and writing.

Text structure serves a dual purpose in print:

1. to help writers communicate their thoughts; and
2. to help readers comprehend what authors are attempting to communicate.

Since reading is an interaction between the thoughts and language of both writers and readers, text structure serves as a convenient vehicle to facilitate this communication.

There is an obvious connection in communication between authors and readers. It certainly cannot be denied that authors attempt to communicate their thoughts to readers through structural patterns in text. These patterns are real, and they are visible on the printed page. On the other hand, one also cannot deny that readers attempt to use their logic in thought and reasoning to understand the printed page. The continuous process that readers employ in imposing their own organizational structure to communicate with authors, though not visible, is also very real, as previously discussed in this text. Meaning construction entails active interchange between writers and readers.

Explicating Text Structure

Knowledge of text structure helps to guide students' comprehension of text. While there are many types of patterns of organization in written materials, the following seem to be most prominent:

1. *Cause/Effect:* This pattern links reasons with results. It is characterized by an interaction between at least two ideas or events, one taking an action and another resulting from that action.

   Example: Because it snowed so heavily, the city traffic came to a standstill.

2. *Comparison/Contrast:* Comparison/contrast patterns of organization demonstrate apparent likenesses and differences between two or more things.

   Example: While a lion and a giraffe are both mammals and bear live young, the lion is a carnivore and the giraffe is a herbivore.

3. *Time Order:* Time order is exemplified by a sequential relationship between ideas or events considered in presence of the passage of time.

   Example: In December Scott took a job with a new company. Things went so well with the new job that he soon became a supervisor. Now, because of continued successes, he is vice-president of the firm.

4. *Problem/Solution:* Similar to the cause/effect pattern, this pattern is exemplified by an interaction between at least two factors, one citing a problem and another providing a potential answer to that problem.

   Example: Certain plants need an environment with a constant, moderate temperature and high humidity or they will die. Consequently, a greenhouse is ideal for those plants.

To further help students recognize such patterns, key words or phrases that signal, or cue, a particular text type should be pointed out. Such *signal words* provide mind sets that enhance the perception of text structure and learning from text. See Table 9.2 for examples of signal words. It should be noted that cue words signaling the problem/solution pattern will be similar to those signaling the cause/effect pattern.

Teaching students to be on the lookout for signal words helps with awareness of an author's text structure and improves their recall. In addition, helping students discern signal words and their related text structures gives them a strategy for distinguishing important concepts from unimportant, or even misleading, information in a text passage. Many of the texts students read in a contemporary medium like the Internet are laden with extraneous items that actually detract from the main idea. Students are bombarded with information and need a means of separating the essential concepts in a text from the surrounding noise. Signal words and text

Table 9.2

Signal Words		
CAUSE/EFFECT	**COMPARISON/CONTRAST**	**TIME ORDER**
because	however	on (date)
since	but	not long after
therefore	as well as	now
consequently	on the other hand	before
as a result	not only . . . but also,	after
	either . . . or	

structure knowledge can be very useful if their application is carefully modeled through teacher think alouds and guided practice. In the section that follows we outline an instructional procedure for developing your students' ability to use text structure to their advantage.

Suggestions for Helping Students Perceive Text Structure

Perhaps the key factor in teaching students to actively use the organizational structure of text is you, the content teacher. It is erroneous to assume students will recognize and utilize organizational patterns. Direct teaching of the recognition of patterns is essential, and all patterns should be pointed out continually to students. The time you spend in stimulating the perception of organizational patterns will take little away from your instructional time and will facilitate comprehension.

Tips for teaching students to perceive Patterns of Text Organization

1. **Modeling.** You should demonstrate the use of text structure first before expecting students to utilize it. Passages drawn from their reading should be used to illustrate your demonstration because they are most relevant to the students. Showing students a particular organizational pattern and pointing out why it is a certain type and how that pattern type is organized is essential. Any signal words that clue the reader to the organization of the material should also be pointed out and discussed.

2. **Recognition.** Next, you should walk students through a particular passage type by asking judicious questions that focus their attention on the text structure. For students experiencing difficulty, you may wish to read the material to them first rather than having them read it. In this way your students can concentrate entirely on perceiving the pattern. You may also wish to start with sentences only and then move to paragraphs and longer passages. Essential to this recognition step is students' verbalization of the how and why of the text structure.

3. **Production.** Producing a communication is a logical extension of receiving one. Writing, therefore, becomes a valuable means to reinforce text structure. From time to time all content teachers require students to write. Requiring logical organization in students' own writing can become a vital extension of perceiving text organization. As part of a writing assignment, you should ask students to frame a logical response by utilizing a particular pattern of organization and the signal words associated with it. Skeletal outlines or a graphic organizer may also be provided to facilitate production of an organized writing sample. We demonstrate how to teach structure awareness through writing in Chapter 11.

Reading and Comprehending Multiple Digital Texts

Throughout the book, we note that the process of reading and navigating digital texts, particularly the Internet, require guidance beyond that associated with the patterns of text organization typical in static, printed texts. Some of these ideas were introduced in Chapter 2 on Technology and they are reinforced in Chapter 12 on Studying. As a prelude to guiding students' reading and search strategies, it is important to observe and note their current approaches (McNabb, 2006). You can note sites students select and their persistence in reading related texts on various sites. If a student exhibits difficulty comprehending hypertext, consider slicing the task into a smaller collection of suggested web pages that make a topic search more manageable. McNabb (p. 118) suggests having students:

1. Think aloud by talking about their rationale for selecting particular sites.
2. Keep an annotated hyperlink log to reflect on the pathway they took on a site.
3. Keep an archival record of their searches using the bookmark function on their search engine.

In many ways, reading digital texts is related to learning how to comprehend and construct connections across printed texts. *Intertextuality,* or the process of reading and making conceptual connections across a range of texts (broadly defined to include Internet and media-based texts), requires careful guidance as students are not necessarily skilled at this process. Recent work on teacher's use of *multiple texts* in content area classrooms offers some guidelines.

Teaching in the Content Areas with Multiple Texts

Accomplished teachers in a variety of content areas often guide students' use of multiple print and non-print texts to enhance their comprehension of key concepts in science, events in history, and the dynamics of economics (Walker & Bean, 2004; Walker, Bean, & Dillard, 2005). Part of the rationale for using multiple texts is a recognition that textbooks alone are best used as one resource among many in a content area (Smith & Wilhelm, 2006). Textbooks, while useful, must be augmented with primary source documents and the Internet, particularly in inquiry and project-based classrooms. For example, Behrman (2003) conducted a study of students in a high school biology classroom where they were asked to determine guilt or innocence based on DNA analysis in a hypothetical murder. In addition to community resource experts (e.g., a director of a county forensic laboratory), students could self-select texts from any source that would help them solve the crime. As might be expected, they gravitated toward information from real life experts in the community and Internet-based information.

Similarly, in an ongoing series of studies exploring content area teachers' use of multiple texts through classroom observations and teacher interviews, Walker and Bean (2005) found that accomplished teachers saw multiple texts as a way to enrich content area teaching for their students. For example, Maria, an 8th-grade physical science teacher, immersed her students in designing and creating roller coasters to grasp scientific principles including potential and kinetic energy. In one interview, Maria talked about her rationale for using multiple texts and using the core textbook in physical science as one resource among many:

> I try to give them the opportunity to learn the information other than the textbook. The articles are pretty good, and they did a better job than the textbook. The textbook gets too technical, and I wanted it to be more interesting for them.

Maria's articles that students used to augment the textbook included material from magazines and Internet sites considering theme parks and roller coaster safety and design. Based on redesigning a financially struggling theme park, students adopted various roles including researcher, engineer, public relations director, and architect.

Many of the integrated strategies in this chapter and those in Chapters 10 and 11 will be useful in guiding students reading, discussion, writing, and application of multiple texts in your content area. A number of sources are available that provide classroom examples of teachers' use of multiple texts. For example, if you are planning to use multiple texts in history, Stahl and Shanahan (2004) have studied and developed an approach designed to maximize students' success. In particular, a strategy we include in this chapter called Questioning the Author (Tierney & Readence, 2005) has been recommended for guiding students' reading and discussion of multiple texts. Information on teaching with multiple texts in science based on Cynthia Shanahan's (2004) work, as well as vignettes of successful biology and English teachers using multiple texts in Sturtevant et al. (2006), offer classroom views of this practice. Finally, recommended readings at the close of the chapter list useful resources as you explore expanding students' use of multiple texts in your content area.

Integrated Approaches

In Chapter 1 we introduced the notion that helping students learn content needs to be integrated throughout all stages of the instructional lesson, i.e., students generally need to be prepared to read a text during prereading, need guidance in searching for selected ideas during reading, and need reinforcement to retain the material learned during postreading. In this chapter we explored further critical principles of comprehension and related instructional stages. While there are strategies which may only focus on certain aspects of the instructional lesson (see Chapter 10 for a discussion of these strategies), we describe here a series of strategies which should be viewed as more comprehensive in nature. Rather than focusing on one aspect of an instructional lesson, these strategies are integrated across all stages of the lesson—prereading, reading, and postreading—and provide a more holistic view of the comprehension process and integrated lesson planning.

K-W-L

Integrated Teaching and Learning Strategies

- K-W-L
- Inquiry Charts
- Listen-Read-Discuss
- Scaffolded Reading Experience
- Questioning the Author
- Critical Media Literacy

Ogle (2007) created a 3-step integrated strategy designed to encourage active reading of expository text. The *K-W-L* strategy consists of a prereading stage aimed at activating prior knowledge, a reading stage where students seek answers to predetermined questions, and a postreading stage where they can distill what was learned through the reading. K-W-L relies on three categories of information:

K—What we *k*now (before reading)

W—What we *w*ant to find out (during reading); and

L—What we *l*earned (as a result of text reading).

In addition, you should assist students in anticipating the organizational structure or likely categories of information a text author will introduce. In the example that follows, the topic of killer bees might present their recent invasion of the southern United States as a problem to be solved. Thus, the category section would include the labels "problem" and "solution." To prepare a K-W-L lesson, create a framework like the one in Figure 9.1 on the board or overhead and ensure that each student has a copy of this framework.

Figure 9.1   K-W-L LESSON FRAMEWORK

K—What we know	W—What we want to find out	L—What we learned
Categories of information		
1.		
2.		
3.		

Steps to Utilize K-W-L Framework

1. Engage students in a brainstorming session on the topic they are about to read in the text. Students can draw their visualization of the topic (e.g., killer bees) to activate prior knowledge. Next, elicit possible categories the author might use to organize this information on killer bees. The lesson framework in Figure 9.2 displays students' comments concerning the killer bees selection they were about to read in the K column.

2. To help students develop a clear purpose for reading a selection, they should create questions the text might answer. The framework in Figure 9.2 shows some of the questions students generated for the killer bee text in the W column.

3. Finally, students need to record the information they have learned in the framework (see the L column on the next page). In addition, you may wish to

Figure 9.2   K-W-L Lesson Framework on Killer Bees

K—What we know	W—What we want to find out	L—What we learned
1. They can kill people.	1. Why are they called "killer bees"?	1. They are more aggressive than the common honey bee.
2. They kill other bees.	2. Where are they found?	2. The southern and western U.S.
3. Their sting is worse than honey bees.	3. Where are they from?	3. Africa originally. They were brought to Brazil by accident in 1956.
	4. How dangerous are they?	4. Very aggressive, but their sting is no more dangerous than other bees. However, they can interfere with the pollination of many fruits and vegetables by the common honey bee, raising the cost of these items.
	5. How can we get rid of them?	5. Scientists claim it is impossible.

Categories of information

1. Problem of killer bees
2. Solution to this problem

have students develop a visual representation such as a graphic organizer or map, or they can write a short summary statement. Students can then share this information in small discussion groups.

Integrated strategies like K-W-L can form a solid foundation for extended research and writing projects. You can have students explore the source and reliability of information gained from reading. Given the vast volume of information on any topic available via the Internet and other media, this is an important, critical reading element. K-W-L also might be extended by having students explore a fourth category of information: What they still need to learn. For example, is it really impossible to rid the United States of killer bees? Perhaps additional reading and research with other texts might provide an alternative viewpoint. Thus, K-W-L can lead into more detailed exploration of a topic or theme spanning a full unit which may take weeks to complete.

Other modifications might be considered for students in diverse classrooms. Small groups might be used to generate the information in steps one and two rather than a large group forum. Students might first work in a small group to record what they know and then report it to the large group. The same can be done for information they might seek. This should enable more students to participate and make the learning environment more collaborative and less threatening. In step three a small group might be a better conduit to get students to record/summarize what they found out. Teachers might also modify the strategy by incorporating more modeling and direction until students are comfortable with it. For particularly difficult topics or topics where little prior knowledge exists, the use of a shorter text or a video might be considered. These could serve as an advance organizer to give the students some familiarity with the topic before they actually have to read the assigned text. Similarly, a video could serve to augment, or even substitute for, the text.

Inquiry Charts

Inquiry Charts, or I-Charts (Hoffman, 1992; Tierney & Readence, 2005), nurture critical reading in content classrooms by having students examine multiple sources of information for points of consistency and inconsistency. Based upon the work of Ogle with K-W-L, students use a data chart to record what they know about a topic, what they want to know about it, and what they found from their readings. The chart allows the students to gather the information they get from multiple sources and organize it for summarization, comparison, and evaluation.

Steps for Using the I-Chart Strategy

1. **Planning.** In planning, teachers must decide what: (a) topic is to be explored, (b) questions will drive the inquiry process, and (c) sources will be used for data collection. For example, let's say the topic is the Civil War, and the teacher decides the questions to be explored are: (a) What were the causes of the Civil War? (b) What were the immediate effects of the war for each side? (c) What were the long-term consequences of the war? and (d) What would the United States be like today if the South had won the war? The teacher might decide that besides the class text, the classroom set of encyclopedias and other textbooks and tradebooks from the school library would serve as resources. Once planning is completed, the I-Chart should be constructed with this information displayed on it (see Figure 9.3).

Figure 9.3

I-Chart: The Civil War • *Potential use* •
Guiding Questions

TOPIC Civil War	1. What were the causes of the Civil War?	2. What were the immediate effects of the war for each side?	3. What were the long-term conse-quences of the war?	4. What would the U.S. be like today if the South had won the war?	Interesting Facts and Figures	New Questions
WHAT WE KNOW						
Sources 1. Class text						
2. Encyclo-pedias						
3. Library trade-books						
SUMMARY						

2. **Interacting.** In this step students work with the teacher to explore their prior knowledge, share interesting facts and new questions, and read and record. First, students respond to each guiding question along the lines of what they already know. This information is recorded on the I-Chart in the "What We Know" row under the appropriate question. This information is recorded whether or not it is accurate or contradictory. Next, any interesting facts the students come up with and any new questions they think of, unrelated to the guiding questions, should also be recorded in the appropriate space on the I-Chart. Finally, students are asked to go to the additional source material to answer the guiding questions. The amount of time this will take depends on the number of available sources as well as the number of questions. Following the discussion of each source, the teacher records the appropriate information for each question on the I-Chart. In this case the information should be as accurate as possible; any new questions or interesting information from the reading should be recorded as well. It is important to understand that the eventual size of the I-Chart will be dictated by the scope of the topic and search required.

3. **Interacting and Evaluating.** In this step the I-Chart is completed, and the findings are evaluated and shared. First, the students are asked to generate summary statements for each of the guiding questions and the interesting facts column. Thus, students are asked to synthesize the information previously recorded, taking into account both converging and conflicting information. Summary statements are recorded on the bottom row of the I-Chart. Next, students compare the information gained from their readings with their prior knowledge and reconcile any misconceptions. Now, students are ready to deal with the new, unanswered questions that arose during their data collection. These questions become the basis for additional research, either individually or in small groups. Finally, students report back to the whole class their findings regarding the unanswered questions.

Once students become familiar with the strategy, teachers can fade their responsibility; students may begin to select their own topics, generate their own guiding questions, and decide what to record on the I-Chart. Eventually, the strategy could be used with small groups or even for individual inquiry. Once students become proficient in synthesizing information into summaries, they may become the basis for students to expand them into paragraphs and, later, complete written reports. Finally, the I-Chart seems to be an ideal tool for exploring multicultural issues in the classroom.

Listen-Read-Discuss

The integrated strategy of *Listen-Read-Discuss* was developed to ensure that students genuinely grasp content information (Manzo, Casale, & Thomas, 2004). Because students receive multiple exposure to concepts through listening, reading, and discussion, they are more likely to learn and retain information you feel is worthy of this intensive process.

Steps for a Listen-Read-Discuss Lesson

1. The first part of the lesson entails presenting a well structured lecture on the material students are about to read in the text. Students need to have a good grasp of the content you are presenting if they are to participate actively in a

listen-read-discuss lesson. Therefore, consider providing a clear lecture guide, perhaps in the form of a graphic organizer, that will serve to cue students to the text's structure. For example, the graphic organizer in Figure 9.4 might be used to assist high school students' comprehension of a lecture on Japan's rise to a world power. Reading in their text would follow about a 15-minute lecture on the topic. Notice that the graphic organizer displays the cause-effect structure of the text. Items one and three would be provided by the teacher on the graphic organizer lecture guide passed out to students. Those items in script would be filled in by students as the lecture progresses, with clear cues from the teacher signaling each important point.

Figure 9.4

Sample Graphic Organizer and Lecture Guide for Listen-Read-Discuss

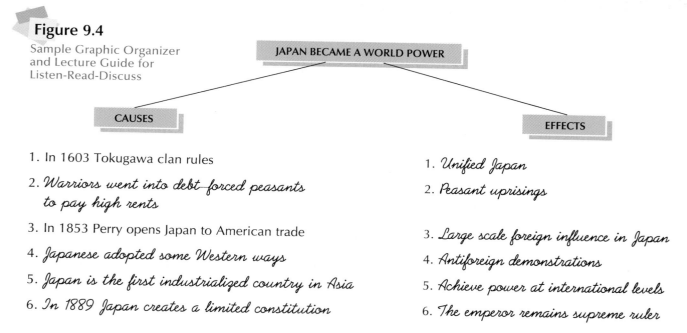

JAPAN BECAME A WORLD POWER

CAUSES

1. In 1603 Tokugawa clan rules
2. *Warriors went into debt—forced peasants to pay high rents*
3. In 1853 Perry opens Japan to American trade
4. *Japanese adopted some Western ways*
5. *Japan is the first industrialized country in Asia*
6. *In 1889 Japan creates a limited constitution*

EFFECTS

1. *Unified Japan*
2. *Peasant uprisings*
3. *Large scale foreign influence in Japan*
4. *Antiforeign demonstrations*
5. *Achieve power at international levels*
6. *The emperor remains supreme ruler*

Once the lecture is completed and students have filled in their graphic organizer lecture guides, the teacher is ready to progress to step two, the reading portion of a listen-read-discuss lesson.

2. The teacher directs students to read the text pages on which the lecture was based. Their purpose for reading should be to compare their understanding of the lecture with the information presented in the text. In addition, they can identify vocabulary and concepts that need clarification and pinpoint any inconsistencies between the text and the teacher's lecture. They are then ready to discuss the information on Japan's rise to international power.

3. The discussion step can begin with small groups and progress to a summary discussion as a whole class. Three major questions should guide students' discussion of the lecture and text reading: (a) What did you understand best from what you heard and read? (b) What did you understand least from what you heard and read? and (c) What questions or thoughts did the topic raise in your mind? This last question is one that is often glossed over in our desire to cover the content. Yet it goes to the heart of students' personal interest in a topic. For example, Japan's influence on our economy has grown considerably over the years. It would be important to raise and consider contemporary issues like this, which have their roots in the mid-1800s.

Scaffolded Reading Experience

The *Scaffolded Reading Experience* (SRE) is a comprehensive lesson framework with a good deal of flexibility in its implementation (Tierney & Readence, 2005). *Scaffolding* refers to the degree of support and guidance a teacher may need to provide to help students engage text that would be too difficult, left to their own devices. As in all lesson frameworks, you need to first carefully consider what prior knowledge students may bring to the topic. For example, in an art history class, it is unlikely that contemporary students would have much knowledge of the Surrealists, let alone specific artists and their beliefs. A sense of students' prior knowledge about the topic helps suggest the level of prereading, reading, and postreading scaffolding needed. For example, in an art history lesson on the Surrealist Salvador Dali (Martin, 1999), students might consider one of his paintings before doing any text reading about his philosophy and beliefs. The actual lesson steps follow, but keep in mind that this is an overall lesson framework with a great deal of flexibility in implementation.

Steps for Implementing an SRE

1. At the prereading stage, the teacher can ask students to pair up with a classmate and look at the slide of a famous Dali painting, *The Persistence of Memory*. The landscape shows three timepieces bent as if melted by a hot fire. There is a sheer stone cliff in the background and the contorted clocks in the foreground. The colors are mainly dark and foreboding, and one clock face hangs from a sparse gray tree limb by the middle of its limp clock face. The teacher uses a prereading question, What does this painting remind you of?, to give students a chance to explore their prior knowledge. They comment on its dreamlike quality and scary looking landscape. The teacher then offers a definition of surrealism with its intense interest in dreams and the unconscious. Because Freudian influences also weighed heavily on Dali during his life (1904–1989), the teacher also offers a brief cultural history based on the text.

2. Based on the foundational information in the prereading stage of the SRE, students are given a broad study guide question to consider as they read the text about Salvador Dali: How was Dali regarded as a Surrealist painter during his lifetime?

The World of Dreams and Salvador Dali's Art

Salvador Dali sought to tap into his dreams and represent the more bizarre dimensions of the unconscious mind. He painted in a realistic style such that familiar objects are easily recognizable, even if juxtaposed in odd ways. Despite the fact that many people now know Dali and perhaps few other famous Surrealists, he was actually tossed out of the Surrealist group by another artist, Andre Breton. Dali tended to reveal his interest in Freud and subconscious dreams in a fashion that many critics thought was too obvious and literal. Indeed, Dali had little use for abstract painting, which may explain some of his appeal and notoriety with the masses. He was on the one hand, irreverent, and, on the other, meticulous in his planning for a painting. He was criticized for being too academic in his planning and execution compared to the more abstract Surrealists. Nevertheless, his 1931 painting, *The Persistence of Memory*, is widely associated with Surrealism and serves as an introduction to this artistic movement for many people.

3. At the postreading stage, a number of options for critical response to the text are possible. For example, questioning, discussion, writing, drama, art, media, and other response modes might be adopted. In the example of the Dali text, the teacher could ask students to write a short play where Dali attempts to defend his contribution to Surrealism in the face of criticism that he was too realistic in his work. Or, students might research other artists of the period that contrasted with Dali's style and include examples of their works in a gallery set up around the classroom. Other students could then browse these posters containing photos and brief text explaining the philosophy of each artist. Slide shows, videos, and other hypermedia might be used. The possibilities are endless, so it may be helpful, before planning and SRE, to consult additional sources.

The Scaffolded Reading Experience helps students grasp key ideas in a text selection. The next two strategies, *Questioning the Author* (Tierney & Readence, 2005), and *Critical Media Literacy* (Stevens, 2001; Stevens & Bean, 2007) emphasize critical thinking. We first introduce Questioning the Author.

Questioning the Author

This strategy is particularly useful for narrative and expository texts that are unfriendly and likely to challenge students. The strategy unfolds in three separate stages: planning, discussion, and implementation.

PLANNING. Start by doing a careful content analysis of the text you plan to use. The teacher's manual may be helpful for major ideas and questions. Then, read the material imagining yourself as a student who is a less skilled reader and likely to struggle with the text. Identify key ideas and logical segments of text. Based on the key ideas you discern and the segmented text, create some queries that will help guide students as they read. You will be asking students to stop reading at particular points in the text and respond to these queries. Unlike much of the prereading and postreading guidance we have emphasized thus far, these queries will interrupt the reader *during reading*. Broad questions such as, What is the author trying to say here?, encourage students to reflect on the material just read.

IMPLEMENTATION. In the example that follows, we accompany a student attempting to read a passage in agriculture on horse communication (adapted from Budiansky, 1997).

Horse Communication

The widely popular 1960s television show, Mr. Ed, featured a horse who could talk. Indeed, Mr. Ed sometimes seemed to be much more on top of things than his human owners. This desire to attribute human-like traits to wild animals is unfortunate. People are prone to anthropomorphism and sentimentality when it comes to animals, particularly domesticated animals like dogs and horses.

Query: What is the author trying to say about our view of horse communication?

In fact, horses use sounds to communicate but in a fashion quite different from that depicted in Mr. Ed. They actually use four basic sounds: (1) the nicker (low pitched like the key of G), (2) the blow (a low nontonal sound),

(3) the squeal (louder and like a C two octaves above middle C), and the (4) whinny (very loud).

Query: How does the author help you understand what each horse signal sounds like?

Each signal has particular uses. For example, the whinny is used for long-distance communication when horses are out of visual range of other horses they socialize with.

DISCUSSION. Based on responses to the various text queries, students can then discuss the section of the chapter they read. This is a good place to raise issues of accuracy in what the author presented and help students make connections to their prior experiences and reading. For example, students who have some experiences with horses and their various signals might offer insights during the discussion stage.

This strategy is flexible and lends itself to the creation of higher-order questions for various queries in a text. Questions can range from those that are variously text-based and guide the reader, to those that are open-ended and extend understanding of the text.

Critical Media Literacy

Contemporary adolescents encounter a broad range of texts that include television, films, and music. This popular media helps engage students' interest, but it is rarely treated as a forum for discussion and critique. Recent efforts to infuse popular culture and critical media literacy in content classrooms show how critical thinking can be developed through the inclusion of contemporary media. The critical media literacy lesson framework that follows will help demystify this process. In addition, recommended readings for this chapter offer additional resources as you begin to work with popular culture material in your content area.

Steps for a Critical Media Literacy Lesson

1. Planning a critical media lesson must involve a clear awareness of district policies regarding appropriate films and music. Movie clips need to acknowledge students' interests, jog their thinking about concepts, and be deemed acceptable within district norms. For example, Stevens (2001) and a middle school physical science teacher collaborated on the development of a popular media lesson involving the three basic laws of motion. At the planning stage, they decided to ask students to critique action sequences in films to judge the degree to which they were consistent with the laws of physics. Movies rated G and PG were selected with a parent consent letter for a 5-minute action sequence from *Jumanji* (1995). They were especially interested in how students reacted and judged those movie sequences where they were expected by the film's producer and director to suspend an understanding of physical laws and what is actually possible.

2. Ask students to watch or listen to the media clip (in this example, a scene from *Jumanji*) and write down their conclusions about the scene's consistency with the laws of physics. They can use their textbook as a reference to cross-check any concepts that may help with their critique. For example, in *Jumanji,* a hunter shoots a bullet, and it stops in the air. Physical laws of motion do not support this scene and students used both the film clip of this action and their book to critique its veracity.

Our definition of what constitutes a text must be expanded to include the wide array of media material students encounter. More importantly, this material offers an exciting platform for the development of critical thinking and critical discourse. Popular film, music, and television offer a readily available means to challenge students' thinking and assumptions.

Needless to say, the Critical Media Literacy strategy, as well as the K-W-L, I-Chart, Listen-Read-Discuss, Questioning the Author, and Scaffolded Reading Experience strategies, will require a good block of time to complete. They should be reserved for topics you feel are important enough to warrant the extra time. Because of the integrated nature of these strategies, students receive multiple exposures to concepts. This may be especially useful for those students who often need extra time to learn content material.

Now go back to the comprehension vignette at the beginning of the chapter. React again to the lesson as you did before. Compare your responses with those you made before you read the chapter.

Mini Projects

Using the CD-ROM excerpt "Ears and Hearing," do one or both of the following:

1. Develop three questions at each of the three levels of understanding and identify the predominant text structure present.

2. Develop a lesson based on K-W-L, the I-Chart, Listen-Read-Discuss, Questioning the Author, or the Scaffolded Reading Experience. Try out the lesson with a small group of students or your peers. Evaluate the success of the strategy upon completion.

Website Activity

To locate and complete Chapter 9 activities, go to [*www.kendallhunt.com/contentarealiteracy*].

10

Comprehension: Guiding Content Literacy

Setting

Lydian Flat's high school band class. In the previous class, Mr. Flat began a lesson on scale theory. In this class he plans to expand on this foundational information by exploring the seven modes of the major scale.

The Lesson

Mr. Flat begins class by reviewing concepts about scale theory introduced in the previous class lesson. He does this by asking students to respond to questions he throws out to the whole class at the beginning of the period. In the scene that follows, T = the teacher, Mr. Flat, and S = the students.

T: "Can anyone tell me what a scale is?"

S: Some students attempt to assemble their instruments, honking on saxes and clarinets, while others raise their hands to answer. Mr. Flat calls on Phil, a guitarist, who answers with a textbook definition:

S: "A scale is a series of tones organized according to a specific arrangement of intervals. An interval is the distance between any two tones or pitches. The smallest interval is the half step which on my guitar is the difference in pitch between two notes one fret apart on the same string."

T: "Okay, Phil, nice answer. Now let's try a tough one. What's a pentatonic scale?"

S: Phil snickers. Clearly this is an easy question for him, but the other students become even more intent on fussing with their instruments, resulting in a growing cacaphony.

T: "Alright, alright. Phil, tell us what a pentatonic scale is."

S: Phil doesn't answer. Instead he cradles his guitar and plays a slow A minor blues riff built on a minor pentatonic scale.

T: "Yes, that's a minor pentatonic scale, but it's a little ahead of where we are in this unit on scales. We need to consider and play the major scales and learn their key signatures first. And today we'll also be looking at the seven modes of the major scale: the dorian mode in jazz and rock, the phrygian mode, which you may recognize from flamenco music, the lydian mode from jazz, the mixolydian mode used in a lot of folk music, and the aeolian mode and the locrian mode used in jazz. But before we go any farther, let's start by playing a C major scale together."

S: Students launch into scale practice under Mr. Flat's guidance.

T: Near the end of the class, Mr. Flat hands out a worksheet that lists the major keys and their relative minor keys (e.g., C major and A minor). He informs students that there will be a quiz over this material next week on Wednesday.

S: Before the bell rings, students take apart and clean their instruments, frantically tossing the worksheet into folders and backpacks.

→ Keeping in mind that this lesson is concerned with understanding scale theory and applying this theory in playing band instruments, jot down your thoughts on the following questions:

1. What are the good points about the lesson?
2. What are the weak points about the lesson?
3. What, if anything, would you change about the lesson?

Rationale

The integrated approaches to comprehension introduced in Chapter 9 all have advocated providing guidance to students before, during, and after reading. To reinforce the integrated notion that this text recommends, these strategies also advocate the use of all language processes and small groups whenever possible.

To continue in that vein this chapter will describe various strategies that can be predominantly classified as prereading, reading, or postreading in scope. While we realize that a holistic view of the comprehension process encompasses all stages of the instructional lesson and that each stage is not necessarily a separate entity, e.g., the postreading stage of one lesson may serve as the prereading stage of the next lesson, the strategies will be divided to facilitate our discussion of each of them. The intent of all of these strategies, however, is similar: to increase students' interaction with the ideas presented in texts so they will acquire and retain important content information. Therefore, the aim of this chapter is to introduce and demonstrate an array of comprehension strategies that will augment those already described in the previous chapter.

Learning Objectives

→ Be familiar with a wide array of prereading, reading, and postreading strategies for guiding students' comprehension of content area concepts.

→ Be able to apply specific teaching strategies in your content area in order to guide students' understanding of your course content.

Graphic Organizer

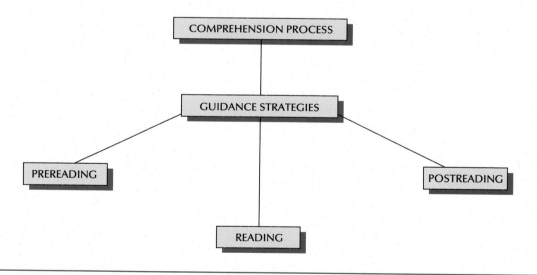

Prereading Strategies

Anticipation Guides

Throughout this text we have been using a number of prereading strategies to introduce each chapter. One of them, the *anticipation guide,* introduces each chapter in Part 1 and is an attractive way to activate your thoughts and opinions about a topic. As you are well aware by now, many of the guide statements are loaded in the sense that we want to challenge commonly held beliefs about content area literacy. Indeed, one of the major features of an anticipation guide is that it brings misconceptions about a topic to the surface (Head & Readence, 2007). Then we can begin to modify these misconceptions through a well-formulated instructional sequence.

Since anticipation guide statements operate at the experience-based level of understanding, they elicit a response based on one's current belief system. Therefore, at the prereading stage a student may adamantly defend a response to a guide statement with little fear of failure. As the learning sequence progresses into the reading and postreading stages, a mismatch between the students' preconceptions about a topic and the information being introduced should result in a subsequent modification of their initial knowledge base.

An additional feature of the anticipation guide is the way in which it functions as an informal diagnostic tool. A teacher can appraise prior knowledge at the prereading stage and evaluate the acquisition of content based on postreading responses to the guide statements. Since anticipation guides encourage a personal, experience-based response, they serve as ideal springboards for large and small group discussion. Furthermore, they seem to work equally well with print and non-print media including films, lectures, and field trips and lend themselves to application in diverse subject areas such as science, art, physical education, and history.

Steps for Constructing an Anticipation Guide in any Content Area

1. Identify the major concepts and supporting details in a text selection, lecture, or film.
2. Identify students' experiences and beliefs that will be challenged and, in some cases, supported by the material.
3. Create statements reflecting your students' prereading beliefs concerning a course topic that may challenge and modify those beliefs. Include some statements that are consistent with both your students' experiential background and the concepts presented in the material or lesson. Three to five statements are usually adequate.
4. Arrange the statements on a sheet of paper, overhead transparency, or the chalkboard. Have students respond positively or negatively to each statement on an individual basis. Have them record their justification for each response in writing, so they will have a reference point for discussion.
5. Engage students in a prereading discussion highlighting their current justification for responding positively or negatively to each statement.

With a little practice you will discover that anticipation guides serve to clarify your content objectives and to motivate students to approach a learning task in an active fashion. Used in conjunction with a film, they can reduce the kind of haphazard, passive processing of film concepts that often characterizes the use of media in a classroom. The following physical education anticipation guide (Figure 10.1) was developed to accompany a fitness film.

Figure 10.1

Anticipation Guide: Stretching

Directions: Before watching the fitness film, put a (+) by those statements with which you agree and a (–) by those with which you disagree. Jot down some notes that will help you defend your point of view in a class discussion.

Anticipation

_____ 1. Most doctors prescribe stretching for relief of tension and stress.

_____ 2. A gymnast and a football player should stretch about the same length of time.

_____ 3. Stretching is neglected because it is painful and boring.

_____ 4. Stretching with the aid of a partner can bring about greater flexibility.

In a social studies class, anticipation guides help students to appraise ideas critically in a text. For example, the following guide (Figure 10.2) was designed to accompany junior high students' reading of a United States history chapter on the Constitution. One student's prereading ideas are included.

Even factual texts in United States history can serve as rich sources for critical thinking when they are supplemented with an anticipation guide like this one. Students begin to see some link between their lives and the often distant concepts in a text. Moreover, they must adopt a critical stance toward a topic, weighing their preconceptions against the author's ideas. Indeed, many educators regard the development and evaluation of arguments as the essence of critical thinking.

As you work with anticipation guides, you may find it helpful to include an "I'm not sure," or "I don't know" response column to accommodate those students who, at the prereading stage, are really not ready to commit to a yes or no re-

Figure 10.2

Anticipation Guide: The Constitution

Directions: Before reading pages 186 to 193, read each statement and place a (yes) by those statements with which you agree and a (no) by those statements with which you disagree under the column labeled Anticipation. Write your reasons for agreeing or disagreeing so you can be part of a class discussion.

Anticipation

__*yes*__ 1. Writers of the Constitution were everyday working class people.
Because they had to work for a living and they were not royalty.

__*no*__ 2. The President, like a king, has complete power to rule the country.
Because he can be kicked out of office by the process of impeachment.

__*no*__ 3. A Ford mechanic cannot become President.
Because it doesn't matter as long as he is the right age and is elected.

__*no*__ 4. People who are rich and people who are poor have equal protection under the law.
Because the rich people have more influence over the law because they can bribe the law.

__*yes*__ 5. Students should have the right to decide what classes they take.
After the 10th grade they should be able to, because by that time they will know what they want from life and they would take courses to prepare for their career.

sponse. This reduces guessing and provides some insight into a student's background knowledge about the topic.

Anticipation guides are best used in small group or cooperative learning pairs. Students can then discuss their perceptions of the topic, which helps them see that these statements are not a test. At first, you may need to make it clear to students that these statements are designed to jog their thinking, not to serve as another true-false test of trivial facts to be memorized. In our experience, students at various levels enjoy reacting to well-constructed guide statements to narrative and expository material as well as to guide statements to lectures and films.

STOP! View the CD-ROM video clip showing a classroom teacher introducing a reading assignment with an anticipation guide.

Text Appetizers

Text Appetizers are teacher-created, introductory paragraphs that offer a framework for comprehending a reading selection by relating the new to the known (Baldwin, Readence, & Bean, 2004; Bean, 2007). By connecting new information in the text to their prior knowledge, students are likely to focus attention on key concepts during reading.

Steps to Develop Text Appetizers

1. **Write the Introductory Paragraph.** Write an interest-building paragraph based on real-life, day-to-day events that would be of interest to your students and are similar in principle to the critical target concepts in a text.
2. **Add Guiding Questions (Optional).** Add guiding questions consisting of one question at each of the three levels of understanding.
3. **Read the Text Appetizer.** Have students read and discuss the appetizer before beginning the reading assignment. The guiding questions can be attached to the appetizer to help students focus attention on important information.

The text appetizer example in Figure 10.3 comes from social studies:

Figure 10.3

Text Appetizer: The Politics of Protest

Suppose that you like to ride a skateboard at the new skate park near your neighborhood. However, due to a small percentage of rowdy skaters taking drugs and extorting money from other kids, your City Council threatens to close down the skate park. How do you feel about this situation? What would you do about it?

The chapter you are about to read shows how groups such as small business people, workers, and farmers in the 1890s protested what they felt were unfair practices by big business, often with the support of the government. Farmers felt they were paying too much interest on equipment loans from big business banks. They banded together to protest this unfair treatment, just as you might protest lumping all teenage skaters together despite only a small minority causing problems at the skate park. Congress was viewed as a governmental body that could help the farmers with the plight, but, like many political systems, this one proved to have its flaws. As you read pages 537 to 549, try to answer the following discussion questions:

Right There on the Page
1. What was the purpose of the Sherman Antitrust Act? (p. 539, paragraph 3)

Think and Search
2. Why didn't the Sherman Antitrust Act work the way it was supposed to in 1890?

On Your Own
3. Do you think the Sherman Antitrust Act is working today?

This text appetizer and its guide questions helped students' comprehension of a potentially dull and distant topic—the farmers' efforts to gain fair treatment in the late 1800s. Having students work on the guide questions in cooperative learning pairs also helps those students who may be unaccustomed to grappling with experience-based, on-your-own issues. Text appetizers can be created for particularly problematic text reading assignments in science and other content areas. They help students approach text reading with a schema for a topic based on prior knowledge.

APPLICATION 10.1

Choose either "The Telltale Heart" or "The Lady or the Tiger" on the CD-Rom and develop a text appetizer to introduce high school students to the story.

ReQuest

This unusual representation of the word "request" is actually a blend of reciprocal and questioning. The *ReQuest* strategy was developed to help students adopt an active, questioning approach to text reading. Students are guided in this process by the teacher, who models the question-asking procedure and attempts to elicit higher-level, text implicit and experience-based questions.

In the ReQuest activity, both the teacher and students silently read specified portions of the text together and then take turns asking each other questions. Students ask the first series of questions. This order gives the teacher an opportunity to appraise the level of their analysis. If the students merely produce text explicit questions (e.g., What color was the main character's hair?), then the teacher attempts to model higher-order questions on that same section of the text after students have fully exhausted their array of questions. The teacher models higher-order questions such as: What is the significance of the main character's iron-gray hair? (text implicit); How would you feel if you were in the main character's predicament? (experience-based); What do you think is going to happen next? (prediction based on text implicit and experience-based factors). Moreover, when students produce similar questions during their interrogative turn, the teacher should praise their efforts with such phrases as: That's a good question! It really makes me think!

Now that you have a general notion of what ReQuest is all about, we want to outline the preparatory steps for a ReQuest session and illustrate the procedure with a story we devised.

Steps for a Successful ReQuest Session

1. Analyze the text selection for major concepts and sections portraying these concepts. For example, a story can usually be divided into the following units: setting and characters; an event that introduces conflict; attempts to resolve the conflict or achieve a goal; resolution of the conflict; and finally, a reaction on the part of the protagonist.

2. Determine prediction points in the story or text selection that allow the reader to form expectations about upcoming events. These prediction points can be labeled in your copy of the material as P_1, P_2, P_3, etc.

    Example: She treaded water, trying to remain calm as the full moon illuminated the last features of her once majestic sloop, now sinking into oblivion.

The tropical air was warm and the Pacific deceptively gentle, yet she knew danger was lurking in the depths that surrounded her.

P_1 _____

Sharks are particularly bold at night. . . .

3. Explain the general ReQuest procedure to your students.

   Example:

   Teacher: We'll each read a portion of the text silently. I will close my book and you can ask me all the questions you can think of, referring to your book as needed.

   Teacher: Let's read the first paragraph. . . .

4. When you reach the final prediction point in the story or text selection, have students generate all the predictions they can think of for the final outcome of the selection. List the predictions verbatim on the board and have students vote on the ones they feel are most plausible. This step is particularly exciting with story selections that have a surprise twist at the end.

The story and ReQuest scenario in Figure 10.4 illustrates one approach to the use of this procedure in an English class. Three prediction points have been established for guiding students' collaborative discussion and comprehension of this story. The teacher and students read the first paragraph (i.e., P_1) silently, then the students ask the teacher questions based on just that section. It has been the authors' experience that even fairly sophisticated students will begin ReQuest by asking rather low-level, text explicit questions. The following hypothetical scenario is representative of a typical ReQuest session:

   Student(s): What was the round swing? (text explicit)

   Teacher: A rope tied to a pine tree. . . .

Notice that this form of text explicit question has a tendency to stifle further discussion. Also note that the teacher did not provide any positive comment on the quality of the question. At this point in the scenario, let us assume that students have exhausted their array of questions on this paragraph and it is now the teacher's turn.

   Teacher: What do you think is going to happen in this story? (prediction via text implicit and experience-based information)

   Student A: Someone's going to fall out of the round swing.

   Student B: We're going to find out how it feels to ride the round swing.

   Student C: It's too early to tell.

   Teacher: Okay, let's read the next paragraph and see what happens!

As you can see, in contrast to text explicit questions, the teacher's question, comprising a blend of implicit and experience-based elements, asked students to predict the next event in the story. This type of question generates discussion and provides a good model for students to emulate when it is their turn. In addition, it is impossible to produce a wrong answer on a prediction question. For the sake of illustration, let us assume that some of the students in this example have grasped the concept of asking higher-order questions as we move into the second paragraph (i.e., P_2).

Figure 10.4
ReQuest Scenario with *The Round Swing*

The Round Swing

The round swing stood in a little clearing behind the Robinson's cabin. It was nothing more than a tall pine tree with all its branches cut off and a long rope hanging from the top to within about three feet of the ground. A piece of cloth was tied to the end of the rope. The tree was set back about ten feet from the edge of a steep ravine, carpeted with pines at the bottom.

P_1 _____

I looked down, far down into the valley below. And the same nervous sickness that overcame me on the thirty-foot diving tower at summer camp bounced into my stomach. But I had to go on the round swing. There wasn't anyone else to refuse with me. I was alone.

P_2 _____

"I'll go first!" Terry said.

"Okay, I'll hold the rope while you get in," Mike Robinson offered.

Terry put his feet through the cloth seat and tested it with his weight.

"I'm no fat man like Mark Rogers. It won't give," he said.

And then he was running hard around the half-circle plateau. Seated and airborne. Yelling his lungs out in nervous excitement. A human puppet soaring over the valley. Stumbling back onto the other side of the plateau and he was off again. Till the rope had coiled itself tightly around the tree and Terry crashed into it panting.

"Wow! It's great, Mike! Hey, you gotta try it, Kev! It's so cool!" "Go ahead, Mike. After all, it's your swing," I said.

"Okay. I'll just go around a few times, then you can try it."

He took off, hooting his way over the ravine like Terry. The third time around he skidded back onto the ledge.

"C'mon, Kev! You can try it now!" Terry said.

P_3 _____

"No, I don't know. I'm not that hot on trying it," I said.

"What? You aren't afraid, are you?"

"No, I just don't care about it that much," I answered.

A car crunched over the dirt road, winding its way into the Robinson's front yard. Mike pulled himself out of the swing.

"Hey, that's probably my parents. Let's go inside. Don't say anything about the swing."

"That's okay. We have to go home now anyway. We'll just go through your backyard and work our way down to the river," Terry said.

"Do you know where the trail is?"

"Yeh, Mike. See you later."

"Too bad you didn't get to try the round swing, Kev," Mike said.

"Yeh, some other time," I answered.

Terry looked disgusted but didn't say anything all the way down the trail. When we reached the river I let myself flow along with it.

Teacher: Okay, you can ask me any questions you can think of from the first two paragraphs.

Student D: What is below the round swing?

Teacher: A valley.

Student E:	What would you do if you were the speaker in the story? (experience-based)
Teacher:	Ah, that's a good question—I'll have to think about that a minute. . . . If it looked sturdy enough I might try the round swing. I think I would test out the cloth seat first!
Student F:	Where do you think this story takes place? (text implicit)
Teacher:	That's interesting to think about. Maybe in the high Sierras somewhere in California? It doesn't really say, so it could be in the hills of Georgia. . . . Probably not in Iowa!"

It should be readily apparent at this point that ReQuest is an attractive method for guiding students' comprehension of a story or text selection. At the final prediction point (i.e., P_3), the teacher would elicit all possible predictions pertaining to the outcome of the story. These would be listed on the board and their probability would be rank-ordered by way of a class vote. Students should be advised that the author's chosen ending is not necessarily preferable to the endings they have generated.

As you can see, ReQuest functions as an effective prereading strategy or, if extended as in the preceding example, it may be useful to guide the entire reading of a selection. Thus, ReQuest overlaps with the reading stage of a well-integrated content lesson.

Comprehension guidance and strategy instruction is especially important for second language learners in your classroom. For example, in a study of low literacy Latina/o students in middle school, Jimenez (1997) found that strategies such as self-questioning and inferencing could be introduced through multicultural literature that captured students' interest. Thus, rather than placing students in text material that may be so frustrating that they reject any attempt to also introduce strategies, you may want to teach self-questioning and other cognitive strategies using more friendly, multicultural literature for second language learners.

Directed Reading-Thinking Activity

Although ReQuest is an ideal means of guiding students toward asking their own questions of well-structured story material, the *Directed Reading-Thinking Activity* (DRTA) works well with expository texts, especially in social studies. The DRTA is a self-questioning strategy that encourages students to predict oncoming information in expository text and set purposes for readings that are personally interesting. Questions not answered by a text may call for supplemental reading, class discussion, consultation with an expert source, or further exploration of a topic.

Steps to Guide a DRTA Lesson

1. Before reading the text in detail, have students survey a chapter topic by considering the title, headings, illustrations, and diagrams. This survey will form the basis for prereading questions. Longer chapters can be broken up into smaller increments, if necessary, or students in small groups can each survey a section of the chapter and share their questions.

2. Have students write questions called to mind in the chapter survey. If you have students keep a journal, they can enter the questions there.

3. As a class, discuss various student-generated questions, emphasizing the value of personal purpose setting.

4. Have students read the text to consider answers to their questions. They can then discuss their answers in small groups or as a class.

5. Have students in small groups develop questions that the text does *not* answer about the topic. Through discussion, help them identify sources such as people and other texts able to supply answers to their questions. Provide time and credit for tracking down these answers.

The DRTA shown in Figure 10.5 was conducted in a diverse junior high geography class. Students were reading a section of the text describing peasant life in China leading up to the peasant revolt. They had to consider two subheadings: (a) Peasants in China, and (b) The Road to Revolt. Here are some of the representative questions and answers they generated for steps one through four.

In this instance, a visitor to the class had spent the previous summer traveling throughout mainland China visiting schools. She was able to provide answers to students' questions. When immediate answers to student-generated questions are not available, it is important to identify available resources that will shed light on

Figure 10.5

DRTA: China

Peasants in China

1. What kinds of jobs do peasants do?
    Farming.

2. Where do most peasants live?
    In the country.

3. Do they have enough food to eat and sell?
    Yes. But they have just a little to sell. To survive, peasants could rent or sell their land. They could sell their children.

The Road to Revolt

4. Why did the rulers dislike peasants?
    Because they thought of them as servants.

5. How did the rulers make life harder for the peasants?
    Peasants did not have enough land to support their rapidly growing population.

Students generated a wide array of interesting questions not answered by the text.

1. *What is life like out in China now?*

2. *Do teenagers go to school, come home, sometimes cook dinner, and do homework?*

3. *Do the Chinese listen to the same music we do?*

4. *Do their homes and houses look like ours?*

5. *Are the parents very strict with their children? Because we get away with a lot of things!*

6. *What do they do when they have free time?*

the questions and allot adequate time and rewards for sharing this information with the class at a later date. In our experience, teachers would do well to pay attention to the experience-based questions students ask in a DRTA lesson because our textbooks do not seem to be responsive to the active interest students display in topics that sometimes seem very distant from their lives. In any case, the DRTA increases students' interest in reading for purposes they set.

Reading Strategies

Sitting down with a textbook in the solitude of your own personal study corner is a lonely activity, devoid of the language interaction afforded by the classroom. You may well wonder what possible strategies exist to help students cope with this inherently solitary task.

Indeed, many text assignments are of the "sink-or-swim" variety. "Go home and read Chapter 13 in your text" is an all too familiar edict for many students. Unfortunately, textbooks are rarely amenable to such independent reading assignments. Texts are instructional tools that require a good deal of guidance if students are to gain anything from them. In the section that follows we will describe some approaches that assist students in coping with their individual text reading assignments.

Reading Strategies

➲ Study Guides
➲ Options Guides
➲ Analogical Guides

Study Guides

The term *study guide* has been used loosely for years to describe almost any form of supplementary material that accompanies a text. Often, study guides are nothing more than a series of text explicit questions supplied by an author at the end of a text chapter. We subscribe to a very different view of the process involved in the development of a good, content area study guide. The sample study guide questions in Figure 10.6 is based upon the previous chapter and contains the basic ingredients necessary to extend students' thinking beyond a mere parroting of text explicit concepts.

Figure 10.6

Sample Study Guide Questions

Directions: Use the information in Chapter 9 to answer the following questions. Compare your answers to those of a colleague.

* 1. What is the second principle of comprehension advanced in the introduction to Chapter 9? (page 170)

** 2. Why is it important for students to be able to produce a text structure in their own writing?

*** 3. Of the comprehension strategies introduced in Chapter 9, which one(s) do you prefer for use in your content area? Why?

*   Text explicit

**   Text implicit

***   Experience-based

Notice that a study guide of this form asks students to react to text concepts at multiple levels of understanding. For example, the first question, which is text explicit, includes a reference to assist students in locating the answer. For some students, this form of guidance may be necessary. Indeed, some students may only be able to answer this form of question, particularly in the early stages of the course. In contrast to question one, question three asks the reader to build a bridge of text concepts and individual teaching needs. Both questions two and three offer the potential for discussion and expanded thinking. Although this study guide example has been presented after the fact, in practice study guides typically accompany a text assignment and the reader completes the guide while reading. Thus, the guide provides a pathway to the major concepts in a content area and counters a more traditional, sink-or-swim reading assignment. A good study guide should mirror the thinking process by which a reader extracts information from text. As such, a teacher-devised study guide should:

1. Focus students' attention on major concepts at three levels of understanding (i.e., text explicit, text implicit, experience-based).
2. Foster student reaction to the text material at each student's own, individual level of understanding.
3. Direct students' thinking processes in extracting information from text material.
4. Serve as a basis for follow-up discussion in small groups to collaborate on the explication of text concepts and extend individual comprehension.

One might expect that students would regard study guides as an additional burden along with the text reading assignment. However, our observations of secondary students' using study guides reveals that they are well received. The majority of students felt they understood text concepts better as a result of completing and discussing guide material.

The development of a study guide involves a process of content analysis similar to the construction of an anticipation guide. Indeed, developing these two comprehension aids simultaneously with a text chapter is a good idea.

Steps to Develop a Study Guide

1. Determine the major concepts and important details in a text chapter or reading selection.
2. Develop questions that reflect these major concepts and details at multiple levels of understanding. Use vocabulary terms students can understand and, in the first few guides you develop, provide page and paragraph indicators to demonstrate the process of locating and extracting information.
3. Assign the study guide as an adjunct to independent text reading. Then, have students discuss and defend responses in small groups.

Since not all students will be able to answer the whole study guide, the discussion step gives everyone exposure to the complete array of information. This study group step is an integral part of the application of study guide material and is essential to its success as an aid to comprehension. Generally, about 10 questions per study guide should be adequate for a text chapter. The guide should look attractive in that adequate space is allowed for student answers, and information does not appear to be crowded on the page.

The study guide shown in Figure 10.7 was used to guide high school students' discussion in United States history. Text explicit questions are labeled "right there on the page," text implicit questions are labeled "think and search," and experi-

Figure 10.7

> ## Study Guide: The Confederation and the Constitution
>
> *Right There On the Page*
>
> 1. What political changes occurred in the 13 colonies as a result of the American Revolution? (pp. 119–120)
>
>   *Colonial self-rule, the recognition of minorities, new constitution, an increase in voting, and the legislature was more responsive to people.*
>
> 2. What social changes took place in the 13 colonies as a result of the American Revolution? (pp. 120–121)
>
>   *The separation of church and state, department of Loyalists, uprooted the Anglican Church, loosening of morals, weakening of slavery, and the development of the feminist movement.*
>
> 3. What economic changes happened in the 13 colonies as a result of the American Revolution? (p. 122)
>
>   *Inventive influences, the loss of commerce because of England, high inflation, great amounts of land available, freedom of trade, a distaste for government.*
>
> *Think and Search*
>
> 4. Can you identify some political, social, and economic disadvantages that resulted from the American Revolution?
>
>   *We did not have many great strong leaders that we had before. We really did not have much control. We were on our own so we needed to spend money to manufacture goods and find people to buy them.*
>
> 5. Why wasn't slavery abolished in the 1770s?
>
>   *Political fighting over slavery was avoided to preserve national unity. Too many people needed workers to make money and get their lives going again.*
>
> 6. Why do you think the authors see the American Revolution as "accelerated evolution" rather than "outright revolution?"
>
>   *Because the Revolution was unknown to many people living in small, isolated villages. And, it wasn't as radical as other revolutions. It made future changes possible.*
>
> *On Your Own*
>
> 7. Would you want to travel through time back to the 1770s during the drafting of the Constitution? If so, why? If not, why not?
>
>   *Yes, so I could maybe put things in or take things out that may help the United States.*
>
> 8. If you decide to travel back in time to visit the drafting of the Constitution you would be taking with you the powerful knowledge of the future! What advice could you give the writers of the Constitution?
>
>   *Be clearer in what is written. Today, interpretations of the Constitution are all different.*

ence-based questions are labeled "on your own." This study guide was developed to accompany reading the Confederation and the Constitution. Students read the text and answered the study guide questions. Then, they engaged in small group discussions of their answers and a large group follow-up discussion focusing on the "on your own" items. One student's answers are included.

Study guides are particularly important in the early part of a course as students are getting a grasp of an author's writing style and dominant text structures. We have used study guides effectively in the early grades and at the academic level.

Study guide questions can form an effective model for student-generated questions. Indeed, study guides help model fluent, efficient text reading. Textbooks are not designed to be read word-for-word. Rather, they should be read selectively with an eye toward important ideas. The following activity is designed to give you further practice with the process of constructing a study guide for a content area text.

APPLICATION 10.2

Directions: The following three study guide questions pertain to the present section of Chapter 10. See if you can generate three additional study guide questions on this same material.

*** 1. Based on your own academic experience, can you think of any courses you have taken where you would have appreciated study guides with the text? Which ones? Why?

* 2. What is the second step in constructing a study guide?

** 3. How does the study guide foster the psychological principle of in-depth processing of text material?

* 4.

** 5.

*** 6.

Options Guides

An *options guide* is another form of study guide that, unlike the focused guidance provided in a traditional study guide, offers possibilities and predictions to be evaluated in subsequent reading. It asks students to function in an active, decision-making role. Unlike a study guide, which is designed to accompany a reading assignment, an options guide is discussed prior to text reading. It then serves as a guide during reading. Options guides are ideal for reading assignments in social studies texts, where students often adopt a passive role, mindlessly turning pages or trying to memorize facts.

Steps to Develop and Introduce the Options Guide

1. Carefully analyze a text reading assignment for major concepts and key sub-headings that foreshadow upcoming events. You want to identify (1) key historical figures and the specific impact they had on other groups of people; and (2) the economy, the arts, religion, and other sociocultural aspects of life.

2. Since up to the time you introduce the options guide, students' previous text reading is all they have to go on in discussing the guide, you should construct a brief background statement that will remind students of the material they have read and studied up to this point.

3. Develop one or two central questions that ask students to consider various options open to specific groups of people within the particular historical context the text is presenting.

4. When students have completed a text reading assignment up to the sub-heading or section of text upon which your options guide is based, have them convene in small groups for about 10 to 15 minutes to discuss and complete the prereading section of the options guide. Then, when they finish reading the assignment, they should check their listed options against actual events in the text and complete the guide's postreading section. Engage students in a fol-

low-up small group discussion to clarify any sections of the guide that need further explanation.

The options guide shown in Figure 10.8 is designed to precede a text reading assignment in world history on the emergence of Japan. Students have read the

Figure 10.8

Options Guide: The Kamakura Shogunate (1192–1333) Began

Background: In 1156, civil war broke out between two large landowning families. Each family had a band of loyal warriors, called samurai. In 1192, one samurai, named Minamoto Yoritomo, became the supreme general of all Japan. The emperor named him the shogun.

During this period of military rule, what *options* for political influence do you think were available to the following groups?

1. Nobles?

    1.1 Before Reading: *They will be even more powerful with the strength of their loyal samurai warriors.*

    1.2 After Reading: *The emperor's power was less but the local "daimyos" (nobles) became supreme rulers of their lands. They fought with other daimyos. There was no effective central government in Japan during this time. Later, in the Tokugawa Era (1603–1868), central government was strong.*

2. Artists?

    2.1 Before Reading: *In this military era, we feel there will be no time for the arts. Artists will be forced to fight or flee. It will be a very backward time.*

    2.2 After Reading: *It seems strange but the arts did flourish. Poetic "No" plays were created, landscape painting was prized, flower arranging, tea ceremonies, and artistic gardens were important in Japanese homes.*

3. Farmers?

    3.1 Before Reading: *With all the fighting, there will be no time for farming. Agriculture will suffer.*

    3.2 After Reading: *Farmers thrived since the daimyos ruled to maintain peace within their own communities. But gradually, cities grew and merchants became important. The landing of the Portuguese in 1543 made the people aware of European trade possibilities.*

4. The Samurai?

    4.1 Before Reading: *They are soldiers, so, like all soldiers, they will have little power. They must follow orders.*

    4.2 After Reading: *Samurai knights were very loyal to their shogun generals. They felt a total moral obligation to do well in battle. If they did not, they would commit suicide or "harakiri." As we suspected, they didn't have much power. The shoguns held the power.*

5. If the Chinese try to invade Japan, how will they do?

    5.1 Before Reading: *Since they are an older, more powerful people, they will win.*

    5.2 After Reading: *Kubla Khan invaded Japan but his Mongol warriors were swept into a big typhoon. The Japanese called this the Kamikaze or "divine wind." As we said before reading, without this typhoon, China's Mongol warriors might have defeated the samurai.*

portion of the chapter on the developing samurai warrior-class. The first sub-heading of the new reading comprises the major heading for the guide. Subsequent sub-headings were used to list various groups affected by shogun society. Representative group answers before and after reading are listed.

As you can see, in some instances students generated options that were borne out in the text. In other cases, their predictions proved far afield of what actually occurred. Options guides make potentially dull text reading assignments considerably more interesting. Indeed, using options guides in conjunction with other strategies (e.g., graphic organizers) will potentially make your lessons even more productive for students. The guides' success hinges in large measure on the small group discussions that precede and follow their use as reading guides. Consider using options guides for selected topics in social studies as a student-centered alternative to traditional study guides. You may want to begin with fairly detailed options guides, like the one on Japan, and slowly fade to skeletal options guides that place the responsibility on students to speculate about the impact of an event on sociocultural aspects of the economy, arts, agriculture, and so on. In our experience, your efforts to develop guide material will be richly rewarded in increased levels of student understanding and participation.

Analogical Guides

Another form of study guide has been developed for application in science classes. The *analogical guide* is aimed at getting students to study new science concepts they are attempting to learn by thinking about the underlying properties of more familiar concepts and comparing these to new, unfamiliar concepts.

We use analogies spontaneously in our everyday speech and thinking. For example, if we plan a field trip to a marine biology laboratory and the trip is successful, we may say the job went like clockwork. If our field trip plans failed, we may say they collapsed like a house of cards.

It is not unusual for scientists to use analogies to explain complex processes or theories. For example, scientists use the analogy of a giant pinwheel or disk to understand the nature of the Milky Way. Texts in biology sometimes feature analogies, but students often do not know how they can use these analogies to comprehend and recall concepts. The analogical guide is designed to make students aware of using analogies to understand concepts. Before we introduce the analogical guide on cell structure, test your knowledge of cell structure by completing Application 10.3.

APPLICATION 10.3

Your last science class may have been quite some time ago, or you may be a science teacher. In any case, we would like you to try the following activity. See if you can correctly match the six cell structure parts on the left with their related functions on the right. Simply write the letter of the correct function on the line to the left of the cell part. Good luck.

Structure

1. _____ mitochondria

2. _____ cell membrane

3. _____ vacuoles

Function

a. controls heredity

b. storage

c. boundary

4. _____ nucleus   d. intracellular transport

5. _____ endoplasmic reticulum   e. cellular respiration

6. _____ ribosomes   f. protein synthesis

These cell structure-function relationships comprise just a small part of a basic chapter on the cell. This material constitutes an important foundation for subsequent chapters that explore more complex aspects of the cell, such as cell division. Most biology texts contain a chart of cell parts and functions for students to study. Many students simply memorize this chart without really understanding how the different cell parts function. In your case, we gave you a small number of cell parts to match to their functions. How did you do? Our guess is that you successfully matched nucleus and cell membrane, but (unless your field is science) you flubbed the other four items. Here are the correct answers: l-e; 2-c; 3-b; 4-a; 5-d; 6-f. Now, consider students who have access to the analogical study guide in Figure 10.9 that a teacher introduces and explains. Do you think your comprehension of these six cell structure-function relations would have been better with such a guide?

Figure 10.9

Analogical Guide: Cell Structure and Function

Directions: You will be studying the parts of a cell and their functions. In some ways a cell resembles a factory, because, like a factory, a cell uses raw materials to manufacture a product. You will find that comparing the different parts of the cell to the parts of a factory will help you remember the functions of the various cell parts. For example, in the guide, the cell walls are compared to factory walls because both provide support and protection.

STRUCTURE	FUNCTION	ANALOGY (LIKE A)
cell wall	support and protection	factory walls
cell membrane	boundary, gatekeeper	security guards
cytoplasm	site of metabolism	the work area
chloroplasts	photosynthesis	snack bar
endoplasmic reticulum	intracellular transport	conveyor belts
golgi bodies	storage, secretion	packaging, storing, and shipping
lysosomes	intracellular digestion	clean-up crew
mitochondria	cellular respiration	energy generation plant
nucleus	controls heredity	boss's office and copy machine
ribosomes	protein synthesis	assembly line
vacuoles	storage	warehouses

The overall factory analogy provides a coherent structure for the whole guide. In a study of this guide's contribution to students' comprehension in high school biology, we found that students who were achieving low grades significantly outpaced peers in a control group when the guide was introduced as a means of studying the text. The control group simply used the cell structure-function chart provided in the text without any analogies.

Steps for Constructing an Analogical Guide

1. Analyze the reading task facing students by identifying those concepts you want them to acquire (e.g., a basic understanding of cell structure and function relationships).

2. This is the most difficult and crucial step—creating appropriate analogies that will connect with students' diverse experiences. A good analogy is one that contains underlying properties similar to the target concept, but it is usually dissimilar at the surface level. For example, comparing the cell membrane to a security guard provides a familiar analogy, because the two share underlying properties of entry and exit control, even though there are no surface level similarities.

3. You need to go over the analogical guide with students, explaining how they can use the analogies on the right side of the guide to comprehend and recall the function of a particular cell structure. Some students may wish to generate their own analogies, so you can gradually transfer responsibility for this process to students.

Whenever we see a glazed look on students' faces during a classroom explanation, we spontaneously search for an appropriate analogy to provide a vivid image of the concept we are introducing. Analogical guides make this process explicit for students by showing them how they can effectively use analogies to link new information with prior knowledge. We recommend that you use analogical guides, when appropriate, for complex topics in science. Although such guides take some time to create, they help alleviate the sink-or-swim experience many students have as they try to fathom science texts. Their feelings are much the same as you experienced trying to complete the cell structure function matching activity. Unguided reading of a complex text simply produces frustration and hostility rather than comprehension and a feeling of power over the material.

In the section that follows we explore the last stage of a content reading, listening, or viewing assignment, the postreading stage.

Postreading Strategies

Despite the intuitive and proven value of review for long-term retention of content area concepts, this activity remains the most often neglected component of a lesson structure. Important concepts are glossed over far too rapidly in an effort to cover the book and get on to new material.

The review stage of a lesson is typically viewed as an independent activity that students perform on their own time. While the phrase, "Now it's time to review the concepts we explored last week," may engender a chorus of yawns, review activities do not have to be a devastating bore. It is true, however, when they consist of nothing more than a teacher-centered lecture recounting previously learned concepts, the outcome is likely to be counterproductive. In fact, classroom observations suggest that small group, collaborative discussions are rare, occupying less than 20 percent of classroom time (Tierney & Readence, 2005). Oddly enough, when we as adults confront some thorny problem, we often collaborate with others in ad hoc groups or more formal committee structures to tackle and solve the problem. Overemphasizing independent review fails to provide experiences that will help students respond to real world challenges in a cooperative fashion.

In contrast to those who see review sessions as teacher-centered activities, we perceive the review process to be a natural outgrowth of the prereading and read-

Postreading Strategies

- Discussion Groups
- Reaction Guides
- Phony Document Strategy
- The Imposter
- Polar Opposites
- Graphic Organizers
- Multiple Text Inquiry Discussion

ing activities in a well-integrated lesson. Activities that acknowledge and, in some cases, refine students' prior knowledge of a topic also can be applied at the postreading stage. For example, the reaction guide you had been filling out at the close of each chapter in Part 1 is essentially a review activity. The graphic organizer and the study guide also lend themselves to the review process. Indeed, we regard review as more than a solitary pondering of text concepts. Review activities should involve active manipulation and collaborative discussion of information. The following are advantages in using discussion groups in a class:

1. Students are more motivated to learn when they are cooperating rather than competing individually with their peers.
2. Students display a more positive attitude toward both the class and the instructor when there are opportunities for this less teacher-centered form of learning.
3. Students in the role of the tutor and the tutee both benefit. They have to know the material in order to effectively teach it to another student.
4. Students' self-esteem is enhanced by helping one another learn content material.
5. Students display more positive perceptions of the intentions of other students. This is especially crucial in multilingual, multicultural classrooms. By working together in cooperative groups, students perceive their peers more positively than when they are isolated from each other. There is a decrease in prejudice and stereotyping.
6. There is a decrease in competitive goal structures. Students come to view other students' ideas as important to their individual learning.
7. Students become less dependent on the teacher as the only source of reliable information. They begin to take charge of problem solving in a cooperative fashion.

We would expect that, given the compelling advantages of using small groups to review content material, teachers would place more emphasis on this mode of instruction. However, many teachers are reluctant to break out of the more controlled teacher-centered role. For instance, Alvermann, O'Brien, and Dillon (1990), who observed 24 content teachers from English, health, science, and other fields in order to determine the match between teachers' idealized comments about what constitutes a good discussion and what actually happens when these same teachers attempt to use discussion in their classrooms, found a marked disparity between teachers' idealized views of discussion—touting active student participation—and the lecture and recitation-based nature of their actual classroom discussions. Teachers worried about releasing classroom control and departing from the rapid fire pace of content coverage.

Using small groups entails a different style of classroom management that is, unquestionably, more of an art than orchestrating instruction from the front of the room and acting as an authority figure. Since we recommend using small groups to discuss material in the various guides introduced in this chapter, and particularly at the postreading review stage of a lesson, what are some of the features that seem to insure small groups work effectively?

Discussion Groups

GENERAL GUIDELINES. It is important to first consider the role you plan to play in guiding small group review. Alvermann, Dillon, & O'Brien (1987) described four possible teacher roles and commented on their characteristic limitations.

The first role they call "the instructor." The teacher retains the normal fountain of truth position and serves to clarify any confusion or difficulties that arise in the small groups. The disadvantage of adopting this role is that it may limit students' sense of their own responsibility for maintaining discussion and resolving problems.

A second possible role is that of "participant." The teacher becomes part of a small group discussion. Although this sounds attractive, you may inadvertently inhibit students from participating. After all, in your normal role you are perceived as the content expert.

A third, and more appropriate role, is that of a "consultant." In this way you are free to rove about the room, responding to requests for help from various groups. It is important to restrain yourself from over-assisting a group. Rather, encourage students to exhaust all their efforts in resolving problems or clarifying information before you offer to step in.

A fourth, and most difficult role, is that of a "neutral observer" of small group discussion. In this case, you remain silent, offering neither opinion, clarification, or conflict resolution. Although this may be an ideal role to adopt, it requires a slow, methodical release of responsibility to students that may span many weeks before students are comfortable and skilled at working in small groups.

An important and often overlooked facet of using small groups effectively is the furniture and layout of your room. If students are in desks arranged by rows, they can easily work in pairs, side-by-side. Or, if you have circular tables, these can be ideal for groups of four to five students. In general, as group size increases, the level of individual participation decreases.

Small groups should be composed of four to five student members of mixed-ability with a clear learning goal. This may range from a discussion of study guide questions or reaction guide statements to debating an issue. Students' learning should be assessed individually, with the small group receiving recognition for the success of its members. This can be accomplished by adding up individual's scores to arrive at team scores for various assessments.

Developing clearly defined student roles within a group is important. One student may be chair for the week, guiding discussion of study guide questions. The group may need a recorder and a gatekeeper to maintain the flow of discussion. These roles can be exchanged periodically. It must be noted that low ability and high ability students both make important contributions to learning. When a small group is discussing a study guide, low ability students often function as excellent fact-finders, while high ability students may see connections from text-based ideas to more global issues. Both types of students offer opportunities for creative debate, and they learn effectively from each other. There is general agreement that it is very important to compose groups that include mixed-ability students, so they can balance each others' strengths and weaknesses.

A recent study of 9th-graders engaged in peer-led discussions of the popular short story, *The Lottery* (Jackson, 1948/1982), found that while students used multiple comprehension strategies, they often skated along the surface of a topic (Berne & Clark, 2006). These authors noted that for a rich discussion to occur, students need to be taught how to actively listen to group members' ideas and questions before darting off on another topic. In addition, they need to be introduced to comprehension strategies (e.g., graphic organizers) aimed at helping them elucidate ideas in a text or short story. Fortunately, you can ensure that small groups function productively in your content area classroom by establishing clear parameters for discussion.

Although these general guidelines for your role in guiding small group learning and review are based on recent synthesis of research in the area of cooperative learning, you must decide how to best use small groups in your own classroom. The next section offers some specific guidelines for developing and managing small groups effectively.

SPECIFIC GUIDELINES. A good way to demonstrate clearly how you want a small group to function is to model this process. Using guide material as a focal point for the discussion, compose a small group at the front of the room and act in the role of a group chair to demonstrate the process for about 10 minutes. Keep early efforts fairly simple and focused. Remember that students are often unaccustomed to working in this cooperative fashion.

If a group is going off course, straying far afield of the task, how should you respond? Unfortunately, this is not a simple issue. As we pointed out earlier, if you adopt the role of the authoritarian instructor and monitor too heavily, you may interfere with the development of independent student problem-solving. On the other hand, total chaos in your classroom is equally undesirable. Fortunately, there are some solutions to this problem.

Small study groups function productively when the teacher sets the stage for the review. To prepare students, the teacher should first explain the goals and advantages of collaborating in the study process via interdependent groups. The key idea here hinges on the phrase, interdependent groups. That is, the success of the group in solving a problem is evaluated collectively, but it also depends on the contribution of the individual members. To achieve such interdependence, stress the following:

1. Explain the desired discussion behaviors that students should strive for (e.g., encouraging each other to respond; valuing each others' ideas; allowing an adequate amount of time for a group member to explain a point without dominating the discussion); and,
2. Explain the reward system by which you would rate group performance. These systems will vary according to the maturity and ability of the students involved.

In addition to these steps, political scientist Walter Parker (2003) offers a teaching model aimed at introducing high school students to thoughtful, deliberative small group discussion about local or global events of interest to students. Using a discussion framework based on one used by public policy professionals, each group must do the following:

1. Identify and explain a public problem (e.g., student dress codes on campus) and related stakeholders.
2. Develop and analyze policy alternatives to include goals, consequences, and trade-offs.
3. Decide what action to take.

However, before getting to the third step, students are introduced to a deliberative process that stimulates active listening to opposing views. In groups of four:

→ Students study the issue under consideration (e.g., dress codes).
→ Each group breaks into pairs of two students.

→ Each pair is assigned a different position on the issue and further reading to support their particular position.

→ Each pair presents their arguments and presents to the other pair.

→ Each pair then reverses their perspective, taking the opposing view.

→ Finally, they combine into a group of four again and, in this deliberative body, seek consensus on the issue or, agree to disagree.

As a model of democratic deliberation that incorporates active listening to content area classroom discussion, this process offers teachers a step-by-step means to ensure that small groups function productively. Issues of war, international cooperation, and global politics all lend themselves to deliberative forums where students move beyond surface understanding of critical issues (Harper & Bean, 2006).

A number of other strategies can serve as jumping off points for vibrant classroom discussion in your content area. Reaction Guides, related to Anticipation Guides, center discussion on key issues.

Reaction Guides

A *reaction guide* provides a good prelude to a more intensive review when it serves as a focal point for small group discussion. When you complete a text selection and then reassess your prereading responses to an anticipation guide, you are using a reaction guide to examine your beliefs about a topic. More than likely, you alter at least some of your prereading beliefs and can defend this change by referencing explicit statements in the text.

A reaction guide is easy to construct since it is essentially another form of the anticipation guide, and the text analysis steps are the same for both comprehension strategies. You can simply add a second column to an anticipation guide for a postreading reaction to the same statements. While the mechanics of the guide are simple, they should not be used as individual worksheets to be completed in silence. Rather, two or three of the most important statements should be considered and discussed by small groups. For example, we might have used the following statement for Chapter 3:

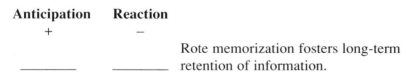

Anticipation   Reaction
        +   –

_____   _____   Rote memorization fosters long-term
                                                   retention of information.

Notice that although many students might have agreed (+) with this statement at the prereading stage, upon considering the psychological importance of deep processing and organization for retention, they would tend to disagree (–) at the postreading stage. More importantly, they would be able to defend this shift by referring to relevant portions of the text that lend support to the respective roles of deep processing and hierarchical organization in the memorial process.

Duffelmeyer and Baum (1992) have suggested an adaptation of the Reaction Guide which promotes students' critical reading and thinking skills as well as requires them to actively confront their potential misconceptions. This adaptation is modeled for you with the anticipation and reaction guides used in Part 1 of this text. In the beginning of each chapter of Part 1 we asked you to agree or disagree with each guide statement and then to be ready to explain your choices. At the end of each chapter of Part 1 we asked you to reconsider your responses to the guide statements. If the information you found in the chapter supported your original choice, we asked you to check the Confirmed column and then write the supporting evidence from the text in your own words in the column marked, Why my choice is confirmed. If the information did not support your original choice, you were asked to check the Disconfirmed column and then write what the text says in your own words in the column marked, Why my choice is not confirmed. The addition of the writing task to the reaction guide facilitates additional interaction with the text as students are asked to justify their claims of agreement or confront their misconceptions.

Phony Document Strategy

This critical reading strategy was initially developed for history classes, but we have found it to be applicable in other fields such as English and science. The *phony document strategy* is based on a teacher-authored letter that purports to be historical and authentic, commenting on a key aspect of a novel, historical event, or scientific experiment (Baldwin, Readence, & Bean, 2004). While it reads as a perfectly plausible account, it is usually embedded with errors that students must ferret out through critical reading. Indeed, the central purpose of this strategy is to engage students in a close reading of the primary source material referred to in the phony document you have written. At the outset, you let them believe in the possible authenticity of this document. However, they must, in the end, refute its authenticity and point out the untruths and flaws embedded in it.

Steps to Using the Phony Document Strategy

1. Create a phony, but plausibly written document such as a letter, critique, news article, and so on. Letters and book excerpts or introductions seem to work best.
2. Ask students to read and judge the accuracy of the document and its value as something the school or district might want to purchase for wide distribution to students. They must engage in a close reading, cross-checking information (e.g., dates, assertions, places, and so on) with other sources.
3. Conduct small group and whole class discussions on the document's accuracy and value.

The following phony letter from a literary scholar illustrates the use of this strategy in an American literature class with high school juniors. Students finished reading Arthur Miller's famous play *The Crucible* (1976). This and other activities in the class prepared the students to write from the perspective of a particular character in the play and extend their thinking about key episodes and events. Students read and critiqued the following phony document:

Student Task for P. J. Pennerd's *The Crucible Revisited*

P. J. Pennerd is the Senior Scholar in Humanities at Boston University and the Danforth Foundation Endowed Chair in Literary Criticism. He is an internationally known expert on Arthur Miller's *The Crucible*. His work is widely quoted by other literary scholars. Our nearby university library recently purchased the complete collection of Professor Pennerd's works for student use and analysis. Copies are currently worth thousands of dollars, and our school district and English Department are interested in purchasing this collection for our English curriculum. Your opinion is important in deciding the value of these documents. Please read and comment on this introductory material.

Introduction

The Salem, Massachusetts, witch trials of 1700 resulted in the execution of 50 Salem witches and far surpassed the number of accused witches put to death in Europe during this period. The Salem girls included Abigail Williams, Ann Putnam, Jr., Mary Warren, and others.

Arthur Miller crafted his popular play around these events by creating characters who best exemplify the play's title, *The Crucible*, defined as a severe test or hard trial, or a container for melting and calcinating ores.

The separation of church and state in Salem made Judge Danforth an objective judge for the trials. Innocent until proven guilty were his watchwords and code of conduct. The community, too, abided by this code of conduct. This is best illustrated by Abigail's willingness to cooperate in the trial's proceedings.

Judge Danforth was not worried about being hemmed in by the law. He was most concerned with seeking justice for the community.

In the pages that follow, I will show how Judge Danforth served as the most dynamic and central character of the play, riveting our attention and earning our compassion and sensitivity.

P. J. Pennerd
January 1998

There are a number of flaws in this document, and even if you have not read *The Crucible* recently, your knowledge of history will reveal some of the erroneous assertions made by the phony P. J. Pennerd! For example, at the most basic level, the date of events is wrong. The Salem witch trials occurred in 1692, and 20 accused witches were put to death, not 50. The second paragraph is okay, but in paragraph three, the presumption of innocence until proven guilty is contrary to the beliefs of this Puritan theocracy. There was no separation of church and state in legal decisions of the time. In paragraph four, Judge Danforth was so blinded by his allegiance to the law that he was unable to discern the truth. Unlike claims in the final paragraph, he is unyielding and definitely not dynamic, at least in the way Proctor and Elizabeth are portrayed by Arthur Miller in the play.

Thus, students had to engage in a close reading of the play and challenge any erroneous information in this lofty document. They ultimately recommended not purchasing this material for wide student use.

As you try out the phony document strategy, be careful to make it look plausible. Of course you can only use this strategy occasionally as students will suspect something is up in subsequent, authoritative documents you circulate in class.

The Imposter

The Imposter (Curran & Smith, 2005) is another strategy that, like the Phony Document Strategy, is aimed at getting students to critically evaluate what they read. This is particularly useful in mathematics and science text. The strategy involves including a contradictory statement, idea, or number in a science passage or mathematical problem. Students must then locate and discover the nature of the contradiction by reading closely. Thus, this strategy motivates students to focus on the text. Curran and Smith recommend the following guidelines for students:

→ Find proof of the error in the text.
→ Errors should be distributed throughout the text.
→ The errors must be somewhat obvious and not so obscure as to be frustrating.

The following example from Curran and Smith demonstrates a quantitative error embedded in an otherwise accurate chemistry passage:

> The pH of a solution is a quantitative assessment of the number of free protons and is measured on a negative logarithmic scale from 0 to 14. Each whole integer, then, is 10 times *greater* than the next highest whole integer. A pH of 5.0 then, has 10 times more free protons than a pH of 6.0. Similarly, a pH of 8.0 has a thousand times *more* protons than a pH of 5.0. (p. 188)

The Imposter error in this passage is embedded in the last sentence where "*more* free protons" should read "a thousand times *less* free protons" (Curran & Smith, p. 188). In essence, any content area passage can lend itself to The Imposter strategy with a little creative thinking. We believe that, as an extension activity, students can create their own Imposter passages. To accomplish this, students must have well-grounded comprehension of the material they are reading. Therefore, we recommend carefully modeling The Imposter strategy and phasing out guidance as students become more adept at detecting embedded errors.

Polar Opposites

When students have a concrete series of reaction guide statements to support or refute, they are more likely to engage in group discussion. *Polar Opposites* is a strategy that also provides a concrete basis for postreading discussion (Bean & Bishop, 2007). A polar opposites guide consists of descriptive adjectives such as happy versus sad that are supported or challenged by events in the text.

Steps to a Polar Opposites Guide

1. Develop four or five polar opposite statements and their accompanying adjectives. Place five blanks between the adjectives. For example:

Cairo's third city is . . .

new ____ ____ ____ ____ ____ old

2. After students have read a selection or listened to a film, have them place a check mark (✓) closest to the adjective that they feel best describes the events or character. They can also score events and characters using a five-point scale.

3. Have students defend their rating in small group discussion or a writing activity by referring to specific examples or events in the selection.

The following example from world geography should help you develop your own polar opposites guide. The passage is from the text, *New Exploring a Changing World* (Schwartz & O'Connor, 1975, pp. 364–365).

On the roofs of Cairo there is a third city—a town of modern roof dwellers. Tens of thousands of people live on Cairo's rooftops. In the days when you could fly a small plane over Cairo, you could clearly see its two levels of life. One is on the ground and one is in the air. . . . I have seen on a roof opposite the Continental Hotel, someone cooking under a bamboo shelter, village women washing clothes, naked children, a goat or two, and a mangy dog. These rooftop slums are mostly servants' quarters but in the old city, they are the result of overcrowding.

Cairo's third city is . . .

	5	4	3	2	1	
new	___	___	___	___	___	old
spacious	___	___	___	___	___	crowded
healthful	___	___	___	___	___	unsanitary
safe	___	___	___	___	___	hazardous
rich	___	___	___	___	___	poor
friendly	___	___	___	___	___	hostile

In this particular guide, Cairo can be viewed either positively, with a possible high rating of 30 (i.e., 5 points × 6 adjectives), negatively with a possible low rating of 6 (i.e., 1 point per item), or somewhere between these polar opposites. Indeed, some of the adjectives entail careful, critical reading to infer a response. For example, the last pair of adjectives, friendly versus hostile, usually engenders heated discussion. If you are a member of Cairo's rooftop culture, then it is undoubtedly friendly, or at least somewhat friendly. However, for the outsider unaccustomed to this overcrowded lifestyle, Cairo's rooftops may well be hostile. Thus, students can critically evaluate the author's perspective. If it seems to be overly ethnocentric, outside sources may be considered to confirm or deny information in the text. In this way, polar opposites can be used to guide students into independent projects involving library and database research.

Polar opposites provides even the most reticent students with a basis for participating in discussion and writing activities. In order to defend or refute a particular rating, students must return to the text for support. Thus, it encourages critical reading in much the same way as the reaction guide.

Graphic Organizers

Although the graphic organizer was suggested as a prereading vocabulary strategy, it is an equally good review guide (see pp. 154–156). Graphic organizers are easy to construct. Teachers find them to be useful across a broad range of content areas. Research reviews on teachers' use of graphic organizers shows that they lead to greater student engagement and support knowledge acquisition and transfer more effectively than simply reading text passages, writing summaries, or outlining (Nesbit & Adesope, 2006). In addition, graphic organizers are particularly helpful for students with low verbal proficiency. In the early stages of a unit, items from the graphic organizer developed by the teacher can be written on notecards or post-it notes. Students working in small groups can attempt to reconstruct the author's conceptual organization or pattern by arranging the notecards in a logical diagram. This review activity can be conducted as a game, if desired, with points awarded for reconstructing successive portions of the unit organizer.

But students need not merely reconstruct information exactly as the teacher's schema portrayed it. Instead, they can use the top-level skeletal structure of the teacher's organizer and add on information they have acquired in text reading. Such student-constructed postreading organizers seem to contribute more to comprehension than a teacher-devised organizer. Application 10.4 illustrates the use of a skeletal graphic organizer as a review guide.

APPLICATION 10.4

Directions: Before we go on, think about the comprehension strategies you have acquired so far in Chapter 10 for each of the three stages of an integrated lesson (i.e., prereading, reading, postreading). In the organizer that follows, one strategy has been listed in each stage. Without looking back at the chapter, see if you can supply at least two additional strategies per stage.

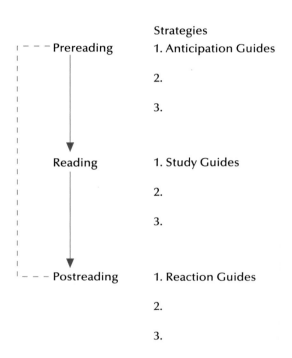

Strategies

Prereading
1. Anticipation Guides
2.
3.

Reading
1. Study Guides
2.
3.

Postreading
1. Reaction Guides
2.
3.

Contemporary content-based ESL programs usually integrate the dual goals of having students work on their second language while simultaneously learning content in history, science, mathematics, and English. Without careful teacher guidance using comprehension strategies, secondary students asked to both learn a new language and to comprehend difficult content in that language will soon flounder. Indeed, visual strategies like the graphic organizer, flow charts, and Venn diagrams are particularly helpful to second language learners. In addition, modeling is essential for students to make the best use of these strategies.

Consider This...

Students in a junior level advanced placement American literature class might explore societal mores and gender roles through reading and discussion of Arthur Miller's play *The Crucible* (1976), the film based on the play, a subsequent reading of *The Scarlet Letter* (Hawthorne, 1850) and Amy Tan's (1991) *The Kitchen God's Wife*. Student discussions should focus on comparing and contrasting elements in the drama, novels, and videos. Their goal would be to build rich conceptual, historical, and literary understanding of what it meant to be a woman and a citizen within the social contexts of these works. Many of the strategies introduced in this chapter can be used to take notes from multiple texts (e.g., graphic organizers), to link ideas that are similar or different across texts (e.g., Venn diagrams), and to extend students' thinking and discussion (e.g., higher-level questioning).

Multiple Text Inquiry Discussion

The use of single texts in many content classrooms is giving way to the use of multiple texts. In addition, definitions of text are being revised to include a broad range of material. Texts can be a book, chapter, story, novel, poem, essay, biography, internet printout, and so on. But texts can also encompass videos, music, photos, a dramatic play, pantomime, and a dizzying array of other ways to communicate. If students are going to become skilled at managing the incredible diversity of information sources at our fingertips today, they need opportunities to explore this process in the content areas. As we mentioned in the previous chapter, a *multiple text inquiry discussion* is designed to generate rich discussions when students read and attempt to synthesize a diverse collection of material on a topic (Walker & Bean, 2003).

Hartman and Allison (1996) offer the following steps for creating an inquiry-based classroom: (1) assemble multiple texts on a topic (ranging from 5 to 20 sources); (2) develop questions that focus discussion on making connections across multiple sources; (3) expect the discussion to extend across many days and, possibly, weeks; and (4) have students record exploratory ideas that emerge in their discussions. Topics should be broad and provocative enough to develop conceptual knowledge that is applicable to other problem-solving lessons students are likely to encounter.

Topics in science on ecological issues lend themselves to the selection of multiple texts, interviews with experts, Internet searches, and conversations with other students in far-away communities. For example, the topic of water quality and population growth is one that permeates news articles throughout the country. Working with the school librarian, local community sources, Internet searches, and so on, you and your students can assemble a collection of sources for multiple text inquiry discussions.

In order to guide students' small group discussion of multiple texts, you need adequate space to lay out all the materials. Large round tables lend themselves to this process far better than individual desks, but desks pulled together in a circle can suffice. Hartman and Allison (1996) recommend sequencing questions that prompt discussions to move from those that connect information within a single text to questions that connect information across two or more texts. Finally, they suggest prompt questions that connect ideas outside the text to information in the text by tapping students' background knowledge. For example, a single text question probe for an initial discussion of *The Crucible* would be: How were female servants like Abigail Williams treated by their employers in 1692? A question probe designed to integrate discussion of multiple texts would be: How are

Proctor's, Hester's, and Winnie Louie's situations alike or different in *The Crucible, The Scarlet Letter,* and *The Kitchen God's Wife*? Finally, a question designed to connect ideas from outside the texts would be: How have women's roles changed since the times depicted in these three novels?

Using butcher paper or some other means of recording small group discussion ideas will be crucial to keeping a continuous record of conceptual growth. Journals and learning logs can be used if space is a problem, or you find yourself teaching in classrooms other than your own. Culminating projects ranging from papers, plays, musical compositions, art, and so on should be a natural outgrowth of days or, in some cases, weeks devoted to exploring a multiple text topic. Evaluation of students' projects can be accomplished through a 4-point rubric focusing on the quality of their work. For example, a 4-point project would display unusual creativity, care in presentation, and evidence of integration of ideas across various texts. In contrast, a 1-point project would appear to be thrown together at the last minute with little evidence of connections across texts read and discussed in small groups.

Postscript

As students become accustomed to your use of a variety of strategies in prereading, reading, or postreading, you may find that a blend of two strategies makes sense. For example, you might introduce the topic of irrational and rational numbers in a math class with a few anticipation guide statements and accompany the reading and problem-solving part of the lesson with a study guide that moves students through successively more involved problems. Indeed, vocabulary strategies from Chapter 8 can be combined with the comprehension strategies in Chapter 9 and in this chapter or those in Chapter 11 on writing in the content areas. In short, don't be afraid to experiment with the strategies offered in this and other chapters. Modify them to fit your own teaching style and student needs. Field-testing the strategies will more than likely improve them. Certainly, you are in the best position to evaluate the success of these strategies in the classroom.

Now go back to the comprehension vignette at the beginning of this chapter. React again to the lesson as you did before. Compare your responses with those you made before you read the chapter.

Mini Projects

Using the text chapter on the CD-ROM entitled, "Smoking and Smokeless Tobacco," do one or all of the following:

1. Pick one of the prereading strategies advanced in this chapter. Develop this strategy and try it out with a small group of students or your peers. Evaluate the strategy in terms of its value as a means of preparing students for a content assignment.

2. Develop a study guide, option guide, or analogical guide on smoking. Try out your guide with a small group of students or your peers. Use the follow-up discussion phase recommended in this chapter for guide material. Evaluate your guide as an independent learning aid.

3. Develop and try out one of the postreading strategies described in this chapter. Use the strategy with a small group of students or your peers. Evaluate its effectiveness in reinforcing concepts about smoking.

4. Develop an integrated unit on smoking containing one strategy from each of the three stages of instruction described in this chapter. This miniproject is a synthesis of projects one through three.

Website Activity

To locate and complete Chapter 10 activities, go to [*www.kendallhunt.com/contentarealiteracy/*].

11

Writing

Setting

Alpha Polonium's high school physics class. Students have been reading in their physics text about various forms of energy, including gravitational force and radiant energy. Toward the end of this class, Ms. Polonium assigns a major research paper on alternative energy due in two weeks.

The Lesson

Ms. Polonium tells students they are to write a research paper on alternative energy sources such as solar energy or hydroelectric power. She mentions that the paper should be no more than 5 pages long with at least 3 sources besides the textbook they use in class. The paper is due in two weeks, she says.

Students look distraught. Ms. Polonium tries to quell their anxiety in a brief question and answer session just before the bell rings.

T: "Are there any questions?"

S: "Ms. Polonium, we only just started on the unit on alternative energy. How do we find the other three sources?"

T: "You could check the Internet for books, magazines and other material that discusses solar cars, hydroelectric dams, windmills, and so on."

S: "But how will we know if our paper is what you want? How will we know if we are reading things that are good descriptions of alternative energy? Personally, I feel lost."

The bell rings and students enter the hallway, still conversing about the alternative energy writing assignment and expressing their anxieties about writing in science.

A week and a half later, we look in on one of the students, Kelvin Newton, at home as he struggles with the assigned paper. He's writing about hydroelectric power, trying to organize the paper around advantages and disadvantages of this gravitational energy source. Kelvin completes a first draft and decides it's good enough since only Ms. Polonium will be reading it and she already knows about hydro power. He flips on the television and relaxes, secure in the knowledge that his paper can be put into a nice folder tomorrow night and turned in on time.

The weekend after the papers were due, we look in on Ms. Polonium, spending her Sunday evening bent over students' alternative energy papers with a red pen, correcting spelling and grammatical errors amidst marginal comments on their many misconceptions about alternative energy. Where did they get these ideas, she wonders?

That following Monday, students get their papers back, riddled with corrections and Ms. Polonium's remarks about paper content. Students console themselves with the knowledge that writing in this class counts for only a fraction of their grade. It's not like English class.

→ Keeping in mind that this lesson focuses on writing about alternative energy in a physics class, jot down your thoughts on the following questions:

1. What are the good points about the lesson?
2. What are the weak points about the lesson?
3. What, if anything, would you change about the lesson?

Rationale

Writing is a powerful way of learning and questioning across content areas. Once the sole province of English classrooms, writing is now seen as an important bridge between students' prior knowledge and ideas expressed in science, social studies, mathematics, and other content area texts. You need to be well informed about the writing process and ways to ensure students can use writing effectively in a variety of subjects. This chapter introduces you to contemporary thinking about the writing process and shows you how to use writing successfully to help students learn and reflect on concepts in your classroom.

Learning Objectives

→ Understand the distinction between composing and transcribing.

→ Be familiar with various teaching strategies that help students use writing to learn and writing to inform.

→ Be able to use various approaches to evaluate students' writing.

Graphic Organizer

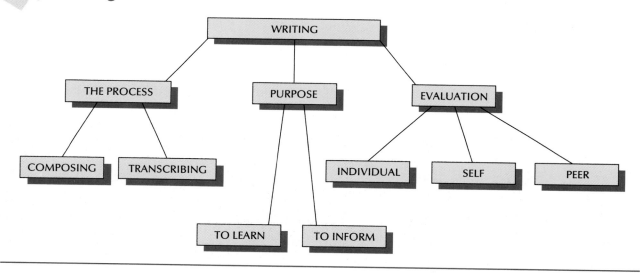

Writing Process

Real writing, the forms of writing most of us use in our daily lives, consists of writing to schedule, rank, plan, map, inquire, record, recall, organize, evaluate, and report. We use writing to share our ideas with others and we use writing as a means of reflection.

Writing is a craft, and like any craft, our writing progresses, sometimes haltingly and in small increments, through many stages. We may let ideas incubate for a time, simply tossing scraps of hastily written notes in a folder, collecting articles, and throwing them in a pile. Eventually, we are ready to organize this collection into categories having a tentative structure. The structure may be a narrative or one of the expository patterns introduced earlier in the text. Writing a draft, revising as we go, and sharing our draft with others eventually leads to a finished piece of writing about which we can feel good. Students need to see some of their writing evolve in this fashion. Other writing may be more exploratory, much like a diary that is not intended for public reading but may contribute to learning in your classroom. Thus, some writing in which you engage students will be designated to help inform others about a topic; other writing activities will assist their learning. Both forms of writing should take place in content classrooms.

In addition to using both expository and narrative forms of writing to develop content area learning in science, math, history, English, and other fields, contemporary classrooms often encourage the use of multiple genres to produce multimedia projects (Bean, 2000; Romano, 2000). Students use a carefully crafted blend of art, music, drama, and personal narrative to explore topics in history and other content areas. Thus, the boundaries of expository and narrative text structures are being expanded by creative teachers and students.

Before exploring specific strategies that help students use writing to learn and to inform, we want to define and consider two important aspects of the writing process, composing and transcribing.

Composing and Transcribing

Composing is the ongoing process of generating and shaping ideas before writing and as the actual writing unfolds. Composing involves thinking about ideas, weighing them, and putting them in some kind of order. Brainstorming, creating, clustering, and categorizing are some of the processes students use in composing. Out of these prewriting musings come new ways of looking at topics in content classrooms.

As students get started composing at a word processor or simply begin writing on a piece of paper, transcribing facilitates or inhibits the development of a finished product. *Transcribing* is a term that describes the mechanics of writing, including spelling, punctuation, capitalization, handwriting, formatting, and neatness. During the early draft stages of writing, when composing dominates students' thoughts, placing too much emphasis on the conventions of transcribing may interfere with the development of ideas. Certainly when students are engaged in reflective journal writing, which they do primarily for their own purposes, transcribing should be less of a concern than when they are preparing a final draft of a paper for a larger audience. As we look at the practice of journal writing in content classrooms, remember that composing issues are at the forefront. Personal journal writing is one of the best ways for students to explore ideas without feeling pressed to produce perfect spelling and grammar. In addition, it is a powerful way for you to carry on a dialogue about the class with individual students. Journal writing is the first writing to learn strategy we will consider.

Writing to Learn Strategies

➲ Journals
➲ Quick Writes
➲ Possible Sentences
➲ Cubing
➲ Writing Roulette
➲ ReWrite
➲ Guided Writing Procedure

Writing to Learn

In many content classrooms, students feel that the authority for their learning resides exclusively with the teacher. Yet in classes where students write often, as much as four and five times a week, they feel like they are in the driver's seat. Writing becomes a powerful vehicle for guiding their learning—a filter through which they can sift and examine concepts and see how these sometimes obscure notions may connect with their lives. Writing-to-learn activities initiate students to various methods for using writing to explore and integrate ideas arising from a content area.

Journal Writing

Observational studies of classrooms reveal far too little sustained writing of a personal nature. Yet in our day-to-day world, we see teachers, business people, scientists, and artists frequently jotting down random ideas or notes in a journal for their own purposes. When ideas wing briefly into short-term memory, a journal is an ideal place to pin them down for later consideration. In social studies, a student's journal may consider how the Bill of Rights might relate to students' rights in a high school environment. In science, a journal entry might wonder about gene splicing and its impact on future generations. In art, a journal comment may state how a student interprets a surrealistic painting. Or, a journal entry may have no higher purpose than to state, "I stayed up late last night. Today I'm having a lot of trouble concentrating on your lecture about the Roman Empire." In this way, *journal writing* can communicate a student's feelings and emotions and provide you with some sense of how your lessons are progressing for individual students on various days. In our crowded classrooms, journals can serve the important need to communicate attitudes and interests beyond the typical rapid fire charge through endless facts and concepts (Martin, 2007).

As you begin to use journal writing in your own subject area, consider the following principles (Bean, 2001):

1. Journal writing should become a regular part of your teaching. Students need to write in their journals on a daily basis.

   During the first five minutes of class, journals can be an ideal way to enter a topic or recap a previous day's lesson. For example, in a social studies classroom, on the first day of a unit students worked through an anticipation-reaction guide activity on the Bill of Rights. One of the statements reads: Students should have the right to select the classes they take. At the beginning of the next day's class, the teacher gives students an opportunity to comment further in their journals on this idea. Jeff writes:

   > I think it's a good idea. But only if we pick our class schedule every other week. That way, at least some of the time we have to take classes that are good for us, even though we may not like them. Like math. Math would be okay every other week. But I know this isn't going to happen. We have to do whatever the government tells us to do. It's depressing.

   Jeff was undoubtedly reluctant to express these opinions in the large class discussion the previous day. But in the privacy of his journal, he is free to explore divergent proposals. Journals can be used to explore content area concepts from a personal perspective, so it is important for students to have opportunities to pick what they want to write about. Therefore, you may want to alternate days devoted to some commentary on previous or upcoming lessons with days devoted to reflections on general topics students choose individually. The next principle suggests how you can demonstrate the range of topics students may wish to explore in their journals.

2. You should model journal writing by keeping your own journal and sharing entries aloud with students.

Just as sustained silent reading works best when you join in by reading a novel of your choice, journal writing takes on real importance in students' eyes when you also participate. For example, your entries may range from commentaries on how a unit is progressing to entries that chronicle your efforts to reduce your 10 kilometer running time.

3. You should look at students' journals and respond to their thoughts.

We recognize that it is unrealistic to expect a teacher to collect endless stacks of journals every day and respond to them. Rather, collect journals randomly so that you see every student's journal a few times in the course of a semester. In order to keep some parts of the journal completely private, you may have students use a looseleaf notebook with dividers labeled public and private. In this way you can at least respond to those sections marked public while not inhibiting opportunities for private comment. How much time should students spend each day writing in their journals?

4. Allot five to ten minutes for journal writing.

These four principles should not imply that journals be used in a rigid, formulaic fashion that may become stultifying over time. Rather, we recommend that you make them a flexible and creative regular part of your teaching repertoire. You can use journals as a way to interrupt a lecture, lab, or activity in order to let students reflect on what they understand at that intermediate phase of a lesson. Using journals fosters students' enthusiasm and personal investment in the content you are trying to teach.

Dialogue journals, where you maintain an ongoing written dialogue with your students, provide a unique window on their concept understanding, confusion, concerns, and complaints (Bean & Rigoni, 2000; Werderich, 2002). In terms of concept understanding, this is a private place where students can express confusion without fear of embarrassment. The dialogue journal offers you a second chance, a chance to reteach information that may not have been understood during the first attempt. In addition, dialogue journals open the door to fluency for second language learners. Students find that dialogue journals are non-threatening because of their uncorrected, ungraded format. Since they are written in a conversational style, dialogue journals reduce the stress of clinging to a dictionary and worrying constantly about translating to the native language. Rather, students can experiment as they would in a free writing activity. Dialogue journals offer students a sense that they do have a voice in how the class progresses. Thus, you might alter your teaching based on this written feedback from students.

Other forms of journal writing allow students to respond to their reading in creative ways. For example, students can write a letter to the author posing questions about a novel or text. Students can take the part of a character in a novel and write a journal entry based on their reactions to a powerful episode. Journal entries can be made on e-mail and sent to students in a far-off classroom for their dialogue responses. The possibilities are endless and, increasingly, involve electronic media (Bean & Moni, 2003).

For example, students can compose and post online fanfiction writing based on popular media, books, music, and video games (Black, 2005). *Fanfiction* can be defined as original works of fiction based on popular media including television, movies, books, music, and video games. Moreover, fanfiction writing offers students a real audience for their work based on the archival website: *www. fanfiction.net*. Because this site offers students a real audience of peers, it provides a forum for second language students to practice language acquisition with a fan community. Along with blogging and Wikipedia writing mentioned in Chapter 2, fanfiction composing opens the boundaries of traditional writing to include visuals and other forms of representation. The social nature of these forms of writing appeals to a variety of students including second language learners and struggling writers.

APPLICATION 11.1

Think about the most challenging group of students you have taught. Write a journal entry describing your feelings now as you think back on the impact your teaching may or may not have had on these students. Exchange your entry with a colleague in class. Discuss the teaching experience you wrote about and your views on journal writing in a content classroom.

Quick Writes

Quick Writes are an informal means of engaging students in thinking about a content topic at the prereading or postreading stages of a lesson or unit (Moore, Moore, Cunningham, & Cunningham, 2003). As the name implies, they are fairly easy to integrate in an overburdened curriculum. They can be used to get an idea of students' prior knowledge at the prereading stage or to synthesize ideas after content learning. Quick Writes are typically based on teacher-generated questions. Students can jot their ideas on note cards and share them with a partner or group, or in their response journals for personal reflection. The teacher may choose to collect them occasionally as an aid to future lesson planning. The Quick Write prompts that follow give you a basic idea of how to generate both prereading and postreading prompts.

Prereading

1. Before we begin our unit on water quality, write down everything you know about this topic. You have one minute.
2. We are going to study recent efforts to achieve a Middle East peace accord. In 30 seconds, write down key political figures you can think are likely to influence this effort.

Postreading

1. We have been studying cloning. Write down some of the ethical issues you think we should discuss in our next class meeting. You have one minute.
2. Today's math lesson dealt with statistical probability. Write down some examples from day-to-day life where knowing the statistical probability of an event might be important. You have three minutes.

Quick Writes are highly flexible so that you can easily adjust the response time to fit your needs. This is a great way to engage students in additional thinking about a topic when you find that some time remains in the class period.

Possible Sentences

Possible Sentences is another writing-to-learn strategy that helps students use technical vocabulary and related concepts in your content area. This strategy places students in an active role in which they predict an author's use of language in a text and evaluate their written predictions against the actual text passage (Moore & Moore, 2007). Possible Sentences engages students in higher order reasoning to identify examples in the text that support their prereading sentences or to revise their sentences after considering the text version. This exercise gives students a vested interest in reading the text to check their prereading possible sentence predictions.

Steps for Creating a Possible Sentences Lesson

1. List on the board or overhead key terms from a chapter or reading selection. The words should be well defined by the context and pronounced several times for the students. For example:

Target Words

pigment

albinism

enzymes

melanin

suntan

albino

Passage

ALBINISM*

The absence of pigmentation in the skin, hair, and eyes in albinos is the result of a deficiency in the manufacture of pigment (melanin) by the body. Albinism is a metabolic disorder resulting from the absence or inactivity of a specific enzyme. Enzymes are complex compounds which act as catalytic agents or mediators of chemical changes in living forms. This enzyme is involved in the formation of melanin. The condition is not restricted to humans and it has been found in many animals: snakes, salamanders, gorillas, rats, mice, Easter bunnies, and even ravens, to name a few.

Human albinos are characterized by white translucent skin and white hair. Because of the lack of pigment in the iris, the eyes are red due to blood vessels. There is no way to overcome albinism. The necessary information to produce the right enzyme has not been inherited and will never be acquired. The specific enzyme or the melanin pigment would have to be injected continuously into each and every pigment cell of the skin, scalp, and eyes in order to produce a normally pigmented individual.

Albinos need continuous protection from sunlight since they burn very easily. Their skin cannot develop a suntan since tans are nothing more than the accumulation of melanin as a response to an increase in the ultraviolet radiation of sunlight. They are also more susceptible to skin diseases and tend to have poor vision. They are otherwise perfectly normal people.

*Brum, G. D., Castro, P., & Quinn, R. D. *Biology and Man*. Dubuque, IA: Kendall/Hunt, 1978, p. 57.

2. Individual students select any two of the words and dictate or write a sentence using them. The teacher writes the sentences on the board exactly as dictated, whether the information in them is accurate or not. For instance:

Possible Sentences

   a. Suntans come from having a lot of enzymes in your skin.

   b. A albino is a person who has no melanin.

   c. An albino can never get a suntan.

   d. Albinism is the missing of pigment in the skin.

3. After an arbitrary number of sentences have been generated, the students search through the passage to verify the sentences on the board. A game twist can be added to this by having teams that are supposed to generate as many sentences as possible with unique pairs of the words listed. In this example there are 15 different possible pairs of words that can be used. Once each team generates its sentences, the opposing teams challenge (with books closed, of course) the accuracy of each set of individual sentences. Points can be given for each accurate sentence. Penalty points can be deducted for inaccurate challenges.

4. The possible sentences are corrected on the board and students are given an opportunity to enter them into their notebooks. For instance:

Revised Possible Sentences

   a. Suntans come from having a lot of melanin in your skin.

   b. An albino is a person who has no melanin.

   c. An albino can never get a suntan.

   d. Albinism is the absence of pigment in the skin.

Possible Sentences will tease out misconceptions students have about a topic. Writing sentences is generally a nonthreatening activity, even for second language learners. We have found that students enjoy Possible Sentences. They enthusiastically pursue text reading to verify their predictions.

Cubing

In order to explore a topic from various dimensions, consider using *cubing* (Tompkins, 2003). The concrete visual of a cube with its six sides serves as a starting point to consider the multiple dimensions of topics in nutrition, science, social studies, mathematics, and other content areas. To introduce cubing, start with a familiar topic and then treat more complex topics once students have a good grasp of how cubing works.

Steps for Cubing

1. Introduce the topic on the board (e.g., ice cream).
2. Have students in small groups examine the topic from the following six sides of the cube:

   → *Describe it* (including its colors, shapes, and sizes, if applicable)

   → *Compare it* (what is it similar to or different from?)

   → *Associate it* (what does it make you think of?)

Figure 11.1

Student Response to the Ice Cream Cube Assignment

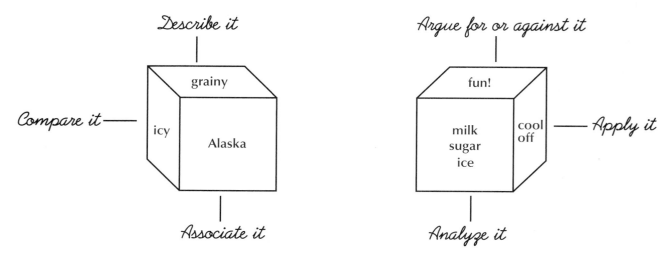

→ *Analyze it* (tell how it is made or what it is composed of)

→ *Apply it* (what can you do with it? how is it used?)

→ *Argue for or against it* (take a stand and list reasons for supporting it)

Figure 11.1 shows one student's response to the ice cream cubing assignment. This particular student *described* ice cream as grainy. She *compared* ice cream with an icy she might buy at a convenience store, and she *associated* ice cream with Alaska because it is cold and snowy. In the second half of the cube, she listed the ingredients as milk (it's actually cream or butter fat), sugar, and ice in the *analyze it* box. In the *apply it* box she said that it helps us cool off, and she naturally *argued for* ice cream because it is fun. In comparing her cube with other students, she revised the ingredients and left the other boxes the same.

Students should spend only 5–10 minutes on each side of the cube. Once they have a good grasp of the process using familiar topics like the ice cream example, you can introduce more difficult content area topics such as solar cars in science, the Bill of Rights in history, and authors in English. Initially, students should begin by using the six sides of the cube to compose descriptive paragraphs. Cubing can then form the basis for longer writing assignments including persuasive essays, letters to the editor, and extended reports treated later in this chapter.

APPLICATION 11.2

Pair up with a colleague in a class from a different content area than your own (e.g., biology and English). Select a passage from your text and guide your partner through either a Possible Sentences or a Cubing lesson.

Writing Roulette

Writing Roulette was originally created to help students become more fluent in writing by having them write about anything at all for a specific period of time. A kitchen timer would be set for five minutes or so, and when it went off, students would pass their writing on to a peer who continues developing the passage for another five minutes or so. Writing Roulette helped students overcome worries about perfect grammar and spelling and moved them into a composing mode.

Bean (2007) modified the original Writing Roulette strategy for use in content learning. First, instead of writing whatever comes to mind, students are told to use a simple three part story structure for the activity so that three different students write each distinct part of the story. Second, they review content material within the framework of the story by selecting key vocabulary words from their expository reading and including these words in each section they write.

Steps for Conducting a Writing Roulette Session

1. Provide a simple structure for the story, consisting of three major elements or divisions.

   a. A setting and characters

   b. A problem or goal for the main character

   c. A resolution

2. Advise students that each section of the story must use at least two words from the lesson or unit they have been studying. These words should be underlined in the story. You can have students review their vocabulary collections, or you can simply supply a list of technical terminology from which they can choose six words.

3. Set a specific time limit for the first story section (e.g., five minutes for the setting). You can use a kitchen timer for this.

4. When time is up, have students exchange papers or collect and shuffle them so that a second author writes the problem or goal section. Advise students to read the paper they receive and continue the story. Set a time limit for this writing as well.

5. Exchange papers one last time so a third author can provide a resolution for the story. Then, have students return the story to the original author and share aloud those stories that are particularly interesting or that use content vocabulary in creative ways.

Writing Roulette is a good way for students to review important vocabulary and concepts before an essay exam or quiz. It is best introduced after students have used other strategies such as graphic organizers and semantic mapping, so that they have a good understanding of content vocabulary. The example that follows is a Writing Roulette story developed by three preservice content teachers. The words are taken from the glossary of our text.

Student 1

Gertrude and Susie were on their way home from school. "Gertrude," said Susie, "that *anticipation guide* we use in class was really great."

"Yeh," replied Gertrude. "And didn't you just love the *graphic organizers?* I can't wait to get home and call all our friends and let them know about our class."

Gertrude and Susie continue down the street, chatting happily.

Student 2

The big history test was rapidly approaching. Gertrude reread her graphic organizer and called Susie on the phone to discuss *study strategies*. She felt her *comprehension* had suffered because she did all of her reading in front of the television. She had never missed an episode of "American Idol" since the show's inception. Susie tried to help Gertrude fill in the blank spaces their teacher had left in the graphic organizer. They stayed on the phone for three hours in anticipation of the big *test*.

Student 3

The next day, Gertrude entered the classroom to face the test. She whispered to Susie, "I hope he gives us an anticipation guide to help us with this test."

The teacher came around and placed a cloze test on each student's desk. Gertrude took a look at it and almost died. Every other word has been deleted. Gertrude whispered to Susie, "Do you have any idea how to do this test?"

Susie said, "Sure, use your knowledge of *morphemic analysis* to *slice* the *response mode,* which will require you to have fewer pieces of information. Then the *scope of information* search will be halved.

Gertrude gave Susie a blank stare. Susie said, "Guess!"

Gertrude knew she would fail, but, fortunately for her, the teacher pulled down the overhead screen, knocking down the wall clock, and a large plastic potted fern onto his big toe. Class was immediately terminated, and Gertrude went whistling out of the classroom, knowing she had escaped a fate worse than death.

Students find Writing Roulette a pleasurable and creative approach to reviewing technical vocabulary and concepts. Since it takes a full period to conduct a Writing Roulette session, you should plan to allot this time just to the activity. Once students have completed their stories, they enjoy exchanging and reading each other's creations in the small group setting. Writing Roulette capitalizes on a familiar narrative structure to review concepts presented in expository material.

ReWrite

ReWrite is a music strategy that combines concept learning and the creation of musical verses within a comprehensive prereading and postreading lesson framework (Bean, 1997; 2000). Music has the power to enhance abstract reasoning. Musical performance typically occurs in high interest cooperative settings with clear, performance-based outcomes. Songwriting can be used to teach concepts in biology, mathematics, history, art, and other content areas.

You do not need to be an accomplished musician to use the ReWrite song writing strategy that follows. Using instrumental music as a foundation for a song your students write or having a music teacher create an instrumental background piece works quite well. Karaoke, the sing-along activity that is popular all over the country, has spawned an endless array of tapes and videotapes of music that can be used for this activity. Or, a teacher can use alternate forms of music like rap and hip hop, which require minimal or no musical accompaniment (Paul, 2000). The lyrics are the important ingredient in the ReWrite song writing strategy.

Day 1

Step One. As in any lesson planning, you need to do a careful task analysis of concepts and strategies needed for the reading assignment. In the example that follows, students were engaged in a science unit on entomology, or the study of insects. The insect students read about in this lesson was the crab spider, a prevalent garden pest on the Big Island of Hawaii since its arrival in 1985 (Nishida & Tenorio, 1993).

To start this ReWrite lesson, concepts that most students would have about crab spiders were incorporated in a blues song. Thus, the song contained commonsense nonscientific knowledge about crab spiders that most students living on the Big Island might know from working around their gardens. The song follows with guitar chords included.

Crab Spiders
(Key of E; Blues Shuffle)

E
Crab spiders hang their webs all over the place
I go outside to work and they just get tangled in my face
      A
Well I hit them with my rake and they stick to my hand
E
Crawling up my arm like Sherman tanks in sand
B7   A   E
I finally decided what I'm gonna do,
collect all my crab spiders and take em to school (repeat)
Well I'll let them go when my teacher isn't lookin and they'll cause
So much trouble she'll send us outside while she's searchin
      A   E
For those crab spiders, crab spiders what a waste
B7   A   E
They just lie in wait to get tangled in my face

Bridge

E
I spray em with Raid, chlorox too but all that does is make my plants look sick and blue
A
Crab spiders, crab spiders how I hate you guys,
      E
you just exist to drive me wild
B7   A
Until I find a way to get rid of this strange insect
E
Maybe I'll just treat my crab spiders with more respect!

The first verse portrayed the pesky quality of these ubiquitous creatures and the next two verses implied the humor of taking them to school and letting them loose in class as a distraction for the teacher. Finally, common approaches to exterminating crab spiders are recounted. The song ends with the author ready to give up trying to fight the crab spider invasion in the yard and just be nice to these pesky, tank-like insects.

Step Two. Students have a copy of the song and follow along while it is played and sung by the teacher. Or, you can have a musician friend perform it and tape the performance. In this example the information in song form was designed to activate students' prior knowledge before they responded to anticipation guide statements based on a science news article about crab spiders.

Step Three. Following the introductory song activity, students gathered in small groups to consider and complete the 5-item anticipation guide on crab spiders that included some factual and critical opinion items. You can use ReWrite without any guide material but, in this instance, we wanted to focus students' discussion on some of the remarkable features of the crab spider. The anticipation guide they completed is shown in Figure 11.2.

Figure 11.2

Anticipation-Reaction Guide
Crab Spiders

Directions: Before reading, consider each statement with a partner. Write *yes* if you agree and *no* if you disagree. Write your reasons below each statement. After reading the text, go back and review each statement.

You   Author

____   ____   1. Crab spiders are harmless.
____   ____   2. A crab spider's web is more deadly than other spider webs.
____   ____   3. We have had crab spiders on our island for many years.
____   ____   4. A crab spider's egg sac can contain more than 100 eggs.
____   ____   5. Fear of spiders is silly.

Most students viewed the crab spider as harmful based on their experiences. They reported receiving bites that swelled up and talked about very painful bites inflicted on their younger siblings who happened to accidentally bump against one of the crab spider's thick webs. They were less sure about statements two through four and very certain number five simply ignored the facts. Fear of spiders was, in their opinion, quite justified.

Day 2

Step Four. Following a prereading discussion of the statements, students were assigned reading of the crab spider article in class. They then engaged in a post-reading discussion of the anticipation guide statements. After reading the article they generally agreed with items two, three, and four from the guide. The more open-ended items, particularly the fear of spiders is silly statement, produced few changes in their initial opinions about crab spiders. Indeed, when they discovered that crab spiders were called "the land equivalent of drift net fleets at sea" and their thick, intricate community of webs termed "walls of death" for flying insects, they were impressed. Students used this text-based information to defend their general fear of all spiders.

Step Five. Students stay in their groups and write a new crab spider song by creating verses that reflect their new knowledge. In our example, each group shared their verse with the other groups by reading it aloud.

Step Six. Students' verses were assembled and typed at home before the next class. Copies were then made of the students' song and Crab Spider Blues was performed at the start of the next class with each group singing their respective verses. This performance served as a review of text information and set the stage for subsequent insect study. The ReWrite version produced by students follows.

CRAB SPIDER BLUES

Crab spiders work in teams hanging walls of death

Between bushes and trees, under eaves, across a doorway or in trees

Big mama in the middle and daddy goofin off on the side

They wait for prey and take their breath away

Thelacantha bevispina down the back of my shirt

They are difficult to remove and darn they hurt

Their bite may swell up like a sting from a bee

Why do these things always happen to me?

The mothers like to lay about a hundred eggs

And when they pop out they like to bite my legs

There's no killin these bugs at all

Smash um when they're big, squash um when they're small

If you're wondering when the crab spider arrived

They've been around since 1985

The Big Island was cursed because they were the first

The answer to how they came is never the same

Students genuinely enjoy this activity, and the ReWrite song becomes a memorable way to learn and critique content area concepts.

STOP! View the CD-ROM video clip demonstrating a ReWrite lesson using the song *Great White Shark Blues*.

The last writing-to-learn strategy we are going to consider is the Guided Writing Procedure, which guides students through the prereading and postreading stages of a lesson.

Guided Writing Procedure

The *Guided Writing Procedure* (GWP) gives students practice in developing a coherent written account of a topic they are studying in the text (Bean, 2001). The GWP helps students examine their prior knowledge of a topic. They can then modify their previous knowledge based on the text reading. In contrast to the strategies we have introduced up to this point, the GWP entails editing writing for both content and form. The GWP is designed to achieve the following teaching objectives:

1. To activate and sample students' prior knowledge of a topic before they do any text reading.
2. To sample and evaluate students' written expression in a content area.

3. To improve students' written expression through guided instruction.
4. To facilitate the synthesis and retention of content area material.

Use of the GWP improves the quality of the writing that students produce. They become more adept at integrating information from text and prior knowledge and produce writing that is more carefully edited and readable. The GWP usually spans three days of content instruction and involves the following steps.

Day 1

Step One. Write the topic heading you are introducing on the board and have students brainstorm words or phrases that come to mind when they think about this topic. For example, social studies students who were about to read a chapter describing conditions during the Depression of 1929 generated six ideas based on their prior knowledge of this topic.

Step Two. Record students' ideas verbatim on the board or overhead. Engage students in a discussion of their ideas, and ask them to explain how they are related to the topic being considered. Students produced the following list for the causes of the Depression of 1929.

no jobs   stocks crash
no money   everything is cheap
poverty   bad investments

Step Three. Guide students in constructing an outline, graphic organizer, or semantic map of these ideas with appropriate category labels. For example:

Causes and Effects of the Depression
I. Causes
   a. bad investments
   b. stocks crash
II. Effects
   a. no jobs
   b. no money
   c. poverty
   d. everything is cheap

Step Four. Tell students to individually write a short paragraph or two as a first draft, with the outline as a guide to content and organization. You should tell them to direct this draft to a specific audience. A reasonable audience for this information is another class member or a classmate who is absent for this lesson.

Step Five. Collect students' first drafts and rapidly analyze the paragraphs, using the GWP checklist shown in Figure 11.3. You should not make any marks on students' papers. The first draft that follows was written by a student based on the six ideas generated in the brainstorming on the Depression.

Causes and Effects of the Depression

The awful Depression of 1929 was caused by the stock market crash. People made bad investments and lost all their money. Some people bought too much stock on credit. They went to far into det.

When the stock market crashed people lost a lot of money. There wasn't money to pay people for work. People without jobs sunk into poverty. Everything was dirt cheap. You could probably go to a movie for a dime!

Figure 11.3

GWP Checklist

(✓ = okay; O = needs revision; ? = can't tell)

Criteria

Organization of Ideas

Clear topic	✓
Supporting details/examples	0
Logical flow	✓

Comments: *Good organization of ideas. The text will give you details and examples.*

Style

Shows variety in

Word choice	✓
Sentence length	0

Comments: *Short sentences need to be balanced by some that are longer.*

Mechanics

Complete sentences	✓
Capitalization	✓
Punctuation	✓
Spelling	0

Comments: *too far (vs. to); debt (vs. det); sank (vs. sunk)*

This student constructed a first draft that has a clear topic sentence and good organization. At this prereading stage, students had only limited knowledge of the causes and effects of the Depression, so the draft is understandably brief. He made some fairly common spelling errors that the teacher simply pointed out in the mechanics section of the GWP checklist. We are now ready for day two.

Day 2

Step Six. Return students' drafts and checklists. Have students make necessary edits and polish their first drafts, based on the guidelines you offered on the checklist. You can circulate among students to provide extra help. You can also use this time for individual conferences with students experiencing real difficulty with the writing process. For example, second language learners generally benefit from extra, one-on-one discussion of their writing efforts. You may want to display some sample drafts on the overhead and model the process of editing for organization of ideas, style, and mechanics.

Step Seven. Have students turn in their second draft and the original GWP checklist they used to guide their editing. You can then record any comments, particularly praise, on the bottom of the original checklist.

Step Eight. Assign text reading, explaining to students that the purpose of this reading is to locate additional information, especially supporting details and examples, that they can include in a final draft of their writing.

Day 3

Step Nine. Now that they have acquired additional knowledge about the topic (in this case, the Depression), *engage students in a group discussion to revise the original outline to include this text information.* Any misconceptions can be cleared up as well. Here, the text that students read added little to their basic understanding of the causes of the Depression. However, it did expand on the effects of the Depression on workers in the cities and on farmers. Thus, their new outline contained a blend of their original ideas about the Depression and the new information discussed in the text.

Causes and Effects of the Depression

I. Causes
   a. bad investments by people and banks
   b. the stock market crash
   c. business downturn for 10 years

II. Effects
   a. people stopped buying goods
   b. factories closed
   c. by 1932, 13 million jobless workers (one of every four)
   d. young people hopped trains to find work
   e. homeless people lived on the outskirts of town in shacks called "Hoovervilles," after President Hoover
   f. farmers had too much surplus corn, which they could not sell
   g. farmers lost their farms—droughts also led to the Dust Bowl in the early 1930s
   h. poverty was common

Step Ten. Students should then revise and expand their compositions, based on new information from the text. You may want to have them include lecture and discussion information if the text is limited in its coverage of the topic. Students can work in pairs or small groups while you come around to help them link text and prior knowledge concepts. Then have students turn in these final drafts for a grade or give a quiz on this information. These compositions can be used as a lead-in to a unit (in this case, on the New Deal). They can also become part of the guide material you use with future classes, creating a very real audience for students' efforts. The student who wrote the original draft on the Depression produced the following final version.

Causes and Effects of the Depression

The awful Depression of 1929 was caused by bad investments in the stock market. People took great risks with money, stringing themselves out in debt by buying too much stock on credit. The banks also made bad investments and many had to close after the stock market crashed. The Depression that started with the stock market crash of 1929 was a business downturn that, different from the ones before it, lasted for 10 years!

The effects of the Depression were many. Because people lost so much money, they stopped buying goods. The factories had to close and by 1932, 13 million people, or one in four, were out of work. Young people hopped trains to seek work in other towns. Homeless people lived on the edge of the big cities in tiny shacks called Hoovervilles, after President Hoover. Even the farms suffered.

Farmers grew too much corn, which they couldn't sell. Since they couldn't sell the corn, they couldn't pay for their tractors and other equipment. They lost their farms, and droughts made things even worse. The Dust Bowl in the early 1930s wiped out even more farmers. People sank into poverty. Everything was dirt cheap. You could probably go to a movie for a dime, but I would rather live now!

This student's final version now contains supporting details from the text. Furthermore, he includes his own views about living during that era.

The GWP is an in-depth exploration of a text reading assignment. Since it is time consuming, you should plan on using it as a lead-in to a unit so that students approach their reading with some power over the text. For example, in the Depression outline stage, students begin to see the text as a cause-effect organizational pattern, which helps them read fluently and selectively for key ideas and details to revise their original GWP compositions.

Writing to Inform

Writing for an audience of peers, especially to argue a particular point of view, can help students become analytical readers. The strategies considered next emphasize both analytical reading and writing.

Autobiographies and Biographies

When students are asked to write an autobiography of their unique literacy histories from the earliest memories they have up to the present, this activity provides a powerful window on their experiences and feelings about reading (Bean, 2002). A *reading autobiography* charting experiences at early, middle, and later stages of reading can be shaped to focus on reading in science, mathematics, and so on. Autobiographies should be shared in class in small groups and discussed. In Application 11.3, we designed this autobiography format for English. You can modify the format to focus the autobiography on your content area and further narrow the scope of writing to encompass a particular period such as middle or high school.

Writing to Inform Strategies

- ⊃ Autobiographies
- ⊃ Biographies
- ⊃ Research Papers
- ⊃ I-Search Papers
- ⊃ Imaginative Writing Assignments

APPLICATION 11.3

Reading Autobiography

Beginning with your earliest memories of reading or being read to, retrace your experiences as a reader up to and including the present time. As you think about these experiences, making notes, try to include as much of the following information as possible:

1. The kinds of books you read or that were read to you at particular ages. If you can't remember specific titles and authors, describe the plots, characters, themes, or content you can recall.

2. Your reading or lack of reading when you first became an independent reader.

3. What you read or what was read to you both at school and at home during your elementary school years. (Don't be embarrassed if no one read to you or if you didn't read. Just write about the lack of reading in your life.)

4. Facts and feelings about what you read as you moved through the grades up to and including senior high and beyond.

5. Your present reading habits and preferences (or lack thereof).

6. The people (family members, teachers, friends, and others) who either turned you off or turned you on to reading and why.

7. Places where you acquired or now acquire books.

8. The feelings and sensations you associate with reading.

After you have taken notes on your experiences as a reader, write a short autobiographical sketch (3 pages maximum) on your reading experiences based on the eight guideline questions above. Put your development into chronological order so that your autobiography shows the stages you have gone through as a reader. In the final section, review your personal history as a reader and discuss how your own experiences might influence you as a content area teacher interested in helping students cope with unfriendly textbooks and interested in developing in your students a desire to read for enjoyment.

As you write your reading autobiography, be candid and honest. If you like, use an informal writing style as though you were writing in your journal. During our next class meeting, I will ask you to share these experiences with a small group.

Once students have written an autobiography, the transition to reading and writing *biographies* about an important figure in science, physical education, mathematics, history, music, or art is fairly easy. Tradebook biographies offer a powerful way to enrich textbook concepts in a fashion that has human interest. In addition, women and minorities are featured in biographies in greater depth than their contributions might display in a content area textbook that surveys many topics.

Steps to Start Using Biographies in Your Content Area

1. Work with your librarian to ensure there is a good collection of biographies for your content area that encompasses women and minorities.

2. Have students self-select a biography to read and write about in some creative format. Possible project options include:
   a. Write about how the world in the biography you read is different from your world.
   b. Write a journal or e-mail message from the perspective of the book character.
   c. Write a movie review of the story in the book.
   d. Write and act out a historical, you-are-there scene, dressed as the character.
   e. Write a biopoem.

The following template is useful in helping students structure their biopoems (Olsen, 2003).

Structure of Biopoems

Line 1. First name
Line 2. Four traits that describe the character
Line 3. Relative of
Line 4. Lover of (3 things or people)
Line 5. Who feels (3 items)
Line 6. Who needs (3 things)
Line 7. Who fears (3 things)
Line 8. Who gives (3 things)
Line 9. Who would like to see (3 items)

Line 10. Resident of
Line 11. Last name

3. Have students share their biography project with a small group or the whole class.

For example, sixth-grader Kristen read a biography about a famous show dog, Duke, and wrote a biopoem about her dog, Lady Kathryn, in her middle school language arts class. Duke was Lady Kathryn's father.

Biopoem

Lady

A smart, loving, and sweet dog

Relative of Duke, a dog show champion

Lover of chewys, people, and attention

Who needs her family, chewy, and soft pillows

Who fears loud noises, new places, and new people

Who gives kisses, cute smiles, and playful attitudes

Who would like to see a huge treat, a huge stuffed animal,
  and other small puppies

Resident of Nevada

Kathryn

Thus, *biopoems* can take many forms and be created on virtually any topic across the content areas. In science, students can write about the heart, various animals, plants, and so on. Biopoems are particularly applicable to biographies but very versatile as a creative way of writing to inform.

Biographies in music range from classical pianists to Jimi Hendrix and Shakira. With the help of your librarian, you should be able to locate biographies relevant to many content fields, including physical education, agriculture, art, music, history, science, mathematics, vocational education, and so on. Searching for and selecting a biography to read and write about forms a great foundation for research paper writing. Use your imagination to create additional project options that involve writing to inform.

Research Papers

At its worst, a research paper assignment may amount to no more than students engaged in the busywork of copying facts laboriously cataloged for a teacher who knows this information in the first place. In this instance, the paper is put off as long as possible and hurriedly thrown together the night before it is due. The teacher then pays an inordinate amount of attention to the form of the paper, poison pen in hand to circle in red any grammar and spelling errors.

At its best, a research paper is the culmination of a student's efforts to become an expert in some subtopic of a field so this knowledge can be shared with an audience of peers. This may range from developing an insider's knowledge of sharks in science to an understanding of how parapsychologists explore phenomena such as poltergeists in a psychology class. You can probably recall writing papers of this sort a few times during your years in school. But notice we said "a few times." Opportunities to become actively involved in pursuing a topic of genuine personal interest are all too rare.

In this section we want to outline some general steps to consider as you assign research papers in your content classroom.

Steps to Assigning Research Papers

1. Selecting and narrowing a topic is often a difficult task for teachers and students alike. Students can form cooperative research groups for this stage of the process. A research team of two to five students with a recorder can brainstorm subtopics within the general area you suggest. For example, if the topic was earthquakes, students might narrow this to a list consisting of famous earthquakes, California earthquakes, the science of earthquakes, and so on.

2. Once the topic has been chosen, the research team can then meet to plan how they are going to tackle the topic. They can brainstorm possible questions for their topic and place them on notecards. For example, if the topic were the science of earthquakes, possible questions might include: What causes earthquakes? Can scientists predict when they will occur? Where do they occur most often? All questions should be considered at this brainstorming stage. Once all possible questions have been elicited, they should be categorized and transformed into statements that will guide the research and notetaking stage.

3. The research team should identify potential sources of information, including encyclopedias, textbooks, films, and experts who may be interviewed. If your school has access to computer databases that contain up-to-date encyclopedias, these may also be a good place to locate information.

   Once each research team has identified their resources for the paper, they should develop a timeline that delineates specific dates when they will finish each task. Thus, they need a date for completing the collection of information in the form of notes, another date for a paper outline, one for the first draft, and a date for the second draft. The search for information can be divided among team members so that a portion of the team reads and annotates encyclopedia information while another dyad interviews an expert on earthquakes.

4. Once information has been collected, students should regroup in their teams to categorize and consider the ideas they have. This is a good time to transform the headings that guided the information search into a tentative outline. The science of earthquakes outline might look like this.

   I. Earthquake
      A. Definition
   II. Cause of earthquakes
      A. Early myths
      B. Modern tectonic theory
   III. Where they occur the most
      A. Pacific belt
      B. Mediterranean belt
   IV. Effect of earthquakes
      A. Landslides
      B. Tsunamis

V. How they are studied
   A. Seismographs
   B. Earthquake waves

Once the outline is prepared, students can begin writing their individual reports. Be sure they realize that the outline is merely a tentative guide—it may be altered as the writing progresses and new insights develop.

5. The first draft of the paper can now be written. Once the first draft is completed, students should exchange papers and use a writing guide checklist like the one that accompanied the Guided Writing Procedure to peer-edit the papers.

6. Based on suggested edits by their peers as well as yourself, students can now complete the second and final draft. Naturally, this process takes time. Students need adequate class time to meet in their groups, and they need enough time to allow for two drafts of the paper. Provide student groups with a form where they can list team members, the topic, categories to be explored, resources, and the timeline proposed. The teacher then reviews this material for each group and signs off to indicate topic approval. Students may also need a checklist, particularly for the group recorder, that indicates the various stages of the process (e.g., brainstorming, researching, organizing, and writing), along with the sub-steps for each procedure (e.g., for brainstorming: generate questions, categorize the questions, and write them as statements; identify sources; and set timelines). This will help focus the group effort on the various steps in the process.

In addition to carefully describing the parameters of a writing assignment as extensive as a research paper, you may want to share with students some model papers that were completed in a previous class. Papers written by former students can become important sources of information for the present class, giving students a functional audience for their writing aside from the usual teacher as examiner-audience. At their best, research papers should be memorable experiences for students that result in in-depth knowledge and appreciation of subtopics that might otherwise go unnoticed in a frenetic effort to cover too much content in too short a time.

I-Search Papers

The *I-Search* paper is an alternative to the more traditional research paper (Macrorie, 1988). Unlike traditional research papers where there is a tendency for students to report on a topic by reading and distilling the works of others, in I-Search papers students investigate a topic of their choosing by interviewing experts, visiting places, and telling the story of their search. The I-Search paper consists of the following steps:

Steps to Construct an I-Search Paper

1. *Choose a topic.* Students should select topics of personal interest. For example, Jennifer, a middle school student, had been a regular visitor to the zoo for years. She was mystified by the pandas and her I-Search paper investigated how they were cared for in the city zoo. Another student, Fabio, wanted to find out more about how guitars are made. His I-Search paper took him on a journey to a local luthier.

2. *Carry out the search.* Share the topic with the class and see if anyone has some ideas about where to find an expert to interview. For example, Jennifer's interest in pandas put her in contact with the head veterinarian at the city zoo. Fabio's search sent him to a luthier. Before contacting and interviewing the veterinarian and luthier, these students did some background reading on their respective topics. Based on this background reading, they created some interview questions on their respective topics. For example, Jennifer asked the veterinarian at the zoo, "Why are pandas on the endangered species list?" Fabio asked, "How much does a handmade koa guitar cost to build?"

3. *Conduct the interview.* Using a tape recorder to retain the information they needed for the I-Search paper, Jennifer and Fabio visited and interviewed the experts they located. They got recommendations for further reading into the topic from these experts. For example, when Fabio interviewed a luthier, the guitar maker said "read *The Guitar Handbook*" (Denyer, 1982).

4. *Write the paper.* Use the I-Search experience as a way of telling the story of how the paper evolved. Anything important in the search process should be included, and the format can follow the four categories of information listed below:

   a. *What the student knew or did not know when the topic was selected.* For example, Jennifer did not know that there are only about 1000 pandas living in the mountains in China. The pandas depend heavily on the food source of their bamboo forests, which are vulnerable to logging and a natural life and death cycle.

   b. *Why the student decided to write on this topic.* In Jennifer's case, she worked as a volunteer at the zoo. She had a long-standing interest in biology and in becoming a veterinarian specializing in the care of large, endangered zoo animals. Fabio played an old koa guitar that once belonged to his grandfather, and he was interested in how it was made. He dreamed about someday making his own guitar.

   c. *The search should be described.* Fabio's paper described his visit to luthier Bob Gleason of Pegasus Guitars. Fabio commented on the old industrial warehouse where the luthier worked and how neat everything was. Fabio spent two afternoons at the guitar maker's workshop and borrowed the book, *The Guitar Handbook,* to further research his paper.

   d. *What the student learned.* Jennifer included information on the panda's diet in the zoo (i.e., bamboo, apples, carrots, sweet potatoes, pans of slurpy ice, and mixtures of milk, eggs, and ground vegetables), sleep habits (i.e., 12 to 14 hours-per-day), and reproduction. In addition, she learned that in China, breeding programs are used to raise pandas in captivity to be released into the wild.

The I-Search paper should conclude with a list of sources, experts, and key people involved in supplying ideas and insights for the paper.

The I-Search paper goes well with cooperative learning. For example, rather than using individual I-Search topics, a small group or team of students can collaborate to investigate a topic about which they share a common interest. The I-Search paper is also a good alternative to the traditional research paper for multi-cultural topics, second language learners, and at-risk students because of its experiential nature.

Imaginative Writing Assignments

Discussing text reading and writing an in-depth research report are mainstays of content learning. But it is equally important to provide a variety of writing opportunities, especially opportunities for imaginative writing. In this section we offer some imaginative writing assignments that lend themselves to a variety of content areas. You can undoubtedly think of other possibilities.

Students can project themselves into the lives of people in historical contexts or animals in various habitats by writing a diary entry from a unique perspective. For example, have social studies students write a diary entry as if they were hobos riding the rail during the Depression. In the area of ecology, they could write a diary entry from the perspective of a whale or dolphin passing through an ocean channel near one of our polluted city harbors.

Similarly, have students write a "Who Am I?" piece in which they portray topics such as: I am your heart, I am your lungs, I am President Roosevelt, I am a camera. This exercise can require researching on a topic in detail to transform what might otherwise be dull expository prose into a lively, personal account.

Imaginative writing expands students' sense of audience and encourages creativity. In business education, students can write real letters to a newspaper column or the Small Business Association, asking for advice about their business interests. They can write a business plan for a small business they wish to start, such as yard cleaning or car detailing. Some students may want to interview a small business owner and create an oral history of the trials and tribulations of business ownership.

In social studies, students can write about a historical event from the perspective of a person experiencing it. For example, what was it like to be a woman on a ranch during cattle drives, isolated from other women, responsible for a family and livestock? Students can write fictional accounts about historical events, transforming expository prose into a more lively narrative form. In mathematics, students can create a story using math symbols in place of some words. In science, defending an unpopular theory, such as the notion that there is such a thing as earthquake weather, and directing this defense to a newspaper or a peer audience requires both research and imagination. In foreign language classes, acting in the role of a visiting student writing a diary entry about the first day in the United States can illuminate cultural diversity.

In music, drama, and art, writing a critical review of a concert or interviewing an artist for the newspaper helps broaden the audience for student writing. In health and physical education, keeping a sports diary that chronicles jogging or swimming progress and diet strategies demonstrates the day-to-day usefulness of writing to inform.

Students can also respond to literature or other forms of text using a variety of genres (Gillespie, 2005; Romano, 2000). *Multigenre writing* helps students experiment in imaginative ways with a host of genres including ad writing, comic strips, editorials, and so on. Consistent with other writing strategies we have introduced, it is important to model new genres for students before they attempt multigenre writing on their own. We include two excellent guides in the recommended readings that offer additional information on multigenre writing.

Responding to Writing

As students develop research papers and lengthy pieces of writing in your content area, your skill at responding to their writing becomes crucial. You may remember having a paper returned from a teacher covered with red marks attesting to your ability to produce sentences that were "awk" (i.e., awkward), and phrases that were, in the teacher's eyes, "frags" (i.e., fragments). When students receive a barrage of negative criticism for their writing efforts, they come to associate writing with frustration, depression, self-doubt, and avoidance. Furthermore, they may come to view revision as a process that involves merely making surface level changes similar to proofreading rather than a process that entails deeper structural and organizational changes. In contrast, we believe that students need to be able to take risks in portraying their ideas in writing without simultaneously balancing total attention to the mechanics of grammar and spelling, except in the revision stage of the second draft. You should avoid riddling a student's paper with red marks that focus on mechanical errors and consider alternate means of responding to students' writing. This is especially important in working with second language learners who may be very intimidated by writing in English.

Valuing students' writing should be at the top of your list when you confer with students. Finding value in the content of their writing, treating students as writers, and encouraging growth through comparisons of early and later writing make a difference. Indeed, evaluation can be defined as finding value in a piece of writing. Teachers should also display their own attempts at writing in content areas and act as co-learners in the writing process. Autobiographies, journals, research papers, and imaginative writing all offer opportunities to participate with your students as writers. In our research in secondary classrooms, for example, we freewrite with students on various topics related to American literature.

When you write responses to a student's writing, consider the following. Begin any comments about a paper with some positive praise. This alleviates anxiety and opens the door for revision. Second, writing marginal questions that probe areas of the paper that need revision directs the student to take responsibility for this process. Third, using an analytical checklist like the GWP checklist provides a means of guiding revision without marking up a student's paper. Fourth, individual conferences in combination with the checklist can be more productive than merely returning a paper with marginal comments. Finally, helping students use effective self-evaluation to revise their writing based on a series of generic questions lessens your paper load and encourages independence.

Three response schemes are discussed in detail—individual conferences, self-evaluation, and peer evaluation.

Individual Conferences

An individual conference is a conversation between a teacher and student for the purpose of evaluating and pointing out areas for revision of a draft of a paper (Bean, 2000). These conferences can be organized with a sign-up sheet on a first-come, first-served basis, or you can circulate about the room meeting with students as needed. The conversations you have with students should be purposeful, resulting in specific ideas for revision of a draft. Having a series of generic questions in mind to guide the individual conference will help the student participate actively in these sessions rather than passively by hoping you will do the revising. The following questions are recommended (Newkirk, 1986, p. 121).

1. What do you like best about this draft?
2. What do you like least?
3. What gave you the most trouble in writing this?
4. What kind of reaction do you want your readers to have—amusement, anger, increased understanding?
5. What surprised you when you wrote this? What came out differently than you expected?
6. What is the most important thing you learned about your topic in writing this?

Sandmann (2006, p. 21) developed a questioning process to assist with revision called the *Focused Question Card* strategy. An overarching revising question guides this process starting with:

→ Does this text say what I want it to say?

Following that question, subsequent questions home in on specific content revisions including:

→ Do I have enough specific detail to make my point or do I need to add more?
→ Did I keep the same point of view?
→ Is my writer's voice coming through? How?

Sandmann provides a list of 24 revision questions and links this process with a related rubric for evaluation of students' writing. This process can be used for peer and individual editing, particularly in the early stages of developing a sense of how to write a research paper. By modeling the use of focused question cards (on note cards), students begin to internalize the steps in revising a paper and the physical note cards can eventually be phased out.

These questions and others you devise, in combination with the GWP Checklist, should place the emphasis on the student's ideas, but there is always a tendency in teaching for the teacher to do most of the talking. Listening carefully and holding back your natural desire to grab the paper and revise in a way you think appropriate gives a student responsibility for this important process.

Ideally, students need to learn effective means of self-evaluation. The individual conferences you conduct using a series of generic questions can form the basis for effective self-evaluation.

Self-Evaluation

The checklist introduced with the Guided Writing Procedure can serve as a guide for self-evaluation. Similarly, a series of questions like the following may also focus the writer on areas needing revision (Bean, 2001).

1. What makes you happy about this writing?
2. Do you excite your reader with a good beginning?
3. Is there a clear topic sentence?
4. Do you back up your ideas with details and examples?
5. Do you use a variety of words to express your ideas?
6. Are your sentences different lengths?
7. Do you use complete sentences?
8. Did you check your writing for correct capitalization, punctuation, and spelling?

Although checklists and questions can help students detect areas needing revision, a writer's distinct style is more difficult to define. Writing that expresses each student's individual interest in his or her own unique style is often a pleasure to read. However, many of the expository texts students read seem to have had the author's voice edited out of them. If these are the only models of writing students read in a content area, their own writing may have this same bland quality. In addition to texts, students need to read tradebooks in science, social studies, mathematics, and business that demonstrate the author's enthusiasm for a topic and unique voice.

In addition to self-evaluation, peer evaluation can play an important role in the revision process. If you have ever tried to evaluate your own writing objectively, you know how hard this process can be. You know what you meant to say, even if the actual version you produced on paper is incoherent. A peer reader will quickly find these problem areas.

Peer Evaluation

Teams of two students can become skilled at evaluating each other's writing when they have some practice and clear guidelines for the process (Porto, 2002). We have found that students can comfortably practice peer editing by starting with some writing samples from a lower grade. They can apply the GWP Checklist to these samples without feeling self-conscious about critiquing a classmate's writing. Once they are skilled at responding to these papers, they can then exchange papers with a peer and collaborate to polish their first drafts.

The GWP Checklist offers a good general series of composing and transcribing considerations for any content area writing. However, students should begin a peer editing session by first complimenting their partner on some aspect of the paper. The following general comments help students grasp this important first step: (1) "I thought the most interesting part of your paper was . . .," (2) "You gave the most complete information about . . ."

It is also suggested that students phrase any negative comments as questions. For example, "Can you tell me more about . . ." The approach avoids engendering any defensive feelings as a peer helps in the revision process.

In peer editing, merely finding problems in a paper is not enough. Unlike the red pen "awks" and "frags" we all remember trying to decipher and resolve, a peer reader should offer some solutions to the problems that have been identified. For example, the reader can suggest alternative organizational structures, revised sentences, correct spellings, and format changes. With the use of word processing among student writers, these changes should not be overwhelming.

Rubrics

Rubrics offer a concrete description of the qualities and criteria expected in a particular piece of writing (Olson, 2003). A good rubric tells students explicitly what is expected for maximum performance in writing. The example rubric that follows was created for a writing assignment involving the development of a biography on a key figure in history from the Revolutionary War. While the actual numeric values associated with performance in writing on this rubric operate on a 4-point scale, you can have a rubric with additional items. Nevertheless, a 4-point rubric is fairly common.

Example Rubric

4 Key information about this Revolutionary War figure is presented in a coherent, carefully edited, well organized two-page biography. Word choice, organization, grammar, and spelling make the figure described come alive for the reader. It is evident that thoughtful library research went into the final product. The writing is highly polished and enjoyable to read.

3 Most key information about this Revolutionary War figure is presented in a coherent fashion. However, greater attention to word choice, paragraph transitions, word choice, spelling, and grammar would be helpful. Overall, the paper displays reasonably thorough library research and the writing is adequate.

2 Some key information about this Revolutionary War figure is not included, and the writing would benefit from more careful editing and polishing, particularly with respect to word choice, organization, grammar, and spelling conventions. In addition, more thorough library research is needed and the writing is incoherent in many places.

1 Little detailed information is supplied about this Revolutionary War figure and the writing is not coherent in many places. Substantial revision is needed to correct numerous word choice, organization, grammar, and spelling problems. Overall, the paper displays a lack of attention to research and editing.

There are many different types of scoring schemes for evaluating writing, and these can be adapted for a wide array of writing assignments across various content areas.

A Final Word

Individual conferences, self-evaluation, and peer evaluation all help content teachers manage the paper load, the biggest single obstacle to writing assignments in many content classrooms. The fact that you can probably remember those content area papers you have written over the years where *you* became the class expert on some topic, whether it was sharks or the stock market, attests to the power of writing as a mode of learning and reflection. It is worth the trouble. It takes real effort to guide students through various drafts for longer papers and real restraint to resist overcorrecting writing that is intended only for the writer's eyes as a bridge to learning.

Calkins (1994) says this about writing, and we agree:

> We write to communicate, plan, petition, remember, announce, list, imagine . . . but above all, we write to hold our lives in our hands and to make something of them. There is no plot line in the bewildering complexity of our lives but that which we make for ourselves. Writing allows us to turn the chaos into something beautiful, to frame selected moments, to uncover and celebrate the organizing patterns of our existence. (p. 8)

Now go back to the writing vignette at the beginning of this chapter. React again to the lesson as you did before. Compare your responses with those you made before you read the chapter.

Mini Projects

1. Visit a content area classroom for at least a week. Keep a log of writing activities you observe. Categorize these activities according to the major headings on the graphic organizer for the chapter: writing to learn, writing to inform, and responding to students' writing. Compare your findings to those of other students in your class.

2. Examine the writing activities recommended in a major student text in your content area. Using the headings from this chapter, determine what types of writing are being emphasized. Compare your findings to those of colleagues in class.

3. Using the text chapter on the CD-ROM entitled, What causes weather patterns?, select one of the writing to learn strategies in Chapter 11. Conduct a lesson with a small group of students or your peers. Write a description and evaluation of this lesson and share it with colleagues in class.

4. Select one of the writing to inform activities and conduct a lesson with students in your content area. Respond to students' writing using the GWP checklist, and conduct at least one individual conference or peer editing session, using the guidelines in this chapter. Write a description of your experience and share it with colleagues.

Website Activity

To locate and complete Chapter 11 activities, go to [*www.kendallhunt.com/contentarealiteracy*].

12

Studying and Preparing for Examinations

Vignette

Setting

Sam Valuta's 10th-grade world history class. Mr. Valuta and his students just completed a unit on the Baltic nations and their efforts to achieve independence. A unit test is scheduled for the next class meeting, and Mr. Valuta is suggesting ways to study for this essay test.

The Lesson

Mr. Valuta reviews material on the Baltic Nations of Latvia, Estonia, and Lithuania covered in this unit. He engages students in a discussion of the three nations' cultural and linguistic differences and problems of banding together politically in the Council of Baltic States and economically in a Baltic common market to develop a unified front in negotiations with Moscow. Mr. Valuta then highlights the general area of essay test questions he plans to ask, and he tells students about various study strategies they might use in preparing for the essay test. These strategies come from his own relatively recent experiences in college as a history major faced with countless blue book essay exams.

T: "I know you are worried about taking an essay test on this material. But if you study hard, you'll do fine. I want to tell you about some study strategies you can use. They work for me, and they should work for you too."

S: Students are listening more than usual and ready to take notes.

T: "You all know how to outline, so you might simply take the section of the text on the Baltic States and outline this information. Just writing it out, even copying it from the book, should help you memorize it."

S: "We do that anyway. Sometimes it works okay, sometimes it doesn't. What else can we do, Mr. Valuta? Personally, I'm really worried about this test. Is it one big question or smaller ones?"

T: "I can't really tell you the exact question, but I can tell you that the difficulty of getting three very different groups of people like the Latvians, Estonians, and Lithuanians together for a common cause is an important part of what you need to know. As for other study strategies, I mostly rely on the outline and memorize approach myself but you could try something like this. Take each subheading in the section of the text on the Baltic Nations and turn it into a question. Then see if you can answer the question based on your memory from reading this section. If you can successfully get most of the information, then you'll probably do fine on the essay test."

S: "But we haven't practiced doing this at all. We've just been reading, taking notes on your lectures, talking about the book, and watching films. How do we know what to expect in an essay test?"

T: "That's the whole idea—you don't. It wouldn't be a test if you already had the question and practiced writing an essay. This way, it will be a true test of your memory, and if you do well, you can feel really good about the study strategy you used."

The bell rings, and students file out talking among themselves. They express high anxiety and a sense of powerlessness in the face of this impending essay exam.

→ Keeping in mind that this lesson was designed to help students prepare for an essay exam on the Baltic Nations, jot down your thoughts on the following questions:

1. What are the good points about the lesson?
2. What are the weak points about the lesson?
3. What, if anything, would you change about the lesson?

Rationale

As teachers, the fruit of your labors will be *learning*, which can be defined as the transfer of information from short-term memory to long-term memory. Hopefully, what your students learn will have much to do with math, English, or the sciences, and little to do with accuracy in hurling paper projectiles—although both entail learning. In a much narrower sense, learning can be defined in terms of the acquisition of specific information in content areas, and the preceding chapters of this text have dealt primarily with the means by which this acquisition process can be facilitated. One focus of the present chapter is on study strategies that help students retain and retrieve information. A second focus of the chapter is on test preparation, especially as it pertains to state reading assessments driven by the new regulations of NCLB. Given the consequences of not making annual yearly progress toward the goals of NCLB, it is crucial that teachers in English, social studies, health, and other subject areas know how to prepare students to take and pass state reading tests.

Learning Objectives

→ Justify the time required to guide students toward effective study strategies in your content area.
→ Understand the general learning principles that underlie the study strategies described in this chapter.
→ Guide students in developing study strategies that improve retention and recall of material from your content area.
→ Understand why as a content teacher you should be involved in preparing students to take and pass state reading assessments.
→ Know how to successfully prepare students for state reading assessments.

Graphic Organizer

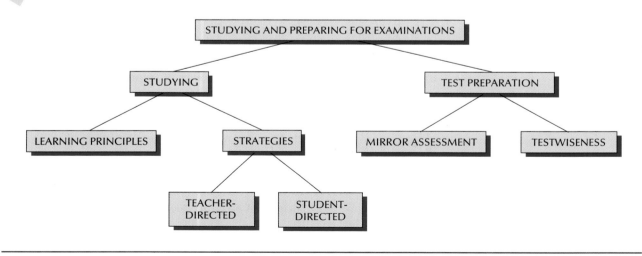

Studying

Everyone has had the experience of walking into an examination, such as the SAT or GRE, only to find the answers to certain questions elusive due to memory failure. For example, the solution to a simple geometry problem may require knowing the formula for finding the circumference of a circle. (Let's see, is that $\pi r2$, $2\pi r$, or $2\pi r2$?) A failure to extract the necessary information from memory may result because: (1) you never bothered to learn the formula in the first place; (2) you learned it at one time but have for some reason failed to retain the formula in your memory; or (3) you did learn the formula and it is still locked in your memory, but you are unable to retrieve or recall the formula. In any event, the net effect is the same, a wrong answer on the test. Clearly, the ability to retain and recall information is as important as the ability to learn it in the first place. For this reason, study strategies are the business of every content teacher. Unfortunately, research has indicated that both preservice and inservice teachers seem to lack knowledge of study strategies and do not value them (Jackson & Cunningham, 1994). A second reason for teaching study strategies in content area classes is to develop in students those habits that encourage and assist independent learning. To the extent that students learn to study effectively on their own, they will be capable of continued reading and learning in the absence of explicit external guidance (Wimmer, 2007).

Principles of Effective Studying

> If I were compelled to sum up in a single word all that is embraced in the expression 'a good memory,' I should use the word attention. Indeed, I would define education, moral and intellectual, as attention (Aiken, 1896, p. 74).

Attention

Read through the following passage one time, and be prepared to answer a single question:

> An *empty* hotel elevator stops and one person enters. The elevator goes up two floors and six people get on; up three more floors and three people get on. The elevator goes down one floor and seven people get off; down one more floor and one person gets off. The elevator then shoots up ten floors and two people get on. Now, without looking back, how many times did the elevator stop?

The answer is six; you probably got it wrong. Why? The second word in this old joke is a distractor. The fact that the elevator is empty has no bearing on the answer to the question. However, the reader, not knowing the question in advance, guesses or assumes that keeping track of numbers of people is the pertinent task. The real rub lies in the fact that tallying the number of elevator stops is much easier than calculating how many people get on and off.

The principle in this example is that comprehension and learning/memory are not at all the same thing. It is quite possible to read with good comprehension and at the same time fail to retain the information. In most instances, the individual's active attention is a powerful factor in placing information in a durable memory store. It is a matter of common sense and common experience. Everyone remembers Miss Frock (the fourth-grade teacher) who said, "If you don't pay attention, you won't remember anything."

Effective Studying Principles

➲ Attention
➲ Goal Orientation
➲ Organization
➲ Rehearsal
➲ Time on Task
➲ Depth of Processing

There is, however, another aspect of attention which has less to do with willingness or appropriateness of attention than capacity to attend. Generally, human beings are capable of attending consciously to only one task at a time. For instance, it is quite impossible to attend to two conversations at precisely the same time, although it is possible to quickly switch attention back and forth between conversations or other tasks which require conscious attention. This principle of capacity limitation for attention will be a critical consideration in discussion of specific study strategies later in the chapter.

Goal Orientation

One of the most serious and frequent impediments to learning is the counterproductive study goal. Students often read a textbook assignment for the sake of completing it, i.e., to be able to tell the teacher, without fibbing, that they have in fact read the assignment. When the student's attention is focused on getting through X number of pages rather than on comprehending and retaining information, the result is almost certain to be inferior comprehension and retention. Students who fail to read the last two paragraphs of a chapter because the teacher accidentally designated reading pages 79–93 instead of 79–94 demonstrate a counterproductive study goal. They meet the letter of the assignment but not its spirit. Constructive purpose, given by the teacher and embraced by the students, is essential to effective study.

Organization

Pronounce each digit in the following number one time, and then try to recall the number from memory:

1248163264128

Difficult, wasn't it? Now, try again.

1 2 4 8 16 32 64 128

Mental Organization

➲ Patterns
➲ Chunking
➲ Mnemonics

The second time should have been much easier. If you sensed the geometric progression, you should have been able to reproduce the original number sequence with minimal strain on memory. It is much easier to remember one number (in this case, 1) and one rule (in this case, digits are produced by doubling the preceding number) than it is to recall what appears to be a random series of digits. This is *organization*, the arrangement of parts of a whole in such a manner that the parts are related to each other. The analogy to study strategies is obvious; whenever information can be organized into meaningful patterns, retention and retrieval of information will be facilitated.

A second type of mental organization is *chunking*. Bits of information are said to be chunked when they are transformed into one large bit of information. For example, the letters *h c r a o* can be transformed into the word "roach." The advantage in chunking is that a larger bit of information, e.g., roach, requires no more memory than a smaller bit of information, e.g., *c*. Because it permits the storage of large amounts of information without placing a corresponding strain on memory, chunking is an efficient means of organizing information.

A third type of mental organization is *mnemonics*, association devices for triggering recall. Perhaps the most familiar mnemonic device is the *acronym*. The process of acronymy is one in which words are formed by combining the initial letters or segments of a series of words. AWOL (absent without leave), VIP (very important person), and radar (radio detecting and ranging) are common examples of acronyms. Tying a string around your finger, remembering how to spell "piece" with the phrase "piece of pie," or improving recall of names by distorting them (e.g., "Baldwin" becomes "bald one") represent other types of mnemonic devices.

APPLICATION 12.1

Directions: Develop a set of at least 10 specific mnemonic devices that could be used to assist in the recall of specific information in your content area. Include acronyms but do not limit your devices to them.

Rehearsal

The acquisition, retention, and recall of information are all assisted by rehearsal or practice. *Rehearsal* is a natural strategy that people use to keep information in memory. In the case of short-term memory, information is repeated over and over until the immediate need for information desists. For instance, it is normal to look up a telephone number, rehearse it rapidly during the act of dialing, and then forget the number as soon as the dialing has been completed.

In the case of long-term memory, recall of information is improved most through *distributed* practice, in which rehearsals are separated by some break. For example, the retention and recall of specific facts and historical trends derived from a social studies lecture will be better with frequent, spaced, and brief periods of study (rehearsal) than with a single massive study session.

Time on Task

While it is almost certainly true that the organization of practice affects retention and recall (e.g., distributed versus massed practice), it is equally true of the raw amount of time spent practicing. In fact, it has been argued that some strategies or teaching techniques appear to improve learning primarily because they result in students spending more time on learning tasks, and not because the techniques are better than others. For example, which of the following strategies would result in the best recall: (1) reading and then outlining a textbook chapter; or (2) reading and then answering teacher-prepared questions over the content? To some degree, the answer would be dependent upon the amount of time each technique caused students to study.

Depth of Processing

Most college graduates are capable of solving an algebra problem such as (a):

$$a. \quad x - 14 = 23$$

On the other hand most college graduates probably could not solve an equation like (b), in spite of the fact that they were undoubtedly forced in high school to work problems at this level of difficulty:

$$b. \quad y = \frac{x^3 \times 5x^2 + 6x}{x + 3}$$

One justification for introducing difficult material is that it helps to guarantee the long-term retention of basic principles and processes. In other words, it is possible that people retain the ability to solve problem (a), not because it is easy but because they were made to expend great mental energies solving problems like (b). This is the principle of *depth of processing*, which asserts that there is a greater likelihood of long-term retention and recall when: (1) the mental activity demands a deeper level of thinking, (2) more schemata are committed to the task, and (3) the degree of semantic analysis is high. The depth of processing principle also explains why a new vocabulary word and its definition will be remembered longer and with greater accuracy by most people if the word is introduced with such elements as context, morphemic analysis, and an etymology. You guarantee better memory for the word and its fundamental meaning by forcing a deeper, more expansive mental processing of the word and its associations.

Specific Strastegies

Strategy implies intent. A strategy is not an accident but is rather the planned means to an end. In general, it is best to plan study strategies that have the following characteristics.

Characteristics of Good Study Strategies
1. They help students focus attention on important information.
2. They provide students with meaningful study goals.
3. They help students organize information.
4. They cause students to practice.
5. They encourage deep processing of information.

The study strategies that follow are plans that teachers and students can implement cooperatively to further the acquisition, retention, and recall of information.

Listening and Taking Notes

Notetaking during lectures and discussions is one of the most common events in the classroom, yet there is considerable confusion over the purposes and best methods of taking notes. In fact, there are many notetaking systems, but none of them have empirical documentation.

Notetaking has two presumed functions, external storage and encoding. The *external storage* (the notes themselves) of information serves as a substitute for memory and gives students an opportunity to review material that might otherwise have been forgotten. The *encoding* function presumably improves the comprehension and retention of information by forcing the notetaker to transform lecture material into personally meaningful language (depth of processing principle). The difference between external storage and encoding is often described as a contrast between taking and having notes. The validity of the encoding function is based on the assumption that during the course of a lecture students will be able to mentally transform what they are hearing. We reject this assumption on the grounds that fast presentation rates during lectures preclude the reflective thought necessary for such encoding. In fact, it is quite possible that taking any kind of notes is detrimental to learning if the material is presented too quickly. The consensus is that the external storage function in notetaking is more important than the encoding function.

In addition to the question of notetaking purposes, there is also disagreement regarding the best procedures for notetaking. For instance, it is customary for students to take notes in *parallel*, i.e., to be writing and listening at the same time. However, *spaced* notetaking seems to improve recall of lecture material. A spaced presentation is one in which the lecture is broken into segments, followed by intervals of silence several minutes long. Students listen during each lecture segment and then make notes at the interval which follows. Why this should be an effective notetaking procedure is explained in part by the limits of human attention. If people can concentrate on only one task at a time, why should we expect students to write and listen effectively at the same time? Most notetakers probably switch back and forth; i.e., they listen for a few seconds and then write, perhaps, but do not listen during those seconds in which individual notes are recorded. The result for many notetakers is incomplete lecture information that has been received in bits and pieces. In contrast, a spaced notetaking procedure permits students to focus their complete attention on listening to the teacher and on encoding lecture information into meaningful notes.

The following statements summarize what is presently hypothesized about listening and notetaking (Spires & Stone, 1989):

1. The external storage of notes is more important than the act of taking notes (encoding).
2. Parallel notetaking may interfere with the reception of forthcoming lecture information, especially when students do not engage in self-monitoring of their comprehension.
3. Teachers should use a spaced lecture format.
4. The rate at which notes are delivered appears to affect the value of notes.
5. The value of notes is much reduced if the notes are not used for practice.
6. Teachers should place important information on the board to cue notetaking.
7. Teachers should use handouts to supplement notetaking.

TEACHER STRATEGIES. It is easy to assume that the quality of student notes is nothing more than a function of students' intelligence and other attributes. However, the lecture situation is a meeting of minds, and the organization and presentation format of the lecture can affect the quality of the notes radically. Following is a list of suggestions that will make notetaking easier and more efficient for students in your lectures and class presentations.

Tips for Making Notetaking Easier

1. Do not lecture if students are expected to write down and remember everything you say. Instead, type the material and hand it out. Lectures are more interesting if they include elements of discussion.
2. Lectures typically follow the same organizational patterns found in texts, e.g., cause/effect and comparison/contrast. Point these patterns out to students while you are lecturing, and tell them about how you have organized your notes. For example, if you have three points to make under each of two headings, let students know so that they can make appropriate room in their notes.
3. Notetaking should not be a game in which the student has to guess about what is important. It is absurd to assume that novices in chemistry or political science should, without guidance, instantly sort essential ideas from trivial details. Write important information on the board, or just tell students when to take notes and when not to.

4. Speak slowly.

5. Use a spaced notetaking procedure. Allow students to listen to your lecture for ten minutes or so. Then give them time to write and ask you questions. This will prevent the students from having to write and listen at the same time (capacity limitation problem).

6. Give students a few minutes at the end of class to revise and/or supplement their notes, and make them do it!

7. Give students distributed practice with their notes. Encourage them to review their notes on a nightly basis or in class. You can give students frequent quizzes over lecture material, allowing them to review their notes before the quiz or even allowing an open-notebook quiz. Another review possibility is to have students create questions strictly from their notes for a class review. In general, anything you can do to get the students to modify and refer back to their notes will boost their recall and retention.

8. Have open-note, but closed-book, quizzes to give students an idea of the quality of their notes. Students who take the time to revise notes and to review them will perform better; this, in turn, will encourage others to revise and review.

STUDENT STRATEGIES. We believe that it is a good idea for students to learn to take good notes, and we define good notes as any notes, however disorganized, sloppy, or idiosyncratic, that will serve as a successful warehouse for lecture information. We know of no one best notetaking procedure for all people of all ages in all subject areas. Therefore, we recommend considerable latitude in individual notetaking systems.

Figure 12.1

	11/24
	-2-
40%	60%
Verbatim Transcription	

Verbatim Split Page Procedure. The notetaking procedure we recommend for students is the *Verbatim Split Page Procedure.* VSPP is a blend of various notetaking systems and is comprised of recording and organizing notes.

1. Recording Notes. Begin teaching VSPP by having students divide their notebook paper so that 40 percent of each page lies to the left and 60 percent to the right (see Figure 12.1). Instruct students to take notes only on the lefthand side during lectures. All notes should be verbatim and clipped. The idea is to expend minimum amounts of mental energy on writing in order that full attention can be focused on listening to the lecture.

2. Organizing Notes. Nearly everyone has had the experience of taking abundant notes for a class, only to find those notes either unreadable or bizarre when it came time to study for the final exam. Abbreviated words, telegraphic sentences, and hasty scribbles may seem quite lucid to the notetaker at the time they are written; however, as the context in which the idiosyncratic shorthand was produced fades, notes of this sort rapidly lose meaning and integrity. For this reason, it is necessary to reorganize notes during significant pauses within the lecture or immediately following the lecture.

The right side of the notebook paper is used for reorganizing and expanding upon the scribbles to the left. Students should be encouraged to:

1. Place lecture information in an outline format;
2. Interpret notes and then encode them in their own words;

3. Expand notes to include lecture information that the student didn't have time to note; and

4. Write out whole words, phrases, and sentences so that notes will be clear in the future. (See Figure 12.2.)

Figure 12.2
Organizing Notes

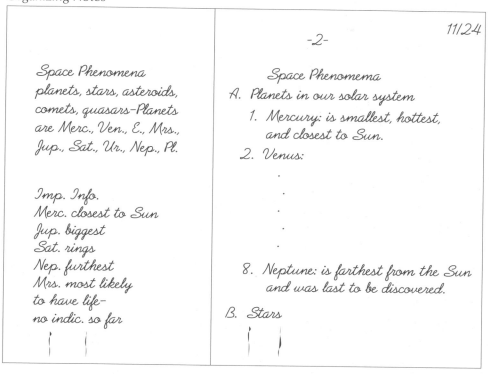

It is sometimes recommended that students take notes in an outline format. This is an extremely difficult task for two reasons. First, deciding which ideas are superordinate and which are subordinate requires attention that notetakers can't spare as they play the role of listener. Secondly, lectures are hardly ever organized and presented in ways which immediately lend themselves to outline notetaking. In Figure 12.2 it is clear that the lecture on space phenomena began with an overview of superordinate concepts and then later presented subordinate bits of information. In reality, most lectures and other teacher presentations are punctuated frequently with digressions and slices of knowledge that are improperly layered within the lecture. With the help of limited verbatim notes, students should be able to rethink and reorganize the lecture material AFTER the lecture is over and when the entire presentation is fresh in their minds.

When the lecture information has been organized in the 60% column, the 40% verbatim column serves as the basis for studying the notes. Students try to recall the reorganized, expanded information using the clipped notes as a prompt.

In addition to the split-page notetaking structure, teaching students to consciously self-monitor their notetaking before a lecture begins, and after the lecture ends, can improve their notetaking performance. Based on teacher modeling of the following self-questioning routine, students should begin and end lecture notetaking with the following questions.

Before the lecture begins:

1. What is my purpose for listening to this lecture?
2. Am I interested in this topic and, if not, how will I increase interest and concentration (e.g., through an argumentative stance where I disagree with the author's point of view)?

After the lecture ends:

1. Did I achieve my purpose?
2. Did I maintain concentration and deal with comprehension failures?

Adding a comprehension monitoring dimension to the split-page procedure increases students' active processing and prepares them for the more advanced lecture and notetaking tasks they will encounter in college.

 STOP! Go to the CD-ROM and practice the VSPP using the lecture entitled, The Effects of Transfer on Learning.

Metacognition

Broadly defined, *metacognition* refers to awareness of one's own mental processes, that is, knowing how you know what to do. It entails an effort to manage one's own thoughts through conscious planning. People who have good metacognitive skills understand their own behaviors, employ mental strategies that they can verbalize, and evaluate the quality of their thinking (Hacker, Dunlosky, & Graesser, 1998). Metacognition is thinking about thinking.

Most children do not have good metacognitive skills. The most common response children give when asked why they have done something is: "I don't know." Sometimes they hide behind the "I don't know" when they do not wish to respond to parents, teachers, or other authority figures. For example:

Dad to teenage Daughter: "I told you to be home at 12 last night. Why did you come home at 3 a.m.?"

Teenage Daughter to Dad: "I don't know."

Of course, the real thought of the teenage daughter is: "Jimmy and I were too busy to pay attention to your stupid rule." On the other hand, young people frequently do not understand or even attempt to monitor their own thought processes, and this is often true in the area of reading comprehension. Too many students rove mindlessly through a textbook assignment without any clearly defined purposes or conscious strategies for learning. Current research in the area of metacognition indicates that students who have good metacognitive skills are better comprehenders (Wade & Reynolds, 1989). Therefore, helping your students to develop their metacognitive awareness is fundamental to study strategies.

TEACHER STRATEGIES. One approach to developing metacognition in students is the think-aloud technique (Kucan & Beck, 1997). The think-aloud technique is a teacher-modeling strategy in which the teacher reads aloud from a text and verbalizes whatever comes to mind in an effort to show students how to reason during reading. The teacher's verbalized thoughts may include questions, predictions, paraphrases, evaluative statements, and even text-irrelevant comments.

Steps for Developing Think-Aloud Strategies

1. Select a passage between 100 and 300 words long in your subject area. The passage should be fairly difficult so that your reasoning is actually useful to the students. If the passage is too easy the students will not see the value of what you are doing.

2. Prepare your comments for the think-aloud based on your experiences. Because the material will not really be difficult for you, you need to plan an idealized set of think-aloud responses. You will be acting the part of a student with good metacognitive skills.

3. Explain to the students exactly what you are doing, e.g., "I am going to show you how I think when I read."

4. Read the passage to the class and insert your planned think-alouds as you go.

5. When you are finished, give students a chance to ask you questions about how you think or about the think-aloud procedure itself.

6. Have students practice thinking aloud with smaller segments of the text.

The paragraph below exemplifies a think-aloud for a biology text. The teacher's questions and statements are indicated by superscripts within the paragraph and referenced after the paragraph.

> Amniocentesis[1] is a technique used by fetologists[2] when the parents are known or suspected to carry one of several types of genetic disease or when the woman is over age 40.[3] Older women are more likely to have a fetus with Down's syndrome.[4] The diseases specifically tested for are caused by having an extra or missing chromosome, a chromosome which has been broken,[5] or a metabolic disease such as phenylketonuria.[6] A hypodermic needle is inserted through the abdomen of the pregnant woman[7] and into the amnion.[8] A small amount of amniotic fluid, containing fetal cells,[9] is drawn into the syringe. These cells are then cultured (grown) for a period of time; when enough culture cells are available, they can be tested for many metabolic defects. Cells can also be specially stained and prepared so that the chromosomes can be seen under a microscope.[10] (Brum, 1978, p. 105).

1. Looks like this is the topic. I better remember this word.
2. What's this? Someone who studies feet?
3. I didn't know people that old could have babies.
4. OK, I know about that. A boy in our church has it.
5. How do you lose a chromosome or get it broken? Could it happen to me if I play football or get in an accident? How will I know?
6. I wonder what nerd made up this word.
7. Ouch!
8. Better ask the teacher what this is.
9. I get it now. Fetal refers to fetus, an unborn baby. That explains what a fetologist is, an unborn baby doctor.
10. Sounds cool; I'd like to see it.

STOP! View the CD-ROM video clip demonstrating a think-aloud.

A second approach to developing metacognition in students is *embedded questions*. Embedded questions are teacher-developed questions inserted in a text at key points which are crucial to understanding the entire passage. This strategy can be used once students have been introduced to, and grasped, the modeling being done in the think-aloud, that is, once students understand what the teacher is demonstrating and see how reasoning occurs during reading. Thus, while think-alouds provide students the awareness and recognition of metacognitive strategies during reading, embedded questions allow students to simulate and produce metacognitive responses as they read.

Planning an embedded questions lesson begins like the think-aloud. A 100–300 word passage is selected, and key points in the passage are identified where students will be able to simulate the metacognitive strategies good readers would employ. Students are asked to read the passage and provide answers to the embedded questions. Following that, a substantive discussion occurs wherein comprehension of the passage is checked as well as verbalization of the metacognitive strategies used to answer the embedded questions. Though only limited to the difficulty of the passage and ability level of the students, some typical embedded questions might be:

→ What do you think will happen next? Why do you think so?

→ What question are you thinking of at this point in the passage?

→ What quality of the character (aspect of the process) do you think the author is emphasizing? Why?

→ What seems to be confusing you the most at this point?

STUDENT STRATEGIES. Most of the strategies in this text will improve metacognitive skills to some extent. For instance, Loxterman, Beck, and McKeown (1994) found that when middle grade students used a think-aloud strategy, they improved their comprehension, particularly with more friendly text. Nevertheless, students need a guiding mental strategy for studying. PLAE (Nist, Simpson, Olejnik, & Mealey, 1991) is an acronym that stands for Preplan, List, Activate, Evaluate.

> *Preplan:* Plan how to study. This may entail asking questions such as: "Should I summarize, take notes, or reread?" "What kind of a test is the instructor going to give?" "Do I want to study by myself or in a small group?"

> *List:* The answers to such questions should result in planned behaviors rather than thoughtless or reflexive ones. The planned behaviors should be written down. For example: "I will read this chapter twice." "I will ask my teacher whether the test will be essay or multiple-choice." "I will ask Marty and Beth if they want to study with me tomorrow."

> *Activate:* This is a monitoring behavior. Basically the student needs to regularly ask, "Am I following my plan?"

> *Evaluate:* Students assess whether or not the plan has worked. For example: "Was it worth studying with Marty and Beth?" "Would I do it again?"

PLAE is deceptively simple, so much so that you may be tempted to dismiss it as superfluous. Yet we believe that a strategy as simple as this is fundamental and not at all too obvious to bother with as you are teaching. How many times have you gotten to school or the office only to discover that you had forgotten your lunch, house keys, wallet, purse, term paper, or other important item? If the average American adult simply stopped at the front door before leaving and asked, "Do I have everything I need to take with me?," it would probably save millions in gasoline and aspirin.

APPLICATION 12.2

Select a textbook from your content area and develop a think-aloud lesson that you can demonstrate for the rest of the class.

Reading and Taking Notes

One of the content teacher's ever-present problems is how to get students to comprehend and retain information from textbook reading assignments. How does the teacher convert the passive page-watcher into a reader who is actively engaged in reconstructing and evaluating the author's thoughts?

Unfortunately, the best method of responding while reading, writing in the text, is not an option for most students because the books belong to the school. Underlining main ideas, starring important terms, asking and answering questions, and making evaluative comments in the margins combine to make a highly personal and convenient response mode during reading. In the absence of this option, however, we must examine what we know about reading and taking notes and consider some alternative study strategies.

Caverly, Orlando, & Mullen (2000) offer the following generalizations about reading and taking notes:

1. Students need instruction in how to take notes. While some students may spontaneously develop notetaking skills, we cannot make the assumption that all students will do so.

2. Students must be able to differentiate important material from supporting detail as well as other irrelevant information for notetaking instruction to succeed.

3. In order for students to benefit from notetaking instruction, review is essential, particularly in delayed recall situations.

TEACHER STRATEGIES. First, avoid giving assignments such as, "OK, read pages 24–43 for Monday." Assignments like this make the completion of page 43 the objective of the assignment. A much better assignment would be "OK, read pages 24–43. When you are finished you should be able to answer these questions . . ." or "As you are reading, write down at least 10 words, facts, procedures, or explanations you didn't understand." By the time you have finished detailing the reading assignment, your students should be able to answer the following questions:

1. What is this reading assignment about?
2. Why am I reading this?
3. What should I know when I have finished?

In fact, students have a right to this information and should be encouraged to ask for it whenever they find themselves facing purposeless reading assignments.

Second, introduce notetaking through the use of think-alouds. Select a passage for demonstration purposes, and hand this out to your students. As you read the passage together, think aloud your reasoning processes and make your notes accordingly. The recording should occur on an overhead projector so students can visualize your recording as they hear you explain your thought processes. Do this several times until students seem to understand the process and then have them demonstrate their notetaking skills. A discussion of these demonstrations should occur. Students may also be placed in small groups to react to each others' notetaking or to produce a set of notes jointly. Joint products should be shared with the entire class. The intention of this instructional recommendation is to model the notetaking process and then have students produce their own notes.

A third teacher strategy is the use of a partial outline developed from a selected passage. The intention here is to provide students structure and guidance until they are eventually able to develop a full set of notes on their own. The first time a partial outline is used, demonstrate how to complete it in conjunction with a passage. Because the outline has a preset number of slots, attention can be drawn to the notion that only a certain amount of information is needed to complete the outline and that there is a difference between subordinate information and information that is supportive or irrelevant. Additional lessons would take the format described previously, that is, teacher demonstrations could be followed by student ones and lessons done in small groups, always with a follow-up discussion of the thinking processes involved. The amount of structure provided in the outline as well as the amount of demonstration and instruction would be based upon the ability level of the students.

STUDENT STRATEGIES. The two strategies we recommend for daily reading assignments are FLIP and Student-Generated Questions.

FLIP, *F*riendliness, *L*anguage, *I*nterest, and *P*rior knowledge (Schumm & Mangrum, 1991), is a textbook previewing procedure designed to teach students how to evaluate the difficulty of daily reading assignments and allocate study time in a realistic manner. The strategy is highly personal and intentionally subjective because students need to learn how to manage reading and study assignments in ways which are consistent with their own abilities, interests, and schedules. The FLIP chart in Figure 12.3 can be used when students are initially learning textbook reading assignments.

Steps for Using the FLIP Procedure

FLIP

Friendliness
Language
Interest
Prior Knowledge

1. Students record the reading assignment on the top of the FLIP chart.
2. Students skim the reading assignment and make a value judgment for each of the four FLIP categories: Friendliness, Language, Interest, and Prior knowledge. In the case of vocabulary, students read three paragraphs at random to check the level of unfamiliar vocabulary. Each of the four categories is given a rating from 1 to 5 with 1 being the most negative and 5 being the most positive.
3. Based on the FLIP category ratings, students make an overall assessment of how comfortable the reading level is for them.
4. Students identify their purpose for reading, estimate how fast they should attempt to read, and then budget their reading time by dividing the assignment into as many chunks as they feel are necessary.

cult for students, yet are ignored as specific instructional objectives in basals and other school texts.

Do not assume that your students will understand even simple pie graphs. If the purposes and designs of graphs have never been explained to them, many students will automatically skip graphs, an unfortunate behavior, since graphs are designed to improve comprehension—not create interference.

As a prereading activity, you should introduce graphs as you would new and important vocabulary. Have students open their texts to the graphs. Then explain the purposes of the graphs to them and demonstrate correct procedures for their interpretations, e.g., how to plot points on a complex quantitative graph. We also recommend that you try the *Graphic Information Lesson* (GIL) (Reinking, 1986).

Steps for Using the GIL

1. In the *introductory* stage the teacher shows the students a graph and explains the mechanics of its use. Then the teacher asks text explicit, text implicit, and experience-based questions that are designed to enlighten the students as to the relationship between the graph and the rest of the text. Students can also learn to judge whether the graph is supplemental, redundant, or complementary to the text.

2. In the *synthesizing* stage the teacher presents teacher-made *pseudographics*, graphs that are related to current text material but which may or may not be accurate or believable. The students have to be able to relate the new graph to what they have learned from the text in order to judge its validity. They must also document their decision with a page number from the text. (See Figure 12.4 for examples of pseudographs.)

3. In the *application* stage students are asked to: (a) develop their own pseudographs to accompany the text, or (b) critique the author's use of graphic aids.

Figure 12.4
Pseudographs

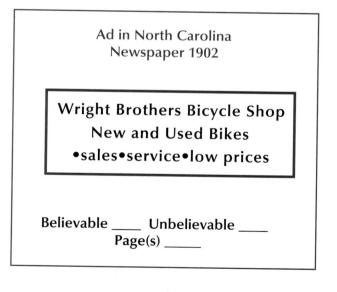

Preparing for Examinations

Test Preparation for State Reading Assessments

There is, of course, nothing that will improve performance on state reading assessments more than improvements in your students' knowledge of American history, chemistry, English, health, and other subject areas. However, to prepare students for the format of the test, there are two general strategies you can use: mirror assessment and principles of testwiseness for multiple-choice tests.

Mirror Assessment

Mirror assessment refers to the practice of preparing classroom examinations in a format that reflects the format students will encounter on the state reading assessment. We are not suggesting that every test and quiz in every classroom should be a mirror assessment, but teachers should use some mirror assessments to guarantee the proper practice and mental readiness for the state reading assessment. According to Figure 5.6, most of the state assessments have the following format: text passages followed by multiple-choice questions followed by a short, writing requirement (performance item). We recommend the following *Mirror Assessment Strategy* (MAS) for subject area test development:

1. Test items should be *multiple-choice* with four or five options depending upon the format for your particular state. State reading assessments do not use true/false, matching, or other item formats. Items should include questions that reflect the reading standards for your state. For example, almost all states have a standard that requires students to distinguish fact from opinion, and questions reflecting this standard are common among the test items released by the various states. If your subject area lends itself easily to this standard, you may want to include such questions.

2. Include at least one performance item—*short essay*—that follows the rubric for your state.

3. The test should be *open-book* so that students have an opportunity to search for information as they would in the state reading assessment.

4. The test should be *timed* so that students develop the ability to pace themselves.

5. Answers to multiple-choice items should be bubbled in on *standardized forms*.

Testwiseness

Testwiseness refers to a series of principles that can be applied to exams independently of subject area knowledge. To be testwise is to be able to (1) exploit the flaws in exams, and (2) apply logic, common sense, and good organization in test-taking situations. There is no substitute for being knowledgeable. However, testwiseness skills can help students to perform better on state reading assessments. The present discussion will be limited to testwiseness in taking multiple-choice tests.

When you are preparing students for MAS tests or state assessments in reading, encourage them to do the following:

→ Read all directions carefully. It is not unusual for students to get poor scores on exams simply because they fail to read and follow directions.

→ Always guess if you don't know the answer. Never leave a multiple-choice question blank.

→ Budget time so that you are certain to finish the test. Students sometimes spend too much time on one part of the test and then fail to finish another.

→ Do not waste time on items that are very difficult. Take a guess and make a light mark in the test booklet—if this is permitted—and go back to the tough questions at the end of the exam. Do not leave answers blank along the way because it is easy to mark answers out of sequence on the answer sheet, which can result in devastating score reductions.

→ Try to come up with the answer to the question before you look at the alternatives. By thinking of the answer first, you are less likely to be fooled by wrong choices that sound good.

→ Look at all the answers before making a choice. Multiple-choice tests typically require you to select the *best* answer.

If the right answer is not clear to you right away, try to eliminate obvious wrong or silly answers and then guess from among those that remain. For example:

The speed of sound is:
    A. 3700 feet per second
    B. 1087 feet per second
    C. 0
    D. 186 miles per second

You should be able to eliminate answer C right away. That would give you a 1/3 chance of guessing right instead of 1/4 chance.

Whenever two of the options are identical, both answers must be wrong. For example:

The universal donor is:
    A. O–
    B. H_2O
    C. AB
    D. water

Whenever two of the options are opposites, one of them is always wrong and the other is often, but not always, right. For example:

A proton is a:
    A. positively charged particle
    B. free atom
    C. negatively charged particle
    D. displaced neutron

Be aware that the answer to a question may appear in the stem of another question. For example, the answer to item I can be found in the stem of item II.

I. A z-score is a:
   A. percentile equivalent
   B. concept in criterion referenced testing
   C. measure of standard error
   D. standardized score

II. Standardized scores such as z-scores and t-scores are based on:
   A. standard deviations
   B. stanines
   C. chi squares
   D. grade equivalents

Other common testwiseness strategies for selecting the correct answer are dependent upon flaws in test item design (e.g., when guessing, select an answer which is neither the first or the last choice) and will not work with most state assessments because the tests are designed by professional test-makers.

Test Preparation for Teacher-Made Assessments

Evaluation tends to be an anxiety-producing situation for teachers and students. Anxiety can be reduced and learning maximized if teachers prepare students for specific examinations and if students learn how to study for and take tests intelligently.

TEACHER STRATEGIES. Middle and secondary students typically fear examinations and mistrust teachers' motivations. Many students develop a neurosis over tests because they have stereotyped teachers as a group of ogres who try to trick them with unfair questions or who purposely do not reveal what material a test will cover so that they can have the pleasure of doling out bad grades. To prove to your students that you are not a test-ogre, we suggest that you: (a) give students precise information about what material an exam will cover, and (b) give students ungraded practice in taking the kinds of tests they will later have to negotiate for grades. We recommend the *Fake Pop Quiz* (FPQ).

Fake Pop Quiz. The FPQ is a quiz designed to reinforce rather than test recently introduced information. The purpose of the quiz format is to stimulate interest. Students are considerably more alert following, "Get your pencils ready; it's time for a fake pop quiz," than they are after hearing, "Get your pencils ready; it's time to do some review exercises." Tests are really a lot of fun once the anxiety over being externally evaluated has been neutralized. In addition, students appreciate test simulations because they know that the teacher is trying to prepare them for the true evaluation that inevitably follows.

FPQs can be brief interludes in daily lessons (placed on the board) or comprehensive reviews prepared on handouts. In either case, the quiz should be preceded by general directions, either verbal or written, along the lines of the following:

> Today we are having a fake pop quiz on earth science vocabulary. Obviously, the score you get on this quiz won't affect your grade in the course, but it will give you some practice and an idea of how well prepared you are for a real test. When everyone has finished the quiz, you will score your own and get two points for each correct answer. Good luck! (The

FPQ may be open- or closed-book depending upon the teacher's objectives and the nature of the exercises.)

Once students have finished the quiz, specific questions can serve as guides to classroom discussion. The FPQ offers a golden opportunity to focus on text implicit and experience-based kinds of questions.

STUDENT STRATEGIES. Students can acquire confidence in their own test-taking abilities if they learn how to prepare for exams and how to cope with them logically. The following information can help your students meet these objectives.

Test-taking skills refer to long-term study strategies as well as to strategies that students can use while taking exams, often referred to as testwiseness. You should be doing frequent reviews of text material, class notes, and other assigned materials. Remember, lots of short study sessions are better than a few giant cramming sessions. Students can be given the following advice for preparing for content area exams.

Tips to Students Preparing for Exams

When you hear about the test.

1. Find out as much as you can about the test itself.
2. Find out exactly when the test will be given.
3. Ask your teachers to discuss the kinds of questions that will be on the test, e.g., multiple choice, true-false, or essay.
4. If your teachers give essay tests, ask them what they look for in a good essay answer.
5. Ask your teachers to give you examples of test items and good test answers. Many will be willing to do this, but almost none will do it if you don't ask.
6. Try to guess which questions your teacher will ask.

The night before the test.

1. A light study session should be enough. Do not cram!
2. Make sure you have pencils, pens, paper, a watch, a calculator (if permissible), and any other materials you may need for the exam.
3. Get a good night's sleep.

The day of the test.

1. Eat a good breakfast.
2. Tell yourself that you will do well on the exam.
3. Make sure you have all the materials you need for the exam.
4. Do not cram right before the test. That is the worst thing you can do. Cramming can cause students to forget important information. Cramming also causes needless test anxiety.

Tips to Students Taking Teacher-Made Multiple Choice Tests

1. Read all directions carefully. It is not unusual for students to get poor grades on exams simply because they fail to read and follow directions.
2. Budget your time so that you are certain to finish the test. Students sometimes spend too much time on one part of the test and then fail to finish another. Nothing hurts a test grade worse than leaving items blank.

3. Do not waste time on items which are very difficult. Come back to them at the end of the exam.

4. Assume that each item has a correct answer and that you are smart enough to figure it out one way or another.

5. Always guess if you don't know the answer. Never leave a multiple choice question blank.

6. Be alert for alternatives that do not match the stem grammatically. Teachers sometimes make this mistake. For example,

The smallest unit of sound capable of making a meaning distinction in language is a
   A. morpheme
   B. allophone
   C. phoneme
   D. tagmeme

7. When alternatives seem equally good, select the one that is longest and seems to hold the most information. For example,

In the United States, inferior intellectual development is most often caused by
   A. poor nutrition
   B. divorce
   C. the combined effects of heritability and environmental deprivation
   D. television

8. When all else fails, select an option which is not the first choice or the last. For example,

The probability of rolling a 12 with two dice is
   A. 3 in 12
   B. 1 in 12
   C. 1 in 36
   D. 2 in 19

APPLICATION 12.3

Identify a course outside your area of expertise. Ask the instructor if you can take one of his or her multiple choice exams to practice your test-taking strategies.

TRUE-FALSE TESTS. True-false questions are actually statements that students must decide are true or untrue. Major examinations are seldom composed entirely of true-false questions. However, many teachers like to include a section of these on their tests. True-false tests are feared by many students, who believe that teachers are trying to trick them into a lower grade. In reality most teachers are just interested in finding out how much the students know. Here are some testwise principles for true-false tests.

Tips to Students Taking True-False Tests

1. Read all directions carefully.
2. Budget your time so that you are certain to finish the test.

3. Always guess if you don't know the answer. Never leave a true-false question blank.

4. If any part of the statement is false, the correct answer for the item is "false." For example, the following item is false because the second part of the statement is false.

   The United States entered World War II after the Japanese attacked San Francisco.

5. Be alert for the words "never" and "always." These absolutes often indicate a wrong answer. For example, item A is false because it does occasionally rain in the desert. On the other hand, item B is true because the word "never" is qualified.

   A. It never rains in the Sahara Desert.

   B. It almost never rains in the Sahara Desert.

6. Long statements are somewhat more likely to be true than short statements. For example, A is true and B is false.

   A. In the poem Ozymandias Shelley uses irony to make a statement about the mortality of man.

   B. Ozymandias was a monk.

7. Assume that the teacher is asking straightforward questions. In other words, do not turn an obviously true statement into a false one by creating wild possible exceptions in your mind. For example, item A is true in spite of the fact that B, C, and D are, if you have a strong imagination, contradictions to the statement.

   A. Shoes are an important part of the business person's physical appearance.

   B. Business people don't wear horse shoes.

   C. Brake shoes are not part of the business person's appearance.

   D. If your pants are too long and cover your shoes, then the shoes won't make any difference.

ESSAY TESTS. Essay tests are among the most difficult exams because they require recall of information, good writing skills, and good organization. Here are some testwise principles for essay tests, followed by an essay test preparation strategy.

Tips to Students Taking Essay Tests

1. Read all directions carefully. Essay tests often use in their directions key words that you must clearly understand. Here are some of the key words and their meanings:

Key Word	Meaning
enumerate	to name one at a time
illustrate	to explain with examples
trace	to tell the history or development of something from the earliest to the most recent time
compare	to point out similarities and differences
contrast	to point out differences
summarize	to give a brief version of the most important points

evaluate	to judge the merit of
justify	to give reasons for
critique	to summarize and evaluate

Two answers (A and B) are given below for the same essay question. Answer B is a better answer because the writer followed directions and compared (noted similarities and differences) the topics under discussion.

Directions: Compare saccadic and pursuit eye movements.

Answer A: There are two basic kinds of eye movements: saccadic and pursuit. Saccadic movements are used when you go from object to object when the objects are at rest. Pursuit movements follow a moving target. During the act of reading saccadic movements allow the reader to stop on a line of print and pick up information. The word saccade means little jerk.

Answer B: There are two basic kinds of eye movements: saccadic and pursuit. They are the same in the sense that both of them are used to locate visual information. However, they are physically different. Saccadic movements are jumps while the pursuit movement is smooth. Another difference is that saccadic movements let the eyes go from one still object to another while pursuit movement follows a moving target.

2. Budget your time so that you are certain to finish the test. Check to see how much each essay question is worth. Spend the most time on the questions that are worth the most points.

3. Always give some kind of an answer, even if you don't understand the question.

4. Unless the directions say otherwise, never give a minimal answer. Teachers will expect you to elaborate and to give full explanations on an essay. For the essay question below, responses A, B, and C technically answer the question, but only C meets the spirit of the essay exam by giving an explanation.

Question: Do you believe that American troops should fight in foreign wars?

Answer A: No.

Answer B: No. I don't think that Americans should fight in foreign wars.

Answer C: No. I think war is immoral. We should not fight unless we are attacked. Besides, when we sent troops to other countries, it makes us look like fascist-capitalistic dogs.

5. Use the technical language of the course when writing an essay. Remember, the teacher wants to find out how much you know. And that includes your knowledge of the appropriate vocabulary. Compare answers A and B for the essay question below. B is a better answer because it uses more technical language.

Question: Summarize the process of conception and the initial stage of prenatal development.

Answer A: The male cell goes up to the egg and digs its way inside. Once this happens, the genetic material from the man and the woman mix to form the genetic pattern for the baby. After this happens, the cell begins to split up again and again as the fertilized egg works its way down to the uterus where it will attach itself to the woman's body.

Answer B: The male sperm cell digs its way into the ovum, and the egg is fertilized. Once this happens, the chromosomes from the sperm cell and the chromosomes from the ovum mix to form the genetic pattern for the baby. After this happens, the fertilized ovum begins to reproduce itself through a process called mitosis. As this process continues, the fertilized egg, now called a zygote, works its way down the fallopian tube to the uterus where it will attach itself to the wall of the uterus.

6. Pay attention to capitalization, punctuation, spelling, grammar, and neatness. Proof for these things as you reread your answers. Remember, the grading of essays is largely subjective. A careless presentation of your answer can only reduce your grade.

PORPE: An Essay Writing Strategy

In addition to general student strategies for essay preparation, Simpson (2007) developed and validated a powerful integrated study strategy under the acronym PORPE which stands for: (a) predict; (b) organize; (c) rehearse; (d) practice; and, (e) evaluate. PORPE involves students in the following sequence of activities:

1. *Predicting* potential essay questions,
2. *Organizing* key ideas using their own words,
3. *Rehearsing* the key ideas,
4. *Practicing* the recall of the key ideas in a self-assigned writing task that requires analytical thinking, and
5. *Evaluating* the completeness, accuracy, and appropriateness of the essay in terms of the self-predicted essay question.

Unlike many sink-or-swim essay exam experiences students have, PORPE does not assume that students readily grasp the preparatory and analytical steps involved in writing a strong essay question response. Rather, PORPE offers a step-by-step process to guide students' independent studying for an essay test. Each of the five steps is elaborated in the following section along with a student-predicted essay question from physical education and a student's response.

STEP ONE: PREDICT. Once students have finished a reading assignment in a unit or lesson where an essay test will be given, have them create potential essay questions, particularly those eliciting higher order thinking through analysis, comparison, and critique. Simpson cautions that you should not assume students grasp the language of essay questions. Rather, she recommends conducting a short session on the language of essay questions, including such common requests as explain, criticize, compare, and contrast. In addition, she recommends teacher modeling of the question prediction step. Following this teacher-directed assistance, ask students to create their own predicted essay questions and share these in small groups.

PORPE

Predicting
Organizing
Rehearsing
Practicing
Evaluating

STEP TWO: ORGANIZE. In preparation for responding to the predicted essay question, students should outline, map, or use a graphic organizer to organize the information they plan to use in their written response. Initial teacher modeling and small group sharing of outlines or graphic organizers are also helpful in this step.

STEP THREE: REHEARSE. The idea in this step is to develop a long-term memory for the information in the outline or graphic organizer that needs to be easily retrieved at the time of essay question response. Simpson recommends self-testing by reciting the overall organizational structure of the outline or graphic organizer and writing it out from memory.

STEP FOUR: PRACTICE. This is a key step as students are asked to write the answer to their predicted essay question from recall. However, prior to actually writing, they should sketch the outline or graphic organizer of their rehearsed response to guide the structure and content of their essays.

STEP FIVE: EVALUATE. An important final step involves having students evaluate their practice essay answers. You may wish to provide students with a checklist that reiterates the criteria for a good essay response. Simpson recommends including a checklist like the one in Figure 12.5.

Figure 12.5

PORPE Checklist

	BELOW AVERAGE	AVERAGE	ABOVE AVERAGE
1. The writer answered the question directly.	1	2	3
2. There was an introductory sentence which restated the essay question or took a position on the question.	1	2	3
3. The essay was organized with major points or ideas that were made obvious to the reader.	1	2	3
4. The essay had relevant details or examples to prove and clarify each point.	1	2	3
5. The writer used transitions to cue the reader.	1	2	3
6. The writer had knowledge of the content and made sense.	1	2	3

In the example that follows, Ardis, a student in physical education carried out the various steps of PORPE to answer her predicted essay question in preparation for a test. The test was based on the topic, Prosocial Skills for Human Movement, and the teacher indicated that there would be a series of short essay questions.

STEP ONE: PREDICT. Ardis predicted that the teacher would ask her to: Explain how games reflect culture, based on a subheading in the text chapter on Multicultural Considerations in Physical Education.

STEP TWO: ORGANIZE. Next, Ardis developed a graphic organizer (see Step Three) showing how games reflect culture based on the information in this section of the text.

STEP THREE: REHEARSE. Ardis then studied, recited, and tested herself on her memory for these key ideas in preparation for writing an essay response.

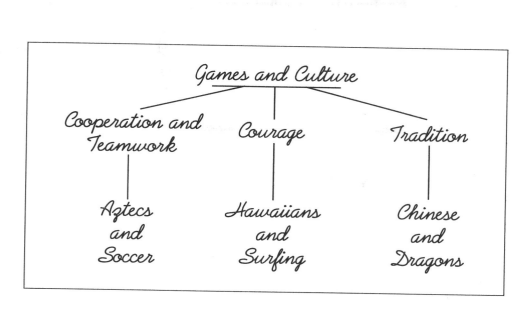

STEP FOUR: PRACTICE. In this most difficult step, Ardis composes a practice answer to her essay question by using the graphic organizer she created as a guide in writing her response.

Ardis' Practice Essay

Games reflect culture because they represent the values of a cultural group. For example, cooperation and teamwork are highly valued by Native American Indians. The game of soccer we play in P. E. that needs careful teamwork was played by the ancient Aztecs in Mexico. Another example is the Hawaiian value of courage or "koa." The ancient Hawaiian royalty fearlessly surfed large waves on heavy koa boards. They tried to ride with a smooth casual style that is now a crucial skill in modern longboarding. And the Chinese value tradition. Their New Year's celebrations maintain the ancient traditions by featuring the dragon, which symbolizes prosperity, authority, and royalty. Each of these games, soccer, surfing, and the folk dance of the Chinese dragon, display the cultural values of their respective cultural groups.

	BELOW AVERAGE	AVERAGE	ABOVE AVERAGE
1. The writer answered the question directly.	1	2	(3)
2. There was an introductory sentence which restated the essay question or took a position on the question.	1	2	(3)
3. The essay was organized with major points or ideas that were made obvious to the reader.	1	(2)	3
4. The essay had relevant details or examples to prove and clarify each point.	1	2	(3)
5. The writer used transitions to cue the reader.	1	(2)	3
6. The writer had knowledge of the content and made sense.	1	2	(3)

STEP FIVE: EVALUATE. Applying the checklist to Ardis' essay response, she has clearly written a very coherent and carefully planned answer.

It is not surprising that Ardis' essay meets each of these criteria. She applied the steps involved in PORPE and was fully prepared for the essay question. Indeed, Simpson points out that students using this strategy outpace students using a more traditional read and answer chapter questions approach. Although PORPE takes time to use with students, it develops a studying approach that will serve students well as they advance into more difficult text material in college. Moreover, the movement away from multiple-choice assessment and the increasing interest in essay questions that tap critical thinking make PORPE an ideal strategy to share with your students. Its acronym is admittedly odd, sounding a lot like "porpoise." But it could be worse—how about SHARK!

 STOP! Go to the CD-ROM and apply the PORPE strategy to the lecture entitled Our Crazy Spelling System and How It Got to Be This Way.

NOW go back to the studying vignette at the beginning of the chapter. React to the lesson as you did before. Compare your responses with those you made before you read the chapter.

Mini Projects

1. Draw an "unbelievable" pseudograph suitable for your content area. Describe the pseudograph and explain how you might use it with a class of students.

2. Try the VSPP notetaking procedure for a lecture in a class you are presently attending. Prepare a written evaluation of the method.

3. Interview a small group of college students to determine the test-taking strategies they use. List the different strategies they report and then provide a written evaluation indicating the quality of their metacognitive skills in test-taking.

4. Develop and administer a mirror assessment for your content area. The assessment should be consistent with evaluation rubrics for reading assessments in your state and should include all of the principles in the mirror assessment strategy.

 Website Activity

To locate and complete Chapter 12 activities, go to [*www.kendallhunt.com/contentarealiteracy/*].

Glossary

Accommodation: the process of adjusting one's existing cognitive structure to accept new information.

Acronym: a word that is formed by combining the initial letters or segments of a series of words.

Adolescent Literacy: moving literacy beyond the notion of school and textbook-based definitions of literacy to one which acknowledges not only that there are multiple literacies and multiple texts but also that texts transcend the adult-sanctioned notions of text forms to include CD-ROM, the Internet, popular music, television, magazines, etc.

Aiming Toward Content: teaching which focuses on content acquisition with no consideration for how to acquire that information.

Analogical Guide: a form of study guide in which students use familiar concepts to learn and retain new information.

Annual Yearly Progress: the improvements a school must make each year in state reading and mathematics test scores, graduation rates, and other measures of performance as defined by *No Child Left Behind*.

Anticipation Guide: a prereading strategy that activates students' ideas about a topic by asking them to react to a series of guide statements related to that topic.

Assimilation: the process whereby new information is simply added to one's existing cognitive structure.

Attitudes: those feelings that cause a reader to approach or avoid a reading situation.

Biographies: reading and writing about an important figure in any content area.

Biopoem: a creative poetry framework for writing about virtually any major figure or topic in the content areas.

Blog: an online weblog that can be circulated but not edited by anyone other than the original blog author.

Body Biographies: a multimedia interpretation of a character in a novel or short story or a major figure in any content area.

Book Clubs: small groups of students meeting to discuss a common reading.

Bound Morpheme: a meaningful language unit that occurs only as an attachment to words or other morphemes, e.g., tele-.

Byte: the amount of space necessary to store one character such as a number or letter.

Capacity Limitation: refers to the theory that human beings are capable of attending consciously to only one task at a time.

Cause-Effect: a pattern of text organization linking reasons with results.

CD-ROM: computer hardware which reads data from a laser disk and is capable of storing large amounts of data.

Censorship: the indirect supervision of morality by regulating films, books, magazines, music, and other information to which people may have access.

Central Questions: a prereading strategy that places students in a problem-solving role.

Chunking: a type of mental organization in which related bits of information are processed as a single unit.

Clues and Questions: vocabulary review procedure that centers on student-generated questions and answers.

Cognitive Structure: the interrelated network of our experiences, organized in memory through a system of categories.

Comparison-Contrast: a pattern of text organization that demonstrates likenesses and differences between things or ideas.

Composing: the process of generating and shaping ideas before writing begins and as the actual writing unfolds.

Connotation: subtle shades of meaning that define a word; there can also be specific grammatical and semantic conditions that delimit a word's appropriate usage.

Content Area Literacy: the level of reading and writing still necessary to read, comprehend, and react to appropriate instructional materials in a given content area.

Content Reading Inventory: a teacher-made and text-based test designed to assess students' ability to effectively read and learn from the text.

Context Clues: a decoding technique that consists of utilizing surrounding words and their meaning to identify unfamiliar words.

Contextual: refers to the connotative meaning of words in context.

Contextual Redefinition: a vocabulary strategy in which the teacher places new vocabulary in self-defining or high utility contexts.

Criterion: a relative standard, or score, that implies adequate achievement without reference to the performance of others.

Criterion-Referenced Test: a test of specific content, measuring individual performances without comparison to the entire group.

Critical Literacy: asks readers to carefully examine power relations in texts in terms of social justice dimensions and is an especially powerful way to consider novels as social constructions that position characters, sometimes in stereotypical ways, to be deconstructed and critiqued.

Critical Literacy Discussion: a strategy that asks students to consider power relations in a novel with a particular focus on which characters have a voice and how race, class, and gender are constructed.

Critical Media Literacy: lesson designed to use the popular media as a forum for discussion and critique.

Cubing: writing strategy which allow students to consider the multiple dimensions of topics; students examine topics by describing, comparing, associating, analyzing, applying, and arguing.

Culture: a collection of values, beliefs, and standards which influences how students think, feel, and behave in various social settings.

Cybrary: a blend of the words cyber and library, referring to a collection of websites accessible from a single site and dedicated to a specific subject area.

Debriefing: feedback by students in the form of self-reports, introspection, and hindsights.

Decoding: any process whereby a coded message is converted back into thought.

Definitional: refers to the denotative meaning of words.

Denotation: the broad meanings of words.

Depth of Processing: a memory principle that asserts that the likelihood of long-term retention and recall is greater when a mental activity involves close semantic analysis and cognitive attention.

Developmental Bilingual Education: similar to transitional bilingual education without a specified phase-out of the native language.

Diagnostic Test: a test employed to determine specific skill strengths and weaknesses of students.

Dialogue Journals: journals in which the teacher maintains an ongoing written dialogue with students.

Dinner Party: a strategy based on the idea that you could invite characters from a young adult novel or any other form of text to your home for dinner and conversation.

Directed Reading-Thinking Activity: a self-questioning process that encourages students to predict oncoming information in text and sets purposes for reading that are personally interesting.

Distributed Practice: rehearsals separated by breaks.

Diversity: the varied student characteristics of language, culture, and learning differences.

DVD: a Digital Video Disk; a device capable of storing 6 gigabytes of electronic data.

Electronic Books: complete works of fiction and nonfiction that have been digitized for reading on computer or on portable ebook readers.

Embedded Questions: a series of teacher-developed questions inserted in a text at key points which are crucial to metacognitive awareness and understanding the entire passage.

Encoding: any process whereby thought or meaning is converted into a code.

English as a Second Language: structured lessons in English while maintaining facility in the native language.

Etymology: study of the history of words and their origins.

Experience-Based: thinking that requires drawing an inference that is not derivable from the text, but rather from one's existing schemata, i.e., reading beyond the lines.

Expressive Vocabulary: words that a person can use properly when speaking or writing.

Extension Activities: pencil and paper exercises designed to reinforce and expand the schemata of newly acquired content area vocabulary.

External Reference: any source of information outside the passage being read.

External Storage: in notetaking, a written substitute for memory.

Fake Pop Quiz: a quiz designed to reinforce, rather than test, recently introduced information.

Fanfiction: original works of fiction based on popular media including television, movies, books, music, and video games.

Feature Analysis: an instructional strategy in which sets of new concepts or vocabulary are defined and discriminated by identifying the unique characteristics of each member of the set.

FLIP: friendliness, language, interest, prior knowledge; a technique for helping students preview a reading assignment.

Focused Question Card Strategy: use of targeted questions on note cards to assist students in revising their writing.

Formal Tests: standardized, norm-referenced tests used to monitor student progress.

Free Morpheme: a morpheme that can stand by itself, e.g., boy.

General Vocabulary: words that are not specifically associated with any one teaching area and are assimilated into existing schemata.

Glossary: an alphabetized list of technical words and their definitions used in a textbook or other work.

Graphic Information Lesson: strategy designed to teach students how to interpret graphs.

Graphic Literacy: ability to interpret graphs and other visual presentations in text.

Graphic Organizer: a visual aid that defines hierarchical relationships among concepts and that lends itself to the teaching of technical vocabulary.

Group Test: a test administered in a group situation.

Guided Listening Procedure: a comprehension strategy employed on a listening level; the purpose is to enhance recall and organization of text information as well as to promote student self-inquiry.

Guided Writing Procedure: an integrated lesson approach that serves as an alternative to the guided reading procedure by capitalizing on writing as a means to commit information to long-term memory.

Hypermedia: hypertext with sounds and pictures.

Hypertext: large and easily programmed linked visual and text databases.

Immersion Bilingual Education: all instruction is in the second language.

Index: an alphabetized list of important terms and topics and the page numbers on which they occur in the text.

Individualization: incorporating the gamut of grouping procedures—whole group, small group, and individual—within the confines of a well-developed instructional plan utilizing the textbook and with the teacher acting as facilitator of learning.

Individual Test: a test that may be administered on only an individual basis.

Informal Tests: teacher-made or published tests that employ a criterion to monitor student progress.

Information Index: a device used to structure the information search by keying students into the location of important concepts.

Inquiry Charts: strategy for nurturing critical reading in content classrooms by having students examine multiple sources of information and charting their findings.

Integrated Thematic Units: teams of teachers from various subject areas collaborate to create units and lessons with a central theme.

Interests: what students like to read about.

Internet: a highly complex, interlinked system of computers forming a worldwide communication network.

Internet Workshop: a set of teacher-directed activities designed to show students how to navigate the Internet and utilize its resources.

Intertextuality: meanings based on reading a particular text and making connections to other texts including media-based and digital texts.

I-Search Paper: an alternative to the traditional research paper such that students investigate topics of their choosing by interviewing experts, visiting places, and telling the story of their search in a written report.

Journal Writing: writing to explore ideas freely without worrying unduly about mechanics.

Jump Drives: a small device for storing and transferring files and data, sometimes called a flash drive.

Knowledge Rating: strategy for establishing what students already know about a topic by having them rate how well they know the vocabulary words.

K-W-L: a three-step integrated strategy designed to encourage active reading of expository text; K = what we know before reading, W = what we want to find out during reading, L = what we learned after reading.

Learning: a change that occurs in an organism at a particular time as a function of experience.

Lesson Planning: teacher planning that includes learning objectives, set induction, content outline, activities, lesson closure, resources and materials, evaluation, and student assignments.

Levels of Text Understanding: the differing levels of thinking involved in reading text material; e.g., text explicit, text implicit, experience-based.

Library Power: strategies designed to expand the reading horizons of children by introducing them to the wealth of books in the school library.

Listen-Read-Discuss: an integrated strategy involving students in a guided lecture, independent reading, and summary discussion to ensure in-depth comprehension.

Listening Guide: used to guide listening to an oral presentation; a skeletal outline of the important concepts arranged in the order and relationship in which they occur to aid students as they listen and fill in the appropriate information.

Literate: being able to read and write.

Literature Circles: a collaborative approach to instruction that integrates the reading of a book with discussion of themes and background information related to it.

Literature Response Journals: journals where students reflect and write their thoughts so they can share their views with the teacher, peers, or parents.

Long-Term Memory: an organized store of information based on a person's cumulative experiences.

Mean: the arithmetic average of a set of numbers.

Metacognition: awareness of one's own mental processes.

Metadiscourse: text intrusions in which the author talks directly to the reader about the information in the text.

Mirror Assessment: a test preparation technique in which classroom exams are designed in a format that is as close as possible to a specific standardized reading assessment.

Miscues: observed responses to printed text that do not conform exactly to the print and may preserve (e.g., auto for car) or disrupt meaning (e.g., cat for car).

Mnemonic: a strategy for remembering one thing by associating it with something else.

Modeling: a report by an individual of the mental operations involved in his or her comprehension process to illustrate its logical steps to others.

Morpheme: the smallest unit of language that has an associated meaning.

Morphemic Analysis: the analysis of affixes and roots to decode unknown words.

Multicultural Literature: literature by and about people who represent groups often on the fringes of the socio-political mainstream.

Multigenre Writing: imaginative writing using a variety of genres including ad writing, comic strips, and editorials.

Multimedia: refers to technological combinations of audio, video, text, graphics, and animation.

Multiple Literacies: the expansion of the meaning of the word *literacy* to include multimedia, the Internet, and other electronic or even non-text mediums for exchanging information.

Multiple Text Inquiry Discussion: students read across various sources to synthesize and discuss a topic.

Multiple Texts: teaching in the content areas using various texts including traditional textbooks, magazines, newspaper articles, young adult novels, video, and a host of other multimedia digital texts available from the Internet and other sources, whose aim is to guide students toward the independent use on multiple sources on topics in science, math, English, social studies, and other subject area domains.

New Literacies: newer forms of texts including Internet-based texts, instant messaging (IMing), blogging, e-zines, and various websites where visual elements, in addition to print elements, carry meaning.

No Child Left Behind: the 2002 revision of the Elementary and Secondary Education Act (ESEA) of 1965.

Norm-Referenced: an assessment in which the performance of an individual is defined relative to the performances of a group of individuals who have taken the same test.

Normal Curve: a symmetrical distribution of scores.

Norms: a set of scores against which the test performance of others may be compared.

Novel Journal: having students write in their journals about their reactions to events occurring in the novels they are reading.

Objectives: the specific learning expectations a teacher plans for a lesson, including students' performance, products, learning conditions, and criteria for successful performance.

Options Guide: a form of study guide in which students predict, discuss, and evaluate options available to key political and historical figures.

Organization: the arrangements of parts of a whole in such a manner that the parts are related to each other.

Parallel Notetaking: listening and taking notes at the same time.

Passage Dependent: in an assessment of reading, it refers to a test question that can be answered only if the text has been read with comprehension.

Passage Independent: in an assessment of reading, it refers to a test question that can be answered without reference to the text.

Passive Failure: a term describing students who are resigned to fail and believe they do not have the ability to succeed in their learning.

PDA: refers to Personal Digital Assistants that now combine the features of cell phones and the Internet to offer remote connectivity.

Percentile Rank: the position of a score in relation to the entire group of scores.

Performance Items: in reading assessments, this refers to test items that require written responses.

Personal Glossary: a strategy to aid students' long-term memory of words that are novel or with which they have had difficulty.

Phony Document: a critical reading strategy where students read, research, and authenticate information in a letter or other document.

PLAE: guidance strategy for studying which consists of preplanning, listing, activating, and evaluating.

Polar Opposites: a teaching strategy using contrasting words to critique a reading selection.

PORPE: essay writing study strategy consisting of predicting, organizing, rehearsing, practicing, and evaluating.

Portfolios: systematic collections of students' work in the classroom used for ongoing diagnosis of their abilities.

Possible Sentences: a vocabulary teaching strategy in which students use new vocabulary to create sentences for verification when reading.

Prediction Guide: a means of assessing students' prior knowledge about a topic through a series of fact-based statements that students determine are true or false before reading.

Presenting Content and Processes Concurrently: teaching that provides direct instruction in the processes necessary to acquire content as well as in what content is to be acquired.

Presenting Isolated Skills: teaching that consists of the direct teaching of skills with no consideration for content.

Prior Knowledge: an individual's background experience.

Problem-Solution: a pattern of text organization exemplified by an interaction of a problem and a potential answer to that problem.

Proficiency: an arbitrarily established level of skill in reading or mathematics sufficient to meet societal demands as defined by parents, a school district, the state, or the federal government.

Pseudographics: student- or teacher-made graphs that may not be an accurate representation of text material.

Qualitative Factors of Readability: non-measurable variables of text selection that include prior knowledge, text organization, and interest, among others.

Quantitative Factors of Readability: language variables of word length and sentence length as counted and measured in readability estimates.

Questioning the Author: designed to help struggling readers to approach segmented text passages with an active mind and critical stance; the use of embedded questions in the form of queries helps guide readers' thinking.

Quick Writes: a brief prereading or postreading written student response to a prompt question about a content area topic.

Raw Score: the number of items answered correctly on a test.

Raygor Readability Estimate: a readability formula based on word and sentence length; noted for ease of administration and reduced potential for error.

Reaction Guide: a postreading strategy used to stimulate review of a selection by asking students to react to a series of guide statements related to the selection.

Readability: a measure of the extent to which a reader finds a given text comprehensible.

Readability Formulas: mathematically derived indices of text difficulty based on an analysis of linguistic variables, the two most common being word length and sentence length.

Readers Theater: students read aloud in a dramatic fashion to present key text concepts.

Readiness Principle: refers to the mental state in which an individual is prepared to derive maximum meaning from a learning situation with a minimum of frustration.

Reading Autobiography: a personalized account of early, middle, and recent reading experiences.

Reading Preferences: the material students might like to read.

Receptive Vocabulary: words that can be read and comprehended in print or heard and understood in spoken context.

Rehearsal: the repeating of information for the purpose of retaining the information in memory.

Reliability: the degree to which a test gives consistent results when administered repeatedly.

ReQuest: a reciprocal questioning procedure that helps students adopt an active, questioning approach to text reading.

Response Bias: writing down what one believes an examiner wants rather than what the examinee really believes.

Response Mode: the type of response required by students' assigned questions, e.g., recall vs. recognition.

ReWrite: a music strategy involving the writing of music verses about content area concepts.

Rubrics: a concrete description of the qualities and criteria expected in a particular piece of writing; usually assigns numeric values to a description of a writing task, ranging from a high quality piece of writing and its related dimensions to a low quality piece of writing.

Scaffolded Reading Experience: comprehensive lesson framework designed to provide students with guidance and support with difficult text.

Scaffolding: refers to the degree of support and guidance a teacher needs to provide to help students engage text that would be too difficult, left to their own devices.

Schema Theory: describes the process by which we add to (assimilate) or adjust (accommodate) our existing cognitive structure in the face of new or discordant information.

Schemata: a category system of the mind containing information about the surrounding environment; the plural of schema.

Scope of Information Search: the number of concepts for which students are held responsible in a given reading assignment.

Self-Concept: how one views oneself.

Semantic Map: a diagram that groups related concepts.

Short-Term Memory: the "working memory" which holds incoming information temporarily until a decision is made to include this information in long-term memory.

Signal Words: the key words that cue a particular pattern of text organization.

Slicing: simplifying the complexity of learning tasks by reexamining those that are required and recasting them to ease the demands placed on students.

Sociolinguistics: the study of language in a cultural context.

Software: refers to applications that run on computers, including word processing applications, games, encyclopedias, and so on.

Spaced Notetaking: taking notes during intervals of silence between segments of a lecture.

Spam: originally an acronym standing for *S*elected *P*arts *A*ll *M*eat, it now refers to Internet junk mail.

Standard Deviation: a measure of dispersion or variability of a group of scores.

Standard Error of Measurement: the variation, or built-in error, in standardized test scores.

Standardized Scores: general term for describing a variety of transformed raw scores that can be compared across other individuals.

Standardized Test: a formal test instrument utilizing norms as a basis for student comparison of achievement.

Standards: a means of delineating what students should know and should be able to do as a result of what they learn in school, with their aim being to make sure all students develop the skills necessary for success in school and in their future careers in the workplace.

Stanines: standardized score with a mean of five and a standard deviation of two.

Strategy: the planned means to an end.

Student-Generated Questions: questions students derive on their own from their reading assignments.

Study Guide: a strategy that focuses students' attention on the major ideas of a selection at three levels of comprehension.

Study Strategies: the specific strategies that focus on locating, retaining, and recalling information.

Survey Test: usually a standardized test that measures global areas of achievement, such as vocabulary or comprehension.

Survey the Text: a prereading strategy that involves some form of preliminary look at a reading selection before more intensive reading is undertaken.

Sustained Silent Reading: a systematic program that establishes regular reading times for students to practice their reading skills on pleasurable and self-selected content-related materials.

Talking Drawings: a prereading and postreading strategy that helps students visualize their knowledge of a topic.

Technical Vocabulary: words uniquely related to particular academic disciplines; the words are accommodated by modifying old schemata or creating new schemata.

Test Ceiling: the upper limit placed on an individual's performance at a particular grade level on a standardized test.

Test Floor: the lower limit placed on an individual's performance at a particular grade level on a standardized test.

Testwiseness: a series of principles that can be applied to exams independently of subject area knowledge.

Text Appetizers: a teacher-devised introductory passage that provides a detailed framework for comprehending a reading selection.

Text Explicit: thinking that requires only getting facts as literally stated by an author, i.e., reading the lines.

Text Implicit: thinking that requires an inference from the text to derive an answer to a question, i.e., reading between the lines.

Text Structure: the various organizational patterns writers and readers use to encode and decode thoughts.

Textbook Adaptations: study guides, graphic organizers, and other guide material a teacher provides to aid student learning of the content material.

Textbook Aids: elements included in a textbook to help students with new vocabulary, for example, a glossary.

The Imposter: critical reading strategy that challenges students to read mathematics and science passages where intentional errors have been embedded in the material.

Thematic Unit: a series of lessons developed around a theme.

Think-Aloud: a teacher modeling strategy whereby one's thoughts about how a text is comprehended are verbalized for students.

Time Order: a pattern of text organization exemplifying a sequential relationship between ideas or events over the passage of time.

TOAST: a strategy for independently studying vocabulary using the acronym derived from the procedural steps—test, organize, anchor, say, and test.

Tradebooks: literature that is found in bookstores.

Transcribing: refers to the mechanics of writing including spelling, punctuation, capitalization, handwriting, formatting, and neatness.

Transitional Bilingual Education: content area instruction in a native language while a student receives second language instruction for a three-year period with the native language slowly phased out.

Two-Way Bilingual Education: both native English and non-native English speakers learn each other's language while they do the bulk of their content learning in the strong, native language.

Unit Blueprint: a unit planning structure that includes the unit topic, goals and objectives, content outline, learning activities, resources and materials, and evaluation plan.

Unit of Instruction: a related series of lessons lasting from 1 to 6 weeks.

Unit Plan: a plan of instruction in which students explore and respond to a selected topic through their interaction with a variety of integrated activities designed to enhance their knowledge and attitude.

Validity: the degree of accuracy with which a test measures what it is intended to measure.

Verbal and Visual Word Association Strategy: a mnemonic strategy in which students associate a word they are trying to learn with personal examples or a concrete drawing.

Verbatim Split Page Procedure: a comprehensive method of taking notes during lectures.

Virtual Reality: an artificially created, electronic environment that extends the sensory abilities of the user and creates the illusion of intimate interaction with the environment.

Vocabulary: a corpus of many thousands of words and their associated meanings.

Vocabulary Self-Collection Strategy: a vocabulary acquisition technique designed to teach students how to select the most important vocabulary from reading assignments.

WebQuest: an inquiry-oriented activity in which some or all of the information acquired from the activity comes directly from the student's interaction with the Internet.

Wikis: software that supports an open editing environment and named after the Hawaiian word for fast.

Word: a pattern of auditory or visual symbols that represent schemata, or concepts.

Word Analogies: exercises requiring students to draw inferences and expose subtle word associations.

Word Map: a visual representation of a definition.

Writing Roulette: a strategy in which students create a simple story containing some of the technical vocabulary they are learning.

Young Adult Literature: selections of interest to readers ages 12 to 20.

Bibliography

Chapter 1, Content Area Literacy: Addressing *No Child Left Behind*

Recommended Readings

Bean, T.W., & Wimmer, J.J. (2006). Resources for adolescent literacy. In Guzzetti, B. (Ed.), *Literacy for a new century*. Westport, CT: Greenwood.

> An annotated list of resources to help teachers support adolescent literacy.

Biancarosa, G., & Snow, C.E. (2004). *Reading next—A vision for action and research in middle and high school literacy: A report to Carnegie Corporation of New York*. Washington, DC: Alliance for Excellent Education.

> Recommends 15 elements to help meet the needs of struggling adolescent readers.

Conley, M.W., & Hinchman, K.A. (2004). No Child Left Behind: What it means for U.S. adolescents and what we can do about it. *Journal of Adolescent & Adult Literacy, 48,* 42–50.

> Examines the connection between adolescent literacy and the No Child Left Behind legislation, citing areas where policy and research should focus their attention.

Franzak, J.K. (2006). *Zoom:* A review of the literature on marginalized adolescent readers, literacy theory, and policy implications. *Review of Educational Research, 76,* 209–248.

> A discussion of how adolescent readers are marginalized and recommendations for policy changes.

Moje, E.B., Dillon, D.R., & O'Brien, D. (2000). Reexamining the roles of learner, text, and context in secondary literacy. *Journal of Educational Research, 93,* 165–180.

> Examines the roles of the learner and text from a sociocultural perspective.

Moje, E.B., Young, J.P., Readence, J.E., & Moore, D.W. (2000). Reinventing adolescent literacy for new times: Perennial and millennial issues. *Journal of Adolescent & Adult Literacy, 43,* 400–410.

> A discussion of major issues surrounding adolescent literacy, including what constitutes best practices and meeting the needs of marginalized readers.

Spor, M.W., & Schneider, B.K. (1999). Content reading strategies: What teachers know, use, and want to learn. *Reading Research and Instruction, 38,* 221–231.

> A survey of K–12 teachers' knowledge of content area reading strategies, revealing that many teachers still rely on the textbook and are not aware of strategies they may use in their teaching but want to know them.

Sturtevant, E.G., Boyd, F.B., Brozo, W.G., Hinchman, K.A., Moore, D.W., & Alvermann, D.E. (2006). *Principled practices for adolescent literacy: A framework for instruction and policy*. Mahwah, NJ: Erlbaum.

> Presents evidenced-based practices for implementing adolescent literacy programs.

References

Bean, T.W., & Harper, H.J. (2006). Content area reading: Current state of the art. In Lapp, D., & Flood, J. (Eds.), *Content area reading and learning* (3rd ed.). Mahwah, NJ: Erlbaum.

Gersten, R., & Woodward, J. (1994). The language-minority student and special education: Issues, trends, and paradoxes. *Exceptional Children, 60,* 310–322.

Kaestle, C.F. (1991). *Literacy in the United States.* New Haven: Yale University Press.

Moore, D.W., Bean, T.W., Birdyshaw, D., & Rycik, J.A. (1999). Adolescent literacy: A position statement. *Journal of Adolescent & Adult Literacy, 43,* 97–112.

O'Brien, D.G. (2006). "Struggling" adolescents' engagement in multimediating: Countering the institutional construction of incompetence. In D.E. Alvermann, K.A. Hinchman, D.W. Moore, & D.R. Waff, *Reconceptualizing the literacies in adolescents' lives* (2nd ed., pp. 29–46). Mahwah, NJ: Erlbaum.

O'Brien, D.G., & Stewart, R.A. (2007). Resistance to content area reading instruction: Dimensions and solutions. In T.W. Bean, J.E. Readence, & R.S. Baldwin, *Content area literacy digital supplement.* Dubuque, IA: Kendall/Hunt.

Sartre, J. (1948). *The emotions: Outline of a theory.* New York: Book Sales.

Wilder, P., & Dressman, M. (2006). New literacies, enduring challenges? The influence of capital on adolescent readers' internet practices. In D.E. Alvermann, K.A. Hinchman, D.W. Moore, S. Phelps, & D.R. Waff, *Reconceptualizing the literacies in adolescents' lives* (2nd ed., pp. 205–229). Mahwah, NJ: Erlbaum.

Chapter 2, Technology and Changing Literacies

Recommended Readings

Benjamin, J.Y. (2003). A checklist for evaluating WebQuests. Retrieved November 9, 2006, from techLearning Website: *http://techlearning.com/story/showArticle.jhtml?articleID=l2803449*

> Provides extensive criteria for evaluating WebQuests and includes links to websites that have model WebQuests.

Geraghty, C.L. (2004). Bernie Dodge puts his life on the line. Retrieved November 9, 2006, from SDS Universe Website: *http://www.sdsuniverse.info/people_content.asp?id= 13409*

> Discusses blogging and the philosophy of long time blogger Bernie Dodge.

Teclehaimanot, B., & Lamb, A. (2004, March/April). Reading, technology, and inquiry-based learning through literature-rich WebQuests. *Reading Online. 7*(4). Available: *http://www.readingonline.org/articles/art_index.asp?HREF=teclehaimanot/index.html*

> Provides a rationale and directions for developing WebQuests using authentic literature.

Valenza, J.K. (2006). Tech.life@school: Imagine textbooks in a new form. Retrieved November 9, 2006, from philly.com Website: *http://www.philly.com/mld/inquirer/business/technology/13905892.htm*

> A Philadelphia Inquirer article about wikibooks and their potential for replacing conventional paper textbooks.

References

Alvermann, D.E. (2001). *Effective literacy instruction for adolescents.* Executive summary and paper commissioned by the National Reading Conference. Chicago, IL: National Reading Conference.

Baldwin, R.S., & Murphy, D.M. (2002). Software for older readers. In B.J. Guzzetti (Ed.), *Literacy in America: An encyclopedia of history, theory, and practice.* Santa Barbara, CA: ABC-CLIO.

Bosco, J. (1989). The organization of schools and the use of computers to improve schooling. *Peabody Journal of Education, 64,* 111–129.

Burke, J. (2002). The Internet reader. *Educational Leadership, 60*(3), 38–42.

CBS News. (2006). *Teens are wired . . . and, yes, it's ok.* Retrieved November 8, 2006, Website: *http://www.cbsnews.com/stories/2006/06/09/gentech/main1698246.shtml.*

Cook, D.L. (1962). The automization of Socrates. *Theory Into Practice, 1,* 9–19.

Cuban, L. (1986). *Teachers and machines. The classroom use of technology since 1920.* New York: Teachers College Press.

Cuban, L. (2003). *Oversold and underused: Computers in the classroom.* Cambridge, MA: Harvard University Press.

Dodge, B. (2006). *The WebQuest Page at San Diego State University.* Retrieved October 30, 2006, Website: *http://webquest.sdsu.edu.*

Esker, F. (2006). *Laptop learning: Classrooms catch up to wireless technology.* Retrieved November 5, 2006, from City Business Website: *http://www.neworleanscitybusiness.com/viewStory.cfm?recID=16787*

Goolsby, K.A. (2006). *Schools toss aside textbooks for eBooks.* Retrieved November 7, 2006, from Dallas News.com Website: *http://www.dallasnews.com/sharedcontent/dws/dn/latestnews/stories/110406dnmetebooks.3255a88.html*

Harris, F.J. (2006). Blogging and the media specialist, part 2. *Learning and Leading with Technology, 33,* 32–33.

Leu, D.J., & Leu, D.D. (2000). *Teaching with the Internet: Lessons from the classroom* (3rd ed.). Norwood, MA: Christopher-Gordon.

McNabb, M. (2006). *Literacy learning in networked classrooms: Using the Internet with middle-level students.* Newark, DE: International Reading Association.

Murphy, D. (2007). Online resources for K–12 education. In T.W. Bean, J.E. Readence, & R.S. Baldwin, *Content area literacy digital supplement.* Dubuque: Kendall/Hunt.

Nettrekker. (2006). Retrieved October 28, 2006, Website: *http://www.nettrekker.com/home/index.html.*

Oppenheimer, T. (1997). The computer delusion. *The Atlantic Monthly, 280*(1), 45–62.

Oppenheimer, T. (2003). *The flickering mind: The false promise of technology in the classroom and how learning can be saved.* New York: Random House.

Pennsylvania Department of Education. (2006). *Classrooms of the Future.* Retrieved November 4, 2006, from Pennsylvania Department of Education Website: *http://www.pde.state.pa.us/ed_tech/cwp/view.asp?a=169&q=118835.*

Postman, N. (1999). *Building a bridge to the 18th century: How the past can improve our future.* New York: Knopf.

Top 500. (2005). *Top 500 supercomputer sites.* Retrieved October 22, 2006, from Top 500 Supercomputers Website: *http://www.top500.org.*

Wilder, P. & Dressman, M. (2006). New literacies, enduring challenges? The influence of capital on adolescent readers' internet practices. In D.E. Alvermann, K.A. Hinchman, D.W. Moore, S.F. Phelps, & D.R. Waff, *Reconceptualizing the literacies in adolescents' lives* (2nd ed., pp. 205–229). Mahwah, NJ: Erlbaum.

Chapter 3, Language, Diversity, and Cognition

Recommended Readings

Banks, J., & Banks, C. et al. (2005). *Democracy and diversity: Principles and concepts for educating citizens in a global age.* Seattle, WA: Center for Multicultural Education, University of Washington. Available from: *http://depts.washington.edu/centerme/home.htm*

This position statement is an excellent resource for any classroom where issues of democracy, citizenship, freedom, and social justice will be introduced.

Garcia, G.E., & Godina, H. (2004). Addressing the literacy needs of adolescent English Language learners. In T.L. Jetton & J.A. Dole (Eds.), *Adolescent literacy research and practice* (pp. 304–320). New York: Guilford.

This book chapter offers a blend of theory and specific strategies content teachers can incorporate to ensure academic literacy for second language students.

Harper, H., & Bean, T.W. (2007). Literacy education in democratic life: The promise of adolescent literacy. In J. Lewis & G. Moorman (Eds.), *Adolescent literacy instruction: Policies, programs, and promising classroom practices.* Newark, DE: International Reading Association.

The authors review useful theories, projects, and strategies aimed at developing students' critical literacy with a focus on social justice issues. These strategies include Structured Academic Controversy and Resident Critic, among others.

Pilgreen, J. (2006). Supporting English learners: Developing academic language in the content area classroom. In T.A. Young & N.L. Hadaway (Eds.), *Supporting the literacy development of English learners: Increasing success in all classrooms* (pp. 41–60). Newark, DE: International Reading Association.

The author offers specific strategies and examples for fostering English as a Second Language (ESL) learners' academic literacy.

Stevens, L.P., & Bean, T.W. (2007). *Critical literacy: Context, research, and practice in K–12 classrooms.* Thousand Oaks, CA: Sage.

This book introduces recent work in critical literacy with an array of classroom examples to help teachers implement these practices in various content area classrooms including science, social studies, mathematics, and English.

References

Alvermann, D.E. (2002). Effective literacy instruction for adolescents. *Journal of Literacy Research, 34,* 189–208.

Au, K.H. (2000). A multicultural perspective on policies for improving literacy achievement: Equity and excellence. In M.L. Kamil, P.B. Mosenthal, P.D. Pearson, & R. Barr (Eds.), *Handbook of reading research: Volume III* (pp. 835–851). Mahwah, NJ: Erlbaum.

Au, K.H. (2006). *Multicultural issues and reading achievement.* Mahwah, NJ: Erlbaum.

Banks, J., & Banks, C. et al. (2005). *Democracy and diversity: Principles and concepts for educating citizens in a global age.* Seattle, WA: Center for Multicultural Education, University of Washington. Available from: *http://depts.washington.edu/centerme/home.htm*

Bean, T.W. (2006, March). *The localization of young adult fiction in contemporary Hawai'i.* Paper presented at the Comparative International Education Society conference, Honolulu, HI, March, 2006.

Bean, T.W., & Readence, J.E. (2002). Adolescent literacy: Charting a course for successful futures as lifelong learners. *Reading Research and Instruction, 41,* 203–210.

Bean, T.W., & Wimmer, J. (2007). Resources for adolescent literacy. In B.J. Guzzetti (Ed.), *Literacy for a new century.* Westport, CT: Greenwood.

Bergknut, L.L. (1997). Stink eye. In A. Von Alemann & M. Kunz (Eds.), *Kanilehua* (pp. 32–33). Hilo: University of Hawaii at Hilo/Hawaii Community College Board of Student Publications.

Cervetti, G., Damico, J.S., & Pardeles, M.J. (2001). A tale of differences: Comparing the traditions, perspectives, and educational goals of critical reading and critical Literacy. *Reading Online.* Available: *http://www.reading.org*

Fleischman, P. (1990). *Saturnalia.* New York: Harper/Collins.

Flores-Gonzalez, N. (2002). *School kids/street kids: Identity development in Latino students*. New York: Teachers College Press.

Franzak, J.K. (2006). *Zoom*: A review of the literature on marginalized adolescent readers, literacy theory, and policy implications. *Review of Educational Research, 76,* 209–248.

Garcia, G.E., & Godina, H. (2004). Addressing the literacy needs of adolescent English Language learners. In T.L. Jetton & J.A. Dole (Eds.), *Adolescent literacy research and practice* (pp. 304–320). New York: Guilford.

Gee, J.P. (2000). Teenagers in new times: A new literacy studies perspective. *Journal of Adolescent & Adult Literacy, 43,* 412–420.

Hadaway, N.L., & Young, T.A. (2006). Changing classrooms: Transforming instruction. In T.A. Young & N.L. Hadaway (Eds.), *Supporting the literacy development of English learners: Increasing success in all classrooms* (pp. 6–21). Newark, DE: International Reading Association.

Harper, H., & Bean, T.W. (2007). Literacy education in democratic life: The promise of adolescent literacy. In J. Lewis & G. Moorman (Eds.), *Adolescent literacy instruction: Policies, programs, and promising classroom practices.* Newark, DE: International Reading Association.

Hudelson, S. (2001). Working with second language learners. In L.W. Searfoss, J.E. Readence, & M.H. Mallette. *Helping children learn to read: Creating a classroom literacy environment* (4th ed., pp. 366–393). Boston: Allyn & Bacon.

Kinney, G. (1993). *W.K. Kellogg transcultural education grant.* Hilo: Department of Baccalaureate Nursing, University of Hawaii at Hilo.

Kist, W. (2005). *New literacies in action: Teaching and learning in multiple media.* New York: Teachers College Press.

Kress, G. (2003). *Literacy in the new media age.* London: Routledge.

Ladson-Billings, G. (1995). But that's just good teaching! The case for culturally relevant pedagogy. *Theory Into Practice, 34,* 159–165.

Laird, D.M., & Jossen, C. (1983). *Wili Wai Kula and the three mongooses.* Honolulu, HI: Barbaby Books.

Lesko, N. (2001). *Act your age! A cultural construction of adolescence.* New York: Routledge Falmer.

Maaka, M. (2001). Forward to S. Florio-Ruane, *Teacher education and the cultural imagination.* Mahwah, NJ: Erlbaum.

McCafferty, S.G. (2002). Adolescent second language literacy: Language, culture, and identity. *Reading Research and Instruction, 41,* 279–288.

McCarthey, S.J., & Dressman, M. (2000). How will diversity affect literacy in the next millennium? *Reading Research Quarterly, 35,* 548–552.

McNabb, M.L. (2006). *Literacy learning in networked classrooms: Using the Internet with middle-level students.* Newark, DE: International Reading Association.

McVee, M.B., Dunsmore, K., & Gavelek, J.R. (2005). Schema theory revisited. *Review of Educational Research, 75,* 531–566.

Moje, E.B. (2002). Re-framing adolescent literacy research for New Times: Studying youth as a resource. *Reading Research and Instruction, 41,* 211–228.

Moje, E.B., & Dillon, D.R. (2006). Adolescent identities as demanded by science classroom discourse communities. In D.A. Alvermann, K.A. Hinchman, D.W. Moore, S.F. Phelps, & D.R. Waff (Eds.), *Reconceptualizing the literacies in adolescents' lives,* (2nd ed., pp. 85–106). Mahwah, NJ: Erlbaum.

Moje, E.B., Dillon, D.R., & O'Brien, D. (2000). Reexamining the roles of learner, text, and context in secondary literacy. *Journal of Educational Research, 93,* 165–180.

Morrell, E. (2004). *Becoming critical researchers: Literacy and empowerment for urban youth.* New York: Peter Lang.

Nieto, S. (2004). *Affirming diversity: The sociopolitical context of multicultural education* (5th ed.). White Plains, NY: Longman.

O'Brien, D. (2006). "Struggling" adolescents engagment in multimediating: Countering the institutional construction of incompetence. In D.E. Alvermann, K.A. Hinchman, D.W. Moore, S.F. Phelps, & D.R. Waff (Eds.), *Reconceptualizing the literacies in adolescents' lives* (2nd ed., pp. 29–46). Mahwah, NJ: Erlbaum.

O'Brien, D.G., & Stewart, R.A. (2007). Resistance to content area reading instruction: Dimensions and solutions. In T.W. Bean, J.E. Readence, & R.S. Baldwin, *Content area literacy digital supplement.* Dubuque, IA: Kendall/Hunt.

Ogbu, J.U. (1992). Adaptation to minority status and impact on school success. *Theory Into Practice, 31,* 287–295.

Pilgreen, J. (2006). Supporting English learners: Developing academic language in the content area classroom. In T.A. Young & N.L. Hadaway (Eds.), *Supporting the literacy development of English learners: Increasing success in all classrooms* (pp. 41–60). Newark, DE: International Reading Association.

Pitre, A. (2007). Critical pedagogy and multicultural education. In T.W. Bean, J.E. Readence, & R.S. Baldwin. *Content area literacy digital supplement.* Dubuque, IA: Kendall/Hunt.

Stevens, L.P., & Bean, T.W. (2007). *Critical literacy: Context, research, and practice in K–12 classrooms.* Thousand Oaks, CA: Sage.

Wade, S.E., & Moje, E.B. (2000). The role of text in classroom learning. In M.L. Kamil, P.B. Mosenthal, P.D. Pearson, & R. Barr (Eds.), *Handbook of reading research: Volume III* (pp. 609–627). Mahwah, NJ: Erlbaum.

Warner, L.S. (1993). *From slave to abolitionist: The life of William Wells Brown.* New York: Dial Books.

Wilder, P., & Dressman, M. (2006). New literacies, enduring challenges? The influence of capital on adolescent readers' Internet practices. In D.E. Alvermann, K.A. Hinchman, D.W. Moore, S.F. Phelps, & D.R. Waff (Eds.), *Reconceptualizing the literacies in adolescents' lives* (2nd ed., pp. 205–229). Mahwah, NJ: Erlbaum.

Chapter 4, Selecting Textbooks and Multimedia Materials

Recommended Readings

Hiebert, E.H. (2002). Standards, assessments, and text difficulty. In A.E. Farstrup & S.J. Samuels (Eds.), *What research has to say about reading instruction* (pp. 337–369). Newark, DE: International Reading Association.

> The author critically evaluates readability indices of text difficulty, along with more recent efforts to use computer-based Lexile systems based on semantic and syntactic difficulty. Hiebert argues for more complex text evaluations that take into account how engaging a text is, along with text format variables (e.g., multimedia, Internet-based text).

Leonard, W.H., & Penick, J.E. (1993). What's important in selecting a biology textbook? *The American Biology Teacher, 55* (1), 14–19.

> Provides a checklist for biology textbook selection, indicating that the concerns discussed in this chapter are also concerns in the subject matter disciplines.

Simmons, J.S. (Ed.). (1994). *Censorship: A threat to reading, learning, thinking.* Newark, DE: International Reading Association.

> This book provides a number of approaches for teachers dealing with censorship.

Singer, H. (2007). Friendly texts: Description and criteria. In T.W. Bean, J.E. Readence, & R.S. Baldwin, *Content area literacy digital supplement.* Dubuque, IA: Kendall/Hunt.

> Describes text features that enhance or inhibit comprehension and provides an accompanying text evaluation checklist.

Zakaluk, B.L., & Samuels, S.J. (Eds.) (1988). *Readability: Its past, present, and future.* Newark, DE: International Reading Association.

> A series of readings on the role of readability in research and practice from its early years to predictions about its future.

References

Edmondson, J. (2002). Asking different questions: Critical analyses and reading research. *Reading Research Quarterly, 37,* 113–119.

Harrington-Lueker, D. (1991). Book battles. *The American School Board Journal, 178,* 18–21, 37.

Leonard, W.H., & Penick, J.E. (1993). What's important in selecting a biology textbook? *The American Biology Teacher, 55*(1), 14–19.

Norman, D.A. (2004). *Emotional design: Why we love (or hate) everyday things.* New York: Basic Books.

Raygor, A.L. (1977). The Raygor readability estimate: A quick and easy way to determine difficulty. In P.D. Pearson (Ed.), *Reading: Theory, research, and practice* (pp. 259–263). Twenty-sixth yearbook of the National Reading Conference. Clemson, SC: National Reading Conference.

Redway, J.W., & Hinman, R. (1916). *Natural school geography.* New York: American Book Company.

Singer, H. (2007). Friendly texts: Description and criteria. In T.W. Bean, J.E. Readence, & R.S. Baldwin, *Content area literacy digital supplement.* Dubuque, IA: Kendall/Hunt.

The Miami Herald. (1982, April 17). Huck Finn is no racist. Miami, FL: *The Miami Herald.*

Zahorik, J.A. (1991). Teaching style and textbooks. *Teaching and Teacher Education, 7,* 185–196.

Chapter 5, Assessment

Recommended Readings

Afflerbach, P. (2004). Assessing adolescent reading. In T.L. Jetton & J.A. Dole (Eds.), *Adolescent literacy research and practice* (pp. 369–390). New York: Guilford.

> Argues that assessments must go beyond multiple-choice items to encompass application of knowledge. Suggests that performance and portfolio assessments offer more comprehensive looks at adolescents' content area knowledge and application.

Afflerbach, P. (2005). National Reading Conference policy brief: High stakes testing and reading assessment. *Journal of Literacy Research, 37,* 151–162.

> Discusses the concerns of high stakes testing and recommendations for improving reading assessment.

Hubbard, R.S., & Power, B.M. (1993). *The art of classroom inquiry: Handbook for teacher-researchers.* Portsmouth, NH: Heinemann.

> Discusses various ways for teachers to collect data in classrooms, with numerous examples of field notes, anecdotal records, etc.

Moje, E.B., Brozo, W.G., & Haas, J. (1994). Portfolios in a high school classroom: Challenges to change. *Reading Research and Instruction, 33,* 275–292.

> Research study of portfolio implementation in a French classroom, with suggestions for their usage delineated.

Tierney, R.J., Clark, C., with Fenner, L., Herter, R.J., Simpson, C.S., & Wiser, B. (1998). Portfolios: Assumptions, tensions, and possibilities. *Reading Research Quarterly, 33,* 474–486.

> A discussion of the uses of portfolios, with illustrative commentaries from practicing teachers.

Tierney, R.J., & Readence, J.E. (2005). *Reading strategies and practices: A compendium* (6th ed.). Boston: Allyn & Bacon.

> Unit 14 of this text presents detailed descriptions of various assessment procedures.

References

Afflerbach, P. (2004). Assessing adolescent reading. In T.L. Jetton & J.A. Dole (Eds.), *Adolescent literacy research and practice* (pp. 369–390). New York: Guilford.

Afflerbach, P. (2005). National Reading Conference policy brief: High stakes testing and reading assessment. *Journal of Literacy Research, 37,* 151–162.

Amrein, A.L., & Berliner, D.C. (2003). The effects of high-stakes testing on motivation and learning. *Educational Leadership, 61*(7), 32–38.

Au, K.H. (2000). A multicultural perspective on policies for improving literacy achievement: Equity and excellence. In M.L. Kamil, P.B. Mosenthal, P.D. Pearson, & R. Barr (Eds.), *Handbook of reading research: Volume III* (pp. 835–851). Mahwah, NJ: Erlbaum.

Blachowicz, C.L.Z. (1991). Vocabulary instruction in content classes for special needs learners: Why and how? *Reading, Writing, and Learning Disabilities, 7,* 297–308.

Gillespie, C.S., Ford, K.L., Gillespie, R.D., & Leavell, A.G. (1996). Portfolio assessment: Some questions, some answers, some recommendations. *Journal of Adolescent & Adult Reading, 39,* 480–491.

Rakes, T.A., & Smith, L.J. (2007). Assessing reading skills in the content areas. In T.W. Bean, J.E. Readence, & R.S. Baldwin, *Content area literacy digital supplement.* Dubuque, IA: Kendall/Hunt.

Webster, B. (1984, December 12). Science sheds light on bats. *The Register.* Santa Ana, CA.

Chapter 6, Unit and Lesson Planning

Recommended Readings

Bean, T.W. (2002). Text comprehension: The role of prior activity theory in navigating students' prior knowledge in content teaching. In C.M. Roller (Ed.), *Comprehensive reading instruction across grade levels* (pp. 133–147). Newark, DE: International Reading Association.

> This chapter provides background information on an alternative lesson and unit planning framework with special attention to classroom sociocultural and contextual dimensions.

Britzman, D. (2003). *Practice makes practice: A critical study of learning to teach* (2nd ed.). Albany, NY: State University of New York Press.

> The update of this now classic book offers a critical examination of the complex social practice elements of teaching. Britzman views teaching and learning as much more than a matter of method. The meanings learners and teachers ascribe to their classroom experiences are crucial in any complex analysis of teaching and learning.

Lesson Plan sites online:

> There are numerous sites, some developed by publishers, to support teachers' lesson planning. To gain an idea of the richness of these sites, see the omnibus site at: *http://www.internet4classrooms.com/lesson.htm.*
>
> This site features multiple links to other lesson and unit planning resources. It spans 8 pages and is divided by grade level.

McNabb, M.L. (2006). *Literacy learning in networked classrooms: Using the Internet with middle-level students.* Newark, DE: International Reading Association.

> This book, also featured in Chapter 3, includes a useful listing of curriculum and lesson plan resources on page 107. For example, if you are planning to create WebQuests in your content area, the following website will be helpful: *www.webquest.org*

Smith, M.W., & Wilhelm, J.D. (2006). *Going with the flow: How to engage boys (and girls) in their literacy learning.* Portsmouth, NH: Heinemann.

> The authors offer a unit planning template (pp. 150–151) that centers on engaging, activity-based inquiry units and lessons aimed at tapping adolescents' sense of competence.

References

Bean, T.W. (2002). Text comprehension: The role of prior activity theory in navigating students' prior knowledge in content teaching. In C.M. Roller (Ed.), *Comprehensive reading instruction across grade levels* (pp. 133–147). Newark, DE: International Reading Association.

Britzman, D. (2003). *Practice makes practice: A critical study of learning to teach* (2nd ed.). Albany, NY: State University of New York Press.

Hinchman, K.A. (2007). How teachers use the textbook: Lessons from three secondary school classrooms (1992). In T.W. Bean, J.E. Readence, & R.S. Baldwin, *Content area literacy digital supplement.* Dubuque, IA: Kendall/Hunt.

Hunt, L.C., Jr., & Sheldon, W.D. (1950). Characteristics of the reading of a group of ninth-grade pupils. *School Review, 58,* 348–353.

McConnell, S. (1993). Talking drawings: A strategy for assisting learners. *Journal of Reading, 36,* 260–269.

McNabb, M.L. (2006). *Literacy learning in networked classrooms: Using the Internet with middle-level students.* Newark, DE: International Reading Association.

Readence, J.E., & Dishner, E.K. (2007). Adapting instruction in content classrooms to meet individual student needs. In T.W. Bean, J.E. Readence, & R.S. Baldwin, *Content area literacy digital supplement.* Dubuque, IA: Kendall/Hunt.

Wiggins, G. & McTighe, J. (2005). *Understanding by design* (2nd ed.). Alexandria, VA: Association for Supervision and Curriculum Development.

Chapter 7, Literature

Recommended Readings

Bean, T.W., & Harper, H.J. (2006). Exploring notions of freedom in and through young adult literature. *Journal of Adolescent & Adult Literacy, 50,* 96–104.

> This article guides the reader through a critical literacy questioning approach with examples from contemporary young adult literature set in international sites of global conflict. Also, see Harper and Bean (2006) in the reference list for a book chapter centered on democracy and citizenship discussions based on young adult literature.

Bean, T.W., & Harper, H.J. (2007). Reading men differently: Alternative portrayals of masculinity in contemporary young adult fiction. *Reading Psychology.*

This article reviews recent research on masculinity and its importance for working with boys and reading. In particular, through an analysis of contemporary young adult books aimed at examining spaces for masculinity to be multifaceted, the article provides student discussion options and examples.

Bean, T.W., & Moni, K. (2003). Developing students' critical literacy: Exploring identity construction in young adult fiction. *Journal of Adolescent & Adult Literacy, 46,* 638–648.

This article walks the reader through a classroom example of how to employ critical literacy in the reading and discussion of contemporary young adult fiction.

Blackburn, M.V., & Buckley, J.F. (2005). Teaching queer-inclusive English language arts. *Journal of Adolescent & Adult Literacy, 49,* 202–212.

The authors offer a comprehensive discussion of gay, lesbian, and transgender young adult literature, along with useful websites and classroom examples incorporating powerful literature and an understanding of difference.

Boyd, F.B. (2003). Experiencing things not seen: Educative events centered on a study of *Shabanu. Journal of Adolescent & Adult Literacy, 46,* 460–474.

This article guides the reader through the use of multicultural literature and various literature response strategies, including journaling, body biographies, and the integration of technology.

Brozo, W.G. (2002). *To be a boy, to be a reader.* Newark, DE: International Reading Association.

This book offers concrete recommendations and resources for influencing adolescent males' reading engagement.

Buscher, K., & Manning, M.L. (2006). *Young adult literature: Exploration, evaluation, and appreciation.* Upper Saddle River, NJ: Pearson.

This contemporary young adult literature text includes resources for linking books to films and offers a chapter on comic books, graphic novels, and magazines. Numerous websites offer teachers additional resources.

Fisher, D. (2004). Setting the "opportunity to read" standard: Resuscitating the SSR program in an urban high school. *Journal of Adolescent & Adult Literacy, 48,* 138–150.

This report of an action research study in a large, urban high school shows in very concrete ways how to turn around an SSR program that is not operating according to key principles. If SSR is to realize its potential to impact students' reading attitudes, interests, and achievement, they must find SSR an engaging and worthwhile time rather than a time to simply rest and recuperate from other text reading.

Landt, S.M. (2006). Multicultural literature and young adolescents: A kaleidoscope of opportunity. *Journal of Adolescent & Young Adult Literacy, 49,* 690–697.

The author explores the concept of cultural authenticity and includes a list of award winning multicultural young adult literature and useful websites.

Nilsen, A.P., & Donelson, K.L. (2005). *Literature for today's young adults* (7th ed.). New York: Longman.

This major text features extensive annotations of books and a compilation of the authors' selections for best young adult literature.

Serafini, F., & Giorgis, C. (2003). *Reading aloud and beyond: Fostering the intellectual life with older readers.* Portsmouth, NH: Heinemann.

The authors present a host of useful ways to make reading aloud to middle and secondary students come alive. Their approaches are designed to foster a lifelong love of reading.

Smith, M.W., & Wilhelm, J.D. (2002). *"Reading don't fix no Chevys": Literacy in the lives of young men.* Portsmouth, NH: Heinemann.

This book, based on extensive interviews with middle and high school young men, provides innovative solutions to the well-documented disconnection between students' in and out-of-school literature.

Smith, M.W., & Wilhelm, J.D. (2006). *Going with the flow: How to engage boys (and girls) in their literacy learning.* Portsmouth, NH: Heinemann.

By centering discussion on essential questions, often from a wide-angle lens perspective, the authors offer an alternative to narrow discussions of literature and other text forms. They include dramatic action strategies and other visual support approaches students find engaging.

References

Achebe, C. (1958). *Things fall apart.* Portsmouth, NH: Heinemann.

Albright, L.K. (2002). Bringing the Ice Maiden to life: Engaging adolescents in learning through picture book read-alouds in content areas. *Journal of Adolescent & Adult Literacy, 48,* 418–428.

Al-Windawi, T. (2004). *Thura's diary.* London, England: Penguin.

Anaya, R. (1972). *Bless me Ultima.* San Francisco, CA: Tonatiuh Press.

Aoki, E.M. (1993). Turning the page: Asian-Pacific American children's literature. In V.J. Harris (Ed.), *Teaching multicultural literature in grades K–8* (pp. 109–135). Norwood, MA: Christopher-Gordon.

Baldwin, R.S., & Leavell, A.G. (2007). When was the last time you read a textbook just for kicks? In T.W. Bean, J.E. Readence, & R.S. Baldwin, *Content area literacy digital supplement.* Dubuque, IA: Kendall/Hunt.

Balliett, B. (2005). *Chasing Vermeer.* New York: Scholastic.

Bean, T.W. (2000). Reading in the content areas: Social constructivist dimensions. In M.L. Kamil, P.D. Mosenthal, P.D. Pearson, & R. Barr (Eds.), *Handbook of reading research: Volume III* (pp. 629–644). Mahwah, NJ: Erlbaum.

Bean, T.W. (2002). Making reading relevant for adolescents. *Educational Leadership, 60*(3), 34–37.

Bean, T.W., & Harper, H.J. (2004). Teacher education and adolescent literacy. In T.L. Jetton, & J.A. Dole (Eds.), *Adolescent literacy research and practice* (pp. 392–411). New York: Guilford Press.

Bean, T.W., & Harper, H.J. (2006). Exploring notions of freedom in and through young adult literature. *Journal of Adolescent & Adult Literacy, 50,* 96–104.

Bean, T.W., & Harper, H.J. (2007). Reading men differently: Alternative portrayals of masculinity in contemporary young adult fiction. *Reading Psychology.*

Bean, T.W., & Moni, K. (2003). Developing students' critical literacy: Exploring identity construction in young adult fiction. *Journal of Adolescent & Adult Literacy, 46,* 638–648.

Bean, T.W., & Rigoni, N. (2000, May). *Exploring the intergenerational dialogue journal discussion of a multicultural young adult novel.* Paper presented at the annual meeting of the International Reading Association, Indianapolis, IN.

Bean, T.W., Valerio, P.C., Money Senior, H., & White, F. (1999). Secondary English students' engagement in reading and writing about a multicultural novel. *Journal of Educational Research, 93,* 32–37.

Benedicty, A. (1995). Reading *Shabanu*: Creating multiple entry points for diverse readers. *Voices from the Middle, 2,* 12–16.

Blackburn, M.V., & Buckley, J.F. (2005). Teaching queer-inclusive English language Arts. *Journal of Adolescent & Adult Literacy, 49,* 202–212.

Boyd, F.B. (2003). Experiencing things not seen: Educative events centered on a study of *Shabanu*. *Journal of Adolescent & Adult Literacy, 46,* 460–474.

Brozo, W.G., Valerio, P.C., & Salazar, M.M. (1996). A walk through Gracie's garden: Literacy and cultural explorations in a Mexican-American junior high school. *Journal of Adolescent & Adult Literacy, 40,* 2–8.

Brozo, W.G., Walter, P., & Placker, T. (2002). "I know the difference between a real man and a TV man:" A critical exploration of violence and masculinity through literature in a junior high school in the hood. *Journal of Adolescent & Adult Literacy, 45,* 530–538.

Bruchac, J. (2006). *Geronimo*, New York: Scholastic.

Cole, J.E. (2003). What motivates students to read? Four literacy personalities. *The Reading Teacher, 56,* 326–336.

Cooney, C.B. (2005). *Code orange*. New York: Delacorte.

Crew, L. (1989). *Children of the river*. New York: Dell.

Csikszentmihalyi, M. (2002). Do students care about learning? A conversation with Mihaly Csikszentmihalyi. *Educational Leadership, 60*(1), 12–17.

Ellis, D. (2000). *The breadwinner*. Toronto, Ontario: Groundwood.

Fisher, D. (2004). Setting the "opportunity to read" standard: Resuscitating the SSR program in an urban high school. *Journal of Adolescent & Adult Literacy, 48,* 138–150.

Flake, S. (2001). *Money hungry*. New York: Hyperion.

Fleischman, P. (1990). *Saturnalia*. New York: HarperCollins.

Franzak, J., & Noll, E. (2006). Monstrous acts: Problematizing violence in young adult literature. *Journal of Adolescent & Adult Literature, 49,* 662–672.

Galda, L., Ash, G.E., & Cullinan, B.E. (2000). Children's literature. In M.L. Kamil, P.B. Mosenthal, P.D. Pearson, & R. Barr (Eds.), *Handbook of reading research: Volume III* (pp. 361–379). Mahwah, NJ: Erlbaum.

Gallo, D.R. (2004). *First crossings: Stories about teen immigrants*. New York: Candlewood Press.

Godina, H. (1996). The canonical debate-implementing multicultural literature and perspectives. *Journal of Adolescent & Adult Literacy, 39,* 544–545.

Gray, A. (2003). Conversations with transformative encounters. In G. Gay (Ed.), *Becoming multicultural educators* (pp. 67–90). San Francisco, CA: Jossey-Bass.

Guthrie, J.T., & Wigfield, A. (2000). Engagement and motivation in reading. In M.L. Kamil, P.D. Mosenthal, P.D. Pearson, & R. Barr (Eds.), *Handbook of reading research: Volume III* (pp. 403–422). Mahwah, NJ: Erlbaum.

Guzzetti, B.J., Kowalinski, B.J., & McGowan, T. (1992). Using a literature-based approach to teaching social studies. *Journal of Reading, 36,* 114–121.

Gwynne, P. (1998). *Deadly unna?* Victoria, Australia: Penguin Books.

Gwynne, P. (2000). *Nukkin ya*. Victoria, Australia: Penguin Books.

Harper, H.J. (2000). *Wild words dangerous desires*. New York: Peter Lang.

Harper, H.J., & Bean, T.W. (2006). Fallen angels: Finding adolescents and adolescent literacy in a renewed project of democratic citizenship. In D.E. Alvermann, K.A. Hinchman, D.W. Moore, S.F. Phelps, & D.R. Waff (Eds.), *Reconceptualizing the literacies in adolescents' lives* (2nd ed. pp. 147–160). Mahwah, NJ: Erlbaum.

Hinton, S.E. (1967). *The outsiders.* New York: Viking.

Ivey, G., & Broaddus, K. (2001). "Just plain reading:" A survey of what makes students want to read in middle school classrooms. *Reading Research Quarterly, 36,* 350–377.

Kincaid, J. (1988). *A small place.* New York: Penguin.

Klass, D. (1994). *California blue.* New York: Scholastic.

Klass, D. (1996). *Danger zone.* New York: Scholastic.

Lee, M. (1997). *Necessary roughness.* New York: HarperCollins.

Lewison, M., & Leland, C. (2002). Critical literacy. In B.J. Guzzetti (Ed.), *Literacy in America: An encyclopedia of history, theory, and practice* (pp. 108–111). Santa Barbara, CA: ABC-CLIO.

Love, K. (2002). Mapping online discussion in senior English. *Journal of Adolescent & Adult Literacy, 45,* 382–396.

Lyons, M.E. (1992). *Letter from a slave girl: The story of Harriet Jacobs.* New York: Charles Scribner's Sons.

McKenna, M.C., Kear, D.J., & Ellsworth, R.A. (1995). Children's attitudes toward reading: A national survey. *Reading Research Quarterly, 30,* 934–956.

McMahon, S.I., & Raphael, T.E. (1997). *The book club connection.* New York: Teachers College Press.

Miller, D.E. (1993). The literature project: Using literature to improve the self-concept of at-risk adolescent females. *Journal of Reading, 36,* 442–446.

Moje, E. (2000). "To be part of the story:" The literacy practices of gangsta adolescents. *Teachers College Record, 102,* 651–690.

Myers, W.D. (1988). *Fallen angels.* New York: Scholastic.

Myers, W.D. (1999). *Monster.* New York: HarperCollins.

Naidoo, B. (2000). *The other side of truth.* New York: HarperCollins.

Nieto, S. (2003). *Affirming diversity: The sociopolitical context of multicultural education* (4th ed.). New York: Longman.

Nilsen, A.P., & Donelson, K.L. (2005). *Literature for today's young adults* (7th ed.). New York: HarperCollins.

Palmer, R.G., & Stewart, R.A. (1997). Nonfiction trade books in content area instruction. Realities and potential. *Journal of Adolescent & Adult Literacy, 40,* 630–641.

Rosenblatt, L.M. (1978). *The reader, the text, the poem.* Carbondale, IL: Southern Illinois University Press.

Savage, J.F. (1994). *Teaching reading using literature.* Dubuque, IA: WCB Brown & Benchmark.

Serafini, F., & Giorgis, C. (2003). *Reading aloud and beyond: Fostering the intellectual life with older readers.* Portsmouth, NH: Heinemann.

Smagorinsky, P., & O'Donnell-Allen, C. (1998). Reading as mediated and mediating action: Composing meaning for literature through multimedia interpretive texts. *Reading Research Quarterly, 33,* 198–226.

Smith, M.W., & Wilhelm, J.D. (2002). *"Reading don't fix no Chevys:" Literacy in the lives of young men.* Portsmouth, NH: Heinemann.

Smith, M.W., & Wilhelm, J.D. (2006). *Going with the flow: How to engage boys (and girls) in their literacy learning.* Portsmouth, NH: Heinemann.

Smith, R. (2005). *Cryptid hunters*. New York: Hyperion.

Soto, G. (1997). *Buried onions*. New York: Scholastic.

Soto, G. (2003). *The afterlife*. New York: Harcourt.

Stevens, L.P., & Bean, T.W. (2007). *Critical literacy: Context, research, and practice in the K–12 classroom*. Thousand Oaks, CA: Sage.

Stover, L.T., & Tway, E. (1992). Cultural diversity and the young adult novel. In V.R. Monseau & G.M. Salvner (Eds.), *Reading their world: The young adult novel in the classroom* (pp. 132–153). Portsmouth, NH: Boynton/Cook.

Vogt, M. (2002). Active learning: Dramatic play in the content areas. In M. McLaughlin & M. Vogt (Eds.), *Creativity and innovation in content area teaching* (pp. 73–90). Norwood, MA: Christopher-Gordon.

Walker, A. (1983). *The color purple*. New York: Harcourt, Brace, Jovanovich.

Warner, L.S. (1976). *From slave to abolitionist: The life of William Wells Brown*. New York: Dial.

Werlin, N. (2004). *Double helix*. New York: Penguin.

Winkler, K.J. (1994, January 12). An African writer at a crossroads. *The Chronicle of Higher Education*, A–9.

Woodson, J. (2002). *Hush*. New York: G. P. Putnam's Son.

Worthy, J., Patterson, E., Salas, R., Prater, W., & Turner, M. (2002). More than just reading: The human factor in reaching resistant readers. *Reading Research and Instruction, 41*, 177–202.

Xu, S.H., Perkins, R.S., & Zunich, L.O. (2005). *Trading cards to comic strips: Popular culture texts and literacy learning in grades K–8*. Newark, DE: International Reading Association.

Young, T.A., & Vardell, S. (1993). Weaving readers' theatre and nonfiction into the curriculum. *The Reading Teacher, 46*, 396–406.

Chapter 8, Vocabulary

Recommended Readings

Balchowicz, C.L.Z., & Fisher, P. (2000). Vocabulary instruction. In M.L. Kamil, P.B. Mosenthal, P.D. Pearson, & R. Barr (Eds.), *Handbook of reading research: Volume III* (pp. 503–523). Mahwah, NJ: Erlbaum.

An examination of the research on vocabulary to see how classroom practice has been impacted.

Baldwin, R.S., Readence, J.E., & Bean, T.W. (2004). *Targeted reading: Improving achievement in middle and secondary grades*. Dubuque, IA: Kendall/Hunt.

Chapter 5 features a number of vocabulary acquisition strategies in a simple format designed for district professional-development days.

Graves, M.F. (2000). A vocabulary program to complement and bolster a middle-grade comprehension program. In B.M. Taylor, M.F. Graves, & P. Van den Broek (Eds.), *Reading for meaning: Fostering comprehension in the middle grades* (pp. 116–135). New York and Newark, DE: Teachers College Press and International Reading Association.

A discussion of the principles and components of a good vocabulary development program.

Graves, M.F., & Watts-Taffe, S.M. (2002). The place of word consciousness in a research-based vocabulary program. In A.E. Farstrup & S.J. Samuels (Eds.), *What research has to say about reading instruction* (pp. 140–165). Newark, DE: International Reading Association.

> This research review provides a good overview of difficulties students have learning new vocabulary, along with useful word learning strategies.

Harmon, J.M. (2000). Assessing and supporting independent word learning strategies of middle school students. *Journal of Adolescent & Adult Literacy, 47*, 518–527.

> This article provides a concrete chart for assessing students' independent approaches to word learning. In addition, it offers specific guidelines for developing independent word learning.

Manzo, A.V., Manzo, U.C., & Thomas, M.M. (2006). Rationale for systematic vocabulary development: Antidote for state mandates. *Journal of Adolescent & Adult Literacy, 49*, 610–619.

> A current state of the art on approaches to vocabulary development.

Nagy, W.E., & Scott, J.A. (2000). Vocabulary processes. In M.L. Kamil, P.B. Mosenthal, P.D. Pearson, & R. Barr (Eds.), *Handbook of reading research: Volume III* (pp. 269–284). Mahwah, NJ: Erlbaum.

> A review of the literature on how students acquire new words into their reading and writing vocabularies.

Tierney, R.J., & Readence, J.E. (2005). *Reading strategies and practices: A compendium* (6th ed.). Boston: Allyn & Bacon.

> Unit 8 contains a variety of meaning vocabulary strategies with appropriate examples.

References

Baldwin, R.S., Readence, J.E., & Bean, T.W. (2004). *Targeted reading: Improving achievement in middle and secondary grades*. Dubuque, IA: Kendall/Hunt.

Blachowicz, C.L.Z., & Fisher, P. (2000). Vocabulary instruction. In M.L. Kamil, P.B. Mosenthal, P.D. Pearson, & R. Barr (Eds.), *Handbook of reading research: Volume III* (pp. 503–523). Mahwah, NJ: Erlbaum.

Butcher, J., & Raminez, M. (2007). Vocabulary development for English Language Learners. In T.W. Bean, J.E. Readence, & R.S. Baldwin, *Content area literacy digital supplement*. Dubuque, IA: Kendall/Hunt.

Cunningham, P.M. (1992). Content area vocabulary: Building and connecting meaning. In T.W. Bean, J.E. Readence, & R.S. Baldwin, *Content area literacy digital supplement*. Dubuque, IA: Kendall/Hunt.

Dana, C., & Rodriguez, M. (1992). TOAST: A system to study vocabulary. *Reading Research and Instruction, 31*, 78–84.

Funk, C.E. (1950). *Thereby hangs a tale: Stories of curious word origins*. New York: Harper & Brothers.

Graves, M.F., & Watts-Taffe, S.M. (2002). The place of word consciousness in a research-based vocabulary program. In A.E. Farstrup & S.J. Samuels (Eds.), *What research has to say about reading instruction* (pp. 140–165). Newark, DE: International Reading Association.

Harmon, J.M., Hedrick, W.B., & Fox, E.A. (2000). A content analysis of vocabulary instruction in social studies textbooks for grades 4–8. *The Elementary School Journal, 100*, 253–271.

Hopkins, G., & Bean, T.W. (1998–1999). Vocabulary learning with the verbal-visual word association strategy in a Native American community. *Journal of Adolescent & Adult Literacy, 42*, 274–281.

Maurer, D.W. (1955). Whiz mob. *Publication of the American Dialect Society*, No. 24.

Ruddell, M.R. & Shearer, B.A. (2002). "Extraordinary," "tremendous," "exhilarating," "magnificent": Middle school at-risk students become avid word learners with the Vocabulary Self-Collection Strategy (VSS). *Journal of Adolescent & Adult Literacy, 45*, 352–363.

Schatz, E.K., & Baldwin, R.S. (1986). Context clues are unreliable predictors of word meanings. *Reading Research Quarterly, 21*, 439–453.

Shu, H., Anderson, R.C., & Zhang, H. (1995). Incidental learning of word meanings while reading: A Chinese and American cross-cultural study. *Reading Research Quarterly, 30*, 76–95.

Tierney, R.J., & Readence, J.E. (2005). *Reading strategies and practices: A compendium* (6th ed.). Boston: Allyn & Bacon.

Chapter 9, Comprehension: Principles and Integrated Approaches

Recommended Readings

Alvermann, D.E. (2002). Effective literacy instruction for adolescents. *Journal of Literacy Research, 34*, 189–208.

> This article provides a comprehensive overview of contemporary issues in adolescent literacy instruction, including information on self-efficacy and engagement, struggling readers, and critical literacy.

Cervetti, G., Damico, J.S., & Pardeles, M.J. (2001). A tale of differences: Comparing the traditions, perspectives, and educational goals of critical reading and critical literacy. *Reading Online*. Online journal of the International Reading Association. Available: *http://www.reading.org*

> This article does an excellent job of clarifying the differences between critical reading and critical literacy. Both are important elements in a comprehensive effort to enhance students' guided and independent comprehension, but they arise from very different philosophical foundations.

Stevens, L.P. (2001). South Park and society: Instructional and curricular implications of popular culture in the classroom. *Journal of Adolescent and Adult Literacy, 44*, 548–555.

> Examples of how to develop critical media literacy lessons in science, social studies, and language arts are provided. In addition, this article shows a teacher how to cope with issues related to district policies regarding popular media so that they can be used to develop concepts in various content areas.

Stevens, L.P., & Bean, T.W. (2007). *Critical literacy: Context, research, and practice in the K–12 classroom*. Thousand Oaks, CA: Sage.

> This book offers an array of classroom examples exploring critical literacy and critical media literacy. Specific strategies such as Resident Critic guide students toward a predisposition to deconstruct and reconstruct multiple forms of texts including traditional textbook accounts, advertisements, media, and Internet sites.

Sturtevant, E.G., Boyd, F.B., Brozo, W.G., Hinchman, K.A., Moore, D.W., & Alvermann, D.E. (2006). *Principled practices for adolescent literacy: A framework for instruction and policy*. Mahwah, NJ: Erlbaum.

> This collection of classroom examples gleaned from a Carnegie project aimed at chronicling outstanding teaching in the content areas provides specific principles and examples of teaching with multiple texts in science, mathematics, English, and other content areas.

Tierney, R.J., & Readence, J.E. (2005). *Reading strategies and practices: A compendium* (6th ed.). Boston: Allyn & Bacon.

Units 7 and 12 describe numerous comprehension strategies.

References

Bean, T.W. (2000). Music in the content areas. In M. McLaughlin & M.E. Vogt (Eds.), *Creativity and innovation in content area teaching* (pp. 91–103). Norwood, MA: Christopher-Gordon.

Behrman, E.H. (2003). Reconciling content literacy with adolescent literacy: Expanding literacy opportunities in a community-focused biology class. *Reading Research and Instruction, 43,* 1–30.

Budiansky, S. (1997). *The nature of horses: Exploring equine evolution, intelligence, and behavior.* New York: Free Press.

Hoffman, J.V. (1992). Critical reading/thinking across the curriculum: Using I-charts to support learning. *Language Arts, 69,* 121–127.

Jumanji. (1995). [Film]. Columbia/Tristar Pictures.

Manzo, A.V., Casale, U., & Thomas, M.M. (2004). *Content area literacy: Strategic thinking for strategic learning* (4th ed.). New York: Wiley.

Martin, T. (1999). *Essential surrealists.* Bath, England: Parragon.

McGee, L.M., & Richgels, D.J. (2007). Attending to text structure: A comprehension strategy. In T.W. Bean, J.E. Readence, & R.S. Baldwin, *Content area literacy digital supplement.* Dubuque, IA: Kendall/Hunt.

McNabb, M.L. (2006). *Literacy learning in networked classrooms: Using the Internet with middle-level students.* Newark, DE: International Reading Association.

Ogle, D. (2007). KWL in action: Secondary teachers find applications that work. In T.W. Bean, J.E. Readence, & R.S. Baldwin, *Content area literacy digital supplement.* Dubuque, IA: Kendall/Hunt.

Raphael, T.E., Highfield, K., & Au, K.H. (2006). *QAR now: A powerful and practical framework that develops comprehension and higher-level thinking in all students.* New York: Scholastic.

Shanahan, C. (2004). Teaching science through literacy. In T. Jetton & J.A. Dole (Eds.), *Adolescent literacy research and practice* (pp. 75–93). New York: Guilford Press.

Smith, M.W., & Wilhelm, J.D. (2006). *Going with the flow: How to engage boys (and girls) in their literacy learning.* Portsmouth, NH: Heinemann.

Stahl, S.A., & Shanahan, C. (2004). Learning to think like a historian: Disciplinary knowledge through critical analysis of multiple documents. In T. Jetton & J.A. Dole (Eds.), *Adolescent literacy research and practice* (pp. 94–115). New York: Guilford Press.

Stevens, L.P. (2001). South Park and society: Instructional and curricular implications of popular culture in the classroom. *Journal of Adolescent and Adult Literacy, 44,* 548–555.

Stevens, L.P., & Bean, T.W. (2007). *Critical literacy: Context, research, and practice in the K–12 classroom.* Thousand Oaks, CA: Sage.

Sturtevant, E.G., Boyd, F.B., Brozo, W.G., Hinchman, K.A., Moore, D.W., & Alvermann, D.E. (2006). *Principled practices for adolescent literacy: A framework for instruction and policy.* Mahwah, NJ: Erlbaum.

Taboada, A., & Guthrie, J.T. (2006). Contributions of student questioning and prior to construction of knowledge from reading information text. *Journal of Literacy Research, 38,* 1–35.

Tierney, R.J., & Readence, J.E. (2005). *Reading strategies and practices: A compendium* (6th ed.). Boston: Allyn & Bacon.

Walker, N.T., & Bean, T.W. (2004). Using multiple texts in content area classrooms. *Journal of Content Area Reading, 3*, 23–36.

Walker, N.T., Bean, T.W., & Dillard, B. (2005). Sociocultural dimensions of multiple texts in two experienced teachers' classrooms. In B. Maloch, J.V. Hoffman, D.L. Schallert, C.M. Fairbanks, & J. Worthy (Eds.), *54th Yearbook of the National Reading Conference*. Oak Creek, WI: National Reading Conference.

Chapter 10, Comprehension: Guiding Content Literacy

Recommended Readings

Baldwin, R.S., Readence, J.E., & Bean, T.W. (2004). *Targeted reading: Improving achievement in middle and secondary grades.* Dubuque, IA: Kendall/Hunt.

This book offers a succinct array of strategies designed for middle and secondary teacher professional development inservices and workshops.

Berne, J.L., & Clark, K.F. (2006). Comprehension strategy use during peer-led discussion of text: Ninth graders tackle "The Lottery." *Journal of Adolescent & Adult Literacy, 49*, 674–686.

These authors offer a number of concrete recommendations for guiding students toward productive discussions in English and other content areas. Their work is based on classroom research with adolescents in English.

Parker, W.C. (2003). *Teaching democracy: Unity and diversity in public life.* New York: Teachers College Press.

This book provides an excellent discussion of democratic processes along with specific strategies and materials teachers in social studies and other content areas can use to help students develop deliberative discussions.

Readence, J.E., Moore, D.W., & Rickelman, R.J. (2000). *Prereading activities for content area reading and learning* (3rd ed.). Newark, DE: International Reading Association.

A succinct and readable explanation of various prereading strategies.

Tierney, R.J., & Readence, J.E. (2005). *Reading strategies and practices: A compendium* (6th ed.). Boston: Allyn & Bacon.

Contains a wealth of practical teaching strategies with appropriate cautions and comments to the reader on their use in classrooms.

References

Alvermann, D.E., Dillon, D.R., & O'Brien, D.G. (1987). *Using discussion to promote reading comprehension.* Newark, DE: International Reading Association.

Alvermann, D.E., O'Brien, D.G., & Dillon, D.R. (1990). What teachers do when they say they're having discussions of content area reading assignments: A qualitative analysis. *Reading Research Quarterly, 25*, 296–322.

Baldwin, R.S., Readence, J.E., & Bean, T.W. (2004). *Targeted reading: Improving achievement in middle and secondary grades.* Dubuque, IA: Kendall/Hunt.

Bean, T.W. (2007). Combining text previews and three level study guides to develop critical reading in history. In T.W. Bean, J.E. Readence, & R.S. Baldwin, *Content area literacy digital supplement.* Dubuque, IA: Kendall/Hunt.

Bean, T.W., & Bishop, A.L. (2007). Polar opposites: A strategy for guiding students' critical reading and discussion. In T.W. Bean, J.E. Readence, & R.S. Baldwin, *Content area literacy digital supplement.* Dubuque, IA: Kendall/Hunt.

Berne, J.L., & Clark, K.F. (2006). Comprehension strategy use during peer-led discussion of text: Ninth graders tackle "The Lottery." *Journal of Adolescent & Adult Literacy, 49*, 674–686.

Curran, M.J., & Smith, E.C. (2005). The Imposter: A motivational strategy to encourage reading in mathematics. *Journal of Adolescent & Adult Literacy, 49,* 186–190.

Duffelmeyer, F.A., & Baum, D.D. (1992). The extended anticipation guide revisited. *Journal of Reading, 35,* 654–656.

Harper, H.J., & Bean, T.W. (2006). Fallen Angels: Finding adolescents and adolescent literacy in a renewed project of democratic citizenship. In D.E. Alvermann, K.A. Hinchman, D.W. Moore, S.F. Phelps, & D.R. Waff (Eds.) *Reconceptualizing the literacies in adolescents' lives* (2nd ed., pp. 147–160). Mahwah, NJ: Erlbaum.

Hartman, D.K., & Allison, J. (1996). Promoting inquiry-oriented discussions using multiple texts. In L.B. Gambrell & J.F. Almasi (Eds.), *Lively discussions! Fostering engaged reading* (pp. 106–133). Newark, DE: International Reading Association.

Hawthorne, N. (1986). *The scarlet letter.* New York: Penguin. (Original work published 1850).

Head, M.H., & Readence, J.E. (2007). Anticipation guides: Using prediction to promote learning from text. In T.W. Bean, J.E. Readence, & R.S. Baldwin, *Content area literacy digital supplement.* Dubuque, IA: Kendall/Hunt.

Jackson, S. (1982). The lottery. In *The lottery and other stories* (pp. 291–301). New York: Farrar, Strauss and Giroux. (Original work published 1948).

Jimenez, R.T. (1997). The strategic reading abilities and potential of five low-literacy Latina/o readers in middle school. *Reading Research Quarterly, 32,* 224–243.

Miller, A. (1976). *The crucible.* New York: Penguin.

Nesbit, J.C., & Adesope, O.O. (2006). Learning with concept and knowledge maps: A meta-analysis. *Review of Educational Research, 76,* 423–448.

Parker, W.C. (2003). *Teaching democracy: Unity and diversity in public life.* New York: Teachers College Press.

Schwartz, M., & O'Connor, J.R. (1975). *New exploring a changing world.* New York: Globe Book.

Tan, A. (1991). *The kitchen god's wife.* New York: Ballantine.

Tierney, R.J., & Readence, J.E. (2005). *Reading strategies and practices: A compendium* (6th ed.). Boston: Allyn and Bacon.

Walker, N.T., & Bean, T.W. (2003, December). *Sociocultural influences in content area teachers' selection and use of multiple texts.* Paper presented at the annual meeting of the National Reading Conference, Miami, Florida.

Chapter 11, Writing

Recommended Readings

Bean, T.W. (2000). Music in the content areas. In M. McLaughlin & M.E. Vogt (Eds.), *Creativity and innovation in content area teaching* (pp. 91–103). Norwood, MA: Christopher-Gordon.

This chapter provides additional examples of the ReWrite strategy as well as rap lyrics and other ways to incorporate music writing in content learning.

Bean, T.W. (2001). Writing across the curriculum. In L.W. Searfoss, J.E. Readence, & M.H. Mallette (Eds.), *Helping children learn to read* (5th ed., pp. 277–309). Boston, MA: Allyn and Bacon.

This chapter includes examples of various writing strategies to use in elementary classrooms along with music and poetry.

Black, R.W. (2005). Access and affiliation: The literacy and composition practices of English-language learners in an online fanfiction community. *Journal of Adolescent & Adult Literacy, 49*, 118–128.

This article describes the various ways fanfiction and the fanfiction Internet site provide a forum for second language students to post their writing about books (e.g., *Harry Potter*), films (e.g., *Snakes on a Plane*), and other media.

Gillespie, J. (2005). "It would be fun to do again": Multigenre responses to literature. *Journal of Adolescent & Adult Literacy, 48*, 678–684.

This article offers a wealth of information on multigenre writing including how to scaffold and model multigenre writing and a comprehensive list of multigenre forms of writing.

Moore, D.W., Moore, S.A., Cunningham, P.M., & Cunningham, J.W. (2003). *Developing readers and writers in the content areas, K–12* (4th ed.). Boston, MA: Allyn and Bacon.

This book provides chapters on writing and inquiry with specific content area examples from mathematics, science, and other subject areas.

Olson, C.B. (2003). *The reading/writing connection: Strategies for teaching and learning in the secondary classroom.* Boston, MA: Allyn and Bacon.

This book offers a comprehensive array of strategies to guide content area teachers efforts to help students gain confidence and independence in their writing. It includes very useful sections on editing, revising, and evaluating students' writing.

Romano, T. (2000). *Blending genre, altering style: Writing multigenre papers.* Portsmouth, NH: Heinemann.

This book guides teachers through the planning and implementation stages of using multigenre papers in various content areas. Art, drama, music, diaries, advertisements, and so on can be combined to paint a vivid picture of topic.

Sandmann, A. (2006). Nurturing thoughtful revision using the Focused Question Card strategy. *Journal of Adolescent & Adult Literacy, 50*, 20–28.

This article includes a table of revision questions that should help guide students' efforts to edit and improve their writing across various content areas.

Tierney, R.J., & Readence, J.E. (2005). *Reading strategies and practices: A compendium* (6th ed.). Boston, MA: Allyn and Bacon.

Unit 9 contains a number of writing strategies and a section on responding to students' writing. Cautions and comments help guide the reader toward effective application of the strategies.

References

Bean, T.W. (1997, May). ReWrite: A music strategy for exploring content area concepts. *Reading Online.* Online journal of the International Reading Association. Available: *http://www.readingonline.org.*

Bean, T.W. (2000). Music in the content areas. In M. McLaughlin & M.E. Vogt (Eds.), *Creativity and innovation in content area teaching* (pp. 91–103). Norwood, MA: Christopher-Gordon.

Bean, T.W. (2001). Writing across the curriculum. In L.W. Searfoss, J.E. Readence, & M.H. Mallette, *Helping children learn to read* (5th ed., pp. 277–309). Boston, MA: Allyn and Bacon.

Bean, T.W. (2002). Literacy autobiography. In B.J. Guzzetti (Ed.), *Literacy in America: An encyclopedia of history, theory, and practice* (pp. 308–310). Santa Barbara, CA: ABC-CLIO.

Bean, T.W. (2007). Combining writing fluency and vocabulary development through writing roulette. In T.W. Bean, J.E. Readence, & R.S. Baldwin, *Content area literacy digital supplement*. Dubuque, IA: Kendall/Hunt.

Bean, T.W., & Moni, K. (2003). Developing students' critical literacy: Exploring identity construction in young adult fiction. *Journal of Adolescent & Adult Literacy, 46*, 638–648.

Bean, T.W., & Rigoni, N. (2000, May). *Exploring the intergenerational dialogue journal discussion of a multicultural young adult novel*. Paper presented at the annual meeting of the International Reading Association, Indianapolis, IN.

Black, R.W. (2005). Access and affiliation: The literacy and composition practices of English-language learners in an online fanfiction community. *Journal of Adolescent & Adult Literacy, 49*, 118–128.

Calkins, L.M. (1994). *The art of teaching writing* (2nd ed.). Portsmouth, NH: Heinemann.

Denyer, R. (1982). *The guitar handbook*. New York: Knopf.

Gillespie, J. (2005). "It would be fun to do again": Multigenre responses to literature. *Journal of Adolescent & Adult Literacy, 48*, 678–684.

Macrorie, K. (1988). *The I-search paper*. Portsmouth, NH: Heinemann.

Martin, S.H. (2007). Using journals to promote learning across the curriculum. In T.W. Bean, J.E. Readence, & R.S. Baldwin, *Content area literacy digital supplement*. Dubuque, IA: Kendall/Hunt.

Moore, D.W., & Moore, S.A. (2007). Possible sentences: An update. In T.W. Bean, J.E. Readence, & R.S. Baldwin, *Content area literacy digital supplement*. Dubuque, IA: Kendall/Hunt.

Moore, D.W., Moore, S.A., Cunningham, P.M., & Cunningham, J.W. (2003). *Developing readers and writers in the content areas, K–12* (4th ed.). Boston, MA: Allyn and Bacon.

Newkirk, T. (1986). Time for questions: Responding to writing. In T. Newkirk (Ed.), *To compose* (pp. 121–124). Portsmouth, NH: Heinemann.

Nishida, G.A., & Tenorio, J.M. (1993). *What bit me? Identifying Hawaii's stinging and biting insects and their kin*. Honolulu: University of Hawaii Press.

Olson, C.B. (2003). *The reading/writing connection: Strategies for teaching and learning in the secondary classroom*. Boston, MA: Allyn and Bacon.

Paul, D.G. (2000). Rap and orality: Critical media literacy, pedagogy, and cultural synchronization. *Journal of Adolescent & Adult Literacy, 44*, 246–251.

Porto, M. (2002). Implementing cooperative writing response groups and self-evaluation in South America: Struggle and survival. *Journal of Adolescent & Adult Literacy, 45*, 684–691.

Romano, T. (2000). *Blending genre, altering style: Writing multigenre papers*. Portsmouth, NH: Heinemann.

Sandmann, A. (2006). Nurturing thoughtful revision using the Focused Question Card strategy. *Journal of Adolescent & Adult Literacy, 50*, 20–28.

Tompkins, G.E. (2003). *Teaching writing: Balancing process and product* (4th ed.). Columbus, OH: Merrill.

Werderich, D.E. (2002). Individualized responses: Using journal letters as a vehicle for differentiated reading instruction. *Journal of Adolescent & Adult Literacy, 45*, 746–754.

Chapter 12, Studying and Preparing for Examinations

Recommended Readings

Brown, R. (2005). Seventh-graders' self-regulatory note-taking from text: Perceptions, preferences, and practices. *Reading Research and Instruction, 44,* 1–26.

> Study demonstrating that, while middle-school students were aware of the importance of note-taking, they were less proficient in their practices than they perceived themselves to be.

Flippo, R.F., & Caverly, D.C. (2000). *Handbook of college reading and study strategy research.* Mahwah, NJ: Erlbaum.

> This collection of papers provides the research foundation for many of the generic principles of studying described in this chapter. Though the title indicates a college level population, the book offers valuable information on independent learning strategies for adolescents.

Hacker, D.J., Dunlosky, J., & Graesser, A.C. (Eds.). (1998). *Metacognition in educational theory and practice.* Mahwah, NJ: Erlbaum.

> A text of readings devoted to the notion of metacognition and its effects on learning in the content areas.

http://www.avidonline.org

> This website describes the AVID project, designed to serve students in grades 5–12 better prepare for their college education. AVID incorporates elements of inquiry and notetaking as part of their literacy support for students.

Jackson, F.R., & Cunningham, J.W. (1994). Investigating secondary content teachers' and preservice teachers' conceptions of study strategy instruction. *Reading Research and Instruction, 34,* 111–135.

> Research which indicated a lack of knowledge and evaluation of study strategies by teachers as well as a confusion of what effective study strategy instruction involved, particularly with preservice teachers.

Kucan, L., & Beck, I.L. (1997). Thinking aloud and reading comprehension research: Inquiry, instruction, and social interaction. *Review of Educational Research, 67,* 271–299.

> A discussion of how thinking aloud encourages students' inquiry and social interaction as well as helps teachers in their instruction with text.

Santa, C.M. (2006). A vision for literacy: Ours or theirs? *Journal of Adolescent & Adult Literacy, 49,* 466–476.

> Emphasizes the importance of metacognition in improving adolescent literacy.

Wimmer, J.J. (2007). iPods, textbooks, and chapter tests: Studying in the digital age. In T.W. Bean, J.E. Readence, & R.S. Baldwin, *Content area literacy digital supplement.* Dubuque, IA: Kendall/Hunt.

> Discusses the use of technology as a study aid, in particular the iPod and online discussions.

References

Aiken, C. (1896). *Methods of mind training.* New York: Harper.

Brum, G.D. (1978). *Biology and man.* Dubuque, IA: Kendall/Hunt.

Caverly, D.C., Orlando, V.P., & Mullen, J.L. (2000). Textbook study reading. In R.F. Flippo & D.C. Caverly (Eds.), *Handbook of college reading and study strategy research* (pp. 105–147). Mahwah, NJ: Erlbaum.

Hacker, D.J., Dunlosky, J., & Graesser, A.C. (Eds.). (1998). *Metacognition in educational theory and practice.* Mahwah, NJ: Erlbaum.

Jackson, F.R., & Cunningham, J.W. (1994). Investigating secondary content teachers' and preservice teachers' conceptions of study strategy instruction. *Reading Research and Instruction, 34*, 111–135.

Kucan, L., & Beck, I.L. (1997). Thinking aloud and reading comprehension research: Inquiry, instruction, and social interaction. *Review of Educational Research, 67*, 271–299.

Loxterman, J.A., Beck, I.L., & McKeown, M.G. (1994). The effects of thinking aloud during reading on students' comprehension of more or less coherent text. *Reading Research Quarterly, 29*, 352–367.

Nist, S.L., Simpson, M.L., Olejnik, S., & Mealey, D.L. (1991). The relationship between self-selected study processes and test performance. *American Educational Research Journal, 28*, 849–874.

Reinking, D. (1986). Integrating graphic aids into content area instruction: The graphic information lesson. *Journal of Reading, 30*, 146–151.

Schumm, J.S., & Mangrum, C.T. (1991). FLIP: A framework for content area reading. *Journal of Reading, 35*, 120–124.

Simpson, M.L. (2007). PORPE: A study strategy for learning in the content areas. In T.W. Bean, J.E. Readence, & R.S. Baldwin, *Content area literacy digital supplement.* Dubuque, IA: Kendall/Hunt.

Spires, H.A., & Stone, P.D. (1989). The directed notetaking activity: A self-questioning approach. *Journal of Reading, 33*, 36–39.

Wade, S.E., & Reynolds, R.E. (1989). Developing metacognitive awareness. *Journal of Reading, 33*, 6–14.

Wimmer, J.J. (2007). iPods, textbooks, and chapter tests: Studying in the digital age. In T.W. Bean, J.E. Readence, & R.S. Baldwin, *Content area literacy digital supplement.* Dubuque, IA: Kendall/Hunt.

Author Index

I

International Reading Association, 136
Ivey, G., 118

J

Jackson, F.R., 249
Johansen, K.V., 138
Jossen, C., 45

K

Kaestle, C.F., 3
Kear, D.J., 117
Kincaid, J., 116
Kinney, G., 36
Kist, W., 45
Klass, D., 130, 131, 138
Kowalinski, B.J., 125
Kress, G., 29, 45
Kucan, L., 256

L

Ladson-Billings, G., 34
Laird, D.M., 45
Landis, J.D., 138
Leavell, A.G., 89, 125
Lee, M., 126, 139
Leland, C., 122
Leonard, W.H., 62
Lesko, N., 47
Leu, D.D., 24
Leu, D.J., 24
Lewison, M., 122
Lipsyte, R., 138
Loughery, J., 137
Love, K., 129
Lum, D.H.Y., 138
Lyons, M., 126

M

Maaka, M., 35
Macrorie, K., 239
Mangrum, C.T., 261, 262
Manzo, A.V., 182
Martin, M.A., 221
Martin, S.H., 221
Martin, T., 184
Maurer, D.W., 141
Mazer, A., 137
McCafferty, S.G., 33
McCarthy, S.J., 48
McConnell, S., 102
McGee, L.M., 174
McGowan, T., 125
McKenna, M.C., 117
McMahon, S.I., 129
McMillen, G.K., 139
McNabb, M.L., 24, 44, 45, 97, 176, 177

McTighe, J., 111
McVee, M.B., 39
The Miami Herald, 54
Miller, A., 210, 214
Miller, D.E., 129
Moje, E.B., 44, 47, 48, 120
Money Senior, H., 125
Moni, K., 122, 129, 133, 222
Moore, D.W., 5, 223, 224
Moore, S.A., 223, 224
Morrell, E., 35
Mullen, J.L., 259
Murphy, D.M., 17, 21
Myers, W.D., 118, 122, 135, 137, 138, 139

N

Naidoo, B., 116, 137
Nesbitt, J.C., 213
Newkirk, T., 243
Nieto, S., 28, 30, 34, 35, 124
Nilsen, A.P., 122, 123
Noll, E., 133

O

O'Brien, D.G., 11, 44, 45, 47, 206
O'Connor, J.R., 212
O'Donnell-Allen, C., 134
Ogbu, J., 48
Ogle, D., 178, 180
Olsen, 236
Olson, C.B., 245
Oppenheimer, T., 19
Orlando, V.P., 259

P

Palmer, R.G., 126
Pardeles, M.J., 35
Parker, W., 208
Patterson, E., 118
Paul, D.G., 229
Penick, J.E., 62
Perkins, R.S., 118
Piaget, J., 39
Pitre, A., 35
Placker, T., 120
Porto, M., 244
Prater, W., 118

Q

Quinn, R.D., 224

R

Rakes, T.A., 74
Ramirez, M., 150
Raphael, T.E., 129, 171

Raygor, A.L., 58
Readence, J.E., 34, 47, 110, 152, 163, 173, 178, 180, 183, 185, 188, 190, 192, 205, 210
Redway, J.W., 52
Reynolds, R.E., 256
Richgels, D.J., 174
Rifa'l, A., 139
Rigoni, N., 124, 222
Rodriguez, M., 164
Romano, T., 220
Rosenblatt, L.M., 122
Ruddell, M.R., 162
Ryan, P., 135, 137
Rycik, J.A., 5

S

Salas, R., 118
Salazar, M.M., 124
Salisbury, G., 135
Sandmann, A., 243
Sartre, J.P., 7
Savage, J.F., 123
Schatz, E.K., 147
Schumm, J.S., 261, 262
Schwartz, M., 212
Serafini, F., 126
Shanahan, T., 10, 178
Shearer, B.A., 162
Sheldon, W.D., 110
Shu, H., 150
Simpson, M.L., 274
Singer, H., 62
Slade, A., 137
Smagorinsky, P., 134
Smith, L.J., 74
Smith, R., 130
Soto, G., 34, 118, 122, 124, 139
Spires, H.A., 253
Stahl, N.A., 267, 270
Stahl, S.A., 267, 270
Stevens, L.P., 35, 122, 133, 173, 185, 186
Stewart, R.A., 11, 47, 125
Stone, P.D., 253
Stover, L.T., 122, 125
Sturtevant, E.G., 178

T

Taboada, A., 170
Tan, A., 33, 214
Tannenbaum, J., 137
Taylor, M.D., 135, 137
Teter, B., 138
Thomas, M.M., 182
Tierney, R.J., 152, 163, 173, 178, 180, 183, 185, 205
Tway, E., 122, 124–25

Subject Index

Note: Page numbers followed by f indicate figures; those followed by t indicate tables.

individual factors affecting, 109
language facility and, 44–45
vs. learning/memory, 249
levels of, 171–172, 172t
memory and, 42–44, 42f, 43f
pattern recognition in, 174–176
principles of, 169–178
prior knowledge and, 38–41,
    169–178. *See also* Prior knowledge
schemata and, 39, 143
standardized testing and, 77
text explicit, 170–172, 172t, 201,
    202f, 258–259
text implicit, 170–171, 172t, 201,
    202f, 258–259
text structure and, 44, 173–176, 175t
Comprehension instruction
analogical guides in, 203–205, 204f
anticipation guides in, 190–192, 191f
critical media literacy in, 186
directed reading-thinking activity in,
    196–198, 197f
discussion groups in, 206–209
graphic organizers in, 213–214
I-charts in, 180–182, 181f
integrated approaches in, 178–184
K-W-L framework in, 178–180, 179f
levels of comprehension and,
    171–172, 172t
listen-read-discuss strategy in,
    182–183, 183f
modeling in, 176
multiple text inquiry discussion in,
    214–216
options guides in, 201–203, 202f
organization of information in,
    173–178
phony document strategy in, 210–211
polar opposites activity in, 212–213
postreading strategies in, 99, 205–216
prereading strategies in, 99, 111,
    190–198
questioning the author strategy in,
    185–186
questions in, 172–173, 199, 200, 200f
reaction guides in, 209–210
reading strategies in, 198–205
ReQuest activity in, 193–196, 195f
scaffolded reading experience in,
    183–185
signal words in, 174–175, 175t
statements in, 173
study guides in, 198–201, 198f, 200f
text appetizers in, 192–193, 192f
text structure explication in, 176–178,
    175t
Computers. *See also* Instructional
    technology
development of, 17
Computer software, 20–21

Concept learning, in content areas,
    40
Concept map, 107, 107f
Conferences, in writing instruction,
    242–243
Connotations, 143–144
Constructivism, 38
Content, aiming toward, 9
Content and processes, concurrent
    presentation of, 9
Content area instruction
aiming toward content in, 9
classroom social context and, 46–49
concurrent presentation of content and
    processes in, 9
debriefing in, 10
integrative approach in, 9–11, 10f
language processes in, 10–11
modeling in, 10
motivational strategies in, 41–42
multiple texts in, 214–216
presenting isolated skills in, 9
prior knowledge and, 38–39
reader interest in, 40–41, 47, 62,
    120–121
reality checks for, 11–12
recommended practices for, 13t
for second language learners, 30–38.
    See also Second language learning
small groups in, 11, 206–209
strategy implementation in, 11–12
technology in, 11, 15–26. *See also*
    Instructional technology
tradebooks for, 125, 136–137,
    137t–139t
Content area literacy, 3–4
assumptions and misconceptions
    about, 6–8, 6t
definition of, 3
instructional recommendations for,
    9–11, 9t
role of teachers and texts in, 7–8
website for, 22–23
*Content Area Literacy: An Integrated
    Approach,* 22
CD-ROM digital supplement for,
    296–301
features of, xiii–xv
integrated instructional
    recommendations in, 9–11
website for, 23–24
Content outline, in lesson planning,
    100–102
Content reading inventory, 84–89, 88f
Context clues, 147
Contextual knowledge, 143–144
Contextual redefinition, 152–153
Conventions, book displays at, 136
Cooperative learning, for second
    language learners, 32–33
Criterion, 76

Criterion-referenced tests, 76
Critical literacy, 35, 122
Critical literary discussions, 133–134
Critical media literacy, 186
Critical policy analysis, 53
Critical thinking, 35
Crossword puzzles, 166
The Crucible (Miller), 210–211
Cubing, 225–226, 226f
Cultural diversity, 30–34, 47. *See also*
    Second language learning
textbooks and, 51–53
young adult literature and, 123–125
Culturally conscious curriculum, 35, 47
Culture, language and, 34–38
Culture wars, textbooks and, 51–57
Curriculum, culturally conscious, 35
Cybraries, 23

D

Danger Zone (Klass), 131
Deadly Unna? (Gwynne), 133
Debate groups, 110
Debriefing, 10
Decoding, 145–148
context clues in, 147
external references in, 148–149
morphemic analysis in, 145–146
strategy for, 149–150
Definitional knowledge, 143–144
Denotation, 143
Depth of processing, 252
Developmental bilingual education, 31
Diagnostic tests, 76–77
Dialogue journals, 33, 222
Dictionaries, 148–149
websites for, 149
Digressive groups, 110
Dinner party, 131–133
Directed reading-thinking activity
    (DRTA), 196–198, 197f
Discussion groups, 206–209
Discussions, teacher-dominated vs.
    collaborative, 48
Distributed practice, 251
Diversity
cultural, 30–34, 47. *See also under*
    Cultural
in lesson planning, 109–114
DVDs, 20

E

eBooks, 20–21
EBSCOhost, 21
Educational mandates, 73. *See also No
    Child Left Behind*
Electronic books, 20–21
Elementary and Secondary Education
    Act of 1955, 4
Embedded questions, 256

Encarta Africana, 20
Encoding, 252
Encyclopedias, CD-ROM multimedia, 21
English as a second language instruction, 30. *See also* Second language learning
ENIAC, 17
ESL instruction, 30. *See also* Second language learning
Etymology, 156–157
Evaluation. *See* Assessment
Examinations. *See* Assessment; Test(s)
Experience-based comprehension, 170, 172t, 199, 200f, 259–260
Expressive vocabulary, 144
Extension activities, in vocabulary instruction, 165–166
External references, in decoding, 148–150
External storage, of information, 252

F

Fake pop quiz, 266–267
Fallen Angels (Myers), 122
Fanfiction, 222–223
  Website, 223
Five-minute lessons, 105–106
FLIP procedure, 260–262, 261f
Formal (standardized) tests, 75–76, 75f. *See also* Assessment; Test(s)
  advantages and disadvantages of, 77
  cautions for, 77–79
  floors and ceilings in, 78–79
Free morphemes, 145
From Slave to Abolitionist: Life of William Wells Brown (Warner), 28, 123
Functional literacy, 3

G

General interest inventory, 120–121, 120f, 121f
General vocabulary, 144–145
Glossaries, 148
  personal, 153–154
Goal orientation, in studying, 250
Goals, in lesson planning, 102
Google Earth website, 21
Grade-level scores, 79
Grammar for the Real World, 20
Graphic comprehension (literacy), 262
Graphic Information Lesson, 263
Graphic organizers
  in comprehension instruction, 213
  definition of, 154
  in second language learning, 214
  in vocabulary instruction, 154–156, 156f

Group discussions, 206–209
  in Guided Writing Procedure, 231–232
Grouping procedures, 110–111
Group tests, 77
Guessing
  on multiple-choice tests, 261
  on standardized tests, 78
Guided Writing Procedure, 231–235, 233f, 243–244

H

Hidden word puzzles, 165–166
High-stakes testing. *See* Assessment
HIP Mathematics, 20
Human Genome Project, 17
Hush (Woodson), 122

I

I-charts, 180–182, 181f
Identity constructions, student, 47
Imaginative writing, 241
Immersion bilingual education, 30
*i*Movie, 20
Imposter, The, 211–212
Index(es), 148
  information, 114
Individualized instruction, 109–114
Individual tests, 77
Informal tests, 76
Information. *See also* Knowledge
  encoding of, 252
  external storage of, 252
  graphic, 263
  retention and retrieval of, 250–252
Information index, 114
Inquiry-based classroom, 214–216
Inquiry charts, 180–182, 181f
Instructional recommendations, 9–11, 9t
Instructional technology, 11, 15–26
  access to, 20
  computer software and, 20–21
  creative use of, 20–21
  downside of, 22–23
  electronic books and, 20–21
  innovations in, 19
  Internet and, 21–24
  limited implementation of, 18
  multimedia software and, 20–21
  resistance to, 18
Instruction groups, 110
Integrated thematic units, 107
Integrative approach, in content area instruction, 9–11, 10f, 107
Interactive approach, vs. transmission approach, 47–48
Interest, reader. *See* Reader interest
International Reading Association (IRA), Commission on Adolescent Literacy, 5, 136

Internet, 21–24. *See also* Website(s)
  cautions about, 22–23
Internet Workshop, 24
I-Search papers, 239–240
Isolated skills, presentation of, 9
ISTE website, 20

J

Journals
  book reviews in, 136
  dialogue, 30, 222
  instructional uses of, 222–223
  literature response, 128–129
  novel, 130–131
  teaching, 98

K

Knowledge. *See also* Information
  contextual vs. definitional, 142–143
  prior. *See* Prior knowledge
Knowledge rating, 90, 90f
K-W-L framework, 178–180, 180f

L

Labels, 33
Language, culture and, 34–38
Language facility, comprehension and, 44–45
Language shock, 33
Learned helplessness, 109
Learning
  category systems in, 38–39, 39f
  collaborative, 48–49
  concept, in content areas, 40
  constructivist view of, 38
  memory in, 38–39, 39f, 42–44, 42f, 43f. *See also* Memory
  misconceptions and, 40
  motivation for, 41–42
  prior knowledge in, 38–39, 62. *See also* Prior knowledge
  topic interest and, 40–41
Learning activities, 102–105
Learning aids, in textbooks, 64, 68–69, 69f
Learning logs, 33
Lectures, listening and notetaking during, 252–256, 254f, 255f
Lesson(s)
  examples of, 100–105
  five-minute, 105–107
  postreading phase of, 99, 205–216
    modifications of, 112–114
  prereading phase of, 99, 190–198
    modifications of, 111
  reading phase of, 99, 198–205
    modifications of, 111–112
Lesson/unit planning, 96–114
  accommodating individual differences in, 109–114

blueprint categories in, 100–107
content outline in, 100–102
for conventional unit, 104t
goals and objectives in, 100
grouping and, 109–110
key elements of, 102–104, 104t
learning activities in, 102–107
lesson objectives in, 102–104, 104t
for lessons within unit structure, 104t
slicing in, 41–42, 112–114
thematic units in, 107–109, 107t
tips for, 98–99
Letters from a Slave Girl: The Story of Harriet Jacobs (Lyons), 126
Libraries
classroom, 123
tradebooks in, 125, 136–137, 137t–139t
community, 116
orientation for, 135
school, encouraging use of, 134–136
Library Power, 134–136
Linguistic factors, in text comprehension, 38–49
Listening, notetaking during, 252–256, 254f
Listening guides, 111–112, 112f
Listen-read-discuss strategy, 182–183, 183f
Literacy
adolescent, 5
content area. *See* Content area literacy
critical, 35, 122, 133–134
critical media, 186
as cultural practice, 29
definition of, 3
functional, 3
graphic, 262
multiple, 19
for non-native English speakers, 30–34. *See also* Second language learning
power and, 26
rates of, 3
Literature, 115–139. *See also* Book(s)
biographies, 235–236
for classroom libraries, 123, 125, 135–136, 137t–139t
interest assessment for, 120–121, 120f, 121f
multicultural, 123–125, 128–129
nonfiction, 125
for sustained silent reading, 126–128
young adult, 121–123
annotated list of, 137t–139t
multicultural, 123–125, 128–129
selection of, 134
sources of, 135–136
Literature response journals, 128–129
Long-term memory, 43, 43f, 42f
Lyric writing, 228–231

M

Macromedia, 20
Maps, semantic, 157–160, 159f, 162–163, 163f
Mean, 75
Memory, 42–44, 43f
aids to, 42, 250–252
capacity limitation for, 42, 249
category systems and, 38–39, 39f
encoding and, 252
external storage and, 252
long-term, 42f, 43–44, 43f
organization of prior knowledge in, 38–39, 39f
short-term, 42–43, 42f, 43f
Metacognition, 256–259
Metadiscourse, 62
Mirror assessment, 264
Mnemonics, 250–251
Modeling, 10
in comprehension instruction, 176
in vocabulary instruction, 150
Morphemic analysis, 145–146
Motivational strategies, 41–42
Movie Works, 20
Multicultural activities, 33–34, 48. *See also under* Cultural
Multicultural literature, 123–125, 128–129
Multimedia, 20
Multiple-choice items, strategies for, 261–262, 264–265
Multiple literacies, 19
Multiple text inquiry discussions, 214–216
Music, in ReWrite activity, 228–231

N

Name sharing, 36–37
Necessary Roughness (Kim), 126
No Child Left Behind, 4–5
annual yearly progress under, 5, 73, 82–84
goals of, 4–5, 82–84, 83t
technological, 18
high stakes testing and, 82–84, 83t
proficiency under, 4, 74
state mandates and, 4–5, 73, 82–84, 83t. *See also* Assessment
Nonfiction tradebooks, 125
Norm(s), 75
inappropriate, 77
Normal curve, 75–76, 75f
Norm-referenced tests, 75
Notetaking
while listening, 252–258, 254f
while reading, 259–260
Novel journal, 130–131
Novels. *See* Book(s); Literature
Nukkin ya (Gwynne), 129

O

One Look Dictionaries (website), 149
Online literature circles, 25
Options guides, 199–203, 202f
Oral tests, 77
Organization, of information, 250–251
Outline, partial, 260
Outlining, 107, 107f
The Outsiders (Hinton), 122

P

Parallel notetaking, 253
Partial outline, 260
Passage independent/dependent test questions, 78, 80–82
Passive failure, 109
Peer evaluation, for writing, 244
Pennsylvania, educational mandates in, 5, 73, 82, 84
Pennsylvania Department of Education, 82, 83f, 84
Pennsylvania State Board of Education, 5
Percentile rank, 76
Performance items, 80
Permanent memory, 42f, 43–44, 43f
Personal glossary, 153–154
Personal review, 262
Phony document strategy, 210–211
PLAE strategy, 257–258
Polar opposites activity, 212–213
Pop quiz, fake, 266–267
PORPE strategy, 271–274, 273f
Portfolios, 89
Possible Sentences, 224–225
Postreading strategies, 99, 205–216
discussion groups, 206–209
graphic organizers, 213–214
imposter, 211–212
modifications in, 112–114
multiple text inquiry discussion, 214–216
phony document, 210–211
polar opposites, 212–213
reaction guides, 209–210
Prediction guide, 90–91, 91f
Prereading strategies, 99, 190–198
anticipation guides, 190–197, 191f
directed reading-thinking activity, 196–198, 197f
modifications of, 111
ReQuest activity, 193–196, 195f
text appetizers, 192–193, 192f
Prior knowledge, 38–39, 62
activation of, 38, 111
assessment of, 89–91
comprehension and, 169–170
linkage of with new knowledge, 40–41
misconceptions and, 39, 40

organization of in memory, 38–39, 39f

prereading strategies and, 99, 111, 190. *See also* Prereading strategies

schemas and, 39

standardized tests and, 78

Problem/solution patterns, 175, 175t

Procedural display, 47

Proficiency, 82

Program evaluation, 74

ProQuest, 21

Pseudographics, 264, 264f

Public education

reform movement for, 73. *See also No Child Left Behind*

undermining of, 73

Puzzles

crossword, 166

hidden word, 165–166

Q

Question(s)

central, 111

in comprehension instruction, 173–174, 199–200, 200f

embedded, 256

ReQuest procedure for, 193–196, 195f

student-generated, 262

Questioning the author, 185–186

Questionnaire, self-report, for reading attitude assessment, 118, 119f

Quick Writes, 223

R

Raw score, 76

Raygor Readability Estimate, 58–59

Reaction guides, 209–210

Readability, evaluation of, 57–59, 60, 61

Readability formulas, 58, 60, 61

Reader interest, 40–41, 47, 62, 120–121

assessment of, 120–121

standardized tests and, 77

Readers theater, 131

Readiness principle

definition of, 151

in vocabulary instruction, 151–152

Reading

notetaking during, 259–260

sustained silent, 126–128

Reading aloud, 112, 126

Reading assessment. *See* Assessment

Reading assignments, length of, 113–114

Reading attitudes

assessment of, 117–118, 119f

definition of, 117

Reading autobiography, 235–236

Reading comprehension. *See* Comprehension

Reading interests. *See also* Reader interest

assessment of, 120–121

Reading preferences, 120

Reading strategies, 99, 198–205

analogical guides, 203–205, 204f

modifications of, 111–112

options guides, 201–203, 202f

study guides, 198–201, 198f, 200f

Receptive vocabulary, 144

Rehearsal, 251

ReQuest procedure, 193–196, 195f

Research groups, 110

Research papers, 237–239

Response bias, 118

ReWrite, 228–231

Robert Frost: Poems, Life, Legacy, 21

Rubrics

definition of, 245

for writing assessment, 216, 245–248

four-point, 216

S

Saturnalia (Fleischman), 35, 129

Scaffolding, 183–185

Schemata, 39, 143

modified, 143

Schema theory, 39

Schools

privatization of, 82

state takeover of, 82

subcultures in, 46–47

Scope of information search, 113

Scrambled words, 166, 166f

Second language learning, 30–34

classroom-community linkage in, 31, 35

cooperative learning strategies in, 33

critical literacy in, 35

culturally conscious curriculum in, 35

cultural sensitivity in, 35

developmental bilingual education in, 30

ESL instruction in, 30

graphic organizers in, 213–214

immersion bilingual education in, 30

instructional design in, 34

instructional strategies in, 30–31

language facility and, 44–45

multicultural activities in, 35

native language in, 30–32

texts in, 44–45

transitional bilingual education in, 30

two-way bilingual education in, 31

Self-evaluation, of writing, 239

Self-report questionnaire, for reading attitude assessment, 118, 119f

Semantic mapping, 157–160, 159f, 163

Short-term memory, 42–43, 43f

Signal words, 174–176, 175t

Silent tests, 77

Sink-or-swim assignment, 198, 199

Slicing, 41–42, 113–114

Small-group discussions, 206–208

in Guided Writing Procedure, 231–235

Small-group instruction, 11

Social context, of classroom, 46–49

Software, 20

multimedia, 20

Song writing activity, 228–231

Spaced notetaking, 253, 254

Standard deviation, 76

Standard error of measurement, 79

Standardized testing, 75–76, 75f. *See also* Assessment; Test(s)

advantages and disadvantages of, 77

cautions for, 77–79

floors and ceilings in, 78–79

Standards-based assessment, 74–75

Stanford Achievement Test, 80

Stanine, 76

State reading assessments. *See also* Assessment

comparative analysis of, 79–80, 80t, 82–84, 83t

mandates for, 4–5, 73, 82–84, 83t. *See also No Child Left Behind*

overview of, 79–80, 80t

preparation for, 264–266

State textbook adoption policies, 56–57

Statistical concepts, in assessment, 75–76

Stink Eye, (Bergknut), 32

Student aids, in textbooks, 62, 68–69, 69f

Student diagnosis, 74–75

Student-generated questions, 262

Student identity constructions, 47

Student portfolios, 89

Study guides, 198–201, 200f, 202f

analogical, 203–205, 203f

options, 201–203, 202f

Studying, 249–256. *See also* Test preparation

attention in, 249–250

depth of processing in, 251–252

distributed practice in, 251

embedded questions and, 256

encoding specificity in, 252

FLIP procedure for, 260–262, 261f

goal orientation in, 250

graphic comprehension and, 262–263

information retention and retrieval in, 250

listening and notetaking and, 252–256, 254f, 255f

metacognition in, 256–257

mnemonics in, 250–251

organization of information in,
250–251
PLAE strategy for, 257–258
rehearsal in, 251
student-generated questions in,
258–259
think-alouds in, 258, 259
time on task in, 251
Stump the teacher, 262
Subject interest, 40–41, 47, 62, 120–121
assessment of, 120–121
standardized tests and, 78
Survey tests, 76
Sustained silent reading, 127–128

T

Talking Drawings, 102
Talk story, 37
Teacher, role of in content area literacy,
7–8
Teacher conventions, book displays at,
136
Teacher-dominated discussions, 47
Teacher-made tests, preparation for,
266–274
*Teachers and Machines: The Classroom
Use of Technology Since 1910*
(Cuban), 18
Teaching, transmission vs. interactive
approach to, 47–48
Teaching journal, 97
Technical vocabulary, 144
Technology, instructional.
See Instructional technology
Test(s). *See also* Assessment
diagnostic, 76–77
essay, 270–274, 271f
floors and ceilings for, 78–79
formal (standardized), 75–77, 75f
group, 77
guessing on, 78, 261
individual, 77
informal (criterion-referenced), 76
multiple choice, 261–262
norm-referenced, 75
oral, 77
passage dependent/independent items
in, 78, 80–82
performance items in, 78, 80
silent, 77
standards-based, 4, 74–75
state-by-state comparison of, 79–80,
93t
survey, 76
teacher-made, preparation for,
266–271
timed, 75, 78
true-false, 269–270
validity of, 80–82
writing sample in, 80

Test preparation, 248–274
for essay tests, 270–274, 271f
mirror assessment in, 264
for multiple choice tests, 261–262
for state reading assessments,
264–265
studying in, 249–259. *See also*
Studying
for teacher-made tests, 266–271
testwiseness and, 261
for true-false tests, 269–270
Testwiseness, 261
Text(s)
multiple, 214
types of, 44
Text appetizers, 192–193, 192f
Textbook(s)
adoption policies for, 56–57
censorship of, 54–55
conceptual difficulty of, 60
cultural diversity and, 32
definition of, 51
evaluation of, 59–62
guidelines and checklists for,
62–64, 63f, 65f
qualitative factors in, 59–62
quantitative factors in, 58–59
readability in, 58–59, 60, 61
instructional technology and, 18
learning aids in, 64, 68–69, 69f,
147–148
politicization of, 52–57, 73
preview of, 64, 66f–68f, 88
publishers of, 55
readability of, 57–59, 60, 61
role of, 7–8
special interests and, 52–53
staying power of, 18
supplementation of, 56–57
time spent using, 51
vocabulary difficulty in, 61
Textbook adaptations, 37
Text comprehension. *See*
Comprehension
Text explicit comprehension, 170–171,
172t, 197, 198f, 258–259
Text implicit comprehension, 170–171,
172t, 197, 198f, 258–259
Text intrusions, 62
Text structure, 44
comprehension and, 176–178, 175t
Thematic units, 107–109, 107f
Things Fall Apart (Achebe), 127
Think-alouds, 258–259
Timed tests, 75, 78
Time on task, 251
Time order patterns, 175, 175t
TOAST, 164
Topic interest, 40–41, 48, 62, 120–121
assessment of, 120–121
standardized tests and, 77

Tradebooks, 123, 135. *See also* Book(s);
Literature
annotated list of, 137t–139t
selection of, 135
sources of, 136–137
Transcribing, 220
Transitional bilingual education, 30
Transmission approach, vs. interactive
approach, 47–48
True-false tests, preparation for,
269–270
Two-way bilingual education, 31

U

Unit blueprint, 100–107
Unit planning. *See* Lesson/unit planning

V

Validity, test, 80–82
Venn diagrams, 129, 129f
Verbal and visual word association,
161–162, 161f, 162f
Verbatim Split Page Procedure (VSSP),
254–256, 254f
Visual and verbal word association,
161–162, 161f, 162f
Visual information, comprehension of,
262–263
Vocabulary, 144–167
decoding of, 145–149. *See also*
Decoding
definition of, 144
expressive, 144
general, 144–145
receptive, 144
technical, 144
in textbooks, 61
words and, 142–144. *See also*
Word(s)
Vocabulary independence strategies,
162–164
Vocabulary instruction, 150–167
analogies in, 165–166, 165f
Clues and Questions in, 160
contextual redefinition in, 152–153
crossword puzzles in, 166
extension activities in, 165–166
graphic organizers in, 154–156, 156f
hidden word puzzles in, 165
modeling in, 150
personal glossary in, 153–154
preteaching in, 150–152
principles of, 150–152
readiness principle and, 151–152
reinforcement in, 151
scrambled words in, 166, 166f
semantic mapping in, 157–159, 159f
student-directed strategies in, 161–164
teacher-directed strategies in, 152–160
TOAST in, 164

verbal and visual word association in, 161–162, 161f, 162f
vocabulary independence strategies in, 161–164
word origins in, 156–157, 158f
word selection for, 152
Writing Roulette in, 226–228
Vocabulary self-collection, 162